An Introduction to Second Language
Acquisition Research

D0000748

APPLIED LINGUISTICS AND LANGUAGE STUDY

General Editor
Professor Christopher N. Candlin, Macquarie University

Error Analysis
*Perspectives on second
language acquisition*
JACK C. RICHARDS (ED.)

Stylistics and the Teaching of
Literature
HENRY WIDDOWSON

Language Tests at School
A pragmatic approach
JOHN W. OLLER JNR

Contrastive Analysis
CARL JAMES

Language and Communication
JACK C. RICHARDS AND RICHARD
W. SCHMIDT (EDS)

Learning to Write: First Language/
Second Language
AVIVA FREDMAN, IAN PRINGLE AND
JANIC YALDEN (EDS)

Strategies in Interlanguage
Communication
CLAUS FAERCH AND GABRIELE
KASPER (EDS)

Reading in a Foreign Language
J. CHARLES ALDERSON AND A.H.
URQUHART (EDS)

An Introduction to Discourse
Analysis
New edition
MALCOLM COULTHARD

Computers in English Language
Teaching and Research
GEOFFREY LEECH AND
CHRISTOPHER N. CANDLIN (EDS)

Language Awareness in the Classroom
CARL JAMES AND PETER GARRETT

Bilingualism in Education *Aspects
of theory, research and practice*
JIM CUMMINS AND MERRILL
SWAIN

Second Language Grammar:
Learning and Teaching
WILLIAM E. RUTHERFORD

The Classroom and the Language
Learner
*Ethnography and second-language
classroom research*
LEO VAN LIER

Vocabulary and Language Teaching
RONALD CARTER AND MICHAEL
McCARTHY (EDS)

Observation in the Language
Classroom
DICK ALLWRIGHT

Listening to Spoken English
Second Edition
GILLIAN BROWN

Listening in Language Learning
MICHAEL ROST

An Introduction to Second Language
Acquisition Research
DIANE LARSEN-FREEMAN AND
MICHAEL H.LONG

Language and Discrimination
*A study of communication in
multi-ethnic workplaces*
CELIA ROBERTS, TOM JUPP AND
EVELYN DAVIES

Translation and Translating
Theory and Practice
ROGER T. BELL

Process and Experience in the
Language Classroom
MICHAEL LEGUTHE AND HOWARD THOMAS

Rediscovering Interlanguage
LARRY SELINKER

Language as Discourse:
Perspectives for Language Teaching
MICHAEL McCARTHY AND RONALD CARTER

An Introduction to Second Language Acquisition Research

Diane Larsen-Freeman and
Michael H. Long

Longman

An imprint of **Pearson Education**

Harlow, England · London · New York · Reading, Massachusetts · San Francisco
Toronto · Don Mills, Ontario · Sydney · Tokyo · Singapore · Hong Kong · Seoul
Taipei · Cape Town · Madrid · Mexico City · Amsterdam · Munich · Paris · Milan

Pearson Education Limited
Edinburgh Gate, Harlow,
Essex CM20 2JE, England
and Associated Companies throughout the world

Visit us on the World Wide Web at:
www.pearsoned.co.uk

First published 1991

BRITISH LIBRARY CATALOGUING IN PUBLICATION DATA
Larsen-Freeman, Diane
   An introduction to second language acquisition
   research –
   (Applied linguistics and language study).
   1. Foreign language skills. Acquisition. Research
   I. Title II. Long, Michael H. (Michael Hugh) III.
   Series
   401.93

ISBN 0-582-55377-6

LIBRARY OF CONGRESS CATALOGING IN PUBLICATION DATA
Larsen-Freeman, Diane.
   An introduction to second language acquisition research/
   Diane Larsen-Freeman and Michael H. Long.
      p.   cm.—(Applied linguistics and language study)
   Includes bibliographical references and index.
   ISBN 0-582-55377-6
   1. Second language acquisition—research. I. Long,
   Michael H. II. Title. III. Series
   P118.2.L37 1990   90–6102
   418–dc20   CIP

20 19 18 17 16 15 14
07 06 05 04

Typeset in 10/12pt and 9/11pt Linotron 202 Erhardt

Printed in Malaysia, CLP

Contents

General Editor's Preface

Workers in the field of second language acquisition are now in the enviable position of having available to them in a readily accessible form a number of core texts which set out the parameters and the perceived objectives of their field of study. Journal articles and journals themselves abound, and the subject itself increasingly finds a place, not only in applied linguistics programs directed at language educators, but also in courses concerned with linguistic and psycholinguistic theory and even in other professional programs targetting, for example, the communicatively disordered and handicapped.

Given this availability, one might ask what new can be contributed at this time, even by a volume as this most comprehensive one by Diane Larsen-Freeman and Michael Long, to the *Applied Linguistics and Language Study* series. Their long-standing position and eminence as researchers in the field would be one argument, but there are two others, the one ineluctably connected to the other.

The first concerns the state of the art in second language acquisition theory and the second, not surprisingly, how we can enable more relevant and appropriate research in the field to be undertaken, by as wide a constituency as possible.

The general set of principles, predicting and explaining natural phenomena, is the objective of such a theory, like all theories. Second Language Acquisition theory, naturally enough, has particular requirements. They are essentially threefold: to explain the particular and variable capacity to acquire other languages (and, incidentally, to relate that capacity to the acquisition of a first language); secondly, to connect the capacity and the processes of second language acquisition to human cognitive capacities and processes in general; and, thirdly, to explain the relationship between acquisition and that which is being acquired, the content and the strategies inherent in the language object and the communicative process. Moreover, in the case of this last requirement, to show how such acquisition proceeds cross-linguistically and the degree to which its path is governed by sets of universal possibilities and constraints generically inherent in the object of acquisition itself. A clear enough agenda: input, cognitive capacity, personality, output, not however independent constructs but interconnected and activated in social milieux which themselves have an advancing or delaying effect on this process. Furthermore, the relative weightings and salience of these constructs vary, not only among individuals but over the lifespan, and second language acquisition research in its legitimate progress towards the definition of its theory must always seek that parsimonious level of generality which will enable the most extensive explanation of data, while, of course, insisting on as broad a variety and range of that theory as possible. Parsimony is important: one may be forgiven in some currently available literature for coming to the conclusion that in some deeply unhelpful way, the potentially influencing variables affecting second language acquisition are so large in number, so relative and various in their potential salience, that the metaphor of interconnectedness that I drew up, has little practical explanatory value. Like many theories before it, in such a scenario second language acquisition theory would be vacuous in its own ornateness.

In short, the theoretical questions are still open, even though the ground has been partly cleared. Accordingly, any book (and this one in particular) which shows us the state of the terrain is of value, and one which examines these constructs and sets them out for the practitioner in a clear yet comprehensive way, is to be valued highly.

I referred earlier in this Preface to two arguments in favour of the existence of this book: what of the second? Theories need theoreticians, they need speculation, but they also require an empirical base. In some ways, the history of second language acquisition research provides a mirror to applied linguistics research more generally, especially in its struggle between a speculative and an empiricist persuasion. Such a struggle is evident both from the literature and from the practice of second language acquisition study and curricula. Often, one feels, the struggle is unhelpfully polarised, seeming to assert a primacy of one over the other, or even more foolishly, that one or the other protagonist is dispensable. The plain fact of the matter, of course, as with other disciplines and fields of inquiry, is that the two are bound, interdependent and both indispensable.

If this is so, then books which have an introduction to research at their masthead must weave a connection between these two persuasions and in an appealing and contingent manner. This Diane

Larsen-Freeman and Michael Long amply provide. The internal structure of the book has been precisely so constructed, culminating as it does with the question of the nature of theories in second language acquisition and how they may reveal themselves as relevant to the context of instruction.

The book begins with methodology, the how of research, both generally and with specific reference to second language acquisition data, targetting in particular interlanguage. Input and its environments constitute a central pivot for the book before the explanatory imperative for research is directed at the influencing variables on the nature, rate, success, and it must be said, the partiality of acquisition.

This latest contribution to the *Applied Linguistics and Language Study* series, like many of its companion volumes, has an instructional purpose. It is directed at the researcher-in-the-making and as such the authors have provided three valuable pieces of apparatus to facilitate this instructional purpose: the problematising questions directed at the issues of the relevant chapter, the activities designed to stimulate limited but nonetheless apposite reader research, and thirdly, possibly the most extensive bibliography of the field currently generally available. Of course, the field is large and its literature growing and prodigious, yet for that very reason we need an organisation and a point of reference to current practice: this is a central objective of this *Introduction*. At the same time, we need to show the way forward to an adequate theory and one which will be the intellectual property of the many, not the few; the democratisation of research into second language acquisition is a primary objective of the authors, myself as General Editor, and of the series itself.

Christopher N. Candlin
General Editor
Macquarie University
Sydney
Australia

Authors' Preface

Our primary aim in writing this book is to introduce readers to research on second language acquisition (SLA). The field is a broad one, and this is reflected in our focus on naturalistic and instructed learning by children and adults, as individuals or groups, in foreign and second language settings.

We have not assumed any prior knowledge of SLA or of SLA research methodology, although some background in language analysis would be helpful. We hope that after completing the book, readers will have become interested enough to delve further into the literature and perhaps even to embark on research of their own.

In Chapter 1 we explain why we think SLA is worth investigating. The methodologies which researchers employ to carry out their work are the subject of Chapter 2. We hope our discussions of the strengths and weaknesses of each methodology will help demystify the research process for readers who have never conducted research themselves. In Chapter 3 we trace the historical development of the field, noting how different data analysis procedures evolved, with each successive type of analysis reflecting a new stage of awareness of what SLA entails. Substantive findings from research to date are detailed in Chapter 4.

After describing SLA and how researchers study it in Chapters 1 through 4, the rest of the book deals explicitly or implicitly with current explanations of the learning process and the search for better ones. This leads us to consider environmental factors, learner differences, the nature of language and the role of instruction. It also means we need to think about forms and functions of theories in social science in general and about some theories of SLA in particular.

Given that learning is an internal process which cannot be observed directly, researchers must make inferences as to the nature of the process in part from an analysis of the product, learner language. In order to improve the quality of these inferences, it is useful to examine the nature of the second language input, something we do in Chapter 5. Since learners vary widely in how successful they are – one of the more obvious differences between first and second language acquisition – we deal in Chapter 6 with learner variables and differential achievement. In Chapter 7 we examine the value of theory in general, and then evaluate some representative SLA theories. Finally, in Chapter 8, we give particular attention to the differences between naturalistic and instructed SLA, and attempt to identify contributions made by language teaching.

In all this, we strive for comprehensiveness but must sometimes make what we hope are forgivable compromises. Two compromises we should acknowledge right up front: we have not reviewed the research literature in the acquisition of specific skills such as reading and writing, nor have we probed in depth acquisition of all the linguistic systems. Thus far, SLA research has primarily concentrated on explaining the acquisition of morphosyntax; the acquisition of phonology, the lexicon and pragmatics have gotten rather short shrift, an imbalance reflected in our text.

The book is intended to be suitable for individual study and for basic literature survey courses in SLA of the kind now common in graduate programmes in TESL, foreign language education and applied linguistics. Since students in such courses are typically required to pursue one or more topics in greater depth, e.g. through a literature review and/or a data-based study of their own, we have made a point of supplying more than the usual number of bibliographic references. These are included in the main body of the text to support generalizations, but also at the end of each chapter as suggestions for further reading. Based on our experience as instructors of SLA courses, this should provide students with easy access to the literature and so save them and their teachers long hours searching libraries and memories.

At the end of each chapter, we have also included activities of two types: the first so that readers can test their comprehension of what they have read, the second so that they can apply what they have learned, and thereby experience what it is like to conduct SLA research and begin to develop the appropriate design and analytic skills. We have found the 'Application' activities to improve critical reading skills for consumers of research articles and in some cases also to serve as a bridge to full-fledged research efforts by readers themselves. Even when that is not the purpose, however, we hope that doing the comprehension and application activities will foster a greater awareness and appreciation of the SLA process.

There are several people whose contributions to this book we would like to acknowledge. We alphabetize their names, as we did our own names as authors. We are very grateful to:

Robert Bley-Vroman, Dominique Buckley, Craig Chaudron, Graham Crookes, Kevin Gregg, Libby Holmes, Malcolm Johnston, David Nunan, Manfred Pienemann, William O'Grady, Kate Parker, Charlene Sato, and Richard Schmidt, for useful comments on parts of the manuscript and discussion of the issues;

Chris Candlin for his expert editorial comments, and to both Chris and Michael Johnson of Longman for their abiding faith in this project;

our students at S.I.T. and U.H. who have survived courses in which early versions of this text were used;

Joy Wallens for her tireless dedication to the preparation of the manuscript;

and last, but not least, to our family members, Elliott, Brent and Gavin Freeman, and Charlene Sato, for putting up with our excuses for too long.

To all these folks, we offer heartfelt thanks.

Diane Larsen-Freeman   Michael H. Long
School for International Training   *University of Hawaii*

Acknowledgements

We are grateful to the following for permission to reproduce copyright material:

Holt, Rinehart and Winston for a diagnostic passage from *Manual of American English Pronunciation* by Clifford Prator and Betty Wallace Robinett; *JHWPESL* for a table (Experimental studies of the effect of input modification on comprehension) from 'The effects of linguistic simplifications and elaborative modifications on L2 comprehension' by K. Parker and C. Chaudron (6, 2:107–33); *Language Learning* for a table (Syntax ratings for pre- and post-puberty learners) from 'The sensitive period for the acquisition of syntax in a second language' by M. Patkowski (30:455), and for a table (Learning strategy definitions) from 'Learning strategies used by beginning and intermediate ESL students' by M. O'Malley, G. Stewner-Manzanares, L. Kupper and R. Russo (35:33–4); National Centre for English Language Teaching and Research of Macquarie University for a table (Tentative developmental stages in ESL) from 'Factors influencing the development of language proficiency' by M. Pienemann and M. Johnston in *Applying Second Language Acquisition Research* edited by D. Nunan (pp. 82–3); Newbury House for an excerpt from 'Instructed interlanguage development' by M.H. Long in *Issues in Second Language Acquisition: Multiple Perspectives* edited by L.M. Beebe, and for a table (Wes's affective profile) from 'Interaction, acculturation and acquisition of communicative competence' in *Sociolinguistics and Second Language Acquisition* edited by N. Wolfson and E. Judd; Sage Publications and Thomas Cook for a table (Attributes of the qualitative and quantitative paradigm) from 'Beyond qualitative versus quantitative methods' by C. Reichardt and T. Cook in *Qualitative and Quantitative Methods in Education Research* edited by T. Cook and C. Reichardt; *Studies in Second Language Acquisition* for seventeen sentences rated for their 'coreness' from 'Transfer and non-transfer:

where we are now' by E. Kellerman (2, 1:49); Teachers of English to Speakers of Other Languages and the authors for a table (Natural order for morphemes) from 'Some issues relating to the Monitor Model' by S. Krashen in *On TESOL '77: Teaching and Learning ESL* edited by H.D. Brown, C. Yorio and R. Crymes (p. 149), for a table (Relationships between instruction, exposure and second language acquisition) in 'Does instruction make a difference?' by M. Long from *TESOL Quarterly* 17 (p. 375), and for a table (A typology of communication strategies) from 'Conscious communication strategies in interlanguage' by E. Tarone in *On TESOL '77: Teaching and Learning ESL* edited by H.D. Brown, C. Yorio and R. Crymes (p. 197).

1 Introduction

1.1 The place of second language in the world today

What comes to mind for many people when they encounter the phrase 'second language acquisition', is the experience they had as school students when they were engaged in the study of one or more foreign languages. Second language acquisition, however, occurs in other forms in schools today as well. Bilingual education, for example, has been a reality in many parts of the world for years. There are several models for bilingual education programmes, but generally they exist for the purpose of helping students to maintain their native language or to continue to grow in their native language while acquiring a second language.

Another form of second language acquisition in an educational context is the immersion programmes popular in Canada and certain parts of the United States. In these programmes, native English-speaking children receive all of their initial instruction in a second language. After the early grades, more and more content courses are taught in the native language.

The acquisition of second languages in a formal school setting, however, is not the only context where second languages have their place in the world today. English, a second language for most of the people of the world, has increasingly become the international language for business and commerce, science and technology, and international relations and diplomacy. Other professional intercourse, such as the proceedings of meetings of health practitioners or educators from many different parts of the world, is often conducted in English, a second language for many of the participants. In fact, it has been estimated that although there are only 325 million of the world's 4.7 billion population who speak English natively, for as many as 1.4 billion additional people, English is an official second language (Crystal 1985).

Another example of second language use linked with occupations is the *gastarbeiter* or migrant worker situation in Europe. In recent years, 11 million workers, primarily from Greece, Spain, Italy and Turkey, have left their homes and families to seek employment in the indus-trialized Western European countries. The migrant workers typically do not speak or understand the language of their new environment when they arrive. This has made for a number of social problems in the host community. It has also afforded a unique opportunity for SLA researchers to study what language is acquired, research about which we will learn more later.

What distinguishes the foreign workers from other migratory popu-lations is that the former for the most part have no intention, initially at least, of residing in the host countries for the rest of their lives. Thus, another instance where second language acquisition becomes an issue is the arrival and assimilation of immigrants. In the 1980s this was brought to mind by the large influx of Indochinese refugees to many different countries around the world.

Second languages frequently enter into consideration in affairs of state. Bitter contests have been fought in multilingual societies over national language policy formulation: Which languages are to be accorded official recognition and which denied it? Which language(s) is to be the medium of instruction in school and which language(s) is to be taught as a second language? And, of course, these same decisions often apply to dialects as well. Many children of the world grow up speaking a 'dialect' at home, only to encounter their national language for the first time as they enter school.

In short, not only do second languages have a place in school, they also affect many other aspects of people's lives. In the interdependent world of today, second language acquisition and use are ubiquitous.

1.2 Why study second language acquisition?

There are almost as many reasons to study SLA as there are places where second languages are acquired and used. First of all, the study of SLA is fascinating in its own right. It is a true conundrum. Understanding it requires drawing upon knowledge of psychology, linguistics, sociology, anthropology, psycholinguistics, sociolinguistics and neurolinguistics, among others. As David Cook (1965) has said:

> We sometimes overlook the fact that there is much that we can know and need to know about our universe and ourselves that is not necessarily useful at the moment of discovery. By the same token, we are too prone to reject knowledge for which we cannot find an immediate practical application.
>
> Yet much of what those who apply knowledge have discovered in their practical pursuits was made possible by those who were

only pursuing knowledge for its own sake. In an ultimate sense all
knowledge is practical. (p. 9)

But there is more to be gained from grappling with the complexity
of SLA than the sating of intellectual curiosity. The most obvious
beneficiary of an increased understanding of SLA is the second
language teaching profession, and through the teachers, the learners
themselves. Indeed, many researchers have been or remain language
teachers who find themselves attracted to SLA research as a source
of insight into the teaching/learning process. As Corder (1981, p.
7) puts it, 'Efficient language teaching must work with, rather than
against, natural processes, facilitate and expedite rather than impede
learning.' This can happen best when we know what those natural
processes are.

Indeed, we have found it helpful to depict the central players,
processes and content in the language teaching field as a triangle.
As the Figure 1.1 implies, we believe that language teachers' decisions
about the teaching process should, to a large extent, be informed by
knowledge of the subject matter they are teaching (i.e. the target
language and culture) and by knowledge of the unique group of
learners with whom they are working and of the language-learning
process. It is the lower right angle of the triangle with which we are
concerned in this book.

Teachers' expectations about what SLA research can tell us at this
point must be modest, though. As Lightbown (1985) reminds us, at the
moment SLA research does reveal to a certain extent what learners do
and what they know. It has not yet, however, reached the point where

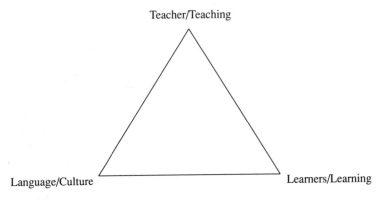

Teacher/Teaching

Language/Culture   Learners/Learning

FIGURE 1.1

we can say with assurance how they have come to do and to know these things, and we are further still from saying what teaching practices should therefore follow. On the other hand, if our research leads to greater teacher awareness of the acquisition process and increased sensitivity towards learners, then it seems to us the effort has been worthwhile.

Then, too, although we have no independent evidence to corroborate their claim, second language learners who have studied SLA research report anecdotally that their awareness of the SLA process facilitates their subsequent attempts at language learning. Clearly a heightened understanding of second language acquisition could also have impact on the other educational programmes involving language acquisition, such as bilingual education and immersion programmes.

But there are other, less obvious areas for which an understanding of SLA may prove helpful. One such example is with certain populations which have specific language-learning needs. For instance, language intervention issues for mentally retarded individuals parallel second language teaching issues to a striking degree (see, for example, Rosenberg 1982). Diagnosing non-native speaking children's learning disabilities as distinct from their second language problems is another example. Facilitating the acquisition of a spoken language by deaf individuals already fluent in sign language is yet a third. Many other potential applications could be cited here.

Mention was made earlier about how knowledge of certain disciplines helps us to understand the SLA process better. Ideally SLA research can and should inform these disciplines as well. SLA provides a good test case for linguists' claims about language universals, and for psychologists' observations on individual learning style differences. It also provides fertile ground for anthropologists' exploration of cultural universals and for sociologists' study of the effect of group membership on task achievement. Psycholinguists should be able to use SLA research findings in order to address a perennial problem for them: how to sort out the effects of cognitive development from normal child language development. Sociolinguists should find second language acquisition research helpful in expanding their understanding of when speakers prefer one speech style over another. Neurolinguists will find that SLA evidence can be brought to bear on issues in human biological development. For example, is there such a thing as a critical period in an individual's development, beyond which it is very difficult or impossible for anyone to truly master something as complex as a second language? These are but a few of the issues which SLA research should shed some light on in these related disciplines.

1.3 Development of the field of study of second language acquisition

People have been interested in second language acquisition since antiquity, but in modern times much of the research emphasis was in fact placed on language *teaching*. Large comparative studies of language teaching methods were conducted. Less ambitious studies focused upon the most efficacious way to teach a particular skill or to sequence structures in a syllabus. The assumption seemed to be that if language teaching methods could be made more efficient, then learning would naturally be more effective.

This assumption may be perfectly valid; indeed, interest in improving language teaching methodology has not diminished. Nevertheless, in the 1960s, as a result of the inconclusive findings from the comparative studies, a debate in psychology over the nature of learning and a revolution in linguistics, a challenge to the dominance of research on language teaching was to take place. Although we will discuss in Chapter 3 the precise nature of this challenge and its implications for second language acquisition, suffice it to say here that for the first time in recent history, many researchers' attention was shifted from the teaching process to the learning process.[1] It was this shift in perspective which introduced a new research agenda and gave definition to the field that has come to be known as second language acquisition.

A dramatic illustration of the results of this perspective shift can be found by simply glancing at the table of SLA studies compiled by Hatch (1978c). Hatch lists only seven studies prior to 1965. Subsequent to this date, there are scores of studies, the mere listing of which consumes almost seven pages. And Hatch's book was published in 1978. Since then there have been hundreds more studies conducted, several new journals begun, and numerous conferences convened.

Raimes (1983) offers an additional indicator of the birth and growth of the SLA field. She conducted an analysis of the topic index of articles which appeared in the *TESOL Quarterly* from 1967 to 1980. For the ten-year period 1967–76, Raimes found 29 articles listed under the topic heading 'second language learning'. Compare this with the 24 articles she counted for the two years 1979–80 in a topical area which was renamed second language acquisition – a four-fold growth! Given the vitality of the field today, it seems prudent to pause here to take stock of twenty years[2] of SLA research and to see where we have been and where we are going.

1.4 The scope of second language acquisition research

Focusing research efforts on the learner and learning process has not meant ignoring the effect of instruction on SLA. On the contrary, one of the fundamental goals of SLA research is to facilitate and expedite the SLA process, and appropriate instruction will undeniably make a contribution. Indeed, there is a group of SLA researchers whose special interest is in conducting classroom-centred research.[3]

Having said this, it is also true that the scope of research has broadened considerably from being solely concerned with what takes place in the classroom. In fact, much of the research these past twenty years has been conducted on SLA in a natural, that is untutored, environment. Sometimes a distinction is made between second language learning which takes place within a classroom and second language acquisition which occurs 'naturally' outside a classroom. We discuss the difference between learning and acquisition in Chapter 7 but prefer to follow most researchers in the field and use acquisition as the superordinate term for all settings. We do, however, retain the traditional term 'learners' to refer to those in the process of acquiring a second language.

A somewhat related matter having to do with setting is that researchers must be able to explain SLA whether the acquisition takes place in a second language or a foreign language environment. A second language is one being acquired in an environment in which the language is spoken natively. For example, a Spaniard acquiring English in England would be acquiring it as a second language. If he or she were studying English in a classroom in Spain, i.e. outside of an environment where the second language is spoken natively, he or she would be acquiring it as a foreign language. In which environment the acquisition takes place is often related to the first variable, whether it takes place in a classroom or not, since foreign languages usually require instruction whereas second languages can often be 'picked up' from the environment. In the second language acquisition field, however, and therefore in this book, we refer to both as instances of second language acquisition, taking up the differential effects of the two settings in Chapter 8.

In addition to setting variables, SLA research must account for learner variables. Age is an example of one such learner variable. The only thing that calling a language 'second' implies is that it is acquired later than a first language. Consequently, SLA research must account for the acquisition of a second language by young learners who may have very little proficiency in their native language, up to the acquisition of a second language by an older learner for whom the native language is very well established. Of course, there are many other learner variables besides age which affect the acquisition process. We will deal with a number of these in Chapter 6.

Even the term 'second language' is not as straightforward as it first seems, as sometimes it refers to a language which is not chronologically the second. SLA really has come to mean the acquisition of any language(s) other than one's native language. Thus, we have 'second' language acquisition studies dealing with the acquisition of third and fourth languages, and we even have 'second' language acquisition case studies of simultaneous bilingualism which in reality are studies of children engaged in learning two first languages.

What complicates our study further is that learners acquire language for a variety of reasons: to fully participate in a society, to travel as a tourist, to pass an examination, to obtain employment, to read scientific texts, etc. It won't do to say glibly that linguistic or communicative competence is what everyone aspires to because, first of all, not all do and second, as McGroarty (1984) reminds us, communicative competence can mean different things for different people.

In sum, the scope of SLA research must be sufficiently broad to include a variety of subjects who speak a variety of native languages, who are in the process of acquiring a variety of second languages in a variety of settings for a variety of reasons. Small wonder Seliger (1984) states unequivocally that it is impossible to describe all the variables in SLA. Nonetheless, Seliger also notes: 'In spite of such infinite diversity there exists the universal fact that human beings of all ages, attitudes, levels of intelligence, socioeconomic background, etc., succeed in acquiring L2s[4] in a wide variety of both naturalistic and formal settings' (p. 37). It is to understand how learners accomplish this and why some fail to do so which has motivated SLA research since its inception twenty years ago.

Notes

1. We say recent history because as Stern (1983) has rightfully pointed out, modern SLA researchers were not the first to discover the SLA learner. Indeed, even though most of the research in the pre-SLA period was devoted to the teaching process, there was some work being done on learner characteristics. Carroll (1963) discusses some of the studies on the relationship between interests, attitudes, motivation, prior language training, age and sex of the learners on the one hand, and their second language achievement on the other.

2. Most researchers date the beginning of the SLA field with Corder's article 'The significance of learners' errors', published in 1967, or Selinker's 'Interlanguage', published in 1972. More will be said about these later.

3. Saying that we have not ignored classroom instruction because there exists a group of researchers interested in classroom-centred research (CCR) is a bit misleading. The goal of CCR researchers is to describe classroom processes, not to prescribe instructional techniques (Allwright 1983, p. 196).

4. L2 and L1 are used as abbreviations for second and first languages, respectively.

Activities

Comprehension

1. Of what value is the study of second language acquisition to language teachers, according to the text?

2. It was said in this chapter that the perspective shift which occurred towards the end of the 1960s brought about a new focus on the learner. What does this mean?

3. Why do you think Seliger says it is impossible to describe all the variables in SLA?

Application

4. A number of ways that people come into contact with second languages were suggested in this chapter. Can you think of any others?

5. Can you think of any reasons for why one should study SLA research in addition to the ones proposed here?

6. Find out if your country has a national language policy. If it does, are there any officially recognized second languages? How are these dealt with in the educational context?

7. Make a list of questions you have about the SLA process. Although we do not promise answers for all, or even any, of them, making a list will help you to identify gaps in your knowledge and will provide you with an initial framework from which to organize what you encounter in subsequent chapters. As you continue to read, this framework, no doubt, will have to be refined.

Suggestions for further reading

We have touched upon a number of different areas in this chapter which we will be unable to pursue in detail since they are beyond the scope of this book. Interested readers may wish to consult the following:

For information on bilingual education, see:
Cummins, J and Swain, M 1986 *Bilingualism in education*. Longman
Paulston, C 1980 *Bilingual education: theories and issues*. Newbury House Publishers, Inc., Rowley, Mass.

For an overview of immersion programmes, see:
Genesee, F 1983 Bilingual education of majority-language children: the immersion experiments in review. *Applied Psycholinguistics* 4: 1–46
Genesee, F 1987 *Learning through two languages*. Newbury House Publishers, Inc., Rowley, Mass.
Swain, M and Lapkin, S 1982 *Evaluating bilingual education: a Canadian case study*. Multilingual Matters Ltd.

For a look at the teaching of English as an international language, see:
Bailey, R and Gorlach, M (eds.) 1984 *English as a world language*. Cambridge University Press
Kachru, B (ed.) 1982 *The other tongue: English across cultures*. University of Illinois Press, Urbana, Ill.
Strevens, P (1980) *Teaching English as an international language*. Pergamon Press

For information on national language policy, see:
Olshtain, E 1985 Language policy and the classroom teacher. In Celce-Murcia, M (ed.) *Beyond basics: issues and research in TESOL*. Newbury House Publishers, Inc., Rowley, Mass.
Povey, J (ed.) 1980 *Language planning and language teaching: essays in honor of Clifford H. Prator*. English Language Services, Culver City, Calif.

For a discussion of the interaction between language acquisition research and populations with specific language learning needs, see:
Cummins, J 1984 *Bilingualism and special education: issues on assessment and pedagogy*. Multilingual Matters Ltd.
Strong, M (ed.) 1988 *Language learning and deafness*. Cambridge University Press

For a discussion of how various related disciplines have contributed perspectives to SLA research, see:
Beebe, L (ed.) 1988 *Issues in second language acquisition: multiple perspectives*. Newbury House/Harper and Row, New York

2 Second language acquisition research methodology

2.1 Introduction

'Research is a systematic approach to finding answers to questions' (Hatch and Farhady 1982, p. 1). Part of being systematic is having a well-planned research design. In this chapter we will see how the SLA field has come to deal with four aspects of research design: the methodology, the setting, the instrumentation and measurement.

In the previous chapter it was mentioned that much of the research in the 1960s comparing language teaching methods was inconclusive and thus unable to quell methodological disputes. At the same time a debate was also ensuing between cognitive psychologists and behaviourists as to the character of human learning. (See, for example, MacCorquodale's 1970 rebuttal of Chomsky's review of *Verbal Behavior* by B. F. Skinner.) Things were no more settled in linguistics, which was itself in an upheaval due to the Chomskyan revolution. It therefore became increasingly apparent to certain European and North American researchers that they could no longer rely on other disciplines for theoretical orientations, but would have to research SLA directly and empirically themselves (Stern 1983, p. 329).

Since SLA was a new, uncharted field, it was by no means obvious how such investigation ought to be conducted. Many of its original research methodologies were consequently borrowed from first language acquisition research. Still others have come from education and the related disciplines mentioned earlier. As their experience grows, however, SLA researchers are becoming more creative in the ways they seek answers to questions in their unique field of specialization.

2.2 Qualitative versus quantitative methodologies

Today it is fair to say that SLA has a varied inventory of methodologies with which to deal with questions, although the methodologies are by no means universally endorsed. Indeed, there is an oft-cited schism in the SLA field between those researchers who favour qualitative methodologies and those who prefer quantitative methodologies. The prototypical qualitative methodology is an ethnographic study in which the researchers do not set out to test hypotheses, but rather to observe what is present with their focus, and consequently the data, free to vary during the course of the observation. A quantitative study, on the other hand, is best typified by an experiment designed to test a hypothesis through the use of objective instruments and appropriate statistical analyses.

For some researchers the distinction between the two represents more than a preference between two types of methodologies; rather it represents a fundamental clash between two paradigms. As Rist (1977) explains: 'Ultimately, the issue is not research strategies *per se*. Rather, the adherence to one paradigm as opposed to another predisposes one to view the world and the events within it in profoundly different ways' (p. 43).

Reichardt and Cook (1979, p. 10) provide a useful summary of the attributes of the qualitative and quantitative paradigms (Table 2.1). As Reichardt and Cook point out, there are two implications for research which relate to this summary. First, it is assumed that if researchers subscribe to one paradigm over the other and thus view the world differently, they must use different methods of inquiry. Second, the paradigms are assumed to be inflexible so that one's only choice is between the two. We find these assumptions to be unjustified. By considering an oft-discussed methodological distinction in the SLA literature, we will demonstrate that the paradigm attributes are not logically linked to one methodology. The distinction we have chosen to exemplify is the one between *longitudinal* and *cross-sectional* studies.

A longitudinal approach (often called a case study in the SLA field) typically involves observing the development of linguistic performance, usually the spontaneous speech of one subject, when the speech data are collected at periodic intervals over a span of time. In a cross-sectional approach, the linguistic performance of a larger number of subjects is studied, and the performance data are usually collected at only one session. Furthermore, the data are usually elicited by asking subjects to perform some verbal task, such as having subjects describe a picture.

Even from these brief descriptions, we can see that each approach is more compatible with one paradigm than the other. The longitudinal approach could easily be characterized by at least three of the qualitative paradigm attributes: naturalistic (use of spontaneous speech), process-oriented (in that it takes place over time) and ungeneralizable

Qualitative Paradigm	Quantitative Paradigm
Advocates the use of qualitative methods.	Advocates the use of quantitative methods.
Phenomeonologism and verstehen: 'concerned with *understanding* human behavior from the actor's own frame of reference'.	Logical-positivism: 'seeks the *facts* or *causes* of social phenomena with little regard for the subjective states of individuals'.
Naturalistic and uncontrolled observation.	Obtrusive and controlled measurement.
Subjective.	Objective.
Close to the data; the 'insider' perspective.	Removed from the data; the 'outsider' perspective.
Grounded, discovery-oriented, exploratory, expansionist, descriptive, and inductive.	Ungrounded, verification-oriented, confirmatory, reductionist, inferential, and hypothetico-deductive.
Process-oriented.	Outcome-oriented.
Valid; 'real', 'rich', and 'deep' data.	Reliable; 'hard' and replicable data.
Ungeneralizable; single case studies.	Generalizable; multiple case studies.
Holistic.	Particularistic.
Assumes a dynamic reality.	Assumes a stable reality.

TABLE 2.1 Attributes of the Qualitative and Quantitative Paradigms

(very few subjects). The cross-sectional approach is easily recognizable from the corresponding attributes of the quantitative paradigm: obtrusive, controlled measurement (use of artificial tasks), outcome-oriented (in that it takes place at only one point in time) and generalizable (larger group of subjects). Upon reflection, however, we realize there is nothing inherent in either approach to prohibit its being practised in a way consistent with the alternate paradigm.

There is no reason, for example, why the natural linguistic performance data obtained through a longitudinal study could not be supplemented by data elicited by some controlled, 'obtrusive' verbal task. Indeed, specific hypotheses generated by an analysis of the natural data are sometimes concurrently tested by means of data collected through elicitation procedures. (See, for example, Cazden et al. 1975.) Moreover, quantifying the data obtained by either means is standard practice in SLA.

The process-oriented versus the outcome-oriented distinction should not be associated exclusively with one approach versus the other, either. It is true that in order to study the SLA process we must be able to trace changes diachronically, or over time, which would seem to suggest the adoption of a longitudinal approach, i.e. one which would allow the researcher to trace the process, not just analyse the product or outcome at any one point in time. However, a synchronic cross-sectional study can be designed in such a way as to emulate the diachronic process of SLA. If the subjects represent a range of language proficiencies, then it is assumed that their aggregate performance at a single point in time will reflect a developmental picture similar to that obtained by a researcher studying the second language development of a single subject over time.[1]

A combination of longitudinal and cross-sectional approaches is also possible. Dato (in Adams 1978), for instance, designed a study of the acquisition of Spanish by English-speaking children using three groups of English speakers with varying levels of exposure to Spanish (Table 2.2). At the start of study, Group (a) had been exposed to Spanish for one month, whereas Group (c) had had three months of exposure. Dato collected data four times from each of the three different groups. The data collected at any one time constitute a cross-sectional study, while all the data for a particular group provide a longitudinal view. The data

		Data collection times (months)			
	Group	*Time 1*	*Time 2*	*Time 3*	*Time 4*
English children's	a	1	2	3	4
length of exposure	b	2	3	4	5
to Spanish	c	3	4	5	6

TABLE 2.2   A Longitudinal/Cross-Sectional Research Design

from all three groups offer a basis for cross-checking generalizations on both the outcome at any one time and of the process over time.

The third attribute cited above was the alleged lack of generalizability of findings from single-case longitudinal studies. It is commonly acknowledged that a difficulty with single case studies is discerning typical SLA behaviour from what is unique to the individual subject. Once again, however, there is nothing inherent in either approach to warrant the imposition of such a rigid distinction. One solution to the lack of generalizability is to conduct a number of concurrent longitudinal studies. This would help in distinguishing the typical from the idiosyncratic, although admittedly such an undertaking might be prohibitively time-consuming. Alternatively, the findings from a number of independent longitudinal case studies might be aggregated.[2]

Moreover, generalizability is not only dependent upon the number of subjects in a study. Even researchers using a cross-sectional study cannot legitimately generalize beyond the subjects they have studied unless the subjects are drawn from a particular population in a random manner – and even then the sample data must be generalized to the population based on proper statistical reasoning.[3] Usually, random selection is not possible and any generalizations drawn are tentative at best. Then, too, as Reichardt and Cook (1979) add: 'While a large and diverse sample of cases can aid in such informal generalizations, so can a depth of understanding of a single case' (p. 115).

From the preceding discussion of paradigm attributes, it can be seen that the longitudinal or cross-sectional approach should not be associated exclusively with either paradigm. This is not to say that one's paradigmatic allegiance is unimportant in designing a methodology; nor is it to deny that certain methodologies are usually associated with specific paradigms. The point is that what is important for researchers is not the choice of *a priori* paradigms or even methodologies, but rather to be clear on what the purpose of the study is and to match that purpose with the attributes most likely to accomplish it. Put another way, the methodological design should be determined by the research question. Nevertheless, as we have said, because extant methods consist of particular clusters of attributes, they are commonly associated more with one paradigm than the other. For the sake of convenience, then, we will introduce them within a paradigmatic context. In keeping with our point that the dividing line between the paradigms is not rigidly fixed, however, we introduce the methods arranged along a continuum with the two paradigms at either pole (Figure 2.1).

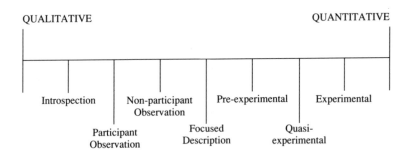

FIGURE 2.1   Qualitative-Quantitative Continuum of Research Methodologies

2.2.1 Introspection

Perhaps the ultimate qualitative study is an introspective one, in which, with guidance from the researcher, learners examine their own behaviour for insights into SLA. Although there is some question about the validity of such self-report data, using introspection as a research method is an old tradition in psychology (see, for example, Titchener 1912).

SLA researchers who challenge the validity of introspective insights do so because they question whether learners' reports of what they are experiencing truly represent what is transpiring within the learner (Seliger 1983). They suggest that introspection be limited to the study of affective factors such as attitudes and motivation. Others, however, argue that observation by the researcher cannot provide access to learners' conscious thought processes (Gaies 1983). In support of this argument, O'Malley et al. (1985a) in their study of learning strategies discovered that they had considerable success in identifying learning strategies when they interviewed the learners themselves; however, they had less success when they interviewed the learners' teachers and very little success in identifying strategies based on the researchers' own observations.

2.2.2 Participant observation

In participant observation, researchers take part in the activities they are studying. They do not approach the study with any specific hypotheses in mind; rather they take copious notes on whatever they observe and experience.[4] The notes are usually recorded immediately after the activities so as to allow the researchers full participation in them. The period of observation is usually long and the number of subjects studied is small.

In an SLA context, an example of a research project carried out using this methodology is K. M. Bailey's study (1980) of her experience as a student of French. The data from the study were collected by means of diary entries recorded by Bailey during her French course. The entries consisted of observations of her fellow students and the teacher. There also were introspective comments since Bailey scrutinized her own experience as well. The positive qualities and the limitations of this type of study will be discussed below.

2.2.3 Non-participant observation

As with its participant counterpart, researchers engaged in non-participant observation do not entertain any hypotheses at the outset of a study. As the name implies, the researchers observe activities without engaging in them directly. This leaves them free to take notes and/or make tape recordings during the observation itself. As with participant observation, the subjects are usually few in number and the period of study relatively long.

In the SLA field, non-participant observations are usually referred to as longitudinal case studies, the classic example being Leopold's study of his daughter's simultaneous acquisition of English and German during the period 1939–49. Leopold made a daily record of his observations, resulting ultimately in a monumental four-volume work. (See a summary in Hatch 1978c.)

Both participant and non-participant observation have many positive qualities to recommend them as research methodologies. Researchers using these methods provide us with a detailed and comprehensive description of subjects' SLA behaviour. Furthermore, such descriptions are psycholinguistically coherent in that they deal with a single subject's development (or only a few subjects' development) over time. Since there are no *a priori* hypotheses to be tested, researchers' attention is freed to discover any potential factors which could significantly influence the SLA process. In fact, such studies are often referred to as hypothesis-generating, since the scope of researchers' perspectives is not restricted – they can look for patterns in naturally occurring data and, once detected, generate hypotheses which might account for them.

There are, however, limitations to these research methodologies. It can seriously be questioned as to whether data gathered in observational studies are in fact natural. Tarone (1979), citing 'the observer's paradox' (Labov 1969), argues that the mere presence of an observer will force the subjects to attend to what they say in a way different than if the observer were not present. It is also not really true to say that the scope of such research is unlimited. The scope is going to be restricted since the observation is being conducted by human beings who are more or less perceptive, more or less biased, more or less objective, more or less experienced, etc. Moreover, in participant observation the scope will be limited by the fact that even the most perceptive researchers' attention is going to be divided between participating in the activities and observing themselves and others while doing so.

Another drawback to these observational studies is that they usually take a long time to complete. Even when they are completed, the researchers will be unable to generalize from their findings. It is impossible to sort out the typical from the unique.

2.2.4 Focused description

Further along the continuum we find focused descriptive studies. These studies are similar to the observational studies just considered since they, too, are descriptive in nature. The difference between them, however, is that researchers who use a focused descriptive methodology do so because they wish to narrow the scope of their study to a particular set of variables, a particular system of language (e.g. morphology) or to explore a particular issue (e.g. the influence of the native language on SLA). According to Van Dalen (in Cook 1965), 'Descriptive studies may classify, order and correlate data seeking to describe relationships that are discoverable in phenomena themselves' (p. 39).

Examples of focused descriptive studies in an SLA context which seek to classify data are those that use interaction analysis. In interaction analysis studies, researchers observe a language class using a data-collection device or instrument to focus and record their observations. The instruments contain pre-established categories of behaviour (e.g. teacher addresses a question to particular students; teacher addresses a question to group as a whole, etc.). Often what is required of the researchers is for them to make a tally next to the category of behaviour when they observe it happening. Specific examples would be FOCUS (Foci for Observing Communication Used in Settings) (Fanselow 1977) and COLT (Communicative Orientation of Language Teaching) (Allen, Fröhlich and Spada 1984). The purpose of these instruments is to classify the communications people send and receive. Questions are addressed such as who talked in the classroom and to what extent.

An example of a focused descriptive study which seeks to order data is Dulay and Burt's (1974) study of morpheme acquisition. These researchers used a cross-sectional approach and an instrument (the Bilingual Syntax Measure) to obtain samples of speech performance in children. They then scored the children's speech for morpheme suppliance. On the assumption that the morphemes which were the least often supplied were the last to be acquired, they determined an order of morpheme acquisition for their subjects. We will discuss this study and others like it more fully in Chapter 4.

Focused descriptive studies which are correlative in nature seek to determine if two phenomena are related, and if so, the degree to which they are. As applied to an SLA context, the usual procedure is for researchers to use instruments to measure certain learner character-istics (e.g. motivation) or characteristics of the learning environment (e.g. amount of native-speaker input) and to correlate these with the learners' second language proficiency. An example of such research is Gardner and Lambert's (1972) study of the relationship between learners' motivation and their second language proficiency. A different form of this procedure has been used by classroom researchers, such as Politzer (1977), where what are correlated with students' second lan-guage achievement are frequencies of teacher or student behaviours.

The fact that these descriptive studies are focused is both an advantage and a disadvantage. What is advantageous is that the scope of the researchers' task is limited: they are not burdened with trying to explain all aspects of second language acquisition simultaneously. Furthermore, once the focus has been established, it is maintained; it does not shift according to the fancies of the researchers. As a natural consequence of these two points, focused descriptive studies are usually less time-consuming than open-ended observational studies, so more of them can be conducted and more subjects can be observed in any one study. Although we have already mentioned that generalizability is not strictly dependent upon the number of subjects in a study, it is also true that researchers can feel much more confident about the generalizability of their findings if they hold for a group of subjects as opposed to a few individuals.

The focus of this type of study can also be disadvantageous, however. Limiting the scope of the research ignores the fact that SLA is a multi-dimensional phenomenon. It is reasonable to question whether findings that result from a focused study will hold when the full context of SLA is restored. Because of the complexity of SLA, it is unlikely that a single isolated factor will be powerful enough to show a relationship to learner success among all learners and in all situations.

The use of an instrument helps to standardize researchers' observations, allowing one to compute the inter-rater reliability of the observations, the degree to which the researchers agree on what they have observed. It also allows researchers to easily compare results from one study to the next. These are very important in observational studies. On the other hand, the use of an instrument precludes the researchers' investigating categories of behaviour apart from those the instrument describes. Whether or not the categories in the instrument are the important ones is also subject to question. They can be just as biased, of course, as a researcher's notes taken during a non-participant observation.

The use of instruments to elicit learner behaviour or measure learner characteristics in the focused studies described above by Dulay and Burt (1974) and Gardner and Lambert (1972) also has its advantages and disadvantages. We will discuss the former in Section 2.4 below and the use of self-report data in the latter in Chapter 6.

2.2.5 Pre-experiment

So far we have been reviewing methodologies that result in descriptions of the SLA process. Researchers who use these methodologies set as their goal understanding the SLA process. True experiments differ in that the goal of researchers using them is to predict and explain human behaviour (Ochsner 1979). As we move along the continuum, we encounter several research designs that approximate, to an increasing degree, true experiments. In a true experiment, researchers attempt to establish a causal relationship between some treatment and some consequence. For example, if we were conducting an experiment in a language classroom, the treatment might be some particular error-correction strategy, and the consequence might be the eradication of certain errors in learners' spoken performance. In order to establish such a relationship in a valid manner, two criteria must be satisfied: (1) there must be experimental and control groups, i.e. groups distinguished by which treatment they have experienced, and (2) subjects must be randomly assigned to one of these groups.

The next type of methodology to be considered here fails to meet both criteria and hence is termed pre-experimental. While researchers using this design are prohibited from making statements about causality, pre-experimental designs can provide useful insights into SLA which later may be tested using more rigorous procedures. One type of pre-experimental design is called the one-group pretest–posttest design. An example of this design in the SLA literature is Gardner, Smythe and Brunet's (1977) study of the effect of intensive French language study on attitudes, motivation and achievement. Sixty-two students of French were administered a battery of attitude and motivation tests as well as a test of oral French proficiency prior to, and upon completion of, a five-week, residential summer programme. Changes in students' attitudes, motivation and French achievement were observed. Although these changes could not be said to be caused by the course, as they could have been due to other factors, the variables which were observed to change could form the starting point for future testable hypotheses.

We will consider the advantages and disadvantages of all experimental methodologies at the conclusion of our discussion of true experiments.

2.2.6 Quasi-experiment

Our next category, quasi-experimental designs, is closer to the true experiment in that one of two criteria of experimental design is met. The result is that one of the two sources of invalidity can be eliminated. Quasi-experimental designs do not require random assignment of subjects to groups but do include one or more control groups. Having said this, it seems contradictory to illustrate this category with a time-series design, since designs of this sort usually involve just one group. Nevertheless, time-series designs are quasi-experiments since they improve upon the one-group pretest–posttest design that was classified as pre-experimental. The improvement in a time-series design is that *multiple* observations of a group are made prior to and following the treatment. Thus, subjects in one group serve both as a control group and as an experimental group. The observations prior to the treatment should show the subjects as a control group, i.e. one should see what the learning curve is without treatment. The learning curve based upon the post-treatment condition is also charted. The observations after the treatment should indicate an upswing in the curve if the treatment had a positive effect on the subjects' performance.

2.2.7 Experiment

The basic premise of an experiment is that all factors save one are held constant. The single factor is varied to see what effect it has on the phenomenon under investigation. As stated earlier, experiments have two criteria: (1) there are at least two groups included in the study, a control group and an experimental group; and (2) the subjects are randomly assigned to one of those groups.

The purpose of having the two groups in the study is that if one group is treated in one manner, and another in a different manner and their post-treatment behaviour differs, we can conclude that the behaviour differs as a consequence of their different treatments. This can only be concluded, of course, if the two groups are comparable to start with. This is the reason for criterion 2. Random group assignment allows the researchers to assume that they have two truly comparable groups at the outset of the experiment. A further safeguard to assure group comparability (especially desirable when subject populations are small) is to compare their performances on a pretest. If the experimental and control groups are equivalent and only the treatment they receive differs, then any post-treatment test differences can be attributed to the treatment itself.

An example of an experiment in the SLA field is Henrichsen's (1984) factorial design studying the effect of sandhi variation on the comprehensibility of English input. Sandhi variation refers to phonological modifications such as contraction (e.g. *gonna–going to*) assimilation (e.g. *watča–what are you*), etc., which reduce the perceptual saliency of morphemes. Henrichsen hypothesized that native English-speaker comprehension would be unaffected by the presence or absence of sandhi variation; non-native speakers' comprehension, on the other hand, would be adversely affected by the presence of sandhi variation. Native English-speakers and ESL learners with high English proficiency and low English proficiency were randomly assigned to one of two treatment conditions: the presence or absence of sandhi variation. Subjects were administered an instrument used to measure their comprehension in the two treatment conditions. The significant interaction found between levels of English proficiency and presence/absence of sandhi variation supported the hypothesis.

The basic idea of an experiment is a powerful one. If one group of subjects is treated in one fashion and another in a different fashion, and there are no other factors influencing the two groups differentially, a cause-effect relationship between treatment and consequence can be determined. Furthermore, a properly controlled experiment allows researchers to generalize findings beyond those obtained from the specific subjects in the study to the population from which the sample was drawn. These are tremendous advantages of the experimental methodology. The use of an experiment is not without cost, however.

In order to enjoy these two advantages, the phenomenon under investigation must be removed from its real-world context. This results in simplification and unnatural manipulation of variables in which the researcher has an interest. The question we are left to face is whether or not such simplification and manipulation change the nature of the phenomenon under study, thereby making generalizations resulting from the findings to the 'real world' invalid. As Hatch and Farhady (1982) state the paradox:

> Our goal should be to approximate as closely as possible the standards of true experimental design. The more care we take the more confident we can be that we have valid results that we can share with others. However, if we reduce our experiments to highly artificial laboratory-type experiments, we must also worry about whether the results can be directly transferred and shared as valid for the classroom. (p. 23)

Another drawback in using an experimental methodology is that experiments are sometimes totally inappropriate for studying human behaviour. An interesting experimental study would be one in which the progress in acquiring a second language of subjects receiving restricted input was compared with that of a control group receiving normal input. However, assuming that the acquisition of the group receiving impoverished input was hindered, it would not be ethical to proceed with the study, unless, of course, volunteers giving their informed consent were used.

At other times, the experimental methodology is inappropriate because one of the conditions cannot be met. For example, SLA subjects are typically composed of pre-existing classes of SL students. The criterion of random selection is not truly met under these circumstances. In these cases, a quasi-experimental methodology may be called for. Quasi-experiments exist as compromises for those interested in studying human behaviour in naturally occurring settings in which complete experimental control is difficult, if not impossible. Although quasi-experimental designs 'are not as adequate as the true experimental designs (since the sources of bias are not amply controlled), they are substantially better than the pre-experimental designs, with regard to control of the threats to validity' (Tuckman 1978, p. 136). Pre-experimental designs, then, are probably best viewed as simply hypothesis-generating. As Underwood (1966) puts it: 'We have no infallible criteria to distinguish between a superstition (a false notion concerning cause and effect) and a "reasonable" hypothesis about cause and effect relationships prior to the time we put each to experimental test' (p. 5).

As we have traversed the continuum between the qualitative and quantitative poles, it may have become apparent that there was no neat separation between one methodology and the next. Indeed, we should probably not think of each methodology as a discrete entity, but rather as a constellation of typical attributes. Moreover, there is no reason why the attributes could not be interchanged so that combination or hybrid methodologies result. We have already illustrated this point with our earlier discussion of the longitudinal and cross-sectional approaches. To give a few more examples, there are focused descriptive studies which use focused introspection to probe some feature of language acquisition. (See, for example, Cohen and Hosenfeld 1981.) Also, there is nothing to prevent a researcher from entertaining hypotheses at the outset of a non-participant observation, nor is there anything in this type of study prohibiting the use of instrumentation to explore the subjects' knowledge of the second language. Kellerman (1974), for example, has suggested supplementing natural data with 'lateralization', in which information is elicited from the learner about specific points of the language he or she is spontaneously producing. To cite one final example, as has been mentioned above, researchers sometimes use correlational designs to look for possible relationships between learner characteristics and learner achievement. They could also, however, use a correlational design to test an *a priori* hypothesis about a relationship, though the results would not demonstrate causality. Only a true experiment will allow claims to be made about causality, although a correlation between two variables provides evidence consistent with a hypothesized causal relationship.

Thus, to some extent, features commonly associated with one methodology can be borrowed by another. In addition, there already exist some established methodologies that attempt to address issues from multiple methodological perspectives. One feature of Mehan's (1978) constitutive ethnography, for example, is that there is an attempted convergence between what non-participant observers note and what participants experience. Asking the participants to comment on the observers' analysis after the observation is one way of doing this. In another procedure, aptly termed triangulation, three perspectives are taken into account. Through a combination of introspection and observation, the teachers', the students' and the researchers' perspective on what transpired during a lesson are all brought to bear on a common experience. (See, for example, Hawkins 1985.)

From these few examples it should be clear that there is much to be gained from approaching the study of SLA using a combination of attributes of both qualitative and quantitative paradigms. Rather than seeing them as competing paradigms, we see them as complementary, implying that it is unnecessary to choose between the two. Similar sentiments have been expressed by Ochsner (1979), who advocates drawing upon both hermeneutic and nomothetic traditions[5]; by Long (1980b), who recommends descriptive anthropological studies as well as large-scale experimental work; by McLaughlin (1980), who supports using careful longitudinal research with single cases and large-scale studies with multivariate analyses; and by Schumann (1983), who calls for the employment of both artistic and scientific modes. The complementarity of the two approaches also has been pointed out by participants in a state-of-the-art session on research methodology sponsored by the TESOL Organization's Research Interest Section (Eisenstein 1986, Wolfson 1986, Henning 1986, Chaudron 1986a).

This ends our somewhat lengthy discussion of research methodologies. Throughout our discussion we have made reference to the desirability of studying the 'natural' process of SLA. Two related design issues are the setting for the study, i.e. 'natural' or in a classroom, and the type of data, i.e. 'natural' or elicited. We will address each of these issues explicitly now.

2.3 Setting

Accompanying the perspective shift from research on the teaching process to research on the learning process was the expressed need to truly understand the acquisition process in its natural state. The assumption was that 'there is a property of the human mind which determines the way language learners process the data of language to which they are exposed' (Corder 1981, p. 72). If this property could be studied operating naturally, researchers might be able to discover some general processing principles. Then, rather than relying on the material developers' intuitions, these principles could be applied to pedagogical concerns such as the selection and sequencing of items in syllabuses.

It was reasonable to assume that instruction could alter natural language processing and thus contaminate SLA data. In an early warning, Selinker (1972) called to our attention idiosyncratic learner errors which were specifically textbook or teacher-induced. More recently Kasper (1982) has identified teaching-induced errors in the discourse behaviour of German students of advanced English.

Felix (1981a) reports finding teaching-induced errors in his study of German high school students learning English as a second language in a classroom. These occurred when students were forced to produce structures for which developmentally they were not ready. For example, in answer to the question 'Is there a flag in the room?', the students would answer correctly, 'No,' but when urged by the teacher to use a full sentence, they would respond, 'No. There is a flag in the room.' According to Felix, the students were unable to negate sentences at this stage in their English development. Felix also found, however, utterances which shared many structural features with the speech of untutored second language learners, leading him to comment that instruction does not apparently suppress the natural process of SLA.

Another obvious difference between instructed and naturalistic settings is in the type of input the learner receives. Pica (1983c) succinctly summarizes the difference here:

> In the classroom setting, language is organized according to the presentation of rules, often given one at a time and in strict sequence, and with the provision of teacher feedback on error, particularly for violations of rules in the linguistic code (see especially Krashen and Seliger 1975). In naturalistic settings, there is no formal articulation of rules and emphasis is on communication of meaning. Error correction, if it occurs at all, tends to focus on meanings of messages communicated. (p. 102)

Despite the setting variations, as with Felix, Pica herself found both similarities as well as differences between the speech of tutored and untutored learners. Her study and others will be discussed in Chapter 8 when we consider how instruction influences SLA. Suffice it to say here that while there are clear differences between the two environments, there appear to be features of the SLA process common to both.

One final consideration has been brought to our attention by Johnston (1985), who points to a problem with naturalistic data themselves. Johnston notes that in his native Australia, many migrants have the opportunity to attend English classes. Thus, the minority of subjects available for the study of naturalistic acquisition in Australia are likely to be more culturally, socially and psychologically distant from native speakers, as compared with their tutored counterparts. While Johnston is quick to point out that there are exceptions to this pattern, it does make it necessary for researchers to recognize the need to sort out any differences in behaviour brought about by the environment from any differences in behaviour due to learner characteristics.

2.4 Instrumentation: production data elicitation

In addition to setting, the issue of naturalness arises with regard to the type of data the researcher collects. As we have seen, one of the features which varies along the qualitative/quantitative continuum is whether or not any instrumentation is used. In theory, researchers who embrace more qualitative methodologies would reject the use of instruments to elicit data, favouring instead spontaneous or 'natural' data. It follows that in theory researchers preferring quantitative methods would choose to use instruments in their studies. In practice, however, as we have seen earlier, no such clear-cut distinction exists.

While it might be desirable to study only subjects' spontaneous production, as was mentioned earlier, the mere presence of an observer is likely to cause the subjects to pay more attention to their speech and thus result in unspontaneous performance. Moreover, even if completely spontaneous production data were available, there are certain drawbacks to relying solely on them for insights into the SLA process. First of all, without the imposition of constraints in terms of the range of possible responses a subject is likely to produce, it is impossible to study all aspects of a learner's developing performance. Certain language features could not be studied because they do not occur frequently in normal conversation. A researcher would have to wait a long time, for example, for subjects to produce enough gerundive complements for the researcher to be able to say anything meaningful about their acquisition.

Second, learners will place limitations on the data themselves (Corder 1981). Learners will often not reveal to researchers their entire linguistic repertoire; rather, they will use only those aspects in which they have the most confidence. They will avoid the troublesome aspects through circumlocution or some other device. And it may be precisely the troublesome aspects of the second language in which the researcher is most interested. Thus, if the occasion does not lend itself for a particular aspect of linguistic performance to be manifest, or if learners are adept at circumlocuting aspects of the language which cause them difficulty, researchers will not be able to adduce any sort of evidence.

Finally, if a researcher were limited to describing what arose spontaneously for a given subject, comparison from study to study would be difficult and generalizations about second language learners would be seriously delayed until a sufficiently large volume of data was amassed.

One of the primary functions, then, of instruments designed to elicit production data is to oblige learners to produce the item the investigator is interested in studying. At the same time, since researchers still want to strive to obtain as natural a performance as possible, it is ideal if the subjects remain unaware of the item under investigation. There are other desirable qualities that one would want to take into account in designing such an instrument, such as the presence of a context, scoring ease, length, sample, ordering effects, ease of administration, etc., but we will be unable to deal with these here. (See Larsen-Freeman 1985b for a discussion of these and other qualities.)

When instruments are used to collect linguistic production data, they are referred to by a variety of names: elicitation procedure, elicitation device, technique for eliciting performance data, data-collection or data-gathering device, a task or even a test, although we will submit later that there is an important distinction between the last two. The purpose of the following is to describe a number, although by no means all, of the elicitation procedures employed in SLA research today. We will present them in a rough order from those that exert more control over the learners' performance to those that exert less control, although admittedly, it is sometimes difficult to order contiguous procedures based on this criterion alone. We will also cite some representative studies in which the elicitation procedure has been appropriated.

(1) *Reading aloud.* This procedure has been used in studies researching pronunciation in a second language (Beebe 1980b; Flege 1980). Subjects are asked to read aloud word lists, sentences or passages which have an abundance of particular sounds in representative environments. The subjects' performance is recorded for later analysis.

(2) *Structured exercises.* Subjects are asked to perform some grammatical manipulation so that researchers can study subjects' performance with regard to specific morphemes or syntactic patterns. Some exercise types which have been utilized are transformation exercises (Cazden et al. 1975), fill-in-the-blanks with the correct form (Larsen-Freeman 1975a), sentence-rewrite (Schmidt and McCreary 1977), sentence-combining (Schmidt 1980) and multiple choice (Bialystok 1982).

(3) *Completion task.* In one form of this task, subjects listen to or read the beginning of a sentence and are asked to complete it using their

own words. Richards (1980) used this procedure to study infinitival and gerundive complements. He gave each subject the start of a sentence including a verb which could take either complement. The subjects were asked to complete the sentence.

Bialystok (1982) had subjects complete a text. Subjects were asked to read a written dialogue and a brief summary statement. The subjects were then asked to complete the dialogue. The task was fashioned so that subjects were required to use one of the six target forms, i.e. forms Bialystok was interested in studying.

Using another completion task of sorts, Natalicio and Natalicio (1971) employed the Berko 'wug' test of first language acquisition fame in their study of Spanish children's acquisition of English. Berko (1958) gave a child a nonsense word – e.g. 'wug' – and then showed the child a picture of 'a wug.' Next the child was shown a picture of two wugs and told: 'This is a picture of . . .' If the child completed the sentence successfully, the researcher determined that the child had the ability to extend morphological rules to new cases. The child had to be using rules, since nonsense plurals, such as 'wugs,' could not have been heard in the input. The Second Language Oral Production English or SLOPE Test (Fathman 1975a) is an SLA completion task, patterned very much like the Berko morphology test.

(4) *Elicited imitation.* The usual elicited imitation procedure is to have the researcher read to the subject a particular set of sentences containing examples of the structure under study (or better, play a taped reading since it standardizes such aspects as rate of delivery). The subject is asked to imitate each sentence after it is read. The procedure is based on the assumption that if the sentence is long enough (Naiman 1974 suggests fifteen syllables), a subject's short-term memory will be taxed and consequently the subject will be unable to repeat the sentence by rote. What the subject will have to do, instead, is to understand the sentence and to reconstruct it using his or her own grammar. Although there is some controversy regarding variability in performance (see Gallimore and Tharp 1981 for discussion), for the most part comparable performances between elicited imitation and spontaneous production have been reported.

(5) *Elicited translation.* Ravem (1968) was one of the first researchers to use translation as an elicited procedure, but the procedure was discussed at greatest length by Swain, Naiman and Dumas (1974). Subjects are given a sentence in their native language and are asked

to translate it into their second language or vice versa. It is thought that such a procedure requires both the decoding of the stimulus sentence and the encoding of the translation, so that subjects' performance approximates natural speech production.

(6) *Guided composition.* Subjects produce oral or written composition in response to some set of organized stimuli. Richards (1980) used picture sequences which tell a story as stimuli. Ioup (1984a) asked subjects to write a composition based on an arrangement of content words she gave them.

(7) *Question and answer (with stimulus).* Conducting a question-and-answer session (with stimuli) is a fairly common means of eliciting SLA data. Researchers using the Bilingual Syntax Measure (Burt, Dulay and Hernandez-Chavez 1975) follow this procedure. Subjects look at a picture or a series of pictures and answer questions designed to elicit particular structures under study. Bialystok (1982) had her subjects listen to sixteen personalized situations which are described in a few sentences and which end with a question. Subjects then were asked to give a contextually appropriate response.

(8) *Reconstruction.* This procedure has also been called 'story re-telling' by Hulstijn and Hulstijn (1984) and 'paraphrase recall' by Connor and McCagg (1983). Subjects read or listen to a story (Larsen-Freeman 1983a) or watch a movie (Godfrey 1980). They are then asked to retell or reconstruct the story orally or in writing.

(9) *Communication games.* Scarcella and Higa (1981) used a procedure which could aptly be classified as a communication game. Native English speakers were paired with both child and adolescent ESL learners. Each pair was asked to use pieces of plastic to replicate a picture they had been given. Their conversations were audiotaped and transcribed. The transcriptions were analysed for the native-speaker input received by the ESL learners of different ages and the negotiation the learners performed to manage the input.

Lightbown, Spada and Wallace (1980) also availed themselves of a procedure which fits this category. Each subject was given ten sets of cards. Each set consisted of four pictures which differed from each other minimally. The subject was asked to choose one of the four and to describe it to the researcher so the researcher would know which picture the subject had selected. The pictures were specifically designed to provide contexts in which the structures under study would be likely to occur.

(10) *Role play.* Fraser, Rintell and Walters (1980) proffer role play as a useful means to study learners' pragmatic competence. So many contextual features (e.g. status of speaker and listener, urgency of the message, relationship between speaker and listener, their sexes, their ages, etc.) are important in determining how a speaker will behave. In a role play, the speech act can be kept constant while the contextual features are varied. In this way, many dimensions of a learner's pragmatic competence may be explored. In Fraser, Rintell and Walters' procedure, the subjects were asked to participate in a more or less structured role play with the researcher. Other researchers have used role plays with puppets when the subjects have been children (Walters 1979).

(11) *Oral interview.* Researchers vary in the way they use oral interviews as an elicitation procedure. Some exercise control over the topics with the hope that they can steer the conversation in such a way that subjects will be encouraged to produce the structure being studied. Other researchers, while acknowledging that an oral interview is constrained in certain ways, allow subjects freedom in choosing what topics should be discussed. In so doing, it is hoped that subjects will tend to become involved in the subject matter of the conversation and consequently produce more spontaneous speech (Johnston 1985).

(12) *Free composition.* Perhaps the least controlled of all elicitation procedures is the free composition. Aside from the establishment of a topic, there is no intervention by the researcher. Of course, a topic itself can encourage the production of certain structures as opposed to others. For instance, if it is the case that the researcher is studying something as ubiquitous as grammatical morphemes (Andersen 1976), then specifying that the writer has to relate some past experience gives the researcher ample data with which to study the acquisition of how the subject expresses past time, although it does not guarantee that subjects will do so using past-tense morphemes. (See, for example, Dittmar 1981.)

2.5 Variability problem

Before moving on in our discussion of instrumentation, we should acknowledge a major problem with the use of elicitation procedures in particular. Earlier we made a case for the indispensability of elicitation procedures: they yield data which complement and expand upon 'natural' data. While we remain resolute in support of the use of elicitation procedures, we now recognize that we must not only be concerned with whether or not performance resulting from elicitation procedures parallels natural performance; we must also be aware that subjects' performance varies from task to task. While this may seem obvious in hindsight, it was once thought perfectly reasonable to expect subjects' performance to be invariant from task to task. The logic was that if subjects had acquired a particular structure, then they should be able to use it in all contexts and modalities.

To test this logic empirically, Larsen-Freeman (1975b) created five tasks in her study of morpheme acquisition by ESL learners. When subject performance was compared from task to task, a great deal of variation was detected. The tasks were deliberately designed so as to require subjects to use different skills. This was expected to result in inflated scores for one task compared with another (e.g. subjects might perform better on all morphemes on the reading task than on the writing task), but it was not anticipated that for some tasks certain morphemes would receive high scores and for other tasks low. Krashen (1975) suggested that Larsen-Freeman's results varied because for some of the tasks the learner was given more time and was encouraged to focus on the linguistic form of his or her performance; other tasks were more communicative in nature so that the learner's attention would be drawn more to the message he or she was trying to convey. The different task demands would therefore yield different performance scores.

In addition to time allotment and the focus on form or communicative intent, Larsen-Freeman (1975a) offered eight other explanations for the varied performance of her subjects. Several of them are as follows: the amount/quality of the context varied from task to task; also, although the morphemes themselves were the same for all five tasks, the lexical items to which they were bound varied from task to task and so perhaps performance on certain morphemes was lexically dependent; another explanation offered was that subjects could avoid producing the target morphemes on certain of the tasks but not on others.

Indeed, it seems to be the conditions accompanying the task itself which cause variable performance. Hulstijn and Hulstijn (1984) found that certain different conditions (where the subjects' attention was focused on form or message; time pressure) they placed on a story-retelling task resulted in different response behaviour on the part of the subjects.

Tarone (1983) claimed in a review of the studies which report task variability that 'when a task elicits a relatively more careful style, that style may contain more target language forms or more prestige native language variants than the relatively more casual style elicited by other tasks' (p. 146). Careful styles, according to Tarone, result when maximal learner attention is focused upon language forms. Crookes (1988b) has more recently demonstrated that the amount of planning time subjects have will also affect their performance on tasks. No matter which explanation for task variability turns out to be correct, the fact remains that different tasks or tasks administered under different conditions yield somewhat different results. And this has been attested to not only for morphology, but also for syntax (Schmidt 1980; Eisenstein, Bailey and Madden 1982; Hyltenstam 1983) and for phonology (Dickerson and Dickerson 1977; Beebe 1980b; Sato 1985a), and not only for non-native speakers, but for native speakers as well (Butler-Wall 1983).

One other difference that has been reported with regard to task differences is in the type of errors associated with learner performance on each. An elicited translation task, for instance, encourages a word-for-word rendition. Thus, it is not surprising that such tasks yield a higher proportion of errors which can be traced back to the influence of the native language (Burmeister and Ufert 1980). Richards (1980) notes that subjects in the Swain, Naiman and Dumas (1974) study exhibited 'errors' even in their native language when translating from their second language; that is, the subjects produced native language forms they wouldn't normally use. It should be noted, however, that this was not true for all learners. In general, the errors subjects made in translation were the same as those they committed in their spontaneous production and imitation (Swain, Naiman and Dumas 1974, p. 76). Then, too, Johnston (1985), reporting on a study by Pienemann, notes that Pienemann's expectation at the inception of his study was that there would be an obvious difference between the data gathered by a linguistic interview and those gathered in natural, spontaneous speech. 'In fact, there turned out to be no palpable difference at all' (p. 80).

So, once again, we see there are no easy generalizations in SLA. Perhaps all we can safely say at this point is that since multiple observations are important in naturalistic observation, by analogy multiple tasks should be used when instrumentation is planned. As early as 1971, Adams (reported in Adams 1978, p. 296) wrote: 'I am convinced that multiple measures are useful in studying SLA.' They certainly demonstrate some stability of performance, but they each also, perhaps, reveal a little different piece of the SLA puzzle. In addition, researchers need to control for task in their studies and to make sure that the tasks used in their studies and those of other researchers are the same before comparing findings *across* studies.

2.6 Instrumentation: intuitional data elicitation

The twelve procedures described in Section 2.4 constitute the primary means by which linguistic production data have been elicited from subjects in SLA studies. Other elicitation procedures have been used to educe the other major kind of linguistic data in SLA. This kind of data has been referred to in a variety of ways. Some call it data on learners' competence (the speaker-hearer's knowledge of his language) (Fraser, Rintell and Walters 1980). Others refer to it as metalinguistic judgement data (Chaudron 1983c) or intuitional data (Corder 1981). Corder explains why it is important in SLA:

> A description based only on textual [i.e. *production* – our term] data cannot achieve more than observational adequacy. As we know, there are an indefinite number of observationally adequate grammars possible of a textual corpus. To be descriptively adequate a grammar must be in accord with the intuitions of the native speaker. (p. 59)

To illustrate Corder's point with a simple example, take the case of a learner who produces the form: 'Is he going to town?' In the absence of other evidence, we do not know if the subject has acquired the rules of yes/no question formation, has memorized this question as a chunk or has merely gotten it right by chance. In short, SLA researchers must be able to account for learners' second language competence, not only their performance. The four following elicitation procedures are what SLA researchers have utilized in an attempt to get at learners' intuitions.

(1) *Error recognition and correction.* Cohen and Robbins (1976) and Schlue (1976) were among the earliest researchers who used error identification and correction tasks. These researchers asked subjects if they could locate an error in a particular sentence that the subjects had produced and if so, if they could supply the correct form. As a final bit of information in the Cohen and Robbins study, the subjects were asked why they thought they had made the errors. Cohen and Robbins found that their subjects did possess the satisfactory metalanguage for

explaining a number of their errors, although Schlue discovered that her subjects were able to locate only 35 per cent of their errors.

Subjects are not always given their own utterances to correct. Sometimes they are given sentences which contain a particular kind of error or in some cases sentences which are correct. Subjects are asked to judge if the sentence is correct or incorrect, and if it is considered incorrect, to correct the sentence. (See also Krashen and Pon 1975.)

(2) *Grammaticality judgements.* Judgements of grammaticality refer to a speaker's intuition concerning the nature of a particular utterance. The subject is asked whether or not a given utterance is well formed. Schachter, Tyson and Diffley (1976) presented sentences containing errors in relative clause formation to groups of second language learners with different native language backgrounds. Each group was asked to judge well-formed sentences as well as those containing errors typically made by speakers sharing their native language backgrounds. They found that whereas the Farsi-speaking group in their study regarded their own deviant output as grammatical, the Japanese group responded randomly to their own unique output. Developmental changes in learner judgements have been studied by d'Anglejan-Chatillon (1975), Arthur (1980) and Gass (1983).

(3) *Other judgement tasks.* In another kind of judgement task, Tucker and Sarofim (1979) asked subjects to rate deviant and well-formed sentences in terms of their social acceptability. Walters (1979) had his subjects make judgements as to the relative politeness of request strategies; Singh, d'Anglejan and Carroll (1982) instructed their subjects to make acceptability judgements; and finally, Eisenstein and Berkowitz (1981) asked ESL learners to rank sentences according to how easy they thought it would be to understand them. In this latter study, subjects listened to three speakers: one standard English speaker, one working-class English speaker and one nonnative speaker.

(4) *Card sorting.* In this procedure, pictures or sentences are placed on cards and subjects are asked to categorize or rank-order them. This type of task was used by Guiora et al. (1982) to test the ability of children to discriminate gender differences; and by Tanaka and Kawada (1982), who had subjects order a set of twelve cards (each bearing a second-language sentence) from the most polite to the least polite (see also Carrell and Konneker 1981).

2.7 Instrumentation: use of miniature languages

Elicitation procedures associated with miniature languages often elicit both linguistic production and intuitional data. In first language acquisition research, subjects have been exposed to a set of sentences of a miniature artificial language created by the researcher. After exposure, the regularities the subjects have observed are determined by asking them to recall or recognize sentences. Since subjects are presented with more sentences than they can have learned by rote, when they are asked to recall, they are actually being asked to produce sentences, and when they are asked to recognize sentences, they are really being asked to make a grammaticality judgement based on the regularities they have induced from the sentences to which they have been exposed. In this way, various principles of human language processing may be determined. (See Smith and Braine 1972 for a review of this work.)

In a second language learning context, Dunkel (1948) used the concept of miniature language to experiment on the effect of instruction. He, however, used a portion of a real language, rather than creating an artificial one. In his study a short series of lessons in Farsi was constructed in alternate forms so that visual and auditory presentation could be evaluated. One group received the material in visual form, the other in auditory form, and the results were compared.

More recently, McLaughlin (1980) has made the case for the use of miniature artificial languages to study the process of second language acquisition.

2.8 Instrumentation: affective variables

Instrumentation has not only been used in SLA research to elicit learner speech or intuitions. It has been used to research affective variables such as attitudes and motivation as well. The five following procedures are those which have been most commonly used to study this area.

(1) *Questionnaires.* Although not always used to measure affective factors (see the Language Contact Profile of Day 1984), questionnaires are often used to get language learners to self-report their attitudes or personal characteristics. For example, in a study of motivation, learners will be presented with a series of statements like the following:

Studying French can be important to me
because I'll need it for my future career.
(Clement and Kruidenier 1983)

Next to each statement will be a Likert-type scale with 'strongly agree'
at one end and 'strongly disagree' at the other. Subjects will be asked
to indicate their appropriate level of agreement with regard to each
statement.

Another format for questionnaires is the use of a semantic differential scale. In an indirect measure of their attitudes, learners have been
asked to rate themselves on unipolar adjective scales and to use the
same scales to rate speakers of the second language. For example,
on a five-point scale ranging from 'very much' to 'not at all', subjects
were asked how well the adjective 'friendly' described themselves and
speakers of the second language (Oller, Hudson and Liu 1977). (For
detailed guidelines for the construction and use of questionnaires, see
Oppenheim 1966 and Bailey 1981.)

(2) *Sociometry*. With young children, direct questions concerning
their attitudes are not appropriate, and so indirect means must be
used. Strong (1984), for example, made use of sociometry, in which
children were asked to nominate classmates who spoke different native
languages as friends or playmates. Based on their nominations, Strong
could identify the subjects' allegiances and plot the group structure
in diagrammatic maps called sociograms. Sociograms are useful in
studying attitudes towards minority-group members within a group
(Anastasi 1968).

(3) *Matched guise technique*. The matched guise technique is used to
elicit attitudes towards speakers of other languages. Several bilinguals
are recorded individually while reading a passage, first in one language
and then in another. Later the tape recordings are played to a group
of subjects. Because the recordings are intermingled, the subjects are
unaware that they are listening to the same speakers in two languages.
The subjects are asked to make judgements about the readers. Since
the readers in both languages are identical, differences in voice quality
and personality of the speaker remain invariant; thus subjects are
thought to be revealing their attitudes towards the languages by the
judgements they make.

The following two procedures have been used to study affective factors;
however, they have also been used to study language-learning strategies
and communicative strategies (Glahn 1980).

(4) *Diary study.* A diary study is an introspective account of a second language experience as recorded in a first-person journal (Bailey and Ochsner 1983). Diaries have been used to study both second language teaching and second language learning. With regard to the latter, the diarist reports on affective factors and on language-learning strategies which would normally escape the attention of an observer.

Schumann and Schumann (1977) were among the first SLA researchers to keep diaries on their language-learning experiences. They recorded their feelings and reactions towards the foreign cultures, the target language speakers and the methods of instruction they were experiencing. The detailed record they kept revealed that for each of them there were a number of personal variables that either promoted or inhibited their second language learning.

(5) *Focused introspection.* Through the use of questionnaires and interviews, subjects have been queried about their feelings and attitudes. For example, one introspection procedure – confrontation – has been used in a large-scale research study conducted by the European Science Foundation and entitled 'The Ecology of Adult Language Acquisition' (Perdue 1982). One of the purposes of the procedure is to confront the subjects with audio or video recordings of themselves and to solicit information from the subjects on what they were feeling during the interaction, their attitudes towards the interlocutor at the time, etc.

As for eliciting data on language-learning strategies, Cohen and Hosenfeld (1981) distinguish between think-aloud and self-observational techniques. Subjects are asked to think aloud as they are performing some language task. They are instructed to let their thoughts flow verbally without trying to direct or observe them. Self-observational techniques are divided by time into 'introspection', which calls for immediate inspection of a subject's mental state, and 'retrospection' (Wenden 1986), in which the subject is queried about what took place after some time has elapsed. (Other introspection techniques and areas investigated are summarized in Wenden 1983.)

2.9 Instruments from other disciplines

Finally, we should point out that SLA researchers have also made liberal use of extant instruments/procedures from other disciplines. These instruments/procedures have almost always been used to analyse learner characteristics. For example, borrowing from psychology, SLA researchers have used various tests (e.g. the Group Embedded

Figures Test) to discover subjects' cognitive styles. (See, e.g., Hansen and Stansfield 1981.) Also from psychology have come various personality assessment measures (e.g. Eysenck's introversion–extroversion scale; Hogan's empathy scale) which SLA researchers have availed themselves of. (See, e.g., Naiman *et al.* 1978.) From neurolinguistics SLA researchers have borrowed dichotic listening tests and eye movement observation to research brain functions and hemisphericity. (See, e.g., Galloway 1981b.)

What these tests and others like them reveal about SLA will be dealt with in Chapter 6. For our purposes here, however, we should acknowledge that many of the instruments/procedures which SLA researchers profit by did not necessarily originate with them.

2.10 Measuring learner performance

Two important methodological issues remain to be dealt with in this chapter. We have blithely been discussing paradigms, setting and instruments for studying SLA. What we have yet to do is to tackle two basic questions, the answers to which have a definite bearing on what and how we research. Before embarking on SLA study we must define what we mean by language/language proficiency and determine how we will know when it is acquired. These issues seem deceptively simple at first glance.

2.10.1 Defining language proficiency

Until recently, most SLA researchers accepted mainstream transformational linguists' portrayal of language in which syntax occupied a central position. Lexical items, phonemes and morphemes were of interest only insomuch as they related to syntax. Following in the same vein, early SLA research dealt largely with the acquisition of syntax and of these so-called 'low-level' linguistic forms. However, even when the quest was limited to explaining linguistic proficiency, there was no consensus as to what such proficiency entailed.

The prevailing view held that language proficiency could be divided into unrelated skills (listening, speaking, reading and writing) and knowledge of language components (vocabulary, phonology and grammar). Oller (1976) challenged this view by hypothesizing that language proficiency is a unitary and indivisible trait, i.e. it cannot be partitioned into distinct components. Moreover, Oller (Oller and Perkins 1978; Oller 1979) claimed this global proficiency factor was strongly related to IQ. This position was supported by a large body of research showing high correlations between verbal and non-verbal abilities on IQ tests (Oller 1981). Since making the initial claim, however, Oller himself has rejected the unitary factor hypothesis, calling it a 'psychometric heresy' (1984, p. 5). Nevertheless, Cummins (1980, 1981a) finds value in the notion of a global language-proficiency factor 'which can be assessed by a variety of reading, writing, listening and speaking tests and which is strongly related to general cognitive skills . . . and to academic achievement' (Cummins 1980, p. 176). This factor Cummins calls cognitive/academic language proficiency (CALP), in place of Oller's global language proficiency. To complement this, Cummins identifies a second, independent dimension of language proficiency. This factor he calls basic interpersonal skills (BICS), which consist of accent, oral fluency and sociolinguistic competence.

Cummins' inclusion of sociolinguistic competence reminds us that it is commonplace these days to speak of students' developing communicative competence rather than mere linguistic proficiency. Canale and Swain (1980) in their original descriptive model suggested that there were three components to communicative competence: grammatical competence, sociolinguistic competence and strategic competence. Having strategic competence means a speaker has a repertoire of communication strategies to invoke to compensate for breakdowns in communication. We will have more to say about communication strategies in Chapter 5. Larsen-Freeman (1981) identified five areas of communicative competence in which SLA research was being conducted: linguistic form, pragmatic/functional competence, propositional content (meaning), interactional patterns (e.g., conversational rules governing how speakers procure and relinquish turns) and strategic competence. Canale (1983), in a revision of his original analysis, include four components of communicative competence: grammatical competence, sociolinguistic competence, discourse competence and strategic competence. Bachman and Palmer (1985) in their descriptive framework of language competence identified two superordinate types of competence (organizational and pragmatic) and four subordinate types: grammatical, discourse, illocutionary and sociolinguistic.

In short, a definitive analysis of communicative competence is just as elusive as was language proficiency. However, even if we were to agree on the components of communicative competence, we would still have a challenge; in order to trace the acquisition process, we must know how to measure the components as well. As Perdue (1982, p. 52) asserts, 'We are studying acquisition at a given time. We wish therefore to know . . . what an informant has acquired, what he has not acquired and what he is acquiring.'[6]

2.10.2 Defining an acquisition point

When attempting to answer these questions with naturalistic data, first language acquisition researchers relied on Cazden's (1968) definition. She defined the point of acquisition of several noun and verb inflections as 'the first speech sample of three such that in all three the inflection is supplied in at least 90 per cent of the contexts in which it is clearly required' (p. 435).

This may seem like a very elaborate definition just to be able to locate when a particular structure is acquired; however, it is necessary to be this precise because the path towards mastery of a structure is full of peaks and valleys. In one given sample of learner language it may be that the learner uses the structure perfectly. By the next time data are collected, however, there has been some regression or *backsliding* and the learner rarely uses the form correctly. Indeed, this type of acquisition pattern is typical for both first and second language acquisition. With only a slight modification, then, Hakuta (1974) was able to adapt Cazden's definition to his SLA study of the development of grammatical morphemes in a Japanese girl learning ESL: the point of acquisition is the 'first of three consecutive two-week samples in which the morpheme is supplied in over 90% of obligatory contexts' (p. 137).

While it works well for what it purports to do, i.e. designate a point of acquisition, there are two limitations to this definition. The first limitation of the acquisition definition involves the notion of *obligatory context*. Sometimes obligatory contexts are easy to identify. For instance, proficient English speakers mark a common count noun preceded by a cardinal number for plurality. The use of such a noun, therefore, establishes an obligatory context for a plural morpheme. What, however, is the obligatory context for a modal verb? The use of a modal verb is entirely dependent upon a speaker's intended meaning, something that is not always available for a researcher's inspection. Clearly the problem becomes even more challenging as researchers begin to study sociolinguistically conditioned use of certain forms. When, for instance, is it absolutely obligatory to use an indirect rather than a direct question in making a request? Some researchers have pointed out an additional problem with the use of obligatory contexts. A point of acquisition should depend not only on how often a structure is supplied appropriately, but should take into consideration how often it is used inappropriately as well (Larsen-Freeman 1975a, p. 89). Acquisition orders determined by subjects' suppliance of forms in obligatory contexts do not take such overgeneralizations into account. Hakuta (1976) offered one solution to this problem by not only reporting his subject's percentage score for suppliance in obligatory contexts, but also reporting her percentage of correct usage.

The second limitation of the acquisition-point definition is that it is often desirable to know how learners are using a particular structure long before the learners have 'acquired' it, in the sense of attained native-like control. Points of acquisition are normative, i.e. the learners' speech is being compared with what native speakers would do; the learners' performance is not being examined in its own right. One solution researchers have found is to focus on the emergence of structures, rather than on their mastery (Cazden et al. 1975; Bahns 1981; Meisel, Clahsen and Pienemann 1981). Acquisition (of a form, only, not its function) then means the first appearance of that form in the learner's language. We return to this issue in later chapters.

2.10.3 Task versus test

The same concern for avoiding comparison with native-speaker performance applies to data that are collected with instruments. Many of the elicitation procedures or tasks such as fill-in-the-blank or multiple-choice exercises described earlier have traditionally been used as classroom tests to assess the learners' mastery of particular structures.[7] There is, however, as we alluded earlier, a difference between a test and a task. The difference has to do with the purposes for which they are devised. Tests are devised to measure what the learner knows and does not know of the target language. A subject's performance is measured against that of target-language speakers. In this sense, a test is normative. A task is devised to reveal what a learner knows: 'the rules he is using and the systems and categories he is working with' (Corder 1981, p. 60). We may sometimes, Corder continues, be able to infer something about the learner's rules, systems and categories from test results, but that is not what the tests are devised to reveal. On the other hand, with regard to tasks:

> The range and nature of the choices or judgements, and the selection of the contexts is based not upon a description of the target language but upon what is known (however limited) [of what the learner knows]. Thus for example the choices in a recognition procedure will be based upon what learners at that stage are known,

believed or may be predicted to do. The contexts for productive elicitation exercises will be selected to elicit lexical items or syntactic forms which learners have already produced or may be predicted to produce in such contexts. (Corder 1981, p. 62)

One more example may be helpful to grasp this important but subtle distinction. Richards (1980) notes that a standard multiple-choice test could not be used as an elicitation procedure or task. The reason is that the distractors are based on the target language and it is entirely feasible that the learner, given the opportunity, would reject all the proffered alternatives. If the distractors instead consisted of forms that learners of the same proficiency level have been known to produce, a multiple-choice format could be used as an elicitation procedure or task. (See Farhady 1980 for one use of this approach.)

2.10.4 An index of development

There are times, of course, when researchers will truly want to be able to measure learners' progress in their L2 development. This sort of information will be needed to characterize a specific subject population (i.e. at what stage of acquisition of the L2 are they?) or to measure the effect of a particular treatment on learners' acquisition (i.e. did the treatment have the effect of moving the particular group of subjects from Stage I to Stage II?) or to measure differences in rate of acquisition among different learners (i.e. how long did it take learner X to move to Stage II versus learner Y and what could account for the difference?).

In addition to traditional integrative tests, other proficiency measures have been used in SLA studies. Several researchers have used native-speaker judgements to gauge learner proficiency. For example, Suter (1976) used a panel of fourteen English-speaking judges to rate the English pronunciation of his non-native speaking subjects. He then correlated the ratings with a variety of learner characteristics.

Scores on standard examinations (e.g. TOEFL, the Michigan Test of English Language Proficiency, the Canadian Forces Language Test, the Modern Language Association Test, the Royal Society of Arts' 'Examination in the Communicative Use of English as a Foreign Language') or proficiency scales (e.g. FSI – Foreign Service Institute, ACTFL – American Council for the Teaching of Foreign Language, ASLPR - Australian Second Language Proficiency Ratings) have been used as measures of second language proficiency.

Sometimes learner proficiency is determined by the teacher's evaluation (e.g. d'Anglejan and Renaud 1985) or by the level of the course to which the student is assigned based on his or her performance on an institutional placement test. Sometimes learner proficiency is merely subjectively gauged and subjects are declared to be beginning, intermediate or advanced with respect to the target language. It is particularly with respect to the vagaries of the latter and recognizing a need for a measure that was sensitive to differences over time that led to Larsen-Freeman's (1976a) call for the creation of an SLA index of development (Hakuta's 1976 term):

> What we need is a yardstick which will allow us to give a numerical value to different points along a second language developmental continuum – numerical values which would be correlates of the developmental process and would increase uniformly and linearly as learners proceed towards full acquisition of a target language. (Larsen-Freeman 1978, p. 440)

First language acquisition researchers employ such a measure. The mean length of utterance or MLU is calculated by averaging the number of morphemes per utterance of a child's speech. The MLU may be somewhat inexact but at least it provides researchers with some estimate of the stage of development of the subjects' native language. Such a measure is, however, obviously not applicable to SLA research where the learner is more cognitively sophisticated and, therefore, capable of producing utterances that are more than a few morphemes in length shortly after initial contact with the target language.

In their search for an SLA 'index', Larsen-Freeman and Strom (1977) examined ESL students' compositions and determined that the written measures which seemed most suitable were the average length of T-units and the total number of error-free T-units per composition.[8] In a later study, Larsen-Freeman (1978) added another measure: the average number of words per error-free T-unit. When these measures were applied to transcripts of spoken language, the results were somewhat disappointing (Larsen-Freeman 1983a). They all worked to a certain extent to discriminate proficiency differences among groups of learners, but they all had some flaws as well, and none appeared to work for all individual subjects. The same findings were reported for an application of T-unit analysis to spoken Japanese as a second language (JSL) by Harrington (1986).

In addition to having it be valid for all subjects, Larsen-Freeman (1983a) listed other desirable characteristics of an SLA index of development: that it be readily available (i.e. not dependent on a particular instrument), that it work well for speakers of different native-language backgrounds and for different target languages, as well as learners of different ages, educational backgrounds, etc., and that it could be applied *post hoc* on data already collected. Whether or not an index of development with all of these characteristics can be developed remains to be seen.

Other researchers have recognized the need for establishing an index of development. Schumann et al. (1982) used the Federal Oral Proficiency Test's five-point scale and attempted to describe grammatical correlates from learner performance at each point along the scale. Researchers in the Heidelberg project developed a cumulative index based on the probability with which certain phrase structure rules are applied. Dittmar (1980) reports that the index the team constructed accorded well with their intuitions about the syntactic elaborateness of their informants. Still, even this index is flawed and admittedly arbitrary to some extent.

More promising results have been obtained more recently in Australia (Pienemann and Johnston 1987). Rejecting the notion that language proficiency, or even communicative competence for that matter, can be atomized and measured in an objective way, Pienemann and Johnston have worked to construct a non-normative language developmental sequence based upon observed learner behaviour. The developmental stages in their sequence are based on speech-processing complexity rather than the accuracy with which learners produce certain target-language structures. We will return to this developmental index when we discuss the Multidimensional Model in Chapter 7.

Since so much of our work in SLA depends on being able to obtain a reliable measure of second language development, we remain sanguine that Pienemann and Johnston's developmental stages will be validated in light of subsequent research. As Singh, d'Anglejan and Carroll (1982, p. 284) have declared, 'Constructing such global indices is always both desirable and *difficult*' (emphasis added).

2.11 Conclusion

In this chapter we have dealt with a number of issues regarding SLA research design:

1. We have recognized that both qualitative and quantitative research have a role to play in enhancing our understanding of SLA. We have also surveyed extant methodologies, acknowledging that each has its strengths and its limitations. We have made the point

that it should not be a case of choosing between the qualitative and quantitative paradigms nor among extant methodologies, but rather of designing a research methodology which possesses the optimal combination of attributes to address the research question under consideration.

2. SLA researchers began their quest for an understanding of the 'natural' SLA process in hopes that language learning would be enhanced when language teaching harmonized with it. There are doubtless numerous differences between tutored and untutored environments for SLA. Nonetheless, we do not want to lose sight of the similarities in the acquisition process which pertain to both environments. This is not to say that instruction has no impact on SLA; clearly it does, certainly on the rate of SLA, at least. We will have more to say about this in Chapter 8.

3. We raised the question of whether any data collected for research purposes could be said to be truly 'natural', and we submitted that well-designed instruments could make production, intuitional and affective data collection more efficient. Such procedures could also yield more complete and comparable data. Nevertheless, we need to recognize that learners perform differently on different tasks and that multiple perspectives need to be brought to bear on a given research question, and that researchers need to be wary of making unqualified generalizations.

4. Finally, we dealt with the nettlesome problem of language proficiency. We saw how difficult it was to achieve agreement on its definition, let alone its measurement. With regard to the measurement issue, we pointed out the value in having the means to study structures as they are developing, i.e. before they conform to target-language norms, as well as having ways of measuring learners' progress.

While some of the issues we have raised here remain unresolved, researchers have not been prevented from addressing issues in SLA. They have had to be realistic about their claims, however, taking care not to generalize beyond what the methodological limitations permit.

Notes

1. It should be noted that it is a point of contention among researchers today as to whether or not both approaches yield identical results. Using a cross-sectional design, first language acquisition researchers de Villiers and de Villiers (1973) were able to corroborate the order of

acquisition of certain grammatical morphemes established by Brown's (1973) longitudinal study of three children learning English as a first language. The picture in SLA is not as clear (see the discussion of morpheme acquisition in Chapter 4).

2. For example, Schumann (1979) has done this for the acquisition of English negation and Bailey (1983a) has done this in her study of competitiveness and anxiety in second-language classrooms.

3. We will encounter the term 'random' sample later in this chapter as well. It is a research concept of some importance. If we are interested in learning about a particular population (e.g. first-year French students at the university level), we cannot possibly study the whole population; we must draw a sample from it. Furthermore, the sample should be drawn randomly to avoid bias. For instance, if we studied only one class of French students at one university, they would not constitute a random sample of all French students, and therefore we could not legitimately generalize to all French students in the country.

4. This is not to say that the observer is objective; as Willis (1976) notes, what is reported says as much about the observer as it does about what has been observed.

5. The nomothetic tradition 'assumes that there is one ordered, discoverable reality which causally obeys the Laws of Nature' (Ochsner 1979, p. 53). Hermeneutic science, on the other hand, assumes that reality is varied, therefore no single method of inquiry will obtain: 'Human events must be interpreted . . . according to their final ends' (Ochsner 1979, p. 54).

6. Of course, when we move into investigating the acquisition of components of communicative competence, we are at another disadvantage. It is often the case that we don't know how native speakers perform. We don't have the necessary native-speaker performance or 'baseline data' against which to measure what learners have acquired (Larsen-Freeman 1981).

7. We use the term 'structure' not only to refer to a syntactic construction but also to any other element of language: a lexical item, a phoneme, a morpheme. A challenge that researchers studying discourse and pragmatics have to contend with is defining their units of analysis (Crookes 1990). What, for example, are the elements of a conversation – adjacency pairs, speech acts, etc. – and how will they be measured once they have been defined? (See Cohen and Olshtain 1981 for their attempt to measure sociocultural competence.)

8. A T-unit is an independent clause and any associated dependent clauses, i.e. clauses which are attached to or embedded within it (Hunt 1965).

Activities

Comprehension

1. Qualitative methods have sometimes been referred to as hypothesis-generating, quantitative methods as hypothesis-testing.

Do you think this is a valid distinction? Give reasons for your answer.

2. Summarize in your own words the advantages and disadvantages of the seven methodologies described in this chapter.
3. What is the difference between a superstition and a genuine cause-and-effect relationship?
4. Why is random subject selection so important? Why is it difficult to achieve?
5. Can you think of any errors which you have heard non-native speakers commit which might have stemmed from formal instruction, i.e., might be teaching-induced?
6. What are the advantages of using more than one task in a SLA research study?
7. How does intuitional data differ from production data? Explain in your own words how the use of a miniature artificial language can yield both types of data.
8. Why is it sometimes desirable to measure attitudes indirectly?
9. What is the difference between language proficiency and communicative competence as the terms are used here?
10. Explain the distinction between a task and a test.

Application

11. If you were interested in researching each of the following questions, which research methodology would you use and why?
   (a) Are there male/female differences in how invitations are extended between native speakers? How does non-native speaker behaviour compare?
   (b) Is there a sequence in which the second language pronouns are acquired? If so, what is it?
   (c) Does practice with sentence-combining exercises result in learners producing longer T-units in their classroom compositions?
   (d) What are word-attack skills learners naturally use when they encounter a word which they don't know?
   (e) What is the relationship between the age at which second language instruction began and the level of second language proficiency achieved after three years of instruction?
12. Choose a structure which occurs fairly frequently in the second language. Collect some naturalistic data and some data through elicited imitation. How do the two types of data compare?
13. The following compositions on 'the most interesting person you have ever known' have been written by a beginner, an intermediate

and an advanced second language student respectively. What objective measures could you use to discriminate among the three performances? Are any of them a candidate for an SLA index of development? (You may wish to consult Larsen-Freeman 1983a, p. 302, for a list of the desirable attributes of such an index.)

Beginning
Last week I went to Disnyland it is a verey good place to met people, and it is verey beautifull. there I met a student from MAXICO she was verey nice. I saw her in coffe sitting alone. So I asked her to seat together she said yeas. So I told he that I am'nt from U.S. and come here just to study. She was verey interesting because I gave her some knowledge about my country. I had a verey good time with her because she could understand me and I feel like I take to my sister also she gave me some idea about her country.

Intermediate
In the refugee camp in Italy, I met the most interesting man in my life. He was interesting because of his misteriousness. Nobady knew anything about him, we could not find explaination about his ever complicated beeing.

His physical appearance was of a bussinessman. He was always running, but it was always unknown from where he came from or where he was going. Whereever I went inside or outside of the camp I always met with him exidently.

The education of my friend was also unknowned. He cliamed that he did not attend even to secondary school, but he seemed to know everything, including the perfect knowledge of twleve languages. He would never tell anybody what was his mother tongue, since apparently his knowledge was outstanding in each language: I thought that he was German according his name, but he speaked Hungarian without a foreign accent, and all the people of different countries said, that he spoked their language just as perfect as they did.

The most misterious of all was his position in the camp. He worked as an interpreter and also sometimes in the coffeeshop. The high office workers were his friend and he was also seened at the International Police Department, where nobody could go in beside the workers.

Inspite of his high standing, he lived the life of the other refugees. He stayed in the dormitory with other men and he eat the same bad food as we did.

Noone could explain his way of living. We was thinking of him as a secret police, interpreter, office worker, or simple refugee the same as we were, but nobady could prove anything. His beeing remained secret all through the years and probably forever.

Advanced

The most interesting person I have ever known is surely my very own stephfather. When I first met this very special man I was only about a year old, and my earliest memories of him are vague. He was a big man, tall and heavy, but his voice was friendly and soft. When I was three years old my mother married him and we moved away from California to live in Holland. My new father was a very influential figure in this small country. He was not only extremely active in the small community in which we lived, but also held several important functions with the Dutch government and managed several large factories. Earlier in life he had served in the army and had won several medals for his services to the people of Holland.

At which when he reached the age of sixty-five, the age most people retire, it seemed that he became even busier. He became active in permoting Dutch trade in foreign countries, and he and my mother visited many countries abroad and met many interesting people. But my stephfather was not only a businessman. During the years he had collected many great works of art and had become the owner of many seventeenth century paintings.

He was also very involved with Unicef, the United Nations Childrens' Fund.

My stephfather is now seventy six years old and is becoming less active. But he stills travels a lot for pleasure, swims every day, and gets up at six o'clock.

I think it becomes clear why I have chosen this man to be the most interesting person I have ever known.

14. Which instrument(s) would be employed in studies where each of the following constitutes the research focus?
    (a) learner anxiety
    (b) understanding cohesive devices
    (c) oral apologies
    (d) r/l pronunciation contrast
    (e) definite versus indefinite article usage in texts
    (f) learner preference for instructional method
    (g) learners' use of *in* versus *on*
    (h) how conversational topics are nominated
    (i) strategies to clarify misunderstanding
    (j) learner judgements as to the deference level of salutations

Suggestions for further reading

For a discussion of qualitative and quantitative methods of conducting research, see:

Bennett-Kastor, T 1988 *Analyzing children's language: methods and theories.* Basil Blackwell

Cook, T and Reichardt, C (eds.) 1979 *Qualitative and quantitative methods in education research.* Sage Publications, Beverly Hills, Calif.

Eisenstein, M 1986 Alternatives in second language research: three articles on the state of the art. *TESOL Quarterly* 20: 683–7, and the three articles which follow Eisenstein's introduction

Ochsner, R 1979 A poetics of second-language acquisition. *Language Learning* 29: 53–80

For a treatment of the experimental continuum, see:

Brown, J D 1988 *Understanding research in second language learning.* Cambridge University Press, New York

Hatch, E and Farhady, H 1982 *Research design and statistics for applied linguistics.* Newbury House Publishers, Inc., Rowley, Mass.

For a book which advocates use of experiments to study SLA, look at:

Cook, V (ed.) 1986 *Experimental approaches to second language learning.* Pergamon, New York

For a collection of articles on the use of introspection in SLA research, see:

Faerch, C and Kasper, G (eds.) 1987 *Introspection in second language research.* Multilingual Matters Ltd.

For a discussion of determining criteria for acquisition, see:

Brindley, G 1986 Semantic approaches to learner language. *Australian Review of Applied Linguistics* 5: 1–43

For an attempt to define communicative competence, see:

Duran, R, Canale, M, Penfield, J, Stansfield, C and Liskin-Gasparro, J 1985 *TOEFL from a communicative viewpoint on language proficiency: a working paper* (TOEFL Research Report 17). Educational Testing Service, Princeton, NJ.

For more on the controversy surrounding language proficiency, see:
Bachman, L 1989 *Fundamental considerations in language testing.* Oxford University Press.
Lantolf, W and Frawley, J 1988 Proficiency: understanding the construct. *Studies in Second Language Acquisition* **10** (2): 181–95

For a discussion of the traits desirable for an index of development, see:
Larsen-Freeman, D 1983 Assessing global second language proficiency. In Seliger, H and Long, M (eds.) *Classroom-oriented research in second language acquisition.* Newbury House Publishers, Inc., Rowley, Mass.

3 SLA: Types of data analysis

3.1 Introduction

In Chapter 2 we focused on the various means that have been employed to collect SLA data. In this chapter we will trace the historical development of types of analyses of these data that researchers have used in an attempt to come to a better understanding of the second language acquisition process. We will be unable to discuss all the substantive findings these analyses have produced here; greater detail will be provided in Chapter 4. The focus here will be on the development of modes of inquiry and on the evolution of issues in the field over the past several decades. (See also Hakuta and Cancino 1977.)

3.2 Contrastive analysis

Before the SLA field as we know it today was established, researchers from the 1940s to the 1960s conducted contrastive analyses, systematically comparing two languages. They were motivated by the prospect of being able to identify points of similarity and difference between particular native languages (NLs) and target languages (TLs), believing that a more effective pedagogy would result when these were taken into consideration. Charles Fries, one of the leading applied linguists of the day, stated it this way: 'The most efficient materials are those that are based upon a scientific description of the language to be learned, carefully compared with a parallel description of the native language of the learner' (1945, p. 9). Such statements inspired a number of contrastive analyses.[1]

The reason language materials were thought to be more efficient when based on contrastive analyses (CAs) was best expressed by Lado, a one-time student of Fries and later his colleague at the University of Michigan:

> Individuals tend to transfer the forms and meanings and the distribution of forms and meanings of their native language and

culture to the foreign language and culture – both productively when attempting to speak the language and to act in the culture and receptively when attempting to grasp and understand the language and the culture as practised by natives. (1957, in Gass and Selinker 1983, p. 1)

Anyone who has attempted to learn a foreign language will be able to corroborate Lado's claim. Foreign-language learners are all too familiar with the interfering effects of their NL causing everything from accented speech to inappropriate non-verbal behaviour.

3.2.1 The contrastive analysis hypothesis

Lado was also responsible for a more controversial position, however, when he claimed that 'those elements that are similar to his native language will be simple for him, and those elements that are different will be difficult' (1957, p. 2). Similarly, Weinreich (1953, p. 1) asserted: 'The greater the difference between two systems, i.e. the more numerous the mutually exclusive forms and patterns in each, the greater is the learning problem and the potential area of interference.' The conviction that linguistic differences could be used to predict learning difficulty gave rise to the contrastive analysis hypothesis (CAH): Where two languages were similar, positive transfer would occur; where they were different, negative transfer, or interference, would result.

We should be quick to point out that many CAs were not merely lists of binary predictions of the form: similarity/difference = ease/difficulty; indeed, those in the University of Chicago series[2] are considerably more sophisticated. Table 3.1 presents a simplified version of Stockwell, Bowen and Martin's (1965a) *hierarchy of difficulty*. Their examples are of an English speaker learning Spanish.

Stockwell, Bowen and Martin's hierarchy is more complicated than this because, among other things, they distinguish between structural and functional/semantic correspondence. Nevertheless, from the table here we can see that they would expect the easiest linguistic point for a language learner to master to be one where the L1 and the L2 correspond structurally and functionally/semantically. Progressively more difficult are those which are coalesced, where several forms in the L1 collapse in the L2; a form which is present in the L1 but absent in the L2; and a form which

Type of Difficulty	L1: English L2: Spanish	Example
1. Split	x < x / y	for < por / para
2. New	ø — — — x	marking grammatical gender
3. Absent	x — — — ø	*Do* as a tense carrier
4. Coalesced	x / y > x	his/her is realized as a single form *su*
5. Correspondence	x — — — x	*-ing* = *-ndo* as a complement with verbs of perception

TABLE 3.1 Hierarchy of Difficulty

is new to the L2. Most difficult of all would be the splits, where a single form in the L1 is manifest as two or more in the L2.

Another characteristic of their system worth repeating is that, unlike Lado, Stockwell, Bowen and Martin do not predict the greatest difficulty in the new and missing categories, where presumably the differences between the two languages are the greatest. Subsequent research has supported their position. Buteau (1970), for instance, found that for English speakers learning French 'the French sentences that correspond literally to their English equivalents are not necessarily the easiest to learn' (p. 138). Psychologist Osgood (1953), had earlier commented on such a phenomenon:

> When two sets of material to be learned are quite different or are easily discriminated by the learner, there is relatively little interaction, that is, learning one has little effect upon learning the other. If they are similar in such a way that the learning of one serves as partial learning of the other, there may be facilitation, or positive transfer. If, however, the similarities either of stimuli or responses are such that responses interfere with one another, then there will be greater interference as similarity increases. (Torrey 1971, p. 226)

As can be seen by the disparity between the dates of Weinreich's (1953) and Lado's (1957) statements and Buteau's (1970) research, more than ten years passed before the statements were put to an empirical test, despite Lado's (1957, p. 72) caveat that

> the list of problems resulting from the comparison of the foreign language with the native language . . . must be considered a list of hypothetical problems until final validation is achieved by checking against the actual speech of students.

3.2.2 Language acquisition as habit formation

In the meantime, the field of language teaching was dominated by the prevailing view of learning at the time – that of behaviourism. The behaviourists held that language acquisition was a product of habit formation. Habits were constructed through the repeated association between some stimulus and some response, which would become bonded when positively reinforced. Second language learning, then, was viewed as a process of overcoming the habits of the native language in order to acquire the new habits of the target language. This was to be accomplished through the pedagogical practices of dialogue memorization, imitation and pattern practice. Overlearning and thus automaticity was the goal. The contrastive analysis hypothesis was important to this view of language learning, since if trouble spots in the target language could be anticipated, errors might be prevented or at least held to a minimum. In this way, the formation of bad habits could be avoided.

3.2.3 The CAH refuted

Ironically, while the association of CAH with behaviourism gave it academic legitimacy, it ultimately led to its downfall. For 1959 saw the publication of Chomsky's classic review of Skinner's *Verbal Behavior*, in which Chomsky seriously challenged the behaviourist view of language acquisition. Moreover, when predictions arising from CAs were finally subjected to empirical tests (see, for example, Alatis 1968), serious flaws were revealed. While CA predicted some errors (see, for example, Duskova 1969; Chamot 1978; Arabski 1979), it clearly did not anticipate all, i.e. it underpredicted (e.g. Hyltenstam 1977). Furthermore, some errors it did predict failed to materialize, i.e. it overpredicted (e.g. Dulay and Burt 1974).

Some of the discrepancies in findings from these studies could no doubt be attributed to the procedures utilized. For instance, the way an error was classified, e.g. due to L1 interference or not, differed from study to study. Moreover, the subjects varied in age and language proficiency, a fact that has been shown to affect the proportion of interference errors committed (Taylor 1975). Nevertheless, it is fair to say that the CAH was not supported by the facts.

Whitman and Jackson (1972), who tested the predictions of four different CAs of English and Japanese by studying the English performance of 2500 Japanese secondary school students on a multiple choice and a cloze test, concluded that 'contrastive analysis was inadequate to predict the interference problems of a language learner', and that

> interference . . . plays such a small role in language learning perfor-
> mance that no contrastive analysis, no matter how well conceived,
> could correlate highly with performance data, at least at the level of
> syntax. (1972, p. 40)

Perhaps the most fatal flaw of the CAH, as pointed out by Long and Sato (1984), was the dubious assumption that one could depend solely upon an analysis of a *linguistic product* to yield meaningful insight into a *psycholinguistic process*, i.e. second language learning.

Despite these criticisms, CAs continued to be conducted, particularly in Europe,[3] and the problem of identifying just where and when L1 influence can be expected to take place has continued to be of interest. We will return to a discussion of language transfer as it is conceived today in Chapter 4. Suffice it to say that, although the CAH was unproven, CA as a methodological option was not abandoned.

3.3 Error analysis

The enduring quality of CA was not due to sheer obstinacy; it was observed earlier that no one could deny that the L1 influenced L2 performance, so that we can often identify with some degree of assurance the native language of a foreign speaker, at least where phonological evidence is available, although we are less successful in identifying the L1 of SL learners based on syntactic evidence alone (Ioup 1984a).

3.3.1 Strong versus weak versions of the CAH

In an attempt to reconcile this observation with the disappointing results of empirical investigations, Wardhaugh (1970) proposed a distinction between a strong version and a weak version of the contrastive analysis hypothesis. The strong version involved *predicting* errors in second language learning based upon an *a priori* contrastive analysis of the L1 and L2, and as we have seen, the predictions are not always borne out. In the weak version, however, researchers start with learner errors and *explain* at least a subset of them by pointing to the similarities and differences between the two languages. Thus, although CAH might not be useful *a priori*, it was still claimed to possess *a posteriori* explanatory power. As such, it was useful in a broader approach to detecting the source of error, namely error analysis.

3.3.2 Language acquisition as rule formation

In the early 1960s, inspired by Chomsky's theory of language acquisition, first language acquisition researchers began studying the speech of children acquiring English as an L1. What these researchers sought to do was to characterize their subjects' performance by writing a grammar – a system of rules which would account for the utterances the children produced. This enterprise was in keeping with Chomsky's view that language acquisition was not a product of habit formation, but rather one of rule formation. Chomsky posited a theory in which humans were thought to possess a certain innate predisposition to induce the rules of the target language from the input to which they were exposed. Once acquired, these rules would allow learners to create and comprehend novel utterances, utterances they would neither have understood nor have produced were they limited to imitating input from the environment.

Chomsky's theory of language acquisition received support from first language acquisition researchers recording the errors of children. Children acquiring English as their L1 were found to commit errors such as

* She doesn't wants to go.
* I eated it.

which suggested that they had internalized rules for subject–verb agreement and past tense formation in English, respectively, but had not yet mastered the limitations of the rules. Furthermore, such original errors indicated that the children were not simply repeating forms from the input they encountered.

Especially noteworthy for SLA was that SL learners were found to commit similar 'developmental' errors, errors that were not apparently due to L1 interference. Thus, by extension, the process of SLA was also thought to be one of rule formation, in which the rules were inculcated through a process of hypothesis formation and testing. After initial exposure to the target language (TL), learners would form hypotheses about the nature of certain TL rules. They would then test their hypotheses by applying them to produce TL utterances. Based on the mismatch learners perceived between what they were producing and the forms/functions of the target language to which they were being exposed, learners would modify their hypotheses about the nature of the TL rules so that their utterances increasingly conformed to the target language.

3.3.3 Interlingual versus intralingual errors

To be sure, SL learners still committed errors which could be traced to L1 interference and as such were termed *interlingual* errors by Richards (1971). The weak version of the CAH, therefore, was regularly invoked to explain a number of errors. What was also found to be the case, however, was that a large number of similar errors were being committed by SL learners, regardless of their L1. These errors were called *intralingual* (Richards 1971). In what was to become a seminal paper in the SLA field, Corder (1967) maintained that learners' errors were invaluable to the study of the language-learning process. By classifying the errors that learners made, Corder submitted, researchers could learn a great deal about the SLA process by inferring the strategies that SL learners were adopting. Such claims motivated a number of error taxonomies. Certain errors were classified as overgeneralization (Richards 1971), caused by the learners' failure to observe the boundaries of a rule, such as in the examples cited above. Other errors were attributed to simplification (George 1972) or redundancy reduction, such as when a plural marker was omitted from a noun preceded by a cardinal number larger than one. Still others were labelled communication-based errors (Selinker 1972), errors which resulted when speakers invoked communicative strategies, and induced errors (Stenson 1974), errors which were brought about by a teacher's sequencing or presenting two linguistic items in a way which created confusion in the mind of the language learner. For examples of these error types, see Table 3.2.

There is, of course, some overlap among these categories: a common simplification error, for example, such as the omission of the copula *be*, could also be due to interference from a language with no such verbs. Nevertheless, what is significant about such attempts to identify and classify errors is the new stature ascribed to errors. In his 1967

Type of Error	Example	Explanation
Interlingual Interference	*Is the book of my friend.	The omission of the subject pronoun and the use of the 'of the' possessive appear to be due to Spanish interference.
Intralingual Overgeneralization	*I wonder where are you going.	The speaker has perhaps overgeneralized the rule of subject–auxiliary inversion and applied it here to an embedded WH-question incorrectly.
Simplification (Redundancy reduction)	*I studied English for two year.	The omission of the plural marker following the noun *year* could be termed redundancy reduction as no information is lost, i.e. the cardinal number already signals plurality.
Communication-based	*The learner uses 'airball' for balloon (word coinage, Tarone 1980)	The learner incorrectly labels an object but successfully communicates a desired concept.
Induced errors	*She cries as if the baby cries FOR 'She cries like a baby'. (Stenson 1974)	The teacher had given the student a definition of 'as if' meaning 'like' without explaining the necessary structural change.

TABLE 3.2 Error Taxonomy

paper, Corder made a distinction between a *mistake* and an *error*. Whereas a mistake is a random performance slip caused by fatigue, excitement, etc., and therefore can be readily self-corrected, an error is a systematic deviation made by learners who have not yet mastered the rules of the L2. A learner cannot self-correct an error because it is a product reflective of his or her current stage of L2 development, or underlying competence. Rather than being seen as something to be prevented, then, errors were signs that learners were actively engaged in hypothesis testing which would ultimately result in the acquisition of TL rules.

3.3.4 Interlanguage

The language system that the learner constructs out of the linguistic input to which he has been exposed has been variously referred to 'as an idiosyncratic dialect (Corder 1971), an approximative system (Nemser 1971) and an interlanguage (Selinker 1972).[4] While these three differ somewhat in their emphases, it was actually the term *interlanguage* which entered common parlance, partly perhaps due to its neutrality of attitude, since the other two terms connote a TL-centred perspective (Sridhar 1980). Nevertheless, all three writers seem to subscribe to the three assumptions put forth by Nemser in discussing his approximative system (La) concept:

> Our assumption is three-fold: (1) Learners' speech at a given time is the patterned product of a linguistic system (La), distinct from LS and LT (the source and the target language) and internally structured. (2) La's at successive stages of learning form an evolving series La^1....La^n, the earlier occurring when a learner first attempts to use the LT, the most advanced at the closest approach to LT.... (3) In a given contact situation, the La's of learners at the same stage of proficiency roughly coincide with major variations ascribable to differences in learning experiences. (p. 116)

Thus, the concept of interlanguage (IL) might better be understood if it is thought of as a continuum between the L1 and L2 along which all learners traverse. At any point along the continuum, the learners' language is systematic, i.e. rule-governed, and common to all learners, any difference being explicable by differences in their learning experience.

According to Selinker, one of the major issues for which any description of IL must account is the phenomenon of *fossilization*:

> Fossilizable linguistic phenomena are linguistic items, rules and subsystems which speakers of a particular NL will tend to keep in their IL relative to a particular TL, no matter what the age of the learner or amount of explanation and instruction he receives in the TL. (p. 215)

Thus, it is not always true that a language learner, given continued exposure to the TL, will steadily grow in his or her mastery of the TL. Perhaps it is the case, as Corder suggests, that once the language learner's IL grammar is sufficiently developed to enable the learner to communicate adequately for his or her purposes, the motivation to improve wanes.

It should be evident that the view of learners from an error analysis (EA) perspective differs vastly from the view of learners from the CA perspective. In the latter, errors were the result of the intrusion of L1 habits over which the learner had no control. From an EA perspective, the learner is no longer seen to be a passive recipient of TL input, but rather plays an active role, processing input, generating hypotheses, testing them and refining them, all the while determining the ultimate TL level he or she will attain. As Jakobovits (1970, p. 2) put it for L1 acquisition: 'The burden of acquisition is now placed on the child, with relatively minor importance attached to the environment as a reinforcing agency.'

3.3.5 Error analysis criticized

While the status of the IL notion has been maintained in the field, EA, like CA, fell into disfavour. It did so for a number of reasons, conveniently summarized in Schachter and Celce-Murcia (1977). By focusing only on errors, researchers were denied access to the whole picture. They studied what learners were doing wrong, but not what made them successful. Furthermore, it was often difficult, if not impossible, to identify the unitary source of an error. As we acknowledged earlier, the source of an error like

* The doges ran home.

is ambiguous. It could be due to the overgeneralization of the syllabic plural, but it also is a developmental error of the type children learning English as their native language (NL) commonly make.

Another charge which has been levelled against EA is that it fails to account for all the areas of the SL in which learners have difficulty. Schachter (1974) reported that, contrary to expectations based on an *a priori* CA, Chinese and Japanese speakers committed fewer errors in English relative clause production than Spanish and Persian speakers. What Schachter discovered was the Chinese and Japanese speakers made fewer errors than their Spanish- and Persian-speaking counterparts because the former attempted to produce fewer relative clauses. In other words, the Chinese and Japanese students avoided producing relative clauses because they knew they would be problematic.

Avoidance of the English passive by Arabic speakers (Kleinmann 1977) and of English phrasal verbs by Hebrew speakers (Dagut and

Laufer 1985) has also been confirmed. On the other hand, with passives in Hebrew and English, and relative clauses in Chinese and English, Seliger (1978) and Houng and Bley-Vroman (1988), respectively, have shown that obtaining baseline data on the L2 learner's L1 is crucial in order to make sure that any under-representation of a structure in the IL is really due to avoidance and not simply to low use of that structure in the native language. What is striking is that in none of these cases would an analysis of errors alone have uncovered these apparent areas of difficulty.

In short, the weaknesses of EA were too blatant for it to continue to serve as the primary mode of SLA analysis. As Harley (1980, p. 4) put it:

> The study of errors that L2 learners make can certainly provide vital clues as to their competence in the TL, but they are only part of the picture . . . [I]t is equally important to determine whether the learner's use of 'correct' forms approximates that of the native speaker. Does the learner's speech evidence the same contrasts between the observed unit and other units that are related in the target system? Are there some units that he uses less frequently than the native speaker, some that he does not use at all?

The narrowness of perspective did not lead to the demise of EA, but rather to its incorporation into performance analysis (PA), an analysis of the learners' IL performance, not limited to analysing the errors they commit.

3.4 Performance analysis

Although narrowly focused themselves, perhaps among the earliest studies which could be termed performance analyses (PAs) were those which came to be known as the morpheme studies.

3.4.1 Morpheme studies

Adopting methodology from Brown's (1973) study of L1 acquisition, SL researchers scored protocols of subjects' speech for suppliance of grammatical morphemes in obligatory contexts, i.e. contexts, as we saw earlier, where the TL requires a particular linguistic structure, such as the plural marker at the end of a common English noun preceded by a cardinal number. Dulay and Burt (1973, 1974) fashioned a scoring scheme which awarded different point values depending upon whether a morpheme was correctly supplied in an obligatory context, supplied but not well formed, or omitted altogether. Applying this scheme to their subjects' speech elicited by means of the Bilingual Syntax Measure (BSM) (Burt, Dulay and Hernandez-Chavez 1975), a picture-elicitation device using coloured cartoons, Dulay and Burt claimed that they had found evidence of a morpheme acquisition order based upon the relative suppliance of eleven English morphemes in obligatory contexts. Furthermore, this acquisition order was characteristic of both Chinese and Spanish children, and thus was thought to be almost impervious to L1 influence. These early morpheme studies attracted a good deal of attention and excited researchers who were searching for evidence of an innate learner-generated or *built-in syllabus* (Corder 1967). They also drew fire, mainly directed at their methodology and their claims of minimal L1 interference.[5] We will return to a discussion of the charges and rebuttals in the next chapter.

3.4.2 Developmental sequence

Another type of PA was also being conducted at this time which some researchers found to be a more elucidating approach. As Wode, Bahns, Bedley and Frank (1978, p. 176) expressed it:

> [The problem] is the fact that the morpheme order approach misses what makes language acquisition attractive for, and subject to, developmental investigations, namely, to discover how language is processed by the child for the purpose of acquisition. This processing is reflected in the way that children decompose complex structural patterns and then rebuild them step by step until they finally reach target-like mastery. Therefore, pre-targetlike regularities must be regarded as an essential part of the total process of acquiring a language.

Studying developmental sequences or the steps leading to acquisition of a particular structure, is intended to do just that.

Typically, investigation of developmental sequences has involved a longitudinal study in which the speech of one or more subjects is recorded and the transcripts are analysed for particular structures. There have been many such studies conducted over the years, making it impossible to be comprehensive here. In this chapter, we will mention some of the early studies (see Table 3.3) and the issues which emerged from them, saving discussion of further examples until Chapter 4.

One of the first major discoveries was the degree of similarity between L1 and L2 developmental sequences. Ravem (1968, 1970)

Researcher	Focus of study	L1 and L2 developmental sequences
Ravem (1968, 1970)	English negation and WH-questions by two Norwegian-speaking children	Similar
Dato (1970)	Spanish verb phrase development of six 6-year-old native English speakers	Similar
Milon (1974)	English negation by 7-year-old Japanese speaker	Similar
Wode (1976)	English negation of four German-speaking children aged 4–10	Different (due to the fact that children relied on their L1 when there was a 'crucial similarity' between English and German)

TABLE 3.3 Summary of Early SLA Research Addressing the Question of the Similarity Between L1 and L2 Developmental Sequences

tracked the development of English negation and WH-questions in the speech of his Norwegian-speaking children. He reported finding strikingly similar developmental sequences to those of Brown and his associates, who studied the acquisition of these structures by children acquiring English as an L1. Milon (1974) confirmed Ravem's findings. Examining the acquisition of negation in a study of a seven-year-old Japanese speaker learning ESL, Milon reported that his subject produced negative utterances which were very much like those of children acquiring English as a native language. Likewise, Dato (1970), studying the acquisition of Spanish by SL learners who spoke English natively, discovered that SL learners follow a pattern of verb phrase development in Spanish similar to that of native Spanish speakers.

Such claims of similarity between L1 and L2 developmental sequences were not without opposition, however. Wode (1974, reported on in 1976) studied the ESL acquisition of four German-speaking children aged four to ten. Wode disagreed with the claims of the equivalence between the L1 and L2 developmental sequences. Instead, he argued that there were differences, that the differences were systematic and that they were due to the children's relying on their L1 only under a structural condition where there was a 'crucial similarity'. For example, Wode's subjects exhibited a stage in their acquisition of the English negative in which the negative was placed after the verb:

* John go not to the school.

Such statements appear to be the result of negative transfer from German. While this is no doubt true, it is not the case that English disallows post-verbal negation. In English the verb *be* and auxiliary verbs are followed by the negative particle:

* He isn't listening.
* She can't mean that.

Thus, Wode argued, the language-transfer error arose since negative placement in English and German were similar enough to encourage the children's reliance on their L1.

3.4.3 Learner strategies

Another contribution of the developmental studies was the identification of strategies employed by SL learners (see Table 3.4). Huang (1970) studied the acquisition of English by Paul, a five-year-old

Taiwanese boy. Huang found that his subject used formulaic utterances such as 'See you tomorrow' in appropriate situations. The other strategy Paul employed was to juxtapose two words with a juncture between them to create an English sentence, such as 'This . . . kite.' Thus, Paul formed a rule perfectly consistent with his topic–comment native language.[6]

Butterworth (1972) was one of the earliest language acquisition researchers to study the acquisition of English by an adolescent, in this case a thirteen-year-old native speaker of Spanish. Ricardo, Butterworth's subject, tended to reduce English structure to simple syntax. He also used the strategy of relexification, replacing Spanish words with English words while retaining the Spanish syntactic patterns.

Hakuta (1974) studied the acquisition of English by a five-year-old Japanese speaker for a one-year period. Hakuta found that, like Paul, his subject, Uguisu, used formulaic utterances, which Hakuta labelled prefabricated routines. Uguisu, however, also used prefabricated patterns in which at least one slot would be filled by other words with the same part of speech. For instance, Uguisu produced the following:

> Do you saw this rabbit run away?
> Do you saw three feet?
> Do you bought this too?
> Do you put it? (Hakuta, in Hatch 1978c, p. 142)

It is clear that studying the developmental sequences of SL learners can yield important insights into the SLA process. One of the times this type of study has met with criticism, however, has been when researchers maintain an exclusive TL perspective. In 1976, Adjemian cautioned that if it is true that an IL is different from both the L1 and L2, then it must be the product of a unique set of linguistic rules and should be studied as a fully functioning language in its own right, not as an incomplete version of the TL. As Corder (1983) put it, it is only from the TL perspective that we can say that simplification is a language-learning strategy, because how can learners be said to be simplifying that which they do not already possess? (For a different view, see Meisel 1983c.) And Bley-Vroman (1983) warns SLA researchers against 'the comparative fallacy', i.e. relying on theoretical constructs which are defined relative to the TL norm. Even such a fundamental construct as an error can be accused of such a bias. In other words, researchers should not adopt a normative TL perspective, but rather seek to discover how an IL structure which appears to be non-standard is being used meaningfully by a learner.

Researcher	Focus of Study	Strategies	Examples
Huang (1970)	English acquisition by 5-year-old Taiwanese child	Imitation of formulaic utterances	See you tomorrow.
		Rule formation	This . . . kite. That . . . bus.
Butterworth (1972)	English acquisition by 13-year-old Colombian child	Reduction to simpler syntax	He champion.
		Relexification	He understand chess? (with rising intonation)
Hakuta (1975)	English acquisition by 5-year-old Japanese child	Prefabricated routines	Do you know? How do you do it? Do you want this one?
		Prefabricated patterns	What do you doing? What do you do it?
Wagner-Gough (1973)	English acquisition by 5-year-old Iranian child	Incorporation	What do you want is truck.

TABLE 3.4 Learner Strategies Identified in Early Developmental Studies

3.4.4 The acquisition of forms and functions

Illustrating the value in studying a learner's speech in its own right is a study by Huebner (1980). Huebner investigated the patterns of '*waduyu*' and 'x *isa* y' (where x and y are slots) in his one-year longitudinal study of a Hmong-speaking adult learning ESL. Not surprisingly, Huebner found that the functions which were assigned to these forms by his subject were not TL functions. *Waduyu*, for instance, functioned as a general WH-question marker, as in

> Waduyu kam from? (Where are you from?)
> Waduyu kam Tailaen? (How did you come to Thailand?)
> Waduyu kam? (Why did you come?)
> Waduyu sei? (What did you say?)

Later, other forms appeared to fill some of these roles; for example, the subject used *matwei* for questions involving means. Finally, *waduyu* disappeared altogether. Huebner's study, therefore, also calls into question whether in fact learners using prefabricated routines or formulas are really using them appropriately right from the beginning. He suggests that the acquisition of appropriate functions for formulaic utterances may be an evolutionary process.

That the mapping of function on form or form on function is an evolving process is undoubtedly true, not only for formulaic utterances, but for other forms in the language as well (Wagner-Gough 1975). Bahns and Wode (1980), for instance, demonstrate that learners do not learn all the functions of a particular form at the same time. Their German-speaking subject used *didn't* as a past-tense marker for some time before he used it as a negator. They concluded that 'it is obvious that one cannot generally claim that the function is acquired before the form or that the form is acquired before the function' (p. 92). Perhaps what is a general principle regarding learning both L2 form and function is that initially, at least, learners attempt to maintain a relationship between one invariant surface linguistic form and a single function, Andersen's (1984c) 'one-to-one principle'. They are motivated to do so in order to keep their IL system internally consistent.

3.4.5 Formulaic utterances

Returning to a discussion of formulaic utterances, we should point out that how their acquisition affects SLA in general has been much disputed. Earlier we cited the work of Huang (1970) and Hakuta (1974), who identified the use of formulaic utterances as one strategy their subjects employed. Wong Fillmore (1976) feels that the memorization of such utterances is indispensable in SLA, for she believes it is the memorized utterances which get analysed and out of which the creative rules are thus constructed.

Krashen and Scarcella (1978) adopt a very different position. They believe that memorized utterances and creative speech are produced in ways that are neurologically different and that, therefore, there can be no interface between them. Schmidt (1983) could find no evolution towards creative rules from his subject's memorized utterances. (See also Hanania and Gradman 1977.) However, Schmidt's subject, Wes, controlled well over a hundred memorized sentences and phrases, and this repertoire considerably enhanced his fluency. For Wes, Schmidt concludes, memorization appeared to be a more successful acquisition strategy than rule formation.

Even if much of Wes's competence in English were due to his having relied on memorized utterances, this would not specifically refute Chomsky's view that language acquisition is a product of rule formation (see Schmidt and Frota 1986 for discussion). As Johnston (1985) reminds us, Chomsky himself has maintained that grammar rules are not psychologically real. Just because a sentence can be explained by the application of a particular linguistic rule, this does not mean that the speaker has applied it each time. 'In fact,' Johnston observes, 'it would seem plausible that a good deal of native speaker linguistic behaviour is quite as routinized as the "formulaic" language of learners' (p. 58).

As CA and EA before, PA served the field well. Also like its predecessors, however, PA was found to be too limiting. An early example of the inadequacy was brought to our attention by Wagner-Gough (1975). Her subject, Homer, an Iranian child aged 5 years 11 months, produced utterances such as 'Where are you going is house.' Homer's utterances are uninterpretable if we limit ourselves to examining his performance. Only when we look at the input preceding Homer's utterance can we make sense out of it. Homer's utterance is offered in reply to an adult's question, 'Where are you going, Homer?' Homer's strategy in answering questions in English was to incorporate the question along with his answer, a strategy referred to as *incorporation* on Table 3.4.

3.5 Discourse analysis

Recognition of the need to examine not only the learner's performance but also the input to the learner, led to a new mode of inquiry being adopted by researchers, namely, discourse analysis (Larsen-Freeman 1980b).

3.5.1 Conversational analysis

One sub-area of discourse analysis (DA) has come to be known as conversational analysis (Gaskill 1980; Schwartz 1980). Hatch (1978b) has perhaps been the SLA researcher who has most promoted the value of examining what learners can be learning when engaged in 'collaborative discourse'. The following conversation between H, a native speaker of English, and Takahiro (T), a non-native speaker, comes from Itoh's (1973) study and is cited by Hatch (1978b, p. 409) to support her contention that 'one learns how to do conversation, one learns how to interact verbally and out of this interaction syntactic structures are developed':

T:	this	
	broken	
H:		broken
T:	broken	
	This /az/ broken	
	broken	
H:		Upside down
T:	upside down	
	this broken	
	upside down	
	broken	

This conversation provides a good example of 'vertical' construction (Scollon 1974), where Takahiro and his interlocutor collaborate to produce a combined social discourse, with Takahiro relying on the strategy of scaffolding (Slobin 1982b), or building his utterances on those of the native speaker. It is thought that through the negotiation of such vertical constructions, learners acquire the 'horizontal' word order of the TL.

Hatch does not deny that SLA takes place through rule formation but suggests (1983, p. 187) that 'other processes which are nonlinguistic may be critical to the learner's discovery of linguistic elements that make up that system. Such processes may make the formation of linguistic hypotheses possible.' But, as Hatch would be quick to admit, 'the connection between conversational interaction and IL development is, unquestionably, a complex one' (Sato 1986, p. 44). In her study of the acquisition of past time reference in English by Vietnamese speakers, Sato found that certain aspects of conversation appeared to facilitate the acquisition of salient linguistic structures (adverbial expressions and lexical past verbs) but apparently did not work for the less salient verbal inflections.

3.5.2 Other applications of discourse analysis

We have mentioned how discourse analysis has allowed the investigation of the relationship between NS input and learner IL forms (Wagner-Gough 1975; also see Chapter 5) and the contribution of conversational interaction to SLA. What ties these two avenues of inquiry together is that both require the interviewer to view language from a discourse perspective, i.e. to work with units of language above the sentence level. Speech events such as conversations (or portions of them) are discourse units, but so are monologues (e.g. oral narratives) and written texts (e.g. compositions).

Another quality of discourse analysis applied to SLA is that researchers are concerned not only with how IL forms evolve, but how learners learn how to use the forms appropriately for a particular discourse function as well (Hatch 1983, p. 109). This has led to the study of speech acts or functions (e.g. apologizing, inviting, complaining, etc.). For example, Giddens, Inoue and Schaefer (as reported on in Hatch 1983, pp. 147–8) constructed-role play situations to elicit complaints from Spanish, Japanese and English native speakers (forty from each native-language group). They discovered that speakers of all three languages structured their complaints in much the same way: speakers began with an opener, provided an orientation for the listener, stated the problem, justified the complaint and the addressee's reason for having wronged the speaker, offered a remedy, concluded the speaking turn and expressed his or her feelings about either the addressee or the wrong committed.

As must be apparent, the broader scope of language and the recognition of the need to view both form and function has opened up many new SLA areas of investigation (Larsen-Freeman 1980b, 1981). We will only mention them here and provide a few references, presenting further detail in subsequent chapters for some of these areas:

1. Foreigner talk discourse (Henzl 1973; Freed 1978; Long 1980a; and for review, Chaudron 1988): Research has primarily centred

around the nature of the adjustments native speakers make when conversing with non-native speakers and how these modifications affect SLA, if at all.

2. Coherence and cohesion (for reviews, see Scarcella 1984 and Hatch 1984): The focus in this area has been on how coherence and cohesion are achieved at the suprasentential level, i.e. in written texts composed of more than one sentence. Studies have been conducted on how SL learners learn to comprehend and produce these texts. Work along these lines has also been conducted as contrastive rhetorical analysis (Connor and Kaplan 1987; Purves 1987).

3. Communicative strategies (Varadi 1973; Tarone 1977; Faerch and Kasper 1983, 1984): Researchers have been identifying what compensatory strategies non-native speakers utilize in order to maintain a conversation when they have an incomplete knowledge of a SL.

4. Contextual analysis (Celce-Murcia 1980): This type of analysis involves the researcher determining the effect of context on linguistic forms. While this has been traditionally a question considered within the realm of theoretical linguistics, SLA researchers must sometimes undertake such analyses themselves (e.g. Vander Brook, Schlue and Campbell 1980); it is impossible to trace the acquisition of a structure if one is ignorant of how native speakers use it variably within contexts.

5. Classroom discourse analysis (Fanselow 1977; Chaudron 1977, 1988; Allwright 1980, 1988; Schinke-Llano 1983; Spada 1986, 1987; Harley, Allen, Cummins and Swain 1987; van Lier 1988): This research deals with the interactions between a teacher and his or her students and among the students in an L2 classroom setting.

6. Discourse/functional analysis (Kumpf 1983; Lynch 1983; Tomlin 1984): Research has centred on how learners use the rudimentary knowledge of SL syntax they possess to accomplish discourse functions in oral narratives. Such discourse functions include foregrounding event clauses in narratives while backgrounding clauses which elaborate on the event line.

7. Speech act analysis (Richards and Schmidt 1979; Fraser, Rintell and Walters 1980; Thomas 1983; Wolfson and Judd 1983; Kasper 1984; Blum-Kulka and Olshtain 1986): Work in this area has dealt with obtaining 'baseline data' on how certain speech acts are realized in language. Once we understand how a particular function (e.g. complaining) is accomplished in the native language and target language of our subjects, then we can proceed with an analysis of

the SLA process (Dechert and Raupach 1980; Ventola 1983; Eisenstein and Bodman 1986; Davies 1987). Such work is now taking place under rubrics such as 'contrastive discourse analysis' (Blum-Kulka and Olshtain 1984b; Edmondson, House, Kasper and Stemmer 1984).

The articulation of the need to investigate pragmatic conventions contrasting L1 and L2 brings us full circle back to the topic with which we began this chapter. Although CA is being investigated with renewed vigour, the motivation for conducting CAs is vastly different from when CA was linked to behaviourism. For one thing, the influence of the native language is no longer thought to affect the SLA process in a deleterious manner. Instead, one's knowledge of another language can be seen to be facilitating in one's attempts to master a SL. We return to a detailed discussion of this issue in Chapter 4.

3.6 Conclusion

As we have traced the development of the modes of SLA inquiry, we have seen how each new type of analysis broadened our perspective and made its own unique contribution. It would be untrue to say that each type of analysis replaced its predecessor, however. Rather, we could say it *subsumed* what came before it. For instance, we saw that those that practised EA appealed to CA to explain a portion of the errors that learners commit. Likewise, since learner errors are part of a learner's performance, EA has a role to play in PA. And finally, the learner's total performance must be taken into account in any DA.

Somewhat surprising is the fact that despite the wave of successive modes of inquiry, the view of language acquisition as a product of rule formation (or in its latest guise, parameter setting – see Chapter 7 for discussion) has still prevailed. This is probably due to the fact that SLA research attention has continued to focus on morphosyntax, which presumably can best be accounted for through such a process. As SLA stretches to consider other aspects of linguistic and communicative competence, however, it would not be surprising to see that other types of learning will have to be considered (Larsen-Freeman in press). For example, we may yet find that habit formation has an explanatory role in the acquisition of L2 phonological features and in the acquisition of formulaic utterances as well. When it comes to the semantic dimension, neither habit formation nor rule formation may be applicable. Instead, verbal association, multiple discrimination and concept learning (Gagne 1965) are more likely to have explanatory power. As we increasingly grapple with the acquisition of pragmatics, we would expect yet again to find a different type of learning to be responsible. All of this is of course speculative and will have to be subject to investigation. The point is, however, that with language as complicated as it is, we should not expect the process of language acquisition to be any less complex.

Notes

1. See, for example, bibliographies compiled by Gage (1961), Hammer and Rice (1965), Thiem (1969), Di Pietro (1971), Selinker and Selinker (1972), Palmberg (1976, 1977), Bausch (1977), and Dechert, Bruggemeier and Fütterer (1984).
2. The University of Chicago Press's *Contrastive Structure Series* (Charles Ferguson, General Editor) includes volumes comparing English to the major European languages taught in American schools. German/English (Moulton 1962; Kufner 1962), Spanish/English (Stockwell and Bowen 1965; Stockwell, Bowen and Martin 1965a), and Italian/English (Agard and Di Pietro 1965a, 1965b) were published. Studies comparing French and Russian to English were prepared but never published (van Els et al. 1984).
3. See, for example, the European studies listed in Fig. 4.3 in van Els et al. (1984), p. 45.
4. The term 'interlanguage' seems first to have been used in 1935 by John Reinecke, in his classic MA thesis, *Language and Dialect in Hawaii*, published by the University of Hawaii Press in 1969. Reinecke, the distinguished pidgin/creole scholar, labor historian and social activist, describes, for example, how in situations like that in plantation-era Hawaii:

    a makeshift dialect will for the most part be used as the means of communication between the several [immigrant] groups. . .[which] will tend to pass into a more formal speech – still imperfect as compared with the standard language – as an interlanguage, until finally this more or less standardized lingua franca becomes the primary tongue of nearly the whole body of inhabitants. (1969, p. 115)

    Reinecke always employed 'interlanguage' to refer to a non-standard variety of a first or second language, used as a means of intergroup communication, gradually approximating the norms of the standard language of some economically and politically dominant group.
5. Dulay and Burt (1975) claimed to have found only 4 per cent of the total number of errors committed by their subjects which could unambiguously be attributed to L1 interference.
6. In a topic–comment language, a speaker typically nominates a topic, 'My head,' and then makes a comment, 'It is aching.' Some researchers (Givon 1979b; Huebner 1983b; Rutherford 1983; Fuller and Gundel 1987) have

suggested that SLA can be characterized by an early topic–comment stage whether or not the L1 is a topic–comment language.

Activities

Comprehension

1. How did the behaviourists view language acquisition?
2. Distinguish between the strong version and the weak version of the contrastive analysis hypothesis.
3. What is a cognitivist view of language acquisition?
4. What are some problems with relying exclusively on error analysis for insight into SLA?
5. Distinguish between an error and a mistake.
6. Explain the term 'interlanguage' using your own words.
7. What are some of the limitations of error analysis?
8. Explain in your own words what the 'comparative fallacy' is.
9. Discuss the different views with regards to formulaic utterances.
10. Explain scaffolding as used by non-native speakers when conversing.
11. It is probably not accurate to say that contrastive analysis was replaced by error analysis and that error analysis was replaced by performance analysis, etc., but rather that each respective analysis subsumed the earlier one. Please discuss.

Application

12. The following is an 'Accent Inventory' devised by Clifford Prator and Betty Wallace Robinett in their book *American English Pronunciation*. In the diagnostic passage, all of the phonemes and many of the intonation patterns of English are contained. Read it over and make a list of predictions about where you think a speaker of a particular native language with which you are familiar is likely to have difficulty. Next, tape a native speaker of the particular language as he or she reads the diagnostic passage. Listen to the tape to determine how many of your predictions were confirmed. Were there other errors that were made that you had not anticipated? What other observations can you make?

Diagnostic passage
(1) When a student from another country comes to study in the United States, he has to find the answers to many questions, and

he has many problems to think about. (2) Where should he live? (3) Would it be better if he looked for a private room off campus or if he stayed in a dormitory? (4) Should he spend all of his time just studying? (5) Shouldn't he try to take advantage of the many social and cultural activities which are offered? (6) At first it is not easy for him to be casual in dress, informal in manner, and confident in speech. (7) Little by little he learns what kind of clothing is usually worn here to be casually dressed for classes. (8) He also learns to choose the language and customs which are appropriate for informal situations. (9) Finally, he begins to feel sure of himself. (10) But let me tell you, my friend, this long-awaited feeling doesn't develop suddenly – does it? (11) All of this takes practice.

[Reprinted with permission of Holt, Rinehart and Winston]

13. Following the Stockwell, Bowen and Martin (1965a) hierarchy of difficulty, identify the type of contrast exemplified by each of the following for a learner of the second language specified.
   (a) French has two auxiliaries, *être* and *avoir*, to mark perfect aspect, depending upon whether the following main verb is a verb of movement (*come, go, arrive, leave*, etc.). English uses one auxiliary, *have*, for all verbs. [English speaker learning French]
   (b) English and Spanish both have one generic word for all types and conditions of snow (*snow* and *nieve*). [Spanish speaker learning English]
   (c) Indonesian marks a distinction between inclusive and exclusive first person plural subject pronouns (*kita* and *kami*). English just uses *we*. [Indonesian speaker learning English]
   (d) English has one word for *corner*, whereas Spanish uses *rincon* for 'internal' corners, e.g. the corner of a room, and *esquina* for 'external' corners, e.g. the corner of the street. [Spanish speaker learning English]
   (e) Indonesian has no auxiliary verb like the *do* of English used in questions and negatives. [English speaker learning Indonesian]
   (f) Indonesian has no interdental fricatives. English has a ð and θ. [Indonesian speaker learning English]
14. The following paragraph completions were written by native speakers of French (compositions a–d) and Spanish (compositions e–i). Conduct an error analysis of each, trying to determine what the cause of the errors might be.
   (a) People have always had many different reasons for traveling. One reason is curiosity about the ways of life in other countries

or even in other regions of a country. Another reason is to change environment, to see and breathe something new which might contrast with the dull life spent in the same place. Some other people travel for a specific purpose; for business affairs, to go find relatives, for a pilgrimage, to explore unknown territories. Some other people move all their lives from camp to camp as nomads, just through customs and habits. Some, because they are forced by circumstances to leave a country or a region in which it is uneasy for them to live. Also, students travel to study in foreign countries. But all travelers would like to be tourists.

(b) People have always had many different reasons for traveling. One of the most important reasons should be certainly the very deep desire of most of them to visit other countries than their native ones, and, by that way, to meet new people and undoubtless learn something else. Another good reason might be conducted by wishing to visit their own families and friends established over there. Many other reasons could bring people to leave for a while their own frontiers. But, at the present time, we may assume that very important factors such as travel publicity by radio, TV or agencies plus all the actual means used to attract public (tours, chartered flights, etc.) are giving, in this respect, a very efficient help. As a result, we may assure that those means develop unconsciously but surely the desire of everyone for traveling.

(c) People have always had many different reasons for traveling. One reason why people travel is because they want to see many different things and places they don't see when they are working steadily. By traveling, you can not only see wonderful sights but you can also meet very interesting people in foreign countries. If you speak the foreign language of this country, you can enjoy discussing with natives about common problems and realities and you can also discover a complete different world specially about their customs and habits, and their way of thinking. Without any doubt the natives of the country will better accept you if you speak their language.

(d) People have always had many different reasons for traveling. One reason, probably the only one in the time of the first civilizations, is to know the world where we live, to discover new countries, or new planets in our time. This conception of traveling always passionated man because it represents something new, the adventure, the unknown. But in the history of mankind, travels have been often caused by wars. Not only the armies are traveling (Alexandre le grand, Hannibal), but also, against their will, the defeated population. This last kind of travel is, without any doubt, the least pleasant of all. It is only recently that traveling occurs at the time of 'vacations'. The modern means of communication, the amelioration of level of life, more and more allow young and older people to travel for their pleasure all over the world.

(e) Some people feel that a woman's place is in the home. Others feel that a woman should be able to enter the same professions and occupations open to a man. I feel I think that the home is a place where woman should be most of the time when they have small children. But I also believe that in our days a woman should have, if not all, but many opportunities that a man has. I am not in favor of women liberation only of some changes.

(f) Some people feel that a woman's place is in the home. Others feel that a woman should be able to enter the same professions and occupations open to a man. I feel that a woman has to work and have the same professions than the man but also she has to take care of the childrens. For me the perfect woman is the one who works the half of a day (morning or afternoon) and stay at home the other half. If a woman doesn't work at all is bad too because she became boring of stay at home doing nothing, but also is bad for her to work all day because I think that she can easily forget her family and dedicates her time to do other things than to be a wife and a mother.

(g) Some people feel that a woman's place is in the home. Others feel that a woman should be able to enter the same professions and occupations open to a man. I feel that the best place for a woman is the home, to me a woman is prettiest when she is a housewife. Men to the war, women to have babies. It is my personal opinion that women Liberation is not a good solution for the women, rather I think, that movement is very disappointed.

(h) Some people feel that a woman's place is in the home. Others feel that a woman should be able to enter the same professions and occupations open to a man. I feel the same as the firts people. I thing they have to participate in all kind of affairs of a member of the community without exception. The woman can regulate the feelings of the more agresive temperament that men have. They can synchronice the structure of the society. They have to have the same rights as the men, in job opportunities and wague pay. They have to be more and more independent and adquire more personal character.

(i) Some people feel that a woman's place is in the home. Others feel that a woman should be able to enter the same professions and occupations open to a man. I feel that woman should have the same opportunities than men in regard of jobs and education, in case they need to work, but if marryed I think is preferable to stay home and do her part that correspond to her take care of the house, have children cook and be the queen.

[We are grateful to Marianne Celce-Murcia for supplying these data from her seminar in contrastive analysis. For many other problems of this type, see Selinker and Gass (1985).]

15. As was stated in the text, the claims for the existence of common acquisition orders excited those who were searching for evidence of a built-in or learner-generated syllabus. Nickel (1973, cited in Corder 1981, p. 94), for instance, has advocated 'teaching a developmental syllabus derived from a study of the progression of forms found in natural language learning situations'. Widdowson (1977) proposed that the teacher's simplifications should be made to approximate those of the learner at any particular stage in the learning process (Corder 1981, p. 94). What do you think about these proposals?

16. If in conducting a performance analysis, one of your low-level ESL subjects produced the sentence 'I don't know' at the same time she was saying things like 'He no go' and 'I no want', you might hypothesize that for this subject 'I don't know' was a prefabricated routine, a conventionalized form (Yorio 1980) or a formulaic utterance. What further evidence would you look for to test your hypothesis?

17. Below are some slightly altered data from Godfrey (1980). Subjects were asked to evaluate a non-dialogue film they had just viewed for its usefulness in the classes at the English Language Institute (ELI). Conduct a discourse analysis of this subject's tense usage:

> I think this films is very useful and excellent for us the students of ELI. It contains much suggestion and fantasy. It had beautiful colors.

How does discourse analysis reveal errors in tense usage that an error analysis conducted at the sentence level does not?

18. If different types of learning are found to be responsible for different aspects of language (e.g. habit formation for phonology, rule

formation for morphosyntax, etc.), what pedagogical implication should be drawn?

Suggestions for further reading

For overviews and critiques of various approaches to the analysis of IL, see:

Bley-Vroman, R 1983 The comparative fallacy in interlanguage studies: the case of systematicity. *Language Learning* 33: 1–17

Long, M and Sato, C 1984 Methodological issues in interlanguage studies: an interactionist perspective. In Davies, A, Criper, C and Howatt, A (eds.) *Interlanguage*. Edinburgh University Press

For an in-depth treatment of contrastive analysis in SLA, see:

James, C 1980 *Contrastive analysis*. Longman

Zobl, H 1982 A direction for contrastive analysis: the comparative study of developmental sequences. *TESOL Quarterly* 16: 169–83

For an anthology containing some of the classic articles dealing with contrastive analysis and error analysis, see:

Robinett, B and Schachter, J (eds.) 1983 *Second language learning: contrastive analysis, error analysis and related aspects*. University of Michigan Press, Ann Arbor

For a collection of key papers in the early error analysis tradition, see:

Richards, J (ed.) 1974 *Error analysis*. Longman

For an excellent discussion of evolving form and function in performance analyses and discourse analyses, see:

Brindley, G 1986 Semantic approaches to learner language. *Australian Review of Applied Linguistics* 3: 1–43

For the role of discourse analysis in understanding SLA, see:

Hatch, E 1978 Discourse analysis and second language acquisition. In Hatch, E (ed.) 1978 *Second language acquisition: a book of readings*. Newbury House, Rowley, Mass.

Hatch, E 1983 *Psycholinguistics: a second language perspective*. Newbury House, Rowley, Mass.

Larsen-Freeman, D (ed.) 1980 *Discourse analysis in second language research*. Newbury House, Rowley, Mass.

4 Interlanguage studies: Substantive findings

4.1 Introduction

As we saw in Chapter 3, the study of SLA can be said to have passed through a series of phases defined by the modes of inquiry researchers have utilized in their work: contrastive analysis, error analysis, performance analysis and discourse analysis. While one impetus for methodological change has clearly been shifts in the issues investigators have chosen to address, many of the basic research questions have remained the same: what is the role of the first language in SLA? Do learners follow common developmental paths? Do they learn as a function of the input, or are they autonomous to some degree? Does SLA mirror first language development?

In this chapter, we summarize some of the major findings in terms of three principles governing IL development:

1. ILs vary systematically.
2. ILs exhibit common accuracy orders and developmental sequences.
3. ILs are influenced by the learner's L1.

The reader should be aware, however, that work in any one area rarely proceeds in isolation from developments in others. The findings are often related, in other words. All studies ultimately seek to answer just one question: how do people learn second languages?

4.2 ILs vary systematically

4.2.1 Free variation

Like all natural languages, ILs are variable; however, the amount of synchronic variability ILs exhibit is especially large. Ellis (1984a), for example, reports an eleven-year-old Portuguese boy producing *No V* and *Don't V* negation ('No look my card' and 'Don't look my card') within minutes of each other during the same game of word bingo, for the same purposes and in equivalent linguistic contexts (discourse-initial utterances), an example of (non-systematic) *free variation* of two ESL negation constructions. Similarly, Eisenstein, Bailey and Madden (1982) found adult ESL learners using simple and progressive verb forms in free variation in a cross-sectional study, and Wagner-Gough (1975) showed that her Assyrian-speaking subject, Homer, initially used both *V-ing* and simple verb forms ('Giving me/Give me the book', etc.) to express a similar, very broad (non-target-like) range of functions. Teachers, as is well known, are often frustrated by their students' erratic suppliance of SL morphology, like English third-person *s*, or their fluctuating pronunciation of certain sounds.[1]

This strikingly high degree of IL variability is probably due to a number of factors, of which two may be particularly important. First, compared with some other forms of language growth, ILs are typically changing rather fast in developmental terms. One reason for this is that most learners' earliest IL grammars are soon being modified towards an accessible, external, target-language norm, a process Andersen (1979b, p. 109) refers to as 'denativization'. Availability of the target-language model means this often happens relatively quickly. Consequently, there is less encouragement from the linguistic environment for the IL to *stabilize*, or for a (temporarily) stabilized IL to become (permanently) *fossilized*. In other words, learners will not hear many language models like their own and so will not receive much linguistic reinforcement for their variety.

A second reason for the rapid developmental change is that older children and adult SL acquirers are less cognitively and psycholinguistically constrained than young children acquiring their native language. Their long-term memory and processing ability, for example, are much improved. This means that, while learners in early stages may, as Andersen (1979b, p. 109) claims, be creating their own internal representation of the SL, a composite of processes he calls 'nativization', even early SLA tends to proceed rather fast.

4.2.2 Systematic variability

While ILs are indeed synchronically variable, much of the internal inconsistency is not due to free variation, like Ellis's example of the interchangeable use of *No V/Don't V*, but *rule-governed*, or, as claimed by Selinker (1969), *systematic*. In other words, at least part of the variability can be predicted and accounted for, as due to the effect of situation, linguistic context, degree of planning, or some other identifiable cause. The same learner on a given day may alternate between supplying and omitting indefinite article, between using plural NPs (noun phrases) with and without a plural S allomorph, or between pronouncing and simplifying a full word-final consonant cluster. Close study of the IL usually reveals patterns in such alternations, however.[2]

An example of *systematic variability* of this sort is well illustrated by another report (Huebner 1983b) from the study mentioned previously of the early IL development of a naturalistic Hmong acquirer of ESL. Huebner found that his informant initially used a (non-target-like) definite article *da* ('the') before an NP which referred to a specific referent which he 'assumed' was known to his interlocutor and which was not a topic or constituent of a topic, whereas other NPs received zero marking at this stage. Thus, while the learner's IL varied with respect to suppliance of *da*, the variability was rule-governed, the rule this time being semantico-pragmatic (and, of course, non-target-like). 'Recognition' that this was wrong subsequently led the learner to neutralize the rule by 'flooding' almost 90 per cent of all NP environments with *da*. 'Flooding' is defined by Huebner (1983b, p. 48) as the process by which 'the use of a given linguistic form is generalized to all environments which share one feature (in this case, [+NP]) with the environments in which the form had previously been used'. Later still, the learner gradually bled *da* from one syntactic environment after another until its function closely matched target *the*. This latter process Huebner terms 'trickling', defined as the revision or neutralization of an erroneous hypothesis, or rule, through the gradual elimination of a form from one context after another, sometimes including environments in which the target language allows or requires the form.

Findings like these provide some insight into the *process* of SLA, revealing the way form–function relationships in ILs evolve over time, partly reflecting patterns of variable use at an earlier point in time. They also have implications for language teaching and language testing. The fact that ILs are shown to be at least partly rule-governed, i.e. systematic, even in those areas where they are variable, means that they are potentially amenable to systematic change, e.g. through instruction. More specifically, the factors that have been found to be related to IL variation, such as the kind of task learners are engaged in or the amount of attention to form involved, are also, on the one hand, likely candidates for manipulation in language teaching, e.g. through the sequencing of pedagogic task types, and on the other, variables needing to be controlled in language testing.

4.2.3 Variability resulting from amount of attention

Building on work on L1 variability by Labov (1970) and others, SL studies have attempted to predict movement from less to more target-like control of phonological or morphological features according to the amount of attention learners are thought to be paying to language production, the predicted relationship being that greater accuracy will be observed in more 'careful', more formal, speech styles, when learners are 'attending to' language. Thus, several researchers have reported higher frequencies of target-like production of L2 sounds when learners are reading aloud or imitating a model, and less target-like production in spontaneous speech (see, e.g., Gatbonton 1978; Tarone 1982, 1983; Beebe and Zuengler 1983). In a study of ten Japanese ESL learners, Dickerson (1975) collected data on production of English /z/ three times over nine months on three tasks: (1) free speech, (2) reading dialogues aloud, and (3) reading word lists aloud. In each data set, the correct /z/ variant was used most frequently on task (3), followed by (2), and least often on (1), with variants also being conditioned by phonological environment. A similar finding for syntax is reported by Schmidt (1980), who studied second-verb ellipsis (e.g. John bought a book and Peter ø a pen) by speakers of various L1s on four tasks. She found that subjects used the second verb in free speech but deleted it increasingly often on tasks (supposedly) allowing more and more attention to form: elicited imitation, written sentence-combining and grammaticality judgements, respectively. (For similar findings, see Lococo 1976.)

Based on her research in this area, Tarone (1979, 1982, 1983) formulated a theory of IL variation which she labels the 'continuum paradigm', utilizing the sociolinguistic notion of speech style. She claimed that at any point in time a learner's IL is really a continuum of *speech styles*, where 'style' is defined in terms of the amount of attention to language form, and operationalized in terms of the tasks eliciting the styles. The 'vernacular' is the speech style used when least attention to form is paid, and is the one exhibiting least variability, i.e. the style showing the greatest systematicity, or internal consistency. At the other end of the continuum, the more careful speech styles are more 'permeable', i.e. more open to native-language and target-language influence, and are as a result the most variable, or least systematic. Tarone claims that new target-language forms will first appear in the most careful style and gradually move to the vernacular.

Sato's (1985a) research, however, would seem to provide counter-evidence to this claim. Sato studied the production of consonant clusters by two Vietnamese learners of English on three tasks (free conversation, oral reading of continuous text, and elicited imitation of words and phrases). Sato sampled the subjects' interlanguage at four points over a ten-month period. What she found was the subjects' production was actually more target-like in the 'vernacular style' (free conversation in her study) than in the 'careful style' (reading aloud) in two of the four samples. In an earlier study focusing primarily on age differences in the pronunciation of foreign sounds, Oyama (1976) also found the reverse relationship. Her subjects produced more target-like pronunciation in casual samples involving less self-monitoring (spontaneous stories of frightening incidents in the subjects' lives) than in the more careful samples (reading a paragraph aloud).[3]

In her own test of her theory, Tarone (1985) conducted a study of the production of IL morphology by ten Arabic-speaking and ten Japanese-speaking adults on three tasks, supposedly increasing in the amount of attention to speech they required: narratives, interviews and written grammaticality judgements (involving recognition of errors and correction). She found no systematic relationship between task and target-like use of two bound morphemes, third-person singular *s* and noun plural *s*, and the *opposite* of the predicted trend with two free morphemes, definite article and direct object pronoun *it*. For free morphemes, that is, the (supposedly) more formal tasks elicited *fewer* target-like uses than the (supposedly) less formal tasks.

From a reanalysis of the Tarone (1985) data, Parrish and Tarone (1986) observe that the connection between task and variation is more complex than had originally been thought. Parrish and Tarone conclude that attention to language form cannot alone account for IL variability. Instead, a complex of variables is at work, of which two are the communicative demands of the task and the cohesiveness of the discourse produced in response.

4.2.4 Free variation as an impetus for development

A different view of variation is taken by Ellis, who adopts Gatbonton's (1978) 'diffusion model' of phonetic variability in SL speech and applies it to IL variability and change in general. Ellis is impressed by the especially high degree of *non-systematic* or free variation in IL. Individual native speakers may use pairs like /iy/ and /ay/ for 'either', 'who' and 'that' in restrictive relative clauses, and even 'variation' and 'variability' interchangeably, but such free variation is limited. IL users, on the other hand, often shift erratically back and forth with a wide range of sounds, grammatical functors and lexical items, as well as evidencing much more systematic (linguistic and situational) variability. Ellis (1985, p. 94) claims that free variability is crucial in that it 'serves as the impetus for development'. New forms, he believes, are first 'acquired' (first enter the IL) in the careful style of planned discourse, when the learner is 'monitoring' or 'attending to' speech, resulting in the greater variability of that speech style. The new forms are in free variation with existing ones at this stage, not having definably separate functions. During the second 'replacement' phase, each form in a pair is gradually restricted in use, i.e. takes on a particular range of (target or non-target) functions.

In Ellis's model, free variability is the force driving development, in that it is the reason posited for the appearance of new forms in the IL. Systematic variability, i.e. that due to linguistic or situational context, then comes into play, determining what subsequently happens to the newly acquired items. Ellis's idea, like Tarone's, is that forms which initially occur only in the learner's careful style spread along the continuum of IL speech styles, from formal to informal styles, and from linguistically simple to linguistically complex contexts. Through practice and a consequent need for less and less attention in their production (cf. McLaughlin, Rossman and McLeod 1983), they eventually permeate the vernacular, the most natural, systematic style, in which they appear fully analysed and automatised.

While interesting, these claims, like Labov's original work, are not without problems. First, no criteria are provided in either the first or second language studies which would enable the tasks used to be classified independently of the speech data in terms of the amount of attention to form they require. In other words, after a task elicits target-like variants, it is assumed to require attention to form. This is circular and effectively rules out a search for task features other than attention to form which might have resulted in the production of more target-like forms. Second, as Sato (1985a) and Parrish and Tarone (1986) point out, it is likely insufficient to define style solely in terms of the attention paid to language form. The differing task demands, the difference in linguistic structures being tracked and the length of discourse produced all presumably will affect learners' performance.

4.2.5 Multiple explanations for variability

Evidence supporting Sato's assumption of the need for a more powerful model is provided by Young's (1987, 1988) study, which begins to probe the true complexity of IL variation. Young's study involved production of plural *s* by twelve Chinese learners, six of higher proficiency (TOEFL scores above 476) and six of lower proficiency (TOEFL scores below 408). Each learner was interviewed twice, once by a native interlocutor, and once by a non-native, yielding a total of 45 minutes of talk from each of 24 one-hour interviews, and a total of 1,564 tokens of semantically plural nouns, of which 1,021 (65 per cent) were marked with a plural *s*.

Using a multivariate VARBRUL analysis,[4] Young found that variation in plural *s* marking could not be explained by any one factor or group of related factors. Thus, while overall ESL proficiency predicted accuracy of suppliance fairly well, other factors combined with proficiency to give better predictions, i.e. to account for more of the variability. For example, *s* was supplied more often in adverbs and complements than in subjects and objects by all twelve learners, but in a wider range of phonological environments by more advanced learners, and also more often by high-proficiency learners in cases of high 'social convergence' with a native-speaker interlocutor. 'Social convergence', a combined measure of the degree to which interlocutors shared certain social attributes (ethnicity, age, sex, education, occupation, and place of origin) was irrelevant when the interlocutor was a non-native speaker, on the other hand. Further, when Young controlled for social convergence, there was no effect for native/non-native interlocutor on *s* suppliance, a result Young interprets as showing (cf. Beebe and Zuengler 1983)[5] that the relevant interlocutor characteristic is not ethnicity but social convergence, and that (Young 1987, p. 21) 'the effect of target language input from the NS will only be felt if the NNS is able to identify with the NS'.

Finally, among a wealth of other detailed results, Young found that, contrary to popular belief, and contrary also to tendencies observed in pidgins and creoles, e.g. in early stages of Tok Pisin (Muhlhausler 1981), plural marking was favoured in contexts where it was communicatively redundant, e.g. following numerals (four *books*) and *these/those*, but more likely to be omitted when number was not marked anywhere else in the NP. Especially salient within the last finding was the close to categorical marking of plural *s* by high- and low-proficiency learners on what Young calls 'measure words', such as *years*, *days*, *hours*, *miles* and *dollars*, which usually follow quantifiers. Many of these items may initially be unanalysed 'frozen' forms, of course, and may also have helped produce the findings regarding syntactic environments favouring *s* plural marking, given their frequent occurrence as adverbials or complements.

In summary, ILs are much more synchronically variable than most other natural languages. Use of powerful enough analytic models reveals, however, that much of that variability is systematic, or rule-governed. Indeed, differences in the ways a learner uses a given form in contexts defined according to two kinds of variation, linguistic and situational, may indicate the future path of development of that form in the learner's IL over time. Synchronic variation, that is, may anticipate diachronic change (Weinreich, Labov and Herzog 1968). Even free variation, which causes most problems for researchers and teachers alike, may play a constructive, perhaps crucial role in development, for it is certainly one, and some have claimed, the single most important, source of growth in the new language.

4.3 ILs exhibit common acquisition orders and developmental sequences

As we saw earlier, although ILs are highly variable, they are also systematic. Documented acquisition orders and developmental sequences show a high degree of uniformity. Explanations for the systematicity vary (see Chapter 7), but most presuppose an innate language-specific endowment and/or a very powerful cognitive contribution by the learner. Acting alone or, more likely, in combination with the linguistic environment, either or both internal resources are held to underlie observable developmental sequences and common error types by learners with different L1s. In Chapter 2 of a prophetic but sadly neglected book for language teachers written in the late 1960s and published only some years later after his tragically early death, Dakin (1973) called attention to these errors, to their positive role in language learning, to the stages of development they signified, and to the need to distinguish external and 'internal syllabuses' in instructed SLA.

4.3.1 Acquisition order: morpheme studies

Early empirical evidence of that systematicity and of the existence of L1-neutral developmental sequences was provided by the so-called 'morpheme studies', noted in Chapter 3, which established the existence of a common acquisition order for a subset of English grammatical morphemes. Early studies by Dulay and Burt (1973, 1974) found that some 250 Spanish- and Chinese-speaking children, aged six to eigh. learning English in the USA, exhibited statistically significantly related orders in speech data elicited using the Bilingual Syntax Measure (BSM).

The finding of a common morpheme order was confirmed, again

using the BSM, for 73 Spanish-speaking and non-Spanish-speaking instructed adults by Bailey, Madden and Krashen (1974), who also showed that the ESL order differed from that obtained for English L1 in a longitudinal study of three children by Brown (1973) and a cross-sectional study of 24 children by de Villiers and de Villiers (1973). Dulay and Burt had already found the child ESL order different from the L1 order.

In another large-scale study conducted during this period, Larsen-Freeman (1975a) tested 24 adults, six speakers each from four L1 backgrounds (Arabic, Spanish, Japanese and Farsi), twice over a six-month period, using five tasks: the BSM, a picture-cued sentence-repetition test, a listening comprehension test (identifying one picture from a set on the basis of a spoken sentence), a modified reading cloze passage (with multiple-choice answers), and a writing test consisting of the same passage, but this time with the subjects filling in the blanks without the multiple-choice items. Larsen-Freeman found statistically significantly similar 'accuracy' orders[6] across L1 groups, and between her listening, BSM and repetition tasks and Dulay and Burt's BSM order, but some differences between these orders and those she obtained for her reading and writing tasks. Certain items rose in accuracy rank on those two tasks, notably plural *s* and third-person *s*, thereby 'disturbing' the order that was becoming familiar. While contrastive analysis of the L1s represented in her sample showed that L1 transfer could not explain the orders obtained, Larsen-Freeman did find some effect for L1, e.g. the low rank for article in the Japanese order. (For similar findings with children, see Mace-Matluck 1977.) In a subsequent study, Larsen-Freeman (1976c) suggested that input frequency might be one factor influencing the order, although not the only factor, of course; articles, for example, are always the most frequent item in the input, but relatively low in the accuracy order.

Reviewing over a dozen ESL morpheme studies available at the time, Krashen (1977) postulated a 'natural order' supported, with few exceptions, by the longitudinal and cross-sectional, individual and grouped SL findings (Figure 4.1). No claims were made for the order of items within a box, but items in boxes higher in the order were regularly found (80 or 90 per cent) accurately supplied in obligatory contexts (SOC) before those in boxes lower in the order. While admittedly not rigidly invariant, Krashen (1977, p. 151) pointed out, the order was also far from random.

Criticisms of the methodology utilized in these and subsequent morpheme studies are well known (for review, see Long and Sato 1984). Not all were well founded. A suggestion, for example, that

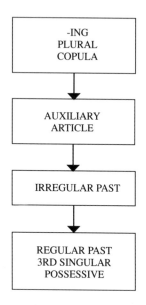

FIGURE 4.1 Krashen's (1977) 'Natural Order' for ESL

the order was simply an artefact of the BSM (Porter 1977) was easily refuted by Larsen-Freeman's data, by a study by Krashen, Houck, Giunchi, Bode, Birnbaum and Strei (1977), which obtained the same order from the spontaneous speech of 22 'intermediate' adult ESL students from various L1 backgrounds, and by studies obtaining the same order using adult free-composition data (Houk, Robertson and Krashen 1978; Krashen, Butler, Birnbaum and Robertson 1978).

A claim by Rosansky (1976) that the order could only be sustained in aggregated, cross-sectional, group data, and that it was contradicted by longitudinal data on individuals, was also refuted. Krashen (1977) showed that for all studies with individual subjects as well as with groups, in which at least ten obligatory contexts per morpheme were included, the 'natural order' held. Using fewer than ten obligatory contexts as Rosansky had done tends to produce unreliable results, as a change of just one extra correct suppliance of a morpheme means a change of more than 10 per cent on a subject's score for that item. Rosansky was undoubtedly correct in positing variability at the level of the individual. Nevertheless, Andersen (1978) showed that individual and grouped morpheme data do, in fact, correlate significantly.

Some other criticisms, however, clearly were more problematic for those wishing to base any strong claims on the findings of the morpheme studies. First, given the 'weak' nature of the inferential statistical tests employed (Spearman or Kendall rank order correlations), showing that orders were statistically significantly related could, and often did, still mean that they differed in significant ways, too (J.D. Brown 1983). Second, very few grammatical items were common to a majority of the studies, meaning that any claims concerning common orders were based on a tiny portion of English grammar (just nine items in Krashen's order, for instance). By definition, they were also language-specific, precluding cross-linguistic generalizations. If they showed anything, in other words, it was likely to be something about ESL, not SLA. And finally, the order, common or not, consisted of a linguistically heterogeneous group of bound and free NP and VP morphemes, which are in fact more revealing of developmental patterns when analysed in subsets, e.g. analysing the subset of morphemes having to do with noun phrases (Krashen 1977; Andersen 1978; J.D. Brown 1983).

Lacking any theoretical motivation, the order was itself in need of explanation (Gregg 1984). Several factors suggested as potential explanations, semantic and syntactic complexity, perceptual saliency, functional transparency and others, may well play a role, but only input frequency has much empirical support to date (Larsen-Freeman 1976c; Long 1980a; Lightbown 1983; Long and Sato 1983; for review, see Hatch 1983, Chapter 3). Another possibility is that suggested by Clahsen, Meisel and Pienemann (1983) and Pienemann and Johnston (1985), namely that the structures of any language, not just ESL, are learned as permitted by a series of underlying processing constraints (for discussion, see Chapter 7). The universality of the constraints potentially explains the commonalities across learners of both the morpheme accuracy/acquisition order and developmental sequences.

The early work reported here was by no means the end of the story. At least fifty SL morpheme studies have now been reported, many using more sophisticated data collection and analysis procedures, notably target-like use (TLU) analysis, in which subjects' performance in supplying morphemes in non-obligatory contexts in addition to SOC is scrutinized (see, e.g., Lightbown, Spada and Wallace 1980; Lightbown 1983; and for review, Pica 1983c). Importantly, Pica (1982) showed that SOC and TLU orders calculated for the same corpus correlated statistically significantly, thus helping allay some of the fears about the earlier findings. Other researchers have extended the range of subjects sampled, finding orders correlating significantly with those from the earlier studies with subjects from Indo-European and non-Indo-European L1 backgrounds (Mace-Matluck 1977; Fuller 1978), on different performance tasks, e.g. Fathman's SLOPE test (Krashen, Sferlazza, Feldman and Fathman 1976), and in different (foreign language and second language) acquisition contexts (Fathman 1978; Makino 1979; cf. Sajavaara 1981). Finally, a small number of studies have appeared documenting accuracy orders for other L2s, e.g. Spanish (van Naerssen 1980, 1986) and Quiche Mayan (Bye 1980).

In sum, despite admitted limitations in some areas, the morpheme studies provide strong evidence that ILs exhibit common accuracy/acquisition orders. Contrary to what some critics have alleged, there are in our view too many studies conducted with sufficient methodological rigour and showing sufficiently consistent general findings for the commonalities to be ignored. As the hunter put it, 'There is something moving in the bushes.'

4.3.2 Developmental sequence: interrogatives

As indicated in Chapter 3, a second striking example of the systematicity of IL consists of common *developmental sequences* within morpho-syntactic domains through which, with only minor variations, all learners seem to pass, regardless of age, native language or (formal or informal) learning context. The sequences consist of ordered series of IL structures, approximations to a target construction, each reflecting an underlying *stage* of development. Stages in a sequence are not discrete, but overlap, and are traditionally identified by ascertaining the most frequently used, not the only, IL structure(s) at a given point in time. To qualify as a 'stage' and to constitute an interesting theoretical claim, however, each potential stage must be ordered (with respect to other stages in a sequence) and obligatory, i.e. unavoidable by the learner (Meisel, Clahsen and Pienemann 1981; Johnston 1985).

One of the first developmental sequences to be identified was that for ESL questions. Following initial work by Huang (1970), Butterworth (1972), Ravem (1970), Young (1974), Wagner-Gough (1975), and Adams (1978), researchers in the famous Harvard Project (Cazden, Cancino, Rosansky and Schumann 1975) studied six Spanish speakers, two children, two adolescents and two adults, learning English naturalistically in the Boston area over a ten-month period, collecting data through tape-recorded biweekly conversations between the researchers and individual subjects. Among many other findings from this study

Stage	Sample utterance
1. Rising intonation	He work today?
2. Uninverted WH (+/− aux.)	What he (is) saying?
3. 'Overinversion'	Do you know where is it?
4. Differentiation	Does she like where she lives?

TABLE 4.1 Developmental Sequence for Interrogatives in ESL

(see, e.g., Chapters 6 and 7) was that interrogatives in ESL emerged in a predictable sequence, shown in schematic and slightly modified form in Table 4.1.

At Stage 1, questions are formed by marking statements with rising intonation. WH-questions appear at Stage 2, but without subject–verb inversion, indeed often without an auxiliary verb at all, e.g. 'Where you go?' and 'Why the Mary not here?' When inversion does enter the system at Stage 3, it is with a vengeance. It is applied correctly to yes/no and WH-questions such as 'Can you speak Spanish?', 'Is he your teacher?' and 'How can you say it?', first with the modal *can* and then the copula *be*, but also overgeneralized to embedded questions, as in 'Do you know what time is it?' and 'I know where are you going.' Finally, at Stage 4, the learner reaches the full target system, differentiating between simple and embedded WH-questions, inverting in the former only.

Most subjects in the studies cited were native speakers of Spanish, which clearly limits the generalizability of any claims made. On the other hand, Huang's subject, Paul, a five-year-old Taiwanese boy, showed the same general pattern, as did Ravem's two Norwegian children, Reidun and Rune, aged six and three. The Norwegian ESL data did suggest some influence for the learners' L1 on the sequence (see Section 4.4 for other examples), the children producing relatively few intonation questions in the subset of yes/no questions formed with copula, such as 'Are you hungry?'. In those cases, they usually inverted, as required, Ravem points out, in copula yes/no questions in Norwegian. Where WH-questions were concerned, however, Norwegian would predict utterances like 'Where go Mary?', but the children instead produced uninverted WH-questions at Stage

Stage	Sample utterance
1. External	No this one / No you playing here.
2. Internal, pre-verbal	Juana no / don't have job.
3. Aux. + neg.	I can't play the guitar.
4. Analysed don't	She doesn't drink alcohol.

TABLE 4.2 Developmental Sequence for ESL Negation

2, like 'Where Mary go?', following what seems to be the ESL IL norm for interrogatives.

4.3.3 Developmental sequence: negation

Another well-known developmental sequence is that for ESL negation (Table 4.2). Learners from a variety of typologically different first language backgrounds have been observed to pass through four major stages: *no* + X, *no/don't* V, aux-neg, and analysed *don't* (for review, see Schumann 1979). Thus, at stages 1 and 2, not just speakers of languages like Spanish, with pre-verbal negation, but also speakers of languages such as Swedish, Turkish and Japanese, with post-verbal negation, all produce pre-verbally negated utterances.

At Stage 1, externally negated constructions like 'No book', 'No is happy' and 'No you pay it' occur, although they seem rare in adult learners, and particularly ephemeral in speakers of L1s with post-verbal negation. Internal pre-verbally negated strings, on the other hand, like 'He no can shoot good', 'They not working' and 'I don't have car' are very common. *No* is the typical (often the only) negator at Stage 1, while *no*, *not* and *don't* are all used at Stage 2. Utterances such as 'I don't like Los Angeles' at Stage 2 can temporarily lead a researcher (or teacher) to believe the learner has mastered English negation. A preponderance of utterances at this stage like 'He/she don't like job', 'John don't come to class (yesterday)' and 'I don't can play good' reveals, however, that *don't* is really being used as an unanalysed negative particle, not as auxiliary + negator.

Stage 3 sees the placement of *not*, usually in its contracted form, following *can* in particular, as in 'I can't play', and the *be* verb as in

'It wasn't so big.'[7] The fact that *can't* and *wasn't* are frequent in the input and are often the first to appear, and that most early Stage 3 items use the contracted *n't* form, suggest that some initial examples, at least, may be unanalysed chunks. If so, the aux–neg rule soon becomes productive. Perhaps by analysis and generalization from it, the learner then moves to Stage 4, with use of the full target system of aux + neg and analysed *don't*. Attainment of the later stages, as Stauble (1981) demonstrated, is related to the development of other VP (verb phrase) morphology. Stage 4, for example, requires control of a full auxiliary system, including the ability to inflect correctly for number and time reference (e.g. *isn't, weren't, don't, doesn't* and *didn't*).

In addition to the commonality of the sequence as a whole, a striking feature of the negation findings is the pervasiveness of initial pre-verbal constructions. Although speakers of L1s with pre-verbal negation tend to spend longer at Stages 1 and 2, while learners whose L1s have post-verbal negation may traverse these stages quite quickly (Gillis and Weber 1976; Gerbault 1978; and see discussion in Section 4.4), pre-verbal negation, as indicated earlier, has been documented as the first ESL stage for learners from a wide variety of L1s (Schumann 1979), and also for other SLs. Hyltenstam (1977), for example, found pre-verbal negation in the early Swedish (which has post-verbal negation in main clauses) of English speakers, and even in that of Turks, whose own L1 also has post-verbal negation.

Cases such as these, where a structure in a common IL sequence cannot easily be accounted for by reference to either the L1 or the L2, are powerful evidence for those who claim that IL development is guided at least in part by language universals. They are also evidence against a pure *restructuring* view of IL development, which holds that learners start from the L1 and develop towards the target language by a process of *relexification* (i.e. use of L2 words in L1 syntactic patterns) and replacement of L1 grammatical features (for discussion, see Nemser 1971; McLaughlin 1987, 1990). Conversely, they are consistent with the notion that IL development is a process of gradual 'complexification', or *recreation* of the L2 in much the same way that children 'recreate' their mother tongue in first language acquisition (see, e.g., Corder 1978 and the 'creative construction process' of Dulay and Burt 1977).

While little experimental research has been conducted, studies so far suggest that these and other 'natural' IL sequences, e.g. those claimed for German SL (GSL) word order (Clahsen 1980; Meisel, Clahsen and Pienemann 1981; Pienemann 1985a; Pienemann and Johnston 1987) and for ESL relative clauses (see Chapter 7) are strongly resistant to alteration by instruction (see Chapter 8) and possibly immutable. Modifications due to L1 influence (see Section 4.4) may delay initiation of a sequence, delay or speed up passage through it, or even add sub-stages to it, but never seem to involve either omission of stages or changes in the sequence of stages. As with the so-called 'natural order' for morpheme accuracy, most of the morpho-syntactic developmental sequences identified to date are language-specific, and so lacking in generalizability, and once again, explanations other than rather general appeals to 'internal learner contributions' are in short supply. Some exist, however, and we return to these in our discussion of theories of SLA in Chapter 7.

4.4 ILs are influenced by the learner's L1

As described in Chapter 3, the widely held belief in the 1950s and 1960s was that the L1 played a decisive and negative role in SLA, termed 'interference', and that this interference could be predicted by systematically comparing and contrasting the learner's L1 and L2, looking to points of difference between the two. As we also acknowledged in Chapter 3, this strong view of the CAH has, quite simply, not been supported by research findings. The CAH is problematic on two counts: the predictions have not been borne out (Hammerly 1982), and often it is the similarities, not the differences, that cause the greatest problems (Koutsoudas and Koutsoudas 1962), stated as a principle by Wode (1978): 'Only if L1 and L2 have structures meeting a crucial similarity measure will there be interference, i.e. reliance on prior L1 knowledge.'

Wode's principle is an example of what has occupied numerous scholars since the mid-1970s, not showing that the learners' L1 influences SLA, but rather when it does. Needless to say, this is not an easy enterprise. K. Flynn (1983) has demonstrated that transfer can easily be overlooked, especially if one is focused solely on linguistic form. Flynn found similar frequencies of present perfect verb forms in the essays of Chinese, Arabic and Spanish learners of English, suggesting a lack of effect for L1. Further analysis revealed, however, clear evidence of transfer in inter-group differences in the functions expressed by these forms.

In addition to *when* the L1 affects SLA, researchers these days have been striving to understand *how* it does. Recall that under the CAH, the prediction was either that the L1 would cause difficulty (i.e. cause errors to be committed) or it would facilitate SLA. Recent research, however, has shown that transfer manifests itself in unexpected ways as well. For example, Schachter and Rutherford (1979) noted that certain of their ESL subjects (one Chinese and one Japanese) *overproduced* extraposed and existential sentences with 'dummy' subjects, e.g.

> It is unfortunate that . . . (extraposed)
> There is a small restaurant . . . (existential)

They hypothesized that the overuse of such sentences was due to the learners' having seized a particular English syntactic pattern to serve a discourse function that their L1s, being topic–comment, require.[8] Later, Schachter (1983) speculates that language transfer is a constraint on the nature of the hypotheses language learners are inclined to make about the L2. Thus, other ways the L1 may affect SLA are through causing learners to overproduce certain L2 forms and by influencing the hypotheses learners are likely to entertain about how the L2 is structured.

The renewed interest in L1 transfer, attested to by such studies, resulted in the appearance of several anthologies of empirical studies (see, e.g., Gass and Selinker 1983, Sajavaara 1983, Kellerman and Sharwood-Smith 1986). Some of these researchers reserve use of 'transfer' for cases of incorporation of features of one language in another, e.g. L1 features in an IL, and have adopted 'cross-linguistic influence' (Sharwood Smith 1983) as a more appropriate, theory-neutral cover term for the far wider range of phenomena that actually result from language contact, including interference, positive transfer, avoidance, borrowing, over-production and L2-related aspects of language loss[9] (Kellerman and Sharwood Smith 1986; Weltens, de Bot and van Els 1986). Such work also increasingly often involves *cross-linguistic SLA research*, in which a variety of L2s being acquired by learners of varying L1s are examined. (See, for example, Andersen 1984b). Researchers have acknowledged for some time that much of the SLA research has tended to focus too narrowly on ESL and thus there was a need to widen the scope of their investigations, particularly when making claims about L1 transfer.

4.4.1 The effect of the L1 on SLA: how

In an early review article of studies of this sort, Zobl (1982) identified two patterns of L1 influence on SLA. These were (1) the pace at which a developmental sequence is traversed, and (2) the number of developmental structures in such sequences. Zobl noted that a learner's L1 can inhibit and/or accelerate passage through a developmental sequence, although apparently not alter the sequence itself, except

Main clause WO	Simple verb	Aux. verb
Dutch/German	SVO	SOV
Turkish	SOV	SOV
Arabic	VSO	SVO

TABLE 4.3 Word Order in Source and Target Languages

by occasionally adding a different initial starting structure. Where an L1 form is similar to a developmental one, this can make the learner persist with the developmental form longer than learners without such a form in their L1, and can also extend the structural domain of the immature form (Zobl 1980a, 1980b, 1983a; Schumann 1982). Thus, Zobl maintains that (pre-verbal L1 negation) Spanish-speakers' initial *No V* ESL negation rule is the result of the developmental creative construction process, as with speakers of other languages without a *No V* construction in their L1, but that both the Spanish-speakers' protracted use of the construction compared, say, with (post-verbal negation L1) Japanese speakers (Gillis and Weber 1976), and also their extension of the rule to modal and copular verbs, are due to the convergence of the L1 and developmental structure. Similar generalizations are captured in Kellerman's (1984) 'reasonable entity principle' and in Andersen's (1983b) 'transfer to somewhere principle', which holds that transfer operates in tandem with natural developmental principles in determining the way ILs progress.

Another example Zobl (1982) provides of congruence causing a delay in traversing a developmental sequence concerns the persistence of verb-final word order in the learning of Dutch and German (see Table 4.3). Zobl notes, first, that in a study of the development of Dutch SL word order by Turkish and Moroccan migrant workers in Holland, Jansen, Lalleman and Muyksen (1981) found that, while the Turks used many more verb-final structures in their early Dutch ILs, as might have been predicted from the SOV order of Turkish, both Turkish and Moroccan Arabic speakers used verb-final structures in the early stages, something one would not expect of the latter group due to the fact that Moroccan Arabic is not verb final. Zobl notes further that overgeneralization of the verb-final order in main clauses with auxiliary verbs to main clauses with simple verbs was also reported for

(SVO) English speakers learning Dutch (Snow and Hofnagel-Hohle 1978). Third, verb-final order is also dominant in early stages of the L1 acquisition of German (Roeper 1973), which has the same word-order distribution as Dutch. From the L1 and L2 data, Zobl argues that the developmental sequence in Dutch and German is clearly verb-final before verb-internal word order. The OV order of Turkish can thus be seen to have caused both the more protracted and the more generalized use of the verb-final developmental structure of the Turks' Dutch SL in the Jansen et al. study. Conversely, the SVO Moroccan Arabic order allowed the Arabic speakers in the same study to move on from the generalized verb-final stage in the developmental order more quickly. The slower abandonment of this initial OV strategy by the Turks, Zobl claims, parallels Spanish speakers' more protracted use of *No V* negation.

While the negation and word-order examples are cases where L1 and developmental structural congruence inhibits learning, Zobl points to several cases where the effect of congruence is positive. When L1 and L2 employ the same device, e.g. inflectional morphology, to encode a given range of meanings, SL learners still start by omitting the marking in the L2, followed by an often lengthy period of variable marking before attaining target-like use. By looking at or across studies involving speakers of two or more different L1s acquiring the same L2 under comparable conditions, Zobl concludes, however, that both the omission phase and the variable marking phase are shorter where the source and target language are congruent. Thus, when the L1 (e.g. Swedish or Spanish) and the L2 (e.g. English or German) both use articles to mark definiteness and indefiniteness, target-like control is achieved more quickly than in cases of zero contrast, i.e. when the L1 (e.g. Finnish or Japanese) lacks articles or some other category present in the L2, a finding obtained for articles in ESL (Fathman 1975a; Hakuta 1975; Granfors and Palmberg 1976; Mace-Matluck 1977; Sajavaara 1978, 1981) and in German as a SL (Gilbert and Orlovic 1975). The same holds true for copular verbs (Henkes 1974; Scott and Tucker 1974), prepositions (Sjoholm 1983 reported in Kellerman 1984) and various kinds of lexical error (Ringbom 1978) in ESL, and for reflexive pronouns in French as a SL (Morsely and Vasseur 1976).

Zero contrast, referred to as 'new' in Table 3.1 (i.e. the L2 possesses a category that is absent in the learner's L1), affects IL development in more subtle ways than originally believed. One effect is to delay passage through a developmental sequence, something we have seen can also result from congruence. An example is provided by Keller-Cohen (1979) from her study of the acquisition of English by three young children, native speakers of German, Finnish and Japanese. Rising-intonation questions are the first question type to emerge in L1 acquisition by speakers of languages which have this option (Wode 1978). Finnish does not use intonation questions, and in L1 acquisition of Finnish, WH-questions develop first, followed by yes/no questions, which require a question inflection and verb transposition (Bowerman 1973). Keller-Cohen found that, while following the same developmental path as the other two children in the learning of yes/no questions in ESL (cf. Table 4.1), the Finnish child progressed much more slowly.

A second possible effect of zero contrast identified by Zobl (1982) involves the addition of a preliminary step to an acquisition sequence. Zobl noted that Paul, a five-year-old Chinese child acquiring ESL (Huang 1970), having no articles in his L1, initially employed deictic determiners, usually demonstrative adjectives (e.g. *this* house), as the first approximation to definite articles in the L2. (For related findings with other SLs, see Orlovic 1974, and Valdman and Phillips 1975.) In contrast, Guero, a three-year-old Spanish-speaking child (Hernandez-Chavez 1977), whose L1 does have an article system, used the English definite article as early as the first appearance of deictics. Again, L1–L2 differences did not alter the developmental sequence but did delay passage through it, this time by postponing the start and adding a sub-stage.

Zobl interprets these findings as showing that transfer, rather than working separately and in competition with the creative construction process, as had once been thought, actually accommodates to natural developmental processes. L1 influence will not change normal developmental sequences but may modify passage through them. Its effects, Zobl concludes, are subject to two constraints. First, it is fairly well established that, in situations of language contact, complex structures typically undergo modification by formally simpler structures. In keeping with this fact about historical language change, the *developmental complexity constraint* (Zobl 1982, p. 180) holds that:

> L1 influence may modify a developmental continuum at that point at which a developmental structure is similar to a corresponding L1 structure and where further progress in the continuum amounts to an increase in complexity beyond that of the L1 structure.

When this condition is met, Zobl predicts, one of three things will happen. First, there may be a delay in the restructuring needed for the learner to progress to the next developmental stage (e.g. the case of prolonged *No V* negation by Spanish speakers). Such structures may be prime candidates for fossilization (Zobl 1983a; White 1985a). Second, the scope of the current developmental structure may be extended (e.g. extension of the Spanish speakers' *No V* negation rule to modal and copular verbs, or Wode's finding that German L1 learners of ESL place the negator after the main verb, as in German, once they begin to place it [correctly] after the English auxiliary). Third, learners may seek development with the smallest possible rule change. In this case, Zobl (1982, p. 180) claims, they are behaving under a second constraint, the *internal consistency constraint* as he terms it, which holds that 'in traversing a developmental continuum, learners will strive to implement rule changes which permit a maximum degree of structural consistency with the preceding developmental forms'. An example of application of this constraint is the transitional use of deictic determiners for articles by learners lacking articles in their L1, thereby allowing them to avoid what would be a more radical restructuring move, from zero marking to full grammaticization (use of an article system). Another example is the Turkish speakers' protracted use of the verb-final Dutch constituent order before making the (for them) more radical switch to VO word order with simple verbs in Dutch.

4.4.2 The effect of the L1 on SLA: when (markedness)

A third 'constraint' on L1 transfer proposed by Zobl and several other theorists is linguistic *markedness*. The general claim is that linguistically unmarked features of the L1 will tend to transfer, but that linguistically marked L1 features will not (e.g. Eckman 1977; Kellerman 1977; Gass 1979; Gundel and Tarone 1983; Zobl 1983b, 1984; Rutherford 1984; Hyltenstam 1984, 1987; Kean 1986; but cf. White 1987a).

Linguistic notions of 'markedness' are usually defined in terms of complexity, relative infrequency of use or departure from something that is more basic, typical or canonical in a language. Thus, one argument for treating masculine members of pairs like *man/woman* and *waiter/waitress* as the unmarked (read 'simpler', base) forms is the fact that English *adds* forms to produce the morphologically more complex feminine form. The feminine form is therefore marked. Similarly, morphemes are added to distinguish past from present, plural from singular, and so on, suggesting that present and singular are unmarked, past and plural are marked.

Markedness can also be ascertained typologically when cross-linguistic comparisons of languages show that the presence of some linguistic feature implies the presence of another feature. Languages which have voiced stops, for example, also have voiceless stops, whereas some languages which have voiceless stops do not have voiced ones, suggesting that voiced (which involves additional complexity in the form of an additional phonological feature) is marked, voiceless is unmarked.

Utilizing this last notion of implicational universals, with 'implied' terms being unmarked or less marked, one of the first and most interesting claims regarding transfer was Eckman's Markedness Differential Hypothesis (MDH) (Eckman 1977, 1985). The MDH makes three predictions (1977, p. 321):

(a) Those areas of the L2 which differ from the L1, and are more marked than the L1 will be difficult.

(b) The relative degree of difficulty of the areas of the L2 which are more marked than the L1 will correspond to the relative degree of markedness.

(c) Those areas of the L2 which are different from the L1, but are not more marked than the L1, will not be difficult.

To support prediction (b), Eckman (1977, pp. 323-7) reanalysed the data on IL syntax in Schachter (1974), showing that the degree of difficulty with English relative clauses experienced by each of the four groups in that study – Farsi, Arabic, Chinese and Japanese speakers – reflected the relative distance of their L1 from English on the Noun Phrase Accessibility Hierarchy markedness scale (Keenan and Comrie 1977). The CAH, he noted, could at most simply predict difficulty for all groups, given that each L1 forms relatives differently from English in several ways, but could not make any principled (non-arbitrary) predictions about relative degree of difficulty. (For discussion of this reanalysis, see Kellerman 1979, 1984.)

Turning to predictions (a) and (c), Eckman further illustrated the explanatory power of the MDH using SL phonology data. Dinnsen and Eckman (1975) had established that of three possible positions in words in which a voiced/voiceless distinction can be made, initial position (*bit/pit*) is the least marked in a markedness hierarchy, followed by medial position (*biding/biting*), with final position being the most marked (*eyes/ice*. Languages like English, Arabic and Swedish, which have voice contrasts in word-final position, will always also have them in medial and initial positions. There are also languages, like German, Japanese and Catalan, however, which have voice contrasts in medial and initial position, but not in final position. Another group, including Corsican and Sardinian, have the contrast in initial position only. There are no languages which make the distinction in medial and/or final, but not initial position, or in final, but not medial and initial position.

With these facts in mind, the MDH predicts (correctly) that German speakers have difficulty making the word-final contrast with obstruents in English, which involves them in adding a more marked distinction in the SL (MDH prediction (a)), whereas English speakers have no difficulty with dropping the (most marked) word-final L1 distinction when learning German (MDH prediction (c)). The original CAH, on the other hand, again could not handle data like these, since an L1–L2 voice contrast difference exists whether English or German is the SL, and so should lead to difficulty in both cases, but does not. Eckman pointed out that a potential modification of the CAH to handle these data, namely, positing that what is difficult is a new contrast or new position of contrast, but not the suppression of a contrast, is not tenable either. While such a revamped CAH would handle the German/English data, it could not explain other cases, such as the fact that English speakers have no difficulty in adding a contrast when they learn to use /ž/ in contrast with /š/ in initial position in French (Gradman 1971), as in 'je'. (English has the /ž/ sound only in medial or final position, e.g. measure, garage.) The MDH correctly predicts the French data, on the other hand. Since English, the L1, has the /ž/–/š/ contrast in the more marked, medial and final, positions for voicing contrasts, adding the contrast in initial position in French involves adding a *less* marked contrast, and so is not expected to be difficult (MDH prediction (c)).

Eckman's MDH seems worthy of more research attention than it has received to date, although it appears that some refinement and modifications will be necessary. First, the precision of the claims needs to be enhanced by adding specific predictions as to the form(s) that 'difficulty' will take in each case, particularly as to whether marked and unmarked structures wil transfer, and under what circumstances. Second, as noted earlier, Zobl has identified cases of difficulty and transfer where both L1 and L2 are marked. Prediction (b) could handle these if each marked structure could be located at different points on a markedness hierarchy (such as Keenen and Comrie 1977), but would need further elaboration in cases of equal markedness. (See Eckman 1985 for discussion of these and other potential modifications.)

4.4.3 The effect of the L1 on SLA: when (perceived transferability)

Two further dimensions that may also need to be added to the model are *perceived transferability* and learner proficiency. Kellerman (1977, 1978, 1979a, 1984) has shown that whether or not learners actually transfer a form can depend in part on how likely they think it to be acceptable in another language, or their perception of the L1–L2 'distance', i.e. how marked its use in their own L1 appears to them. Demonstrating such principles, he argues, often requires elicitation and experimentation, rather than simple observation and description. (See also Kohn 1986; Sharwood Smith 1986.)

Kellerman (1977) presented adult Dutch speakers with grammatical English sentences which contained twenty Dutch idiomatic expressions in translation, and asked them which usages they thought were acceptable in English. He found that they improved in their ability to identify acceptable and unacceptable idioms with increasing proficiency but, especially at lower proficiency levels, were conservative in their judgements. They were more likely to accept idioms which seemed semantically transparent to them and likely to be language-neutral (e.g. I don't think he should have insulted her *behind her back*), and to reject those which to them seemed semantically opaque, language-specific ('typical' of Dutch), unusual, and so marked (e.g. to have a victory *in the bag*). Similar findings were obtained for German SL by Dutch speakers in studies by Jordens (1977, 1978), who showed that the same criteria governing transferability, whether an item seemed marked and whether it seemed semantically opaque, applied not only to idioms but also to syntax. In another study, Gass and Ard (1984) found that ESL students judged sentences illustrating core uses of progressive aspect, such as 'He is working now', as more acceptable than sentences containing more peripheral uses, such as 'He is leaving tomorrow.'

In a second experiment, Kellerman (1978) tested the hypothesis that core, unmarked, meanings of a word will be transferred before others, e.g. that learners would expect 'blue' to be more likely to signify 'a colour' in a SL than 'depression', 'jazz' or 'pornographic'. Kellerman first used a card-sort technique (Miller 1969) to obtain a baseline NS ranking, aggregated from judgements by 50 Dutch NSs, of more and less core meanings of the Dutch verb *breken* (break) used in sentences, as well as rankings of the sentences from concrete to abstract uses of the verb. When English translations of the sentences were later presented to 81 Dutch learners of English, the judgements they gave as to which uses of 'break' they thought possible in English correlated strongly with the NS 'coreness' ranking, but not with the concrete/abstract ranking. The same result was obtained from 291 learners using a subset of nine of the sentences. Table 4.4 shows how learners generally projected the uses of 'break' in English as decreasingly acceptable, i.e. uses nearest the top of the list as most transferable, uses nearest the bottom as least transferable.

Kellerman concludes from his studies, combined with those of Jordens, that transfer is a strategy available to compensate for lack of L2 knowledge. However, its use with idioms, lexis and syntax, at least, and probably with all aspects of language except phonology, will be constrained by the learner's perception of L1–L2 distance, with marked forms (here meaning those which are less frequent, less productive, less semantically transparent, less core) being potentially less transferable than unmarked ones.

A learner's proficiency level seems also to be a relevant factor in determining when transfer will occur, something we already noted in the last chapter in the study by Taylor (1975). Kellerman (1983) notes interesting examples in his and Jordens' data of so-called 'u-shaped behavior'. Beginners were more willing to transfer

---

1. He broke his leg.
2. The cup broke.
3. After the accident, he became a broken man.
4. She broke his heart.
5. The waves broke on the rocks.
6. The light rays break (refract) the water.
7. Thanks to a couple of jokes, the ice was finally broken.
8. He broke his word.
9. The man broke his oath.
10. 'Necessity breaks law'.
11. She broke the world record.
12. His fall was broken by a tree.
13. His voice broke when he was 13.
14. Some workers have broken the strike.
15. Which country has broken the ceasefire?
16. The underground resistance was broken.
17. A game would break (break up) the afternoon a bit.

TABLE 4.4 Coreness Ranking of 'Break' (Kellerman 1979a, p. 49)

marked items along with unmarked ones, perhaps recognizing general typological similarities between these L1s and L2s. Intermediate students were more conservative about transferring marked uses, possibly because they had committed enough errors by this stage to know that, while similar, the languages really differed in detail a great deal. Finally, advanced learners once again became willing to assume transferability. Error frequency in the three phases, consequently, was initially low, then rose, and finally fell again. Accuracy, conversely, was initially high, then fell, and finally rose again, giving the 'U' shape to a graphic representation of the performance data.

Elementary-level learners have also been found willing to transfer marked L1 forms in other studies. About half the English learners of Spanish studied by Liceras (1985), for example, accepted (marked) preposition stranding constructions ('*Where* did you leave *from?*', etc.) in a grammaticality judgement task. Preposition stranding is possible in English, but not in Spanish, which requires pied-piping, i.e. requires the preposition to be fronted along with the WH-question word (*De donde* saliste? – *From where* did you leave?). Intermediate and advanced learners, on the other hand, generally rejected the stranding construction.

In conclusion, the role of the L1 is considerably more complex, but fortunately not as negative, as was first thought by proponents of the CAH. It can lead to errors, overproduction and constraints on hypotheses; however, L1–L2 differences do not necessarily mean difficulty in SLA. On the contrary, it is similarities between native and target language which tend to cause many problems. However, structural identity between two languages does not necessarily result in positive transfer either. When L1 transfer occurs, it generally does so in harmony with developmental processes, modifying learners' encounters with IL sequences rather than altering them in fundamental ways. The modifications take at least six forms:

1. The L1 can delay initiation of passage through a sequence.
2. It can add sub-stages to a sequence in the form of approximations to an IL structure where abrupt movement to the L2 system would require too great a one-time change.
3. It can speed up passage through a sequence, as when strong dis-similarity between a developmental structure and the L1 provides little incentive for learners to stick with the IL form.
4. It can prolong the period of error commission in areas of typological contrast between L1 and L2, e.g. where one language

has grammaticized a domain, such as definiteness, but the other has not.

5. It can prolong use of a developmental form similar to an L1 structure (potentially resulting in fossilization).
6. It can extend the scope of a developmental structure.

In addition to operating in cooperation, rather than in conflict, with universal developmental processes, transfer seems to be constrained by various kinds of linguistic markedness:

7. Transfer of unmarked forms is more likely than transfer of marked ones.
8. Transfer of marked forms may occur, however, if the L2 form is also marked.
9. Learning difficulty generally results from L1–L2 differences involving greater L2 markedness, not from differences involving less L2 markedness, with degree of difficulty reflecting degree of markedness.
10. Transfer is affected by learners' perceptions of L1–L2 distance, and by the perceived transferability of an item, as measured by its apparent degree of markedness.
11. Item 10 notwithstanding, L2 limitations make beginners especially dependent on the L1, and so initially more willing to transfer marked as well as unmarked items.

Clearly, much has been learned about transfer in the last decade or so; equally clear is the fact that there remains much to be learned before we can predict with any confidence when and how L1 transfer will occur.

Notes

1. Of course, what might look like free variation syntactically, morphologically, or phonologically, could be functionally systematic (Schachter 1986a).
2. When they do receive deviant peer input, errors may become fossilized. Such is apparently the case with the so-called 'classroom-dialects' of L2 immersion programmes (Harley and Swain 1978).
3. There also seems to be some discrepancy as to how the formality of tasks affects the transfer of sociolinguistic rules from the L1. Schmidt (1977) found that his subjects used a target-like /ø/ from Classical Arabic on a formal task and a non-target /s/ or /t/ from colloquial Arabic on an informal task. Conversely, Beebe (1980b) reports that Thais' socially conditioned L1 use of R allophones resulted in more non-target-like performance on the more formal tasks in her study.

4. A VARBRUL analysis is a statistical procedure for modelling multidimensional variation in the data.
5. Beebe and Zuengler (1983) claim that more target-like performance can be expected when learners converse with native speakers as opposed to non-natives, due to the general tendency, given a positive affective disposition, for speakers to accommodate to the speech norms of the interlocutor.
6. Larsen-Freeman used the term 'accuracy' order rather than 'acquisition' order. She felt a more modest term was warranted at the time as at that point only cross-sectional studies had been carried out, *and* what was being ascertained was the subjects' ability to use the morphemes accurately in obligatory contexts; no heed was given, for example, to the fact that the subjects may have overgeneralized the morphemes to inappropriate contexts.
7. Negation with the main copular verb *be* comes in this stage, although this stage is usually referred to as the aux + neg stage.
8. It is also interesting to note that errors produced by subjects in their study, e.g.

> * Most of the food which is served in such restaurant
> have cooked already.

were misdiagnosed by ESL teachers as errors in using the English passive voice. Instead, Schachter and Rutherford argue that what the learner was attempting to say was:

> * Most of the food which is served in such restaurants
> [they] have cooked [it] already.

Given this interpretation, it seems such errors could be attributed to the fact that the learners' L1s were topic prominent (Mandarin) and subject-prominent/topic-prominent (Japanese) and thus the subjects were attempting to preserve the topic-comment discourse function in their English utterance. (See Jordens 1983, 1986 for another example of the effect of L1 discourse on L2 morphosyntax.)
9. There is a growing body of research on the issue of language attrition or language loss which regrettably we are unable to deal with here. Interested readers may wish to consult Lambert and Freed (1982), Weltens, de Bot and van Els (1986), Weltens (1987), and Buckley (1988).

Activities

Comprehension

1. What are the differences between free and systematic variation? Give one example of each. How do you know the examples are correctly classified as 'free' and 'systematic'?

2. What is the difference between stabilization and fossilization?
3. Does IL performance vary systematically according to the amount of attention paid to speech?
4. Which factors cause IL variation? Cite one study or piece of evidence for each.
5. Define 'stage' of IL development.
6. What are the methodological problems associated with the morpheme studies, and how serious do you consider each one?
7. List the major stages observed in the development of ESL negation, and provide illustrative utterances for each stage. What could explain the observed sequence?
8. Schachter (1983) speculates that the L1 constrains the nature of the hypotheses that language learners of an L2 are likely to make. What difference in understanding of the role of the L1 in SLA is reflected in this observation in terms of 'interference', 'transfer' and 'cross-linguistic influence'?
9. Provide three pieces of evidence against the claim that L1–L2 difference causes difficulty in SLA.
10. Why would it be unjustified to claim that 'No have money', uttered by a Spanish speaker (Spanish has *No V* negation), is an unambiguous case of L1 transfer? What are the potentially relevant sources of data when attempting to identify L1 influence as a cause of L2 error?

Application

11. How could knowledge of the factors affecting IL variability be exploited in language teaching?
12. The following utterances (data courtesy of Benabe 1981) were produced by a five-year-old Spanish-speaking girl acquiring English naturalistically in the USA. What stage of ESL interrogative development is the learner at, and what rules underlie her production of questions?
    (a) How come God made the rain so loud?
    (b) Is God made the rain too loud?
    (c) Is your room is dark?
    (d) Is a ballet was fine?
    (e) Is your teacher is big or little?
    (f) What color mask color you have for Halloween?
    (g) What you did last night?
    (h) What kind of school you go?
    (i) Where you went after you went to the ballet?

    (j) Where you going first?
    (k) Where is my pastilla grande?
    (l) What you have to do?
    (m) Where you got that, tita?
    (n) Can I go with you to the supermarket?
    (o) That's yours?
    (p) Are you going to give me a happy face?
    (q) How come there's a lot of kids there?

13. Why might IL variability and systematicity be relevant for teachers when giving feedback on learners' errors? What practical ways can you suggest for teachers to assess these dimensions of their students' ILs?

14. In light of what is known about cross-linguistic influence, what differences (if any) do you think desirable between language teaching materials for use with classes of learners with the same L1 and those for use with learners with a variety of different L1s? Are 'English for Japanese speakers' or 'French for speakers of German' meaningful titles for textbooks?

15. What (if any) cases of transfer can Eckman's MDH not handle? How might the MDH be modified to deal with such cases?

16. Andersen (1978) recommends the use of implicational scaling analysis as one way of displaying data with regards to variability and systematicity in SLA. An example applied to SLA would be where the researcher applied implicational scaling analysis to morpheme suppliance in obligatory contexts. A particular morpheme is given a + if it meets a criterion (e.g. 90 per cent SOC) or a – if it is supplied less often. Next, an implicational table is prepared. Subjects are rank ordered along the vertical axis according to the number of structures that met criterion in their IL. The morphemes are ordered along the horizontal axis with the one that was supplied most often occupying the left-most position. Table 4.5 is idealized, but if the results look something like it (have a correlation of reproducibility higher than .9), we could say an implicational scale results. This means one morpheme implies the presence of another. The presence of third-person singular *s* in a subject's IL, for example, implies the presence of the three other morphemes.

    Such a display allows us to examine individual performance and the group as a whole. For example, Hyltenstam (1977) used implicational scaling analysis on his data of 160 learners acquiring Swedish negation. From the tables he was able to check for individual variable behaviour and to conclude that the learners used a regular route in their acquisition process.

Subjects	Morphemes			
	Copula	Article	Irregular Past	3rd Person Singular 's'
1	+	+	+	+
2	+	+	+	−
3	+	+	−	−−
4	+	−	−	−
5	−	−	−	−

TABLE 4.5 Implicational Table

Another analytical tool which comes to us from those concerned with sociolinguistic variation is the variable rule. In his work on the English copula, sociolinguist Labov (1969) proposed incorporating systematic variation into linguistic description and theory by writing variable rules which reflect the relative frequency of a rule's application. According to Labov, variability of rule application results not only from the presence or absence of elements in the linguistic environment, but can also be affected by extra-linguistic factors such as age, social status and ethnicity of the speaker. Dickerson (1975) was one of the first SLA researchers to show that the IL of the SL learner can be described in terms of variable rules.

While Stauble and Larsen-Freeman (1978) acknowledge the contributions of variable rules and implicational scales to the study of variability in IL research, they also point out the inadequacy of both for the study of SLA. The sociolinguists' type of variable rule does not seem adequate for describing SLA data since its primary concern is with the linguistic and social environments which favour or disfavour rule application *at a single point in time.* (See also Grotjahn 1983.) Tarone, Swain and Fathman note: 'To date we have been unable to find linguistic rules capable of handling *both* the variability *and* the instability of interlanguage' (1976, p. 29). The implicational scaling approach would also seem to distort the gradient and variable nature of the IL of a SL learner since the learner must be scored as having acquired a given feature categorically + or −. In addition, implicational scales do

Negative ⟶ (NO) / ——— { [+ auxiliary] }
                         { [+ copula]   }
                         { [+ main verb] }

Stage I	Early Stage II	Mid Stage II	Late Stage II	Stage III
79%	32%	1%	.9%	—

FIGURE 4.2 Variable Rule: Negation

not necessarily show the linguistic environment in which variant forms occur. However, this approach has the advantage over variable rules in that it reveals directionality in the development toward the target language. Stauble and Larsen-Freeman (1978), therefore, propose their own version of variable rules that would both formally describe any single point of development exhibited in the learner's IL and would also generate the learner's variable output at the various points along the developmental continuum. This is accomplished through a rule which specifies the variant forms and the percentage at which they are thought to occur at each stage of development. For example, at an early stage of development, we would expect the rule in Figure 4.2 to apply: The percentage is the percentage of negative utterances accounted for by this rule in the ILs spoken by the NSs of Spanish in Stauble's study, a percentage which would obviously change as more subjects were included.

Compare implicational scaling analysis and Larsen-Freeman and Stauble's version of the variable rule. Are there any advantages or disadvantages of each besides what has already been mentioned?

Suggestions for further reading

For an early discussion of the tricky question of defining systematicity vs. variability, see:

Tarone, E, Frauenfelder, U and Selinker, L 1976 Systematicity/variability and stability/instability in interlanguage systems. *Language Learning* Special Issue Number 4: 93–134

For work on IL variation, see:

Adamson, H 1988 *Variation theory and second language acquisition*. Georgetown University Press, Washington, D.C.

Crookes, G 1989 Planning and interlanguage variation. *Studies in Second Language Acquisition* 11 (4): 367–83

Ellis, R 1985 Variability in interlanguage. In Ellis, R *Understanding second language acquisition. Oxford University Press*

Tarone, E 1983 On the variability of interlanguage systems. *Applied Linguistics* 4: 143–63

Tarone, E 1988 *Variation in interlanguage.* Edward Arnold

Young, R 1988 Variation and the interlanguage hypothesis. *Studies in Second Language Acquisition* 10 (3): 281–302

For a critique of variationist positions on IL development, see:

Gregg, K (to appear) The variable competence model of second language acquisition, and why it isn't. *Applied Linguistics*

For studies of developmental sequences in IL, see:

Johnston, M 1985 *Syntactic and morphological progressions in learner English.* Department of Immigration and Ethnic Affairs, Canberra

Meisel, J, Clahsen, H and Pienemann, M 1981 On determining developmental stages in natural second language acquisition. *Studies in Second Language Acquisition* 3: 109–35

Schumann, J 1979 The acquisition of English negation by speakers of Spanish: a review of the literature. In Andersen, R (ed.) *The acquisition and use of Spanish and English as first and second languages.* TESOL, Washington, D.C.

For the role of the L1 in SLA, see:

Faerch, C and Kasper, G 1987 Perspectives on language transfer. *Applied Linguistics* 8: 111–36

Gass, S 1984 A review of interlanguage syntax: language transfer and language universals. *Language Learning* 34: 115–32

Gass, S and Selinker, L (eds.) 1983 *Language transfer and language learning.* Newbury House, Rowley, Mass.

Kellerman, E 1984 The empirical evidence for the influence of the L1 in interlanguage. In Davies, A, Criper, C and Howatt, A (eds.) *Interlanguage.* Edinburgh University Press

Kellerman, E and Sharwood Smith, M (eds.) 1986 *Cross-linguistic influence in second language acquisition.* Pergamon Press

Odlin, T 1989 *Language transfer: cross-linguistic influence in language learning.* Cambridge University Press

Ringbom, H 1987 *The role of the first language in foreign language learning.* Multilingual Matters

5 The linguistic environment for language acquisition

5.1 Linguistic input for first language acquisition

While revolutionizing linguistics in the late 1950s and 1960s, transformational-generative grammarians alienated many social scientists by dismissing language *use* (performance) as a source of data for doing linguistic research. Chomsky (1965) defined the goal of their work as describing language *knowledge* (competence) underlying performance. Performance data were irrelevant for this task, he explained, because they contained too much 'noise' – false starts, slips of the tongue, repetitions, run-on sentences and the like – to provide an undistorted window on competence. The linguist's or other native speakers' intuitions of grammaticality would substitute for what people actually say, Chomsky asserted, and would do so more reliably.

A corollary of this view, for Chomsky, was that the human infant must be endowed with a highly sophisticated innate ability to learn language – a Language Acquisition Device (LAD) – for in learning the rules of its mother tongue from natural speech, the young child could apparently do what the adult linguist could not: induce the rules of a grammar from performance data. The language young children heard around them was supposedly 'degenerate' (Fodor 1966) in the ways Chomsky described, yet children mastered most of the rules of their first language by the age of five, regardless of intelligence, social class, or any of those environmental factors thought to play a role in other aspects of development. Children could not possibly be using their native-speaker intuitions to do this, because they were not yet native speakers. Further, what they learned was not the actual sentences they heard, but the underlying sentence structures of the language (types), plus the rules for manipulating them, which they then put to use in producing good original sentences (tokens), as well as errors of overgeneralization. That is, children heard 'surface structures', but were able to learn 'deep structure'. The net product, command of a human language, Chomsky argued, was extremely complex and its mastery something accomplished quickly at a time when the child was cognitively very limited. The innate ability, therefore, must be qualititatively different from any other human genetic inheritance (language-specific) and, of course, unique to the human animal (species-specific). (Hence, the interest in whether chimps and other primates can learn to talk.) So went the argument.

But just how 'degenerate' was the child's linguistic environment? Chomsky's claims inspired numerous studies, beginning in the 1960s, of the ways mothers, fathers and other caretakers in different cultures speak to language-learning children. In general, these studies have shown that the linguistic input for first language acquisition – that is, language addressed to children, as opposed to other language they might hear in their environment but ignore – is not very 'noisy' at all. Rather, it is 'simpler' than the full adult version in many ways, closer to the 'core' structure of the target, apparently designed for easy learning.

To begin with, the research has consistently shown that speech to language-learning children is *well formed*. For example, Cross (1977) found that only 3.3 per cent of utterances in mothers' speech to children were disfluent, 2 per cent unintelligible, and 9.8 per cent run-on sentences. Newport, Gleitman and Gleitman (1977) found a disfluency in only one utterance in a corpus of 1,500. This pattern has prevailed in second language studies, too, as we shall see.

The child's linguistic environment has also been found to be 'simpler' than adult speech in other ways – syntactically, phonologically and semantically. In the syntactic domain, utterance length of speech to children is shorter and less varied, as is pre-verb mean length of utterance (MLU). Maternal input is transformationally less complex, with fewer verbs per utterance, fewer coordinate and subordinate clauses and fewer sentence embeddings. It contains fewer adjectives, adverbs and pronouns than adult speech, and has a higher ratio of content (vocabulary) words to functors (grammatical words, like articles, prepositions and auxiliary verbs).

In the area of phonology, speech to children is pitched higher, has more exaggerated intonation, and uses a wider pitch range. It is characterized by frequent reduplication of syllables (*choo-choo* for 'train'), clearer articulation, pauses between utterances and an overall slower rate of delivery. For example, in two studies (Remick 1971; Broen 1972), speech to two-year-old children was found to proceed at half the speed of speech to other adults.

In the semantic domain, vocabulary is more restricted, as measured by type–token ratio (TTR), usually calculated as the number of different words (types) divided by the total number of words (tokens). Talk is firmly anchored in the 'here and now', and it expresses a more limited range of semantic relationships. Caretakers tend to talk about the names of objects, their location and whom they belong to (Phillips 1972; Snow et al. 1976). These factors result in higher frequencies of content nouns and present time marking on verbs.

From these findings – a small sample of those available – it can safely be concluded that linguistic input to the language-learning child is quantitatively different from speech addressed to linguistically competent adults, and not a degenerate corpus. It is also safe to conclude that we do not yet know all the ways in which child input differs. Volumes of empirical studies continued to appear on the subject (e.g. Lewis and Rosenblum 1977; Schaffer 1977; Snow and Ferguson 1977; Waterson and Snow 1978), as did useful reviews of the literature (e.g. Farwell 1973; Landes 1975; Vorster 1975; Clark and Clark 1977; Rondal 1978, 1979; de Villiers and de Villiers 1978).

5.2 Linguistic input for second language acquisition

The work on speech to language-learning children was partly responsible for prompting researchers in the mid-1970s to ask how much environmental assistance was being provided to the SL learner. Although of more recent lineage than the first language work, research on linguistic input to SL learners has a somewhat broader focus. First, like its child language counterpart, it seeks to determine how speech addressed to non-native speakers (NNSs), whether children or adults, differs from language used in adult native speaker (NS) conversation, and whether the differences aid comprehension and/or acquisition or perhaps are necessary for acquisition to take place at all. The role that modified input plays in this regard is of even greater potential importance in SLA, given that many learners are adults, and given the evidence that the innate capacity for language learning declines with age (see Chapter 6 for review). Second, some of the work is motivated by broad sociolinguistic interest in describing what Ferguson (1971) has called one of the 'conventionalized varieties of "simplified" speech available to a speech community'. Third, still other interest has arisen from the search for features common to 'simple codes' of various kinds, including foreigner talk, child language, pidgins, early second language, telegraphese and lecture notes, and for common processes in their creation (Corder 1975; Meisel 1977; Schumann 1978a; Andersen 1979; Bickerton 1979; Janda 1985).

5.2.1 Linguistic adjustments to non-native speakers

Some of the first descriptions of NS speech to foreigners made it look as if the linguistic environment might prove to be an important area of difference between first and second language acquisition. Several early studies, notably Ferguson (1975) and Meisel (1975), reported that NSs of English, French, German, and Finnish switched to an *ungrammatical* variety of their language when addressing NNSs. This, Ferguson claimed, was a socially conditioned speech variety, which he named 'foreigner talk'.

The ungrammaticality was the result of three main processes: omission, expansion, and replacement/rearrangement (Ferguson 1975; Ferguson and DeBose 1976). Examples of omission include the deletion of articles, copulas, conjunctions, subject pronouns and inflectional morphology. An example of expansion is the addition of unanalysed tags to questions, e.g. *yes?*, *no?* and *okay?* Another example is the insertion of subject pronoun *you* before imperatives. Replacement/rearrangement includes forming negatives with *no* plus the negated item (*no like*), replacing subject with object pronouns (*him go*), converting possessive adjective-plus-noun constructions to noun-plus-object pronoun (*sister me* instead of *my sister*), and a preference for uninverted question forms. Thus, sentences like those on the left in Table 5.1 might appear like those on the right in foreigner talk (FT).

As can be seen from these hypothetical examples, this is roughly the way Tarzan starts out talking to Jane ('Me Tarzan, you Jane') and the way many other characters in films and comic books try to communicate with 'the natives' (cf. Hinnenkamp 1982). Such speech often has racist and/or class overtones, involving 'talking

Normal NS–NS Version	*FT Equivalent*
1. Why did you go?	1'. Why you go?
2. Come here at once!	2'. You come now!
3. My sister doesn't like the man.	3'. Sister me no like man.

TABLE 5.1 Ungrammatical FT Translations

down' to inferiors, when the 'inferiors' are imported cheap plantation labour, undocumented migrant fruit pickers in the USA, assembly-line workers in a European car factory, or illegal aliens working in 'sweat shops' in the Los Angeles or New York garment industry. Could it be that this ill-formed linguistic input accounts for the oft-noted lack of success at SLA in populations of this sort? We return to this possibility later.

Ferguson's results were obtained in an elicitation study which involved having students at Stanford University rewrite sentences as they thought they would say them to a group of illiterate, non-European aliens who spoke no English. Asking subjects to introspect about what they imagine they would say in a situation few have ever experienced, and then to write down the answers, is clearly artificial. Nevertheless, the findings have since been confirmed by other researchers observing FT in real settings. Clyne (1977, 1978), for example, found many instances of ungrammaticality in the speech of Australian factory foremen addressing foreign workers, and the same phenomenon has been reported for Germans talking to 'guest workers' (Heidelberger Forschungsprojekt 1978). In a study conducted in Holland, Snow, van Eeden and Muysken (1981) found that Dutch municipal employees used ungrammatical Dutch to foreigners during conversations through government office windows, and also that the frequency of deviant forms in the NSs' speech tended to reflect the number of errors in the Dutch IL of the foreign addressees. Ungrammatical input has been reported from sales clerks in US department stores (Ramamurti 1977) and from passers-by giving street directions to a middle-class American tourist in Portugal (Walter-Goldberg 1982). It has also been noted in young children addressing non-native age peers (Wong Fillmore 1976; Andersen 1977; Katz 1977).

Ungrammatical FT is by no means confined, then, to written elicitation studies. Nevertheless, it has become clear that deviant input is not the norm in SLA. Soon after the Ferguson study, more and more researchers began reporting very similar findings on FT to those obtained previously in studies of caretaker speech. The input described by these researchers was almost wholly *well formed*, although a *modified* version of the target. The data for most SLA, in other words, were no more 'degenerate' than those for first language acquisition by young children.

The most commonly observed features of *grammatical* FT include shorter utterances in T-units (Gaies 1977; Freed 1978; Arthur et al. 1980; Long 1980a; Scarcella and Higa 1981), and utterances which are syntactically and/or propositionally less complex in various ways, e.g. fewer S-nodes per T-unit (Freed 1978), fewer clauses per T-unit, fewer adjectival, adverbial and noun clauses per T-unit (Gaies 1977) or fewer relative clauses and appositives per T-unit (Scarcella and Higa 1981). Modified but grammatical speech to foreigners tends to be a more 'regular' version of the language, avoiding forms which constitute exceptions to general rules in the language concerned. Thus, Long, Gambhiar, Gambhiar and Nishimura (1982) found that the canonical word orders of English, Hindi-Urdu and Japanese occurred more frequently in FT than in informal NS-NS conversation in those languages. The Japanese and Hindi-Urdu FT also contained more utterances which retained the optional (S, V or O) constituents in surface structure needed to form the full canonical orders. In this study and another of Japanese FT by Onaha (1987), there was also more overt marking of grammatical and semantic relations in the FT of languages (Japanese and Hindi-Urdu) which often delete these markers, e.g. Japanese particles indicating topic, comment, subject, object, directionals and locatives, when compared with NS-NS conversational baseline data, i.e. data considered to be exemplary of what native speakers do.

Unmarked patterns are more 'basic', more frequent, more regular, and so perhaps 'easier' for the NNS to process. Recourse to unmarked forms can lead to marked *use* of those forms, however. Consider, for example, the native English speaker's marked use of anaphoric reference in the following extract:

> NS: . . . uh you're from Kyoto, right?
>
> > NNS: Yeah.
>
> Yeah. What does your father do in
> Kyoto?

In NS-NS conversation, the NS's second question would normally be 'What does your father do (there)?' Similarly, use of high frequency lexical items in an effort to avoid comprehension difficulties for the NNS can also result in marked use of the 'easier' item:

> NS: I use ten dollars every day for food.

where 'spend . . . on' would be normal NS usage. This is something some SL teachers occasionally do in an effort to keep within a class's 'known' vocabulary. (For further discussion, see Chaudron 1983a, 1987; Zobl 1983a). Examples of the regularization process in the lexical domain possibly account for the last main finding concerning grammatical input, namely that NSs employ a more restricted range of vocabulary in speech to non-natives, as measured by type-token ratio (Arthur et al. 1980), with idiomatic expressions impressionistically occurring less often (Henzl 1973, 1975, 1979).

Why is input to NNSs sometimes grammatical, sometimes not? The answer to this question is unclear. Long (1981a) identified four factors which tend to predict deviant speech by the NS:

1. zero or very low SL proficiency in the NNS
2. perceived or genuinely higher social status of the NS
3. prior FT experience, but only with NNSs of low SL proficiency
4. spontaneity of the conversation

Unfortunately, however, while most findings reflect these conditions, there exists at least one counter-example to each, suggesting that there is a great deal of variability at the level of the individual where recourse to ungrammatical speech is concerned.[1] The best generalization available is that 1, 2 and 4 appeared to be *necessary* for ungrammatical FT to occur, but that no single condition alone seems to be *sufficient*. A combination of factors is at work.

5.2.2　Conversational adjustments to non-native speakers

In addition to their examination of modified but grammatical speech to NNSs, another feature of several more recent FT studies is their shift in focus from the *input* alone to the structural characteristics of the NS-NNS *conversation* in which FT occurs, i.e. to the study of 'foreigner talk discourse' (Hatch, Shapira and Wagner-Gough 1978; Long 1981b). Some studies have found few or no statistically significant differences between FT and NS speech to other NSs in traditional morpho-syntactic areas of analysis, yet have at the same time found the NSs to be doing considerable 'work' at the discourse level. For example, the following two (constructed) sample conversations exhibit identical NS utterance structure, but differ in their *interactional* structure because of the NS's use of exact and semantic repetition:

(1a)　*NS-NS conversation*
　　　 NS1: Do you like California?
　　　　　　　　　　　　　　　NS2: I love it.

(1b)　*NS-NNS conversation*
　　　 NS: Do you like California?
　　　　　　　　　　　　　　　NNS: Huh?
　　　 Do you like Los Angeles?
　　　　　　　　　　　　　　　Uhm . . . .

Do you like California?

Oh! Yeah, I like it.

To date, some of the ways in which NS-NS and NS-NNS conversations have been found to differ are as follows. Conversational topics are treated simply and briefly in foreigner talk discourse (FTD), as measured by the number of 'information bits' supplied by the NS on any topic (Arthur et al. 1980) or by the ratio of topic-initiating to topic-continuing moves (Gaies 1981; Long 1981b):

(2) NS: Yeah. Exactly. I have *not*
seen them. Yeah. Do you
live
in Tokyo?

NNS: Yes.

Yeah?

I come from
(Ngunga) Tokyo,
near-near Tokyo.

Aha.

But I live in
Tokyo.

Aha. Do you study?
Or . . .

No.

do you work?

There is some evidence that the very nature of the topics preferred in FTD differs, too. Scarcella (1983) compared NSs of Spanish (Mexicans) and English (Americans) conversing with each other (informally, the first encounter between strangers), and each of these types of conversation with NS-NNS encounters between members of the two groups. The Spanish NSs in NS-NS conversation spoke freely about personal matters (home, age, family, marriage, etc.), whereas English NS pairs or dyads tended to discuss only impersonal topics (classes, careers, places of residence, etc.). When the language groups were mixed in NS-NNS dyads, neither American nor Mexican interlocutors introduced personal topics. Scarcella suggests that this was perhaps because the Spanish NSs had lived in the other culture long enough (a minimum of twelve years) to learn which topics were considered appropriate by the English NSs for discussion with strangers. Possibly arising from the need to negotiate topics across cultural boundaries, the FTD in Scarcella's study was also found to contain more abrupt topic-*shifts* than the NS-NS conversations in either language. Note the examples of this in the excerpt in (2), above, from the Long (1981a) study. The FTD in Scarcella's study also exhibited a less predictable *sequence* of topics than the English or Spanish baseline data.

FTD has been found to contain at least three additional indications of the topic-negotiation process, but these features seem to be motivated by the NS's attempt to cater to the NNS's linguistic ability rather than to cultural differences. First, even though the NNS is an adult, with no cognitive limitations, FTD, like caretaker speech (Cross 1978), has been found to be significantly more oriented to the 'here and now' than the NS-NS conversation, as measured by the relative frequencies of verbs marked temporally for present and non-present (Long 1980a; Gaies 1981; cf. remarks on this topic by Krashen 1982a, p. 51). This avoidance of reference to displaced time and place is even more apparent in the classroom FTD of ESL instruction (Long and Sato 1983). Second, NSs have been found to use significantly more of what Hatch (1978a) calls 'or-choice' questions in FTD than with other NSs (Long 1981b). Hatch has pointed out that such questions allow the NNS to choose from a list of potential topics (or comments), and make his or her participation easier still by containing the 'answer' to the question, as illustrated in (3):

> (3) NS: Well what are you doing in the
>   United States? . . .
>   Are you just studying?
>   Or do you have a job?
>   Or –
>
>   NNS: No.
>   I have job.

Third, there is a tendency for NSs to accept unintentional topic switches by NNSs in FTD when a communication breakdown occurs. The NS may, for example, skilfully treat an inappropriate response as a topic-nomination, thereby repairing the discourse:

> (4) NS: Are you going to visit San
>   Francisco? Or Las Vegas?
>
>   NNS: Yes I went to
>   Disneyland and to
>   Knottsberry Farm.
>
>   Oh yeah?
>   (Long 1981a, p. 264)

Several other conversational adjustments have been noted in FTD which concern not the choice of topics but the way they are introduced by the NS. For example, there is a well-documented preference for questions over statements (Freed 1978; Long 1980a; Scarcella and Higa 1982), with questions being especially favoured for topic-initiating moves (Gaies 1981; Long 1981b). Thus, a NS is more likely to open up a new topic in FT with (5a) than (5b):

(5a) NS: Do you like going to the movies?
(5b) NS: I like going to the movies.

and is more likely to use utterances like (5a) throughout a conversation with NNSs than with other NSs.

The preference for questions in topic-initiating moves, and in FTD generally, probably has several motivations. First, questions are more likely to draw the NNS into the conversation. Second, yes/no questions in particular make the NNS's linguistic task easier by making his or her conversational role easier. They contain a complete proposition, which the NNS need only confirm or deny, whereas WH-questions contain a missing element, and statements require a complete new proposition from the other speaker. Consider the increasing complexity required of an appropriate response to (6a)-(6c):

(6a)	Do you live in Los Angeles?	Yes/No.
(6b)	Where do you live?	In Orange County.
(6c)	I live in Los Angeles.	(Do you?) I live in Orange County.

Third, questions are useful as comprehension checks (Do you understand?), which help NSs assess whether they are communicating successfully with NNSs,[2] and also as clarification requests (What do you mean?) and confirmation checks (The library?), which tell them whether they are understanding what the NNSs are trying to communicate to them. All three functions of questions occur statistically significantly more frequently in FTD than in NS-NS conversation (Long 1981b). This suggests that Varonis and Gass (1982, pp. 131–2) are correct in claiming that questions occur frequently as a reflection of the NS checking his/her assumptions about the comprehensibility of the NNS's speech, but not correct when they claim this is the main or only reason they occur more frequently in FTD.

Further devices noted as having more frequent use in FTD than in NS-NNS conversation for introducing topics and/or making them more salient include the use of stress and/or pauses before topic words (Hatch 1978a; Long 1980a):

(7)   NS: Did you . like San Diego? [. = one-beat pause; underlined = increased volume]

left-dislocation (Hatch 1978a):

(8)   NS: Did you . like San Diego? . San Diego . did you like it?

question and answer (Long 1980a):

(9)   NS: When do you take the break? At ten thirty?

and 'decomposition' (Long 1980a):

(10a) NS: When do you go to the uh Santa Monica?
       . . You say you go fishing in Santa
       Monica, right?

                                    NNS: Yeah

       When?
(10b) NS: Uh what does your
       father do in uh you're from Kyoto,
       right?

                                    NNS: Yeah.

       Yeah. What does your father do in
       Kyoto?

As shown in (10a) and (10b), decomposition starts with a request by the NS for the NNS to comment on a new topic introduced by a WH-question. This proves too difficult for the NNS. The task is then broken down (decomposed) into two more manageable parts. First, the (sub)topic is established by its repetition in isolation, usually in the form of a yes/no question or uninverted (intonation) question, and often with a tag (*right?*). When the NNS confirms that the topic has been established, the comment, in the form of a question about the new topic, is restated. (10a) and (10b), respectively, also show that this device, like most of those described, can serve two functions: to repair the discourse following a breakdown in communication, and to avoid such a breakdown occurring. These devices have been classified as *tactics* and *strategies*, respectively, and their realizations quantified and compared (Long 1981a, 1983a). Among the most frequent in FTD are (exact or semantic) self- and other-repetitions, expansions, confirmation checks, clarification requests and comprehension checks. See Table 5.2 for a taxonomy of linguistic and conversational adjustments to NNSs.[3]

In closing this descriptive section on conversational adjustments to NNSs, one or two methodological points are in order. First, it bears repeating that it is not the use of devices like those illustrated which distinguishes FTD from NS–NS conversation, but

---

Linguistic adjustments

Phonology
> slower rate of delivery
> more use of stress and pauses
> more careful articulation
> wider pitch range/exaggerated intonation
> more use of full forms/avoidance of contractions

Morphology and syntax
> more well-formed utterances/fewer disfluencies
> shorter utterances (fewer words per utterance)
> less complex utterances (fewer S-nodes per T-unit, fewer clauses per T-unit, fewer adjectival, adverbial and noun clauses per T-unit, fewer relative clauses and appositives per T-unit)
> more regularity/use of canonical word order
> more retention of optional constituents
> more overt marking of grammatical relations
> more verbs marked for present/fewer for non-present temporal reference
> more questions
> more yes–no and intonation questions/fewer WH-questions

Semantics
> more overt marking of semantic relations
> lower type–token ratio
> fewer idiomatic expressions
> higher average lexical frequency of nouns and verbs
> higher proportion of copulas to total verbs
> marked use of lexical items
> fewer opaque forms (greater preference for full NPs over pronouns, concrete verbs over dummy verbs, like *do*)

TABLE 5.2 Linguistic and Conversational Adjustments to NNSs in Grammatical Foreigner Talk Discourse

---

Conversational adjustments

Content
  more predictable/narrower range of topics
  more here-and-now orientation
  briefer treatment of topics (fewer information bits per topic/lower ratio of
    topic-initiating to topic-continuing moves)

Interactional structure
  more abrupt topic-shifts
  more willing relinquishment of topic-choice to interlocutor
  more acceptance of unintentional topic-switches
  more use of questions for topic-initiating moves
  more repetition (self- and other-, exact and semantic, complete and partial)
  more comprehension checks
  more confirmation checks
  more clarification requests
  more expansions
  more question-and-answer strings
  more decomposition

TABLE 5.2 (*continued*)

rather their statistically significant higher *frequency of use* in FTD. Most, and probably all, of them also occur in NS–NS conversation among normal adults, in caretaker–child conversation, and in talk between adults and the mentally retarded, although documentation is limited with respect to the last two populations. We are dealing, therefore, with quantitative, not qualitative differences between FTD and NS–NS talk.

Second, unlike features of linguistic input to NNSs, the analysis of *interactional* characteristics of FTD requires looking at speech by both participants in a conversation, as well as at previous speech by each of them. Acts like repetition, expansion and confirmation checks only have life across utterances and speakers in context. They result from a process in which negotiation of meaning takes place between NS and NNS. Thus, FT is dynamic, constantly being adjusted to what the learner is perceived to be understanding. For this reason, a NNS's ability to keep a conversation going is a very valuable skill because by maintaining the conversation, the NNS can presumably benefit from receiving additional modified input. Indeed, conversational maintenance is a major objective for language learners who regularly invoke communicative strategies (Tarone 1980b).[4] Figure 5.1 lists some of the communicative strategies learners have been observed to employ.[5]

Paraphrase	
Approximation	– Use of a single target-language vocabulary item or structure, which the learner knows is not correct, but which shares enough semantic features in common with the desired item to satisfy the speaker (e.g., 'pipe' for 'waterpipe').
Word coinage	– The learner makes up a new word in order to communicate a desired concept (e.g., 'airball' for 'balloon').
Circumlocution	– The learner describes the characteristics or elements of the object or action instead of using the appropriate TL structure ('She is, uh, smoking something. I don't know what's its name. That's, uh, Persian, and we use in Turkey, a lot of').
Transfer	
Literal translation	– The learner translates word for word from the native language (e.g., 'He invites him to drink' for 'They toast one another').
Language switch	– The learner uses the NL term without bothering to translate (e.g., 'balon' for 'balloon' or 'tirtil' for 'caterpillar').
Appeal for assistance	– The learner asks for the correct term or structure (e.g., 'What is this?').
Mime	– The learner uses nonverbal strategies in place of a meaning structure (e.g., clapping one's hands to illustrate applause).
Avoidance	
Topic avoidance	– Occurs when the learner simply does not talk about concepts for which the vocabulary or other meaning structure is not known.
Message abandonment	– Occurs when the learner begins to continue due to lack of meaning structure, and stops mid-utterance.

FIGURE 5.1 A Typology of Communication Strategies (from Tarone 1978)

While suprasegmental units are notoriously difficult to define operationally and to quantify, quantification is as necessary here as it is for the grammatical input features, given that it is the relative *frequency of use* (see above) that is at issue. Thus, it is not enough, as some researchers have done, simply to look at FTD (or at FT) and then to assert, e.g., that utterances are short or less complex, or that repetition is used. The question is whether utterances are shorter, syntactically less complex, or more repetitious, than those in NS–NS conversation in comparable situations.

Last, most of the work done on FTD thus far, as well as on teacher–NNS student conversation in classrooms (e.g. Schinke-Llano 1983; Early 1985), has considered such devices as confirmation checks, clarification requests, repetition and restatement in fairly gross terms. Yet such moves in discourse often have multiple functions, and also multiple realizations, choice among which is not arbitrary. The multi-functionality of such devices as confirmation checks and clarification requests, which may simultaneously serve as corrective feedback, was shown by Chun, Day, Chenoweth and Luppescu (1982). Work by Chaudron (1982, 1983b) demonstrates the potential of finer-grained analyses of different realizations of these devices, some of which he has shown to facilitate comprehension by the NNS better than others (see below). This looks to be a promising area for future research.

5.3 Does the linguistic environment make a difference?

As noted in the introduction to this chapter, research on the linguistic environment is of considerable theoretical interest. The role (if any) of environmental factors in first or second language acquisition affects the power and scope of any innate linguistic or cognitive contribution it becomes necessary to posit in the learner. As is the case with the nature/nurture debate in any area of animal behaviour, various claims have been made concerning language learning which range from strong nativist positions through interactionist to equally strong environmentalist ones. We treat some of these in Chapter 7.

The linguistic environment is not just of theoretical interest, however. It has potentially great practical importance for educators of various kinds, too, since input (and the structure of conversation) is something that can be manipulated. Research findings are of interest to SL materials writers, SL curriculum developers and classroom teachers, and also to teachers of the deaf and to those designing language intervention programmes for mentally retarded children and adults. (See, e.g., Mahoney 1975 on 'language ecology' programmes for caretakers of children suffering from Down's Syndrome.)

5.3.1 The effect of deviant input

The first area we discuss in which an effect for input might be expected to show up has attracted surprisingly little research to date. This is the effect of ill-formed, or deviant, input on subsequent language learning. It seems reasonable to expect that a SL acquirer exposed only (or predominantly) to ungrammatical FT will acquire at best a marked, substandard variety of the target language, and there is some suggestive evidence that this is the case. Thus, while no causal relationship has been established, the kinds of SLA environments most often associated with ungrammatical input are also those in which a 'pidginized' variety of the SL has been found to develop (Clyne 1978; Heidelberger Forschungsprojekt 1978; Schumann 1978). It is crucial to note, however, that these results could, of course, be due wholly or in part to *insufficient* as well as, or instead of, ungrammatical input. Pidginization, after all, Bickerton (1983) and Schumann (1978a) claim, is SLA with restricted input. Regrettably, from the researcher's perspective, the two phenomena, deviant and restricted input, are almost always confounded in any natural acquisition setting. One can envisage artificially created laboratory environments which could distinguish them, however (perhaps using miniature artificial languages – see Chapter 2). This issue is of some importance as deviant peer input in immersion programmes has been noted as a possible cause of persistent output errors even when well-formed input is available from the teacher (Plann 1977 for Spanish immersion in the USA; Harley and Swain 1978 for French immersion in Canada).

Meanwhile, SL teachers favouring the use of group work in their classes can derive some comfort from the findings of three recent studies of non-native/non-native conversation ('interlanguage talk') in and out of classrooms. All three studies concur that conversational practice of this sort is as useful for SLA as NS–NNS conversation (Porter 1983; Pica and Doughty 1985; Varonis and Gass 1985), the first and last even claiming it to be a *better* environment in some respects. This is because the fact that both parties are NNSs means that communication breakdowns are more frequent, more obvious to both speakers, and have to be resolved by them (not by skilful SL teachers with plenty of FT experience), and are so resolved through the normal process of negotiation for meaning documented for NS-NNS conversation. (Long and Porter 1985 review these and other studies of IL talk; see also Aston 1987 for some important caveats, and Bygate 1988 for an interesting recent study.)

The same situation apparently obtains between NS and NNS children. While the input an adult provided NNS children in Cathcart-Strong's (1986) study was reliable because the adult tended to respond to every utterance initiated by the children, the NNS children received the largest quantity of negotiated input from NS peers, especially in situations in which the NNS was able to suggest an interesting motivating play scenario to the NS. Peck (1980) adds that the repetitious and non-literal nature of language play in which children engage may provide NNSs with many practice opportunities, particularly of phonological form. The NS adult in Cathcart-Strong's study, on the other hand, offered NNS children an expanded response to their utterances, i.e. one containing non-imitative phrases or sentences related to the NNS's utterance, which may aid SLA. Another important type of input that adults may be better providers of is what Schachter (1986b) calls metalinguistic input, information provided to the learner, perhaps indirectly, that something in what the learner just produced is in some way 'insufficient, deviant, unacceptable or not understandable to the native speaker' (p. 215).

At this point, we would like to see further research directed at studying the effects of varying proportions of conversational experience with natives and non-natives on the SLA process for learners of different proficiency levels and ages, and also studies of ultimate attainment under these conditions.

5.3.2 The role of conversation in developing syntax

A second claim made concerning the role of the linguistic environment in SLA concerns the possibility that it is through participating in conversations in a SL that we learn the SL syntax (see Chapter 3). Echoing previous arguments to this effect by first language acquisition researchers (e.g. Macnamara 1972; Scollon 1973; Keenan 1974; Ervin-Tripp 1976; Atkinson 1979), Hatch (1974, 1978a, 1978b, 1979) has suggested that thinking of SL learners acquiring syntactic structures which they then put to use in conversation is putting the cart before the horse. Speaking of child first language acquisition, she writes:

> Our basic premise has long been that the child learns some basic set of syntactic structures, moving from a one-word phase to a two-word phase, to more complex structures, and that eventually the child is able to put these structures together in order to carry on conversation with others. . . The premise, if we use discourse analysis, is the converse. That is, language learning evolves *out of* learning how to carry on conversations. (Hatch 1978a, pp. 403–4)

While no studies have yet been conducted to test directly Hatch's claim about the move from conversation to syntax in SLA, the arguments seem just as compelling as they do for child first language development. While less constrained by processing and short-term memory limitations, which, it should be noted, could partly account for the use of vertical constructions by young children, older children and adult SL acquirers also seem to utilize the conversational assistance they derive from native (and non-native) interlocutors in formulating their first ideas in a SL. In a longitudinal study of two Vietnamese adolescents acquiring ESL naturalistically, Sato (1982, 1985, 1988) documented use of past time reference previously established by interlocutors as the initial means learners use to compensate for a lack of overt inflectional past time marking. Similar phenomena (again for temporal reference) have been noted for German SL in studies of the speech of adult Spanish, Italian and Turkish 'guest workers' (Dittmar 1981; Klein 1981; Meisel 1987; von Stutterheim and Klein 1987), and for Japanese-, Chinese- and Spanish–English basilangs (Schumann 1987a,b). Meisel (1987), for example, reports use of a range of discourse strategies to compensate for missing inflectional marking: an early preference for adverbials and connectives, interlocutor scaffolding, implicit reference, order of mention, and contrast of two or more events.

The conversation-to-syntax argument also surely has implications for SL teaching. Note that most (though not all) SL teaching methods prescribe just the opposite of what seems to be the normal sequence of events in naturalistic SLA. Classroom learners are typically asked to produce full sentences, often with native-like accuracy, from the earliest stages, usually centring around selected syntactic 'patterns' in the language. Some methods do very little more than this until the learner is quite advanced – advanced enough to begin to carry out conversations in the new language. Further, the same teachers tend to 'correct' errors (of morphology and syntax) rather than to serve as a cooperative source of help in constructing dialogue. The latter is the role they would assume more often if Hatch's claims are correct.

All of this is not to say that participation in conversation is the answer to a learner's problems, however. Both Hatch (1983) and Sato (1986) suggest that conversational assistance is probably differentially useful to learners, depending on the structures involved. Sato argues that the expendability of overt past time marking in most contexts, due precisely to the facilitating effects of scaffolding and situation on *communication*, may actually work against the learner where *acquisition* is concerned by easing what would otherwise be greater pressure to encode the function grammatically. And Hatch (1983, p. 432) suggests: '(M)istakes in the marking of verbs . . . would not be caught by "when?" questions. Such question corrections would more likely elicit a time adverb rather than a verb correction for morphology.' This is exactly what Sato found in her data.

The picture at the global level is also far from clear. Various studies report positive associations between such variables as leisure-time contact with NSs and SL proficiency (Heidelberger Forschungsprojekt 1978; St Martin 1980), out-of-class conversation practice and proficiency (Montgomery and Eisenstein 1985) and classroom participation and achievement gains (Seliger 1977). There are counter-findings, however. Day (1984) found no relationship between either in-class or out-of-class contact with NSs and attainment among adult university students receiving formal instruction in a SL environment. Day and Iida (1988) reported the same lack of relationship in a foreign language context, and Johnson (1983) found no relationship between children's participation in an out-of-class NS peer-tutoring programme in a SL environment and proficiency gain scores. Finally, cases of language learning without any production at all (e.g. Fourcin 1975) show that conversation, although probably facilitative in some cases, is not necessary for success.

5.3.3 Input frequency–accuracy order relationships

A third potential effect of the linguistic environment in SLA is the influence it may have on acquisition sequences. Hatch (1974, 1978a) suspected that the rather limited range of potential topics for conversation with children determined the frequency of different NS question types, and that relative frequencies might in turn help to explain the orders observed by other researchers for accurate production of certain forms. Several studies have set out to investigate this possibility.

Butoyi (1978) found a significant positive correlation between the relative frequencies of noun phrase complement structures in speech addressed to adult ESL students and the rank order in which they appeared accurately supplied by the learners. In an analysis similar to that conducted by Hatch (1974) on English questions in Homer's speech, Lightbown (1980) found a close relationship between the relative frequencies of certain French question forms in speech addressed to child French SL learners and the order in which those forms appeared in the learners' speech.

Larsen-Freeman's work on establishing an adult morpheme accuracy order for ESL has already been described in Chapter 4. Turning her attention to possible explanations for the order, Larsen-Freeman (1976c) found that the accuracy orders in her study were positively correlated with the frequency of occurrence of the same morphemes in the adult NS speech to three children acquiring English as a first language studied by Brown (1973). In another study (Larsen-Freeman 1976c), this time of input in the ESL classroom, she also found statistically significant positive correlations between the relative frequency order of the nine grammatical morphemes in the classroom speech of two ESL teachers and the same accuracy orders.

As part of a larger study, Long (1981b) compared several relative frequency orders for the same nine grammatical morphemes. The relative frequency in NS–NS conversation was significantly correlated with Krashen's (1977) 'natural order' (rho = .63, $p<.05$);[6] the frequency order in NSs' speech to 36 elementary-level Japanese ESL students was also significantly related (rho = .75, $p<.05$). The relative frequencies of obligatory contexts for production of the same morphemes by the NNSs during the conversations was not significantly related (rho = .58, $p>.05$), although this value of rho is not far short of significant at the .05 level. These results suggest that input frequency is more important (for these items, at least) than practice opportunities.

In another study, Long (1980a) obtained similar results. This time, however, the strength of association (rho = .77, $p<.05$) was identical between Krashen's (1977) 'natural order' and both the frequency order in speech to 16 NNSs, on the one hand, and the order in speech to 16 NSs, on the other. (The two relative frequency orders themselves correlated positively (rho = .97, $p<.01$.). While providing further support for the notion that input frequency of these grammatical items is related to their order of difficulty in the acquisition process, there was no evidence here that the relative frequency order in speech to NNSs was itself altered by the structure of NS–NNS conversation, as had seemed plausible following the earlier study. There, it was noted, the input frequency to NNSs (rho = .75) was more strongly correlated than was that to NSs (rho = .63).

The findings reviewed above are consistent with a hypothesized input frequency/accuracy order relationship, as posited by Hatch and by Larsen-Freeman. Two cross-sectional studies (Lightbown 1983; Long and Sato 1983) did not find statistically significant relationships between accuracy orders and input frequencies for morphology in ESL teacher speech at the elementary level. (Larsen-Freeman's findings concerned intermediate ESL students.) Also, a longitudinal study of three Spanish-speaking children by Davis (1986) found variable developmental sequences for several grammatical morphemes and no effect on them for input frequency. Nevertheless, it appears that there exist preliminary data supporting a frequency effect. While such factors as perceptual saliency, semantic complexity, and the influence of the learner's L1 seem to play some role (R. Brown 1973; Hatch and Wagner-Gough 1975; Larsen-Freeman 1976c, 1979), frequency of occurrence was the only factor to have been significantly correlated with production orders in the one SL study (Larsen-Freeman 1976c) which looked at all those possible explanations.

Despite these generally encouraging findings, a few qualifications are in order. First, advocates of a frequency explanation have to account for the fact that articles, which are always by far the most frequent item in (ESL) input, are relatively late acquired, and, like other items in accuracy orders, clearly subject to L1 influence (see Chapter 4). Clearly, in other words, no claim is being made that frequency is the *only* factor at work. Second, most (L1 and L2) studies to date have compared frequency and accuracy relationships at the same point in time, yet there is reason to expect a delayed effect for frequency, meaning that time-lagged designs (see, e.g., Skehan 1982), including time 1 input frequency × time 2 accuracy comparisons, would be more appropriate (see, e.g., Moerk 1980 for a first language study of this kind). Third, all the results described above are correlational only, and based on the fairly weak Spearman rank order correlation coefficient at that (see J.D. Brown 1983 for discussion). They are not a basis for causal claims, therefore, and no such claim is being advanced upon them here.

5.3.4 Input modification and second language comprehension

A fourth potential area of influence of modifications to the linguistic environment is SL comprehension. Implicit in the linguistic controls placed on the majority of textbooks, listening materials and 'graded readers' published for SL learners is the belief that manipulating the range of structures and vocabulary items they contain enhances comprehension and thus learning. Since removal of unfamiliar linguistic items (unknown grammatical constructions and lexis) obviously cannot help a learner acquire those items, it becomes interesting to determine whether it is possible to modify target-language samples in other ways which improve comprehension without denying learners access to the new items.

A number of researchers have addressed this question, and Parker and Chaudron (1987) provide a useful survey of both methodology and findings (Table 5.3). As Table 5.3 shows, Parker and Chaudron found that the twelve studies they reviewed compared comprehension of NS versions of lecturettes or reading passages with versions which the

Study	List./ Read.	Text Versions and Types of Modifications	Level and N	Measure	Significant Outcomes	Simplification?	Elaboration?
Cervantes 1983	List.	A) NS passage B) Repeated passage	ESL University N = 16	Dictation exact morpheme equivalent meaning	B) > A)	–	Yes
Long 1985 (two studies)	List.	A) NS passage B) FT passage less complex (1.68 vs. 1.94 S/T) slower rate (128 vs. 139 wpm) rephrasings/restatements	ESL University N = 87	Comprehension multiple choice while listening	B) > A)	?	?
Kelch 1985	List.	A) NS passage (191 wpm) B) Slower rate (124 wpm) C) FT modifications (200 wpm) synonyms, paraphrases, parallelism D) FT modifications + slower rate (140 wpm)	ESL University N = 26	Dictation exact word equivalent meaning	B,D) > A,C) (exact word) B,D) > A,C) D) > C) (equiv. meaning)	– – –	Yes Yes Yes

TABLE 5.3 Experimental Studies of the Effect of Input Modification on Comprehension (from Parker and Chaudron 1987)

Study	List./ Read.	Text Versions and Types of Modification	Level and N	Measure	Significant Outcomes	Simplification?	Elaboration?
Speidel, Tharp, Kobayashi 1985	List.	A) Complex syntax B) Simple syntax	Standard and Hawaiian English 2nd graders $N = 120$		Not significant	No	–
Mannon 1986	List.	A) NS lecture (live) 123 wpm, 16 repetitions 1.99 S/T uncontrolled discourse B) lecture to NNSs (live) 112 wpm, 28 repetitions 1.72 S/T uncontrolled discourse	ESL University $N = 28$	Multiple choice following list	Not significant but trend for B) > A)	?	?
Pica, Doughty and Young 1986	List.	A) Modified input B) Modified interaction	ESL University $N = 16$	Correct choice and location of items in communication game	B) > A)	–	Yes
Fujimoto, Lubin Sasaki and	List.	A) NS passage 140 wpm, 2.11 S/T	ESL University $N = 53$	Multiple choice following list	B) > A)	?	?

TABLE 5-3 *(continued)*

Study	List./ Read.	Text Versions and Types of Modification	Level and N	Measure	Significant Outcomes	Simplification?	Elaboration?
Long 1986		B) Modified input 117 wpm, 1.15 S/T C) Modified 'interaction' 124 wpm, 2.15 S/T repetitions and paraphrases					
Chaudron and Richards 1986	List.	A) Normal lecture B) Micro-level discourse markers C) Macro-level discourse markers D) Micro and macro level	ESL University $N = 146$	Cloze recall while listening	C) > B)	−	?
Johnson 1981*	Read.	A) Regular B) Modified simplified syntax paraphrases	ESL University $N = 46$	Multiple choice following reading Recall protocols	B) > A) (on recall from culturally unfamiliar texts)	?	?
Blau 1982	Read.	A) Simple passages B) Complex with surface clues	ESL University $N = 85$ ESL 8th grade $N = 111$	Multiple choice following reading	Not significant (univ.) Trend for B, C) > A) (8th grade)	No	−

TABLE 5.3 (*continued*)

Study	List./Read.	Text Versions and Types of Modification	Level and N	Measure	Significant Outcomes	Simplification?	Elaboration?
		C) Complex without surface clues					
Brown 1985	Read.	A) NS passage 10th grade readability B) Modified input syntactically simplified 5th grade C) Modified 'interaction' paraphrase, synonyms 9th grade readability	ESL 9th – 11th $N=30$	Multiple choice during reading	B, C) > A)	Yes	Yes
Tsang 1987	Read.	Same passages as Brown (1985)	ESL 9th – 13th $N = 401$	Multiple choice during reading	B, C) > A) (effect for 9, 10th grade)	Yes	Yes

Key: S/T = S nodes per T-unit – =not tested
* This study involved other factors not relevant to the present study

TABLE 5.3 *(continued)*

researchers had modified in various ways, some using 'simplification', or linguistic adjustments, some using elaborative, or 'interactional structure', adjustments (see Table 5.2), and some using both. Studies also differed as to the specific examples of each type of adjustments made (see 'Text versions and types of modification' column) and as to how they measured comprehension, which included various kinds of dictation, multiple-choice items, cloze tests and recall protocols.

While these modality and methodological differences across studies made comparisons tricky, some generalizations did emerge. Comprehension was consistently improved when elaborative modifications were present. (These were confounded with linguistic modifications in some, but not all, studies.) Linguistic modifications helped comprehension, too, but were not consistently superior in studies in which their effects could be isolated. There was some evidence, as might be expected, of an inverse relationship between proficiency level and the effect on comprehension of either type of modification. Parker and Chaudron (1987, p. 114) conclude:

> As several studies have suggested . . . if one is inclined to present the most native-like TL input, one should modify the input in the direction of elaborative alterations rather than syntactic simplification, for these would allow more native-like complexity and be at least equally successful in promoting comprehension, if not better.

There appears to be substantial evidence of beneficial effects for various kinds of adjustments on comprehension, with elaborative, or 'interactional structure', modifications being successful, and having the added advantage of providing learners with continued access to the very linguistic items they have yet to acquire. Elaborative, or 'interactional structure', adjustments would therefore seem educationally more appropriate than what is commonly offered in current commercially produced materials. Further research is needed, however, both to provide a firmer empirical base for this claim and to identify precisely which members of this class of adjustments (repetitions, topic-fronting, paraphrase, decomposition, rhetorical signalling and other types of redundancy) are most beneficial in which situations.

5.3.5 Comprehensible input and second language acquisition

Following on from work showing a relationship between input adjustments and comprehension, a final claim made for the importance of the linguistic environment concerns the role of *comprehensible* input in SLA, or the relationship between comprehension and acquisition. In a series of papers, Krashen (1980, 1981, 1982 and elsewhere) put forward what he calls the Input Hypothesis. This says that development from a learner's current stage of IL development, i, to the next stage, $i + 1$,[7] is achieved through the learner *comprehending* language which contains linguistic items (lexis, syntax, morphology, etc.) at $i + 1$. Comprehension is necessary, Krashen believes, in order for the input to become *intake*, i.e. data taken in or assimilated by the learner and used by the learner to promote IL development.[8] The ability to understand items not yet in the IL grammar derives, Krashen maintains, from the speech adjustments made to learners, plus the learner's use of shared knowledge and (linguistic and extralinguistic) context. Krashen stresses that the learner's focus of attention during this process is not on the new forms themselves, but on the message being communicated.

The Input Hypothesis became a central claim of later formulations of Krashen's Monitor Theory of SLA (see Chapter 7). In its support, Krashen cited literature on four topics:

1. caretaker speech
2. foreigner talk
3. the 'silent period' in child L1 and SL acquisition
4. comparative methods studies of language teaching.

He noted that caretaker speech and FT accompany all successful cases of language acquisition, first and second, and believes they play a facilitating role. The period of 'silence' by children in the first few months of any kind of language acquisition, he claimed, indicates that the child is listening to and comprehending speech addressed to him or her, prior to beginning to produce. The comparative methods studies, as reviewed in Krashen (1982b), show a general superiority for any 'input-based' method over any production-oriented method. Thus, methods such as Total Physical Response, Suggestopedia and (especially) the Natural Approach, which begin by providing large amounts of simple, comprehensible language to the learners, do better, Krashen claimed, than methods such as audiolingual, Silent Way, audiovisual or Community Language Learning, which insist on early production of almost everything the learners hear from the teacher, and often after minimal exposure. (This problem is made worse, Krashen said, by such accompanying features as a focus on form, not meaning, in some methods in the second group, usually accompanied by frequent error correction.)

While these arguments are initially appealing, some qualifications are in order. To begin with (as Krashen is, of course, aware), the fact that caretaker speech and FT co-occur with successful acquisition does not necessarily mean that they cause it. Next, a 'silent period' is by no means observed in all learners. Gibbons (1985) argues that the evidence for silent periods is in fact very weak, and that there is great individual variation among children as to their duration, where they occur at all. He suggests that they initially signify incomprehension, not intake processing,[9] that prolonged silent periods seen in some children probably indicate psychological withdrawal rather than the acquisition process at work, and that pedagogic recommendations for delayed production are not justified (on the basis of this evidence, at least). Finally, the comparative methods studies, often with problematic designs (see Long 1980b), did not systematically manipulate the $+/-$ comprehensible input characteristic Krashen now claims was the crucial variable in interpreting their findings.

On the other hand, three additional pieces of evidence exist which are supportive of the hypothesis (Long 1983b). These are:

5. the superiority of immersion over F/SL programmes
6. the lack of an effect for additional out-of-school SL exposure for children in immersion programmes
7. *non*-acquisition *without* comprehensible input.

Immersion programmes, in which the provision of large amounts of comprehensible input is a salient characteristic (achieved by use of the L2, appropriately adjusted, to teach subject matter to linguisticially homogeneous groups of NNSs), have consistently produced such good results in Canada (for review, see Swain 1981; Genesee 1983) that their students are typically compared against age-peers who are monolingual (native) speakers of the immersion language – something unthinkable where most F/SL teaching programme evaluations are concerned. Again, however, this is evidence derived from co-occurring phenomena, and may be due to the greater amount of exposure to the SL that immersion children receive (time on task), and to the fact that the children are self-selected, as much as to the type of input they receive.

The lack of effect for additional out-of-school SL exposure is based on a reinterpretation of the outcome of a large-scale study by Swain (1981), which compared the French SL achievement of groups of Anglophone children in various immersion programmes in towns across Canada. Mostly English was spoken on the streets of the towns in the West which had programmes in the study. Increasing amounts of French were used as one moved eastwards, rising to a high of about 65 per cent French in Montreal. Despite what seemed like differential opportunities for out-of-school acquisition of French, Swain in fact found no difference in the French achievement of children from comparable immersion programmes. Long (1983b) suggests that this may have been because the samples of NS French available to these children on the street, on TV, at the movies or in newspapers, was not adjusted for their benefit, and so remained incomprehensible to them, and therefore was unusable for acquisition. This, again, however, is admittedly a *post hoc* interpretation, and only one of those available.

The best evidence for Krashen's viewpoint has to be the fact that children or adults who are not provided with comprehensible input, but only NS-NS models, either do not acquire at all or acquire only a very limited stock of lexical items and formulaic utterances, such as greetings, leave-takings and advertising jingles. This generalization holds across studies of first and second language acquisition, by children and adults, in normal and abnormal populations (for review, see Long 1981, 1983b). Thus, Dutch children, for example, do not learn German by watching large amounts of German TV (Snow, van Eeden and Muysken 1981). Hearing children of deaf parents do not learn spoken language through watching TV, either, yet catch up with age-peers once exposed to normal conversational opportunities for children (Sachs, Bard and Johnson 1981). The *amount* of input in these and other cases is unlimited. It is the *quality* of input – unadjusted, so incomprehensible – which distinguishes them.

Conversely, all cases of successful first and second language acquisition are characterized by the availability of *comprehensible* (not necessarily linguistically modified) input. Cases like Western Samoan mothers (Ochs 1982) and Guatemalan mothers (Harkness 1971) not using simplified speech with their children do not constitute counter-evidence to this claim (cf. Hatch 1983, pp. 185–6). The data Ochs presents on mother–child conversation show clear modifications by the mothers, not of the input *per se*, but of the 'interactional structure' of conversation (Long 1980a), exemplified by the self- and other-repetitions, clarification requests, comprehension and confirmation checks, expansions, and so on, described in Section 5.2.2. Harkness, too, talks of the Guatemalan mothers using exact repetitions following communication breakdowns. The findings from naturalistic and laboratory studies converge here, suggesting in each case that it is interactional, not input, adjustments that are more basic and more important for learning.[10]

Cases of learning a SL through reading only are also understandable, since an initial choice of material with appropriate content can again be combined with modifications to the interactional structure of, this time, the written discourse, e.g. by varying the pace, and thereby processing time, through controlling reading speed, and by exact repetitions through re-reading phrases and sentences. (For further discussion and details of relevant studies, see Long, 1983a, 1983b, 1983c, 1985b; Chaudron 1985a; Krashen 1985; Swain 1985; Parker and Chaudron 1987.)

By suggesting ways that readers can modify the interactional structure of written discourse, we are also acknowledging that learners should not be viewed as passive recipients of input made comprehensible for them by others. We have already mentioned that comprehensible input results from a negotiated process. To this we add C. Brown's (1985) observation that learners themselves are responsible for the differences in the input they receive from the teacher due to the nature of the in-class requests they make. Not every learner, of course, has to manage his or her own input. Allwright (1980) cites the case of Igor, an extroverted language learner who procured many more conversational turns in class than his classmates. Ironically, Igor did not make as rapid progress in learning the TL as some of the other students, leading Allwright to speculate that Igor's communicative attempts with the teacher were perhaps more productive for the 'audience' than for Igor himself (p. 185).

It thus is possible for learners to obtain their own comprehensible input even when they are not negotiating with an interlocutor themselves. Larsen-Freeman (1983a) cites anecdotal evidence of her own 'selective listening' strategy which worked to improve her Spanish proficiency in a Spanish course which was geared for a higher level of proficiency than her own and which she was auditing, i.e. not verbally participating. Larsen-Freeman also relates the case of a Dutch native speaker who claimed to learn some German from radio broadcasts. Due to the similarity between Dutch and German, this learner, at any rate, was able to attend selectively to the input and relying on his NL as a crutch, to make some of the TL comprehensible. The TL radio broadcast was thus not all 'noise'.[11]

The picture that emerges from studies on input is as follows. Neither production nor participation in conversation is necessary for language acquisition, although certain types of each probably facilitate growth (see Swain 1985). Nor are input (linguistic) modifications necessary. Although they often help comprehension when they do occur (as shown in Section 5.3.4), the very process of removing unknown structures and lexical items from the input in order to achieve an improved level of understanding simultaneously renders the modified samples useless as a source of new acquirable language items. Modification of the interactional structure of conversation or of written discourse during reading, on the other hand, is a better candidate for a necessary (not sufficient) condition for acquisition. The role it plays in negotiation for meaning helps to make input comprehensible while still containing unknown linguistic elements, and, hence, potential intake for acquisition.

Notes

1. Other features of FT are no doubt subject to individual variation. Wesche and Ready (1985) detected individual variation in the linguistic modifications made by two NS professors lecturing to NNS students.
2. Hawkins (1985) warns, however, that a learner's response need not be reliable. NNSs can give signals that they understand the FT they are receiving, when in fact they do not understand.
3. Although we term these 'linguistic adjustments', we should not lose sight of the fact that they have a pragmatic motivation. Avery, Ehrlich and Yorio (1985), for instance, found that phonological adjustments made during FT were only made on discourse segments dealing with 'core' information.
4. For a very different perspective on the function of communicative strategies, see Lantolf and Frawley (1984).
5. Of course, it might also be argued that if learners are skilled in the use of communicative strategies, have achieved *strategic competence* (Canale and Swain 1980), then their motivation to continue to acquire the TL might decrease as their communicative goals can be achieved despite syntactic inaccuracy.
6. The rho, better termed the Spearman rho, is a statistic used in correlational analysis to compare two sets of rankings. The closer the rho gets to 1.0, the closer the two orders are correlated. Usually a correlation with a probability of less than .05 ($p<.05$) is considered statistically significant.
7. Cf. Vygotsky's 'zone of proximal development' (1962, p. 104) and Piaget's (1929) principle of optimum level of novelty.
8. The distinction between *input* and *intake* was first made by Corder (1967, p. 165) when he noted that simply presenting a linguistic form to a learner does not qualify it for the status of input because 'what goes in is not what is available for going in'. Much of the input contains 'noise'.
9. Gattegno, of course, maintained this position for years. He claimed that what the baby is doing during the pre-verbal period is learning to control its own articulatory system and is learning to listen to itself. (See, for example, Gattegno 1985.)
10. Similarly, cases like that of 'John' (Blank, Gessner and Esposito 1979), who learned to produce utterances, but did not do so in coherent

conversational contexts, does not constitute counter-evidence. John was immersed in normal caretaker–child conversation, according to the original researchers' account, presumably learning his 'syntax' thereby (as well as through 'symbolic play'), even though not putting it to use in the normal ways for a three-year-old.

11. Beebe (1985) further cautions researchers not to view learners as simply 'passive recipients of comprehensible or incomprehensible input from native speakers but as active participants in choosing the target language models they prefer'. Goldstein (1987) exemplifies this with a study where the target language for an ESL learner was Black English rather than Standard English.

Activities

Comprehension

1. List several features of the speech input to children learning their L1.
2. What is meant by the following terms: 'linguistic', 'conversational', 'interactional' and 'elaborative' modifications? Give an example of each.
3. The transcript in Table 5.4 contains one or more examples of almost all of the linguistic or conversational adjustments listed below (although, lacking NS-NS baseline data, you will be inferencing in some cases). Identify one example of as many as you find, indicating the line(s) of transcript on which it occurs. Transcription conventions can be found at the end of the transcript.

(a) exact repetition
(b) semantic repetition question
(c) self-repetition
(d) other-repetition
(e) confirmation check
(f) comprehension check
(g) clarification request
(h) or-choice question
(i) decomposition
(j) acceptance of an unintentional topic-switch
(k) (impressionistically) abrupt topic-change

(l) repair of *wh* to yes/no
(m) (impressionistically) marked use of a question for topic-initiating move
(n) left-dislocation
(o) question-and-answer
(p) acceptance of ambiguity
(q) lexical switch
(r) stress for topic saliency
(s) expansion

Background
The native speaker (NS) is female, Caucasian American, in her late twenties, and a speaker of 'educated West Coast (Los Angeles) English'. She is a trained ESL teacher with three years of teaching experience. The non-native speaker (NNS) is a male Japanese office worker in his mid twenties, in Los Angeles for an intensive summer course in ESL. He is a 'beginner'. This is their first meeting, which has been arranged by the researcher. It is taking place in a small office on the UCLA campus in 1978. The researcher has introduced the speakers, using first names, and has left the room. The speakers are now seated facing each other (at a slight angle). A cassette tape recorder is running on a desk nearby, visible to the speakers, who know they are being recorded, but who do not know the purpose of the research.

NS	NNS
1. [Name], how are you, [name]?	
2.	(How are you?)
3. How are you?	
4.	I am fine thank you
5 Good good How long have you been	
6. here in the United States?	
7.	I've been . about uh three
8.	weeks about three weeks
9. Oh Do you like it? . Do you like it	
10. here?	
11.	Yes, I like it (xx) very much
12. Are you here for the first time? . . .	
13. Are you in Los Angeles for the	
14. first time?	
15.	Yes I . . . uh first time
16. First time (oh)	
17.	First experience to come
18.	America
19. Good Are you a student in Japan?	
20.	No I am not . . I am worker
21. You're a worker What kind of	
22. work do you do?	
23.	Uh I'm a /ošer/ . /ošer/
24. Official!	
25. Official	Official
26.	of . (pu-) public
27. Ah you work for the <u>government</u>	
28.	Uhm (pref-?) . . No?

TABLE 5.4 Native Speaker/Non-native Speaker Conversation (from Long 1981)

29. (I don't understand) No	
30. Pre?	/prifek/
31.	/prif ker/ S- Japan has uh . .
32.	. . many /prifkers/
33. Factory .	
34. Factory?	No
35. What is it? Can you tell me? What	
36. is that?	
37.	Uhm city
38. Aha	
39.	city
40. Right	city
41.	have /afsr/ [means 'officials']?
42. Ah You work for the city What do	
43. you do?	
44. What do you do? . . . . Do you	
45. talk ⌒ to people? Do you write ⌒	
46. letters?	
47.	(write write)
48. You write Good Uh how long ⌒	
49. have you been working?	
50.	. . . . Mmm I was - I was
51.	working three years
52. Three years Do you like ⌒ the	
53. work?	
54.	Yes I
55. Aha	like (xx)
56. Where did you study English?	
57.	. . . I studied English at uh
58.	school
59.	. . . . . high school and the
60.	university
61. (oh) university What university?	
62.	(yeah)
63. Alright What university did you	
64. go to?	
65.	/aꞔia/ university. .
66. What city is that?	
67.	At /nostaši/ city
68. I don't know Japan I have never	
69. been there	
70. [slight giggle]	[slight laugh]
71.	I see
72. So I don't know Good Alright	
73. Do you like your English class?	
74.	Yes I like . . . very much
75. What do you do in the English	
76. class?	

TABLE 5.4 *(continued)*

77. What do you do?	
78.	. . At at UCLA?
79. Aha	
80.	I studied I studied conversation
81.	English conversation and
82.	grammar
83. Aha . . . How many students are in	
84. your class?	
85.	. About uh my class i- i- uh
86.	ten ten t- ten person ten students
87. Ten students	
88.	About te-
89. Good (that's good) How many	
90. hours every day?	
91. How many hours of English do you	
92. have?	
93.	Uh it's uh eight thirty
94. Aha	
95.	to . around eight thirty
96.	to . three thirty
97. Mmm very long	
98.	Yes
99. That's a long day	
100.	But uh but uh . . we take we
101.	take a break . .
102. oh	
103.	You know thirty minutes
104. oh	
105.	Break time
106. oh good	thirty minutes
107. At ten thirty ⌒ you take a break?	
108.	Thirty minutes
109. Right When do you take the break? ⌣	
110. At ten thirty?	
111.	Uhm . ten fifteen
112. Ten fifteen	ten fifteen
113.	From ten fifteen to ten fifty-five
114. Ten forty-five	
115.	Ah ten f- forty-five
116. Right right Have you seen	
117. Los Angeles?	
118.	Yes
119. What have you seen?	
120.	I went to uh Disneyland
121. Aha Good	
122.	Knottsberry Farm
123. Aha	

TABLE 5.4 (*continued*)

124.	Farmer's Market
125. Aha　What did- Did you <u>like</u>	
126. Disneyland?	
127.	Yes　I like(d)　very much　I
128.	enjoyed I enjoyed Disneyland
129. Right　It's very nice	
130.	Yes
131. Yes　Did you go on the rides　. Did	
132. you go in uh-	
133.	No uh I take I take uh uh . . by
134.	bus
135. You go by bus, right　But in	
136. Disneyland you can walk	
137. or	Yes
138. you can go in a car and you can uh	
139. there's many things for children	
140.	Yes
141. to do　Did you go on the games for	
142. the children?	
143.	Yes
144. Did you go?　Did you go on the big	
145. mountain?	
146.	. . . . . Yes I-
147. (the) Matterhorn?　Did you go on	
148. the big mountain?	
149.	No
150. There's a big mountain . .	
151.	In Disneyland
152. At Disneyland,　right,　a very big	
153. mountain with snow	
154. sn-　right?	(xx)　Ah
155. Did you go?　In the mountain?	
156.	No I didn't go mountain
157. Ah okay (xxxx)　What will you do	
158. when you go back to Japan?　Will	
159. you study more English?	
160.	Yes I uh . . . uhm I come back
161.	. . .

Key to Transcription Conventions

[ ]	transcriber's comments		
.	one-beat pause	2 speaker	overlap
∧	half-beat pause	turns on	
(xx)	inaudible	same line	
(word)	unclear, but sounded like this	‿	run-on (no pause)
word--	false start; cut off		
<u>word</u>	increased volume		

TABLE 5.4 *(continued)*

4. Define and give some examples of communicative strategies.
5. What benefits might accrue to NNSs interacting with one another that they wouldn't necessarily get by conversing with NSs?
6. How does Hatch's view that language learning evolves out of learning how to carry on conversations differ from the traditional sequence in the language classroom?
7. Why must the effect of frequency on accuracy orders be considered a non-causal one at this time?
8. Why are elaborative modifications presumably better to use in simplifying texts for language students than linguistic modifications?
9. Distinguish between input and intake.
10. What does it mean to say that comprehensible input results from a negotiated process? How can this concept apply to the printed word?

Application

11. Meisel (1975, 1983c) compares 'simplification' processes in input to NNSs and in various kinds of IL development (see Chapter 4). Why are such comparisons of interest? What does Meisel mean by 'restrictive' and 'elaborative' simplification? Which is FT supposed to exhibit? What other kinds of common processes do you think occur in FT and some ILs? What evidence can you offer? What other kinds of modifications can you think of that distinguish speech to and by NNSs?
12. What is the input for creolization? How could the development of creoles be used as counter-evidence to a theory of language acquisition which attributed a causal role to input factors?
13. Does the work on caretaker speech and/or FTD affect your views as to the degree to which learning a first or second language is determined by an innate (language) learning capacity? Why or why not?
14. Some language educators have argued for the desirability of using 'authentic', i.e. unmodified, TL materials in the classroom. Do you agree with this? Why or why not?
15. Many of the differences observed between speech to foreigners and other NSs concern the relative frequency of certain linguistic items or the relative simplicity/complexity of talk. Such properties of FT, by definition, can only be established by comparing two (or more) speech corpora. The NS baseline data must be *comparable*, however. Not any speech will do. What factors make corpora

comparable? What factors must you control for, in other words, when collecting data? Can you think of any claims made about differences between FT and speech to/conversation with other NSs that may be due to the use of non-comparable baseline data?

16. We do not yet understand why input to NNSs is sometimes grammatical, sometimes not. Why might it be important to determine whether and when this is the case? What factors do you think are involved? Explain your choice, and make predictions (in the form of hypotheses) about when you expect to find deviant input. Then design a simple study to test one or more of your hypotheses.

17. Display questions for which the speaker already knows the answers, are often posed to language students by language teachers (e.g. What's my name?). Are there any examples of error correction or display questions in the transcript for question 3? How do you account for this?

18. It has occasionally been claimed that NSs unconsciously act as language teachers when they converse (even informally) with NNSs. (See, e.g., Moerk 1974 and Snow 1977 for similar claims about motherese.) Can you find any sequences in the transcript for question 3 that you think could be functioning as miniature SL lessons? Is there any implicit correction going on, for example? What other kinds of covert language teaching (if any) can you find? What arguments can be made *for* and *against* the idea that the adjustments NSs make aid acquisition, as opposed to simply help communication? How could you test the 'acquisition by conversation' claim made, for example, by Hatch (1978a)?

19. Tape yourself or a friend teaching an SL class and also talking informally to one of the non-native students from the same class outside the classroom. Transcribe the two tapes. What similarities and differences do you notice between FT and SL teacher talk? What relevance might the similarities and (especially) the differences have for the success/failure of language teaching and/or for naturalistic (uninstructed) SLA?

20. Tape-record NSs engaged in speech modification to different kinds of interlocutors, e.g. plants, pets, the hearing impaired, mentally retarded individuals, foreigners, lovers (if you can get the data), or other NSs who are not specialists in the areas being talked about (e.g. physicians talking to other physicians, to nurses, and to patients about a medical matter). Using any data you collect, and sources in the literature, what claims can you make about

universals of modification? Are any of your 'universals' likely to be language-specific?

Suggestions for further reading

For the role of input in first language acquisition, see:
Gleitman, L, Newport, E and Gleitman, H 1984 The current status of the motherese hypothesis. *Journal of Child Language* 11: 43–79
Ochs, E 1982 Talking to children in Western Samoa. *Language in Society* 11: 77–104
Ochs, E and Schieffelin, B (eds.) 1979 *Developmental pragmatics*. Academic Press, New York
Snow, C and Ferguson, C (eds.) 1977 *Talking to children: language input and acquisition*. Cambridge University Press

For works dealing with the role of input in SLA, see:
Gass, S and Madden, C (eds.) 1985 *Input in second language acquisition*. Newbury House, Rowley, Mass.
Krashen, S 1985 *The input hypothesis: issues and implications*. Longman, New York

For a discussion of conversation and its relation to SLA, consult:
Day, R (ed.) 1986 *Talking to learn: conversation in second language acquisition*. Newbury House, Rowley, Mass.
Hatch, E 1978 Discourse analysis and second language acquisition. In Hatch, E (ed.) *Second language acquisition: a book of readings*. Newbury House, Rowley, Mass.
Hatch, E 1983 *Psycholinguistics: a second language perspective*. Newbury House, Rowley, Mass.
Long, M 1983 Native speaker/non-native speaker conversation and the negotiation of comprehensible input. *Applied Linguistics* 4: 126–41

For a thorough analysis of teacher talk in SL classrooms, consult:
Chaudron, C 1988 *Second language classrooms: research on teaching and learning*. Cambridge University Press

For some pedagogical applications of what is known about input and SLA, look at:
Long, M and Porter, P 1985 Group work, interlanguage talk, and second language acquisition. *TESOL Quarterly* 19 (2): 207–28
Parker, K and Chaudron, C 1987 The effects of linguistic simplifications and elaborative modifications on L2 comprehension. *University of Hawaii Working Papers in ESL* 6 (2): 107–33

For a collection of articles on communicative strategies, see:
Faerch, C and Kasper, G (eds.) 1983 *Strategies in interlanguage communication*. Longman

6 Explanations for differential success among second language learners

6.1 Introduction

One of the major conundrums in the SLA field is the question of differential success. While it is surely the case that some people are more dextrous than others in using their mother tongue, all children with normal faculties and given normal circumstances master their mother tongue. Unfortunately, language mastery is not often the outcome of SLA. Furthermore, there is a much broader range of language proficiency achieved among second language learners than first. One of the most obvious potential explanations for the comparative lack of success of second language learners is that SL learners begin acquiring the language at a later age than do first language learners. Thus, the effect of age is the first explanation we will consider in this chapter. There is, however, a host of other factors which have been proffered to explain differential success among SL learners, to explain why some acquire a SL with facility while others struggle and only meet with limited success. Thus, whereas in the three chapters that have preceded this one we have dealt with how SLs are acquired, here we are more concerned with why they are and are not acquired. In addition to age, then, we will explore the following explanations for differential success: language aptitude, social-psychological factors, personality, cognitive style, hemisphere specialization, learning strategies, and a few others.

We do not mean to imply that these are the only factors that have an influence on the SLA process. Other factors also clearly have an impact on success. We have already dealt with native language variables and input variables. In Chapter 8 we will deal with instructional variables. In this chapter, however, we will focus on individual variables, leaving our definition of 'individual' broad enough to include an individual acting as a member of a peer or social group. It is undeniable that important individual differences exist among second language learners and, as Selinker has written, 'a theory of second language learning that does not provide a central place for individual differences among learners *cannot* be considered acceptable' (1972, p. 213, fn. 8).

6.2 Age

A good deal of controversy has been generated around whether the age at which someone is first exposed to a SL, in the classroom or naturalistically, affects acquisition of that language in any way. Some writers claim that SLA is the same process and just as successful whether the learner begins as a child or an adult and/or that adults are really better learners because they start off faster (e.g. Genesee 1976, 1988; Neufeld 1979; Snow 1983, 1987; Ellis 1985; Flege 1987). Others think the data ambiguous and/or that adults are at a disadvantage only in a few areas, especially phonology (e.g. Hatch 1983; McLaughlin 1984). Still others are convinced that younger learners are at an advantage, particularly where ultimate levels of attainment, such as accent-free SL performance, are concerned (e.g. Oyama 1976; Seliger 1978; Krashen, Long and Scarcella 1979; Scovel 1981; Patkowski 1980; Harley 1986).

The issue is important for both theoretical and practical reasons. At the theoretical level, i.e. when trying to understand SLA, people who conclude from the data that, for example, children and adults (however defined) go about acquisition differently and/or achieve differentially will presumably posit alternate learning mechanisms and processes in child and adult learners. Conversely, theorists who conclude that children and adults are capable of and/or achieve much the same in SLA may feel freer to posit something closer to an L1 = L2 model, with the same mechanisms and acquisition processes at work regardless of learner age.

In the applied domain, people planning language teaching pro-grammes want to know the optimal timing for such programmes. Should foreign languages be introduced in the elementary school, for example, or is it as good or better to wait until secondary school? And what is the optimal timing of successful bilingual or immersion education programmes? (For discussion and review, see Cummins 1979; Swain 1981; Genesee 1983.) When dealing with adult foreign or second language learning, is it reasonable to try for native-like standards of pronunciation, or is that just wasting teachers' and students' time and frustrating both? How about native-like levels in other linguistic domains, such as lexis, syntax and pragmatics? And do learners of different ages learn (languages) in different ways and so perhaps benefit from different approaches, syllabuses or materials? (See, e.g., Oskarsson 1972; C. Brown 1985.)

In the main body of this chapter we will discuss the research findings for each variable posited to have some bearing on SLA. Then in the conclusion to this chapter, we will discuss possible implications of these findings. Readers should be forewarned, however, that the research findings are even less definitive in the area of individual variables than they have been in the other areas we have considered so far. Thus, any implications we are able to draw must be considered tenuous at best.

6.2.1 Studies of age and SLA

At first sight, the SL age results look chaotic, some studies appearing to show child superiority, some favouring adults. As noted by Krashen, Long and Scarcella (1979), however, some fairly clear patterns emerge once short-term and long-term studies are distinguished. The conclusion they drew from the research literature is that *older is faster, but younger is better.*

As revealed by long-term studies, younger is better in the most crucial area, *ultimate attainment*, with only quite young (child) starters being able to achieve accent-free, native-like performance in a SL. As revealed by short-term studies, older learners are at an advantage in *rate of acquisition* (adults faster than children, and older children faster than younger children). The rate advantage is limited in several ways, however: it refers mainly to early morphology and syntax; it is temporary, disappearing after a few months for most language skills; and it only holds if the 'younger' learners in a comparison involve children or adolescents. Younger *adults* outperform older adults even in short-term studies (Seright 1985).

Short-term studies, ranging from a few minutes to a few months, speak only to differential *rate* of acquisition, not to absolute abilities. They probably favour older learners because of their 'teach and test' or laboratory interview formats and also through their occasional use of tasks which allow older subjects to exploit their greater cognitive development and test-wiseness. Asher and Price (1967) taught Russian to a total of 134 students (a mix of eight-, ten- and twelve-year-olds and college-age adults) for twenty-five minutes using Total Physical Response, and found that adults outperformed all the child groups. Snow and Hoefnagel-Hohle (1978) studied the naturalistic acquisition of Dutch by 96 English-speaking children (eight to ten years old), adolescents (twelve to fifteen years old) and adults, measuring each group's performance on pronunciation, morphology, imitation and translation tasks after three, six, and nine to ten months' residence in Holland. In general, the adolescent and adult groups outperformed the children after three months and (less so) six months in-country, but the children had caught up on most tasks by the time of the third testing. Similar results favouring adults have also been found in short-term studies of phonology involving either teaching and testing phonemic contrasts in a new language (Olson and Samuels 1973) or simply testing subjects' ability to imitate target language sounds in nonsense words (Snow and Hoefnagel-Hohle 1977).

Even some short-term (laboratory) studies have found immediate superiority for younger over older children, however. Tahta, Wood and Loewenthal (1981a), for example, found that the ability of a group of 231 five- to fifteen-year-old English school children to imitate French and Armenian pronunciation of isolated words and phrases after one model *declined* steadily with increasing age. The children's ability to replicate intonation in longer phrases remained steady in the five- to eight-year range, and then dropped rapidly between ages eight and eleven, plateauing again in the eleven to fifteen range. The reverse pattern was observed in the number of models and trials the children required before they could produce the intonation patterns well, the most marked increase in trials needed by older children coming from eight to eleven. (See also Yamada, Takatsuka, Kotabe and Kurusu 1980.)

While further research is clearly needed to disambiguate these findings, the initial generalization proposed by Krashen et al. (1979) still holds: adults proceed through early stages of syntactic and morphological development faster than children (where time and exposure are held constant). The apparent counter-evidence from findings like those by Tahta et al. can be accounted for by assuming that age-related constraints begin to set in as early as six for suprasegmental phonology, and soon after that for segmental phonology, as discussed below. These constraints would make it increasingly difficult for learners to acquire the SL without an accent and have led researchers to hypothesize the existence of a *critical period* (Lenneberg 1967) after which complete mastery of a language is impossible, or at least a *'sensitive'*
period (Lamendella 1977) during which language acquisition is most efficient. Note that such a view would fit with findings by Payne (1980) to the effect that children moving to King of Prussia, a town near Philadelphia, only reach native-like levels in the second *dialect* phonology if they arrive by age six and have parents who speak with the King of Prussia accent in the home.

A second generalization made by Krashen et al. is that older children acquire faster than younger children (again in early stages of morphological and syntactic development where time and exposure are held constant). Representative results are those by Ekstrand (1976) and Fathman (1975a). Ekstrand studied 2,189 eight- to seventeen-year-olds learning Swedish as a SL over a two-year period. He found a linear improvement with age, and that older children performed better than younger children on measures of listening comprehension, reading, free writing, pronunciation and speaking. In an analogous ESL study, Fathman looked at 200 children aged eight to fifteen, resident in the USA for from one to three years, assessing their English morphology, syntax and pronunciation using the SLOPE (a picture-cued sentence-completion test) and a picture-description task. Eleven- to fifteen-year-olds outperformed six- to ten-year-olds on morphology and syntax, although the younger group did better on pronunciation. Similar findings regarding the superiority of older learners on rule-governed aspects of language are reported by Ervin-Tripp (1974), Chun (1978), Snow and Hoefnagel-Hohle (1978), and Harley (1986).

Collier (1987), too, found that older ESL learners (ages eight to eleven) outperformed younger ESL learners (ages five to seven) in second language and content-area achievement as measured by the Science Research Associates tests. Collier attributes this finding to Cummins's (1981b) observation that for older children the academic skills they had 'acquired in their L1 transfer to the L2 and [thus] the process of SLA occurs at a faster rate than for younger children' (Collier 1987, p. 619). Interestingly enough, the twelve- to fifteen-year-olds in Collier's study did less well than both younger groups, a finding which would appear to contradict Cummins's explanation. Collier, however, proposes that the drop in the adolescents' scores may specifically be due to the schools' greater demands on students at the secondary level.

The most interesting SL findings concern ultimate attainment, where the focus is not relative learning speed but absolute abilities – or their decline and (possibly) categorical loss. In long-term studies, those comparing achievement after several years of foreign language study and/or residence in the SL environment, younger starters consistently outperform older ones, and only quite young children seem to be capable of native-like attainment, even after many years of target-language exposure. Learners starting later than about six often become communicatively fluent but typically finish with measurable accents in phonology; and with progressively later starts, the data are beginning to show 'accents' in other linguistic domains as well.

In one of the largest and most carefully conducted studies of this issue to date, Oyama (1976) looked at the pronunciation ability of 60 Italian immigrants with different age of arrival (AO) in the USA (from six to twenty) and who had lived in the USA for different periods (five to eighteen years). Oyama found a clear main effect for AO, and no effect for length of residence (LOR) once the effect for AO was partialled out.[1] Child arrivals performed in the range of native speakers; those older than twelve on arrival did not; and accents were also evident in some who arrived earlier than twelve – an outcome consistent with the short-term results of Tahta et al. (1981) and Fathman (1976). Oyama's findings also echo those of a study by Asher and Garcia (1969), in which 71 Cuban students with AO in the USA of one to six were judged closest to native-like on a sentence-repetition task, followed by those with AO of seven to twelve, and those with AO of thirteen to nineteen doing poorest. Dramatic evidence can also be marshalled from Major (1987) to support the critical period hypothesis for accents. Major examined the pronunciation of certain English phonemes by 53 adult Brazilian Portuguese speakers and 7 NSs. Ten NSs of American English served as judges. The judges heard three short phrases said by each of the 60 subjects and they were asked to determine the degree of foreign accent. None of the 53 NNSs received a higher score than did the lowest-rated NS and, furthermore, there was a considerable score gap between the two groups.

The findings by Oyama, Asher, Garcia and Major, together with those of Payne (1980) for the acquisition of phonology in a second dialect, suggest that SL phonological attainment is strongly conditioned by learner age; specifically that (a) attainment is inversely related to AO, and (b) a native-like accent is impossible unless first exposure is quite early, probably around age six. Very high standards can be attained starting later than six, of course, but not, it would seem, native-like standards. The idea that some ability is irreversibly lost by age six is consistent with the Tahta et al. findings too, although coming from a short-term study, they alone would not constitute sufficient basis for the claim.

Apparent counter-evidence to the idea of a sensitive period for phonology is offered by Neufeld (1979). Since Neufeld's research is relied upon heavily by critics of the sensitive period notion in SLA (e.g. Ellis 1985; Flege 1987; Snow 1987; Genesee 1988), it is important to evaluate his findings carefully.

In an interesting series of studies, Neufeld (1978, 1979) has demonstrated that high levels of pronunciation and intonation can be achieved by both foreign and second language learners. In one study (Neufeld 1978), after receiving eighteen hours of intensive instruction in Japanese and Chinese phonology, twenty adult NSs of English recorded ten statements in each language, the tape later being played to three NSs of each language. Three of the twenty subjects received NS rating in one language, one of the three doing so in both languages. In other studies (Neufeld 1979), a small minority of tapes made by adult learners of French (with lengthy naturalistic French SL exposure and use) were good enough to lead some individuals among groups of linguistically sophisticated and naive judges to misclassify them as those of NSs when hearing a tape of randomly ordered NNS and genuine NS read-aloud speech samples. His findings have led Neufeld to claim that accent-free SL performance is possible and that, therefore, there is no sensitive period for SLA.

This is arguably to overstate the case, however, since the studies suffer from some important limitations and possibly from some methodological flaws. Most obvious is the question of ecological validity, or the generalizability of Neufeld's findings. First, the non-native speakers tested in the French studies were an elite few, drawn from a true bilingual environment (the English/French-medium University of Ottawa). After responding to a public request for subjects who considered themselves highly proficient bilinguals, they survived an initial screening interview for accentedness, and therefore were by definition not representative even of the attenuated sample volunteering for the study, much less of the population at large. This in no way invalidates them as potential test cases for the sensitive period hypothesis, of course, but severely limits any generalizations from the studies about pronunciation abilities.

Second, the speech sample in all Neufeld's studies was extremely limited, consisting of tape-recordings either of isolated model sentences or of very short (fifty-word) rehearsed passages read aloud by the subjects, and in some cases re-recorded by them if not in their opinion as native-like as they felt capable of sounding. The judges' task was to identify these (admittedly very proficient) speakers as non-natives, based on hearing the tiny careful speech samples presented on tape, mixed in random order with renditions of the same passage read by a number of native speakers. How valid a sample even of those subjects' normal spontaneous speech is such 'language-like' behaviour? Is the test to be whether some subjects can fool some of the raters some of the time, or as we would argue, whether some subjects can fool all of the raters all of the time? 'All of the time' obviously has to be circumscribed for the hypothesis to be testable at all, but not nearly as circumscribed as in Neufeld's research.

Third, Scovel (1981) has pointed out that the wording of the instructions given to raters implies that the subjects they are about to hear include native speakers rather than non-natives who have learned the raters' native language as L2, thereby increasing the likelihood that accented speakers will be accepted as natives.

In summary, Neufeld's studies seem most valuable as demonstrations of the high standards both foreign and second language learners sometimes achieve. The findings do not, in our view, constitute counter-evidence to the idea that there is a sensitive period for SL (and second dialect) phonology.

The need for an adequate language sample in such work is clearly shown by a cleverly designed study by Scovel (1981) of the ontogeny of the ability to recognize a spoken or written foreign accent. Scovel had four groups of judges (adult NSs, child NSs of different ages, adult NNSs and adult aphasics) rate twenty eight-second read-aloud taped speech samples as produced by a NS or a NNS; the adult NS judges were also asked to distinguish the same twenty natives and non-natives on the basis of short written pieces (unspeeded, free paragraphs on 'the importance of sleep') which they wrote for the study. There were ten NSs and ten NNSs in the sample, and Scovel made sure the NNSs were very good by first having three experienced ESL teachers screen out from a larger group any whose pronunciation they determined was not excellent.

The children's ability to make correct identifications increased steadily from 73 per cent accuracy at age five (the youngest children Scovel could get to understand the task) to near perfect classification (97 per cent accuracy) by age ten. The adult NSs also had no problem with the oral samples (95 per cent accuracy) but performed at chance level (47 per cent) on the written samples, presumably because, again, the writing represented subjects' best monitored production and allowed subjects to avoid problem areas that might have revealed them to be highly proficient but non-native. Adult NNSs improved in their detection ability with increasing ESL proficiency, but even the advanced group achieved an accuracy rate of only 77 per cent, similar to the five-year-old children's performance and poorer than the 85 per cent average of the group of aphasic patients. In addition to offering several methodological lessons for this type of research, Scovel's findings provide evidence of the age-related evolution of accent recognition in native speakers and of a sensitive period for accent recognition in non-natives.

Evidence of age-related barriers to SLA is also available for other skills/areas of language. In a second study with the same group of 60 Italian immigrants, Oyama (1978) found a strong negative effect for subjects' AO in the USA and their ability to comprehend masked speech.[2] Children arriving before age eleven performed similarly to NS controls, with later arrivals showing a progressive (linear) decline with age. Once again, there was no LOR effect.

In another large-scale study, Patkowski (1980) obtained global syntactic proficiency ratings of transcribed five-minute excerpts from the spontaneous speech of 67 non-native speakers of English, immigrants to the USA, and 15 NS controls during interviews with NSs. Use of written transcripts removed any phonological clues as to the speakers' backgrounds or proficiency. Two trained raters used a scale (with 0 indicating no ability and 5 meaning native-like performance) to rate the ESL speakers. Unknown to the raters, the subjects had varying AO, LOR (minimum of five years) and amount of formal ESL instruction. Patkowski found a strong (negative) main effect for AO, no effect for any other variables (LOR, informal exposure or formal instruction), and no interaction effects. Thus, the earlier the immigrants arrived in the United States, the higher the syntactic proficiency rating they received. Most striking, as shown in the histogram (Figure 6.1), was the clear bimodal distribution among the NNS subjects, indicating that they represented two populations, identified by Patkowski as those who had arrived in the USA pre- and post-puberty. Thus, Patkowski's results seem to be consistent with the notion of an age limitation on the acquisition of syntax in a second language.

There is no published work we know of on the age issue in the area of lexis/collocation, but an unpublished small-scale study by Matsunobu (1981) found NS judges easily able to distinguish writing samples obtained under the same conditions from NS freshman composition students and non-native speakers in the same remedial writing classes at a US college. Judges indicated the basis of their classifications had been both the collocation errors in the NNSs' writing, which were absent in the NS samples, and conversely, idiomatic phrasing in the NS samples which the NNS writing did not exhibit. (Matsunobu used three groups of raters, incidentally, finding ESL teachers best at classifying the samples as NS or NNS, followed by freshman composition teachers, with college-level content teachers bringing up the rear.) Matsunobu's findings were later confirmed in a small-scale replication using NNSs, 'standard' English NSs, and NSs of Hawaiian Creole English (Toutaiolepo 1984).

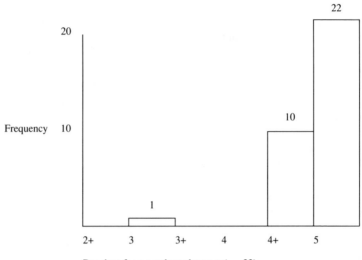

Bar chart for pre-puberty learners (*n* = 33)

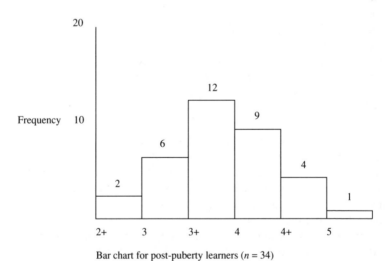

Bar chart for post-puberty learners (*n* = 34)

FIGURE 6.1 Syntax Ratings for Pre- and Post-Puberty Learners
(from Patkowski 1980, p. 455)

There is a need for research in the areas of discourse and pragmatics too. A small-scale study by Devenney (1986) suggests that future work will find age-related abilities in L2 pragmatics. A study by Scarcella (1983), while not directly addressing the age factor, produced results consistent with the idea that late starters will not be able to achieve true native competence in such subtle (but as Scarcella shows, measurable) areas as culturally appropriate topic choice and sequencing, back-channel cues, and other conversational strategies.

6.2.2 Explanations for age-related differences

Even among those scholars who agree that age-related differences in SLA exist, there is disagreement as to the explanation for such differences. At least four major causes have been suggested:

(1) *Social-psychological explanation.* The thrust of the argument here is that adults differ from children in that, for example, they might be more inhibited or that their identity as a speaker of a certain L1 might be more firmly established (H.D. Brown 1987, p. 51). As such, they may resist the socialization that is the end product of child language acquisition (Taylor 1974). With regards to the latter, it has been suggested that an adult learner may prefer to speak accented L2 speech which identifies him as a speaker of a particular L1. Also, if negative attitudes towards speakers of the target language hinder SLA of the particular TL, children, whose negative attitudes may not be fully formed (Lambert 1967), may be immune to the deleterious effects of such attitudes.

(2) *Cognitive explanation.* Several researchers, including Rosansky (1975), Felix (1981b) and Krashen (1982b), have implicated cognitive development, particularly attainment of Piaget's formal operations stage, as negatively affecting SLA. Piaget's formal operations stage involves the ability to think abstractly. The argument is that child SLA and adult SLA might actually involve different processes; the former utilizing a LAD (language acquisition device) as in L1 acquisition, the latter employing general problem-solving abilities. While the ability to think abstractly might give adults a tremendous advantage in solving problems, the claim is that the trade-off is an inability to make use of the LAD for SLA. (See also Johnson and Newport 1989).

(3) *Input explanation.* Features of the input have been suggested as potential explanations by Hatch (1976) and Snow (1983). Younger

learners are said to receive better (i.e. more 'here and now', less complex) input (see Hatch 1976) than adults, input which provides the children with clearer L2 samples from which to learn syntax. Children also enjoy opportunities for language play with their native-speaking peers, through which they get phonological practice (Peck 1978). Moreover, it is argued that younger learners typically receive a larger amount of input, in some cases because earlier AO often also means greater LOR.

(4) *Neurological explanation.* There are two main positions in the literature regarding the effect of neurological factors on SLA. First, Penfield and Roberts (1959) and Lennenberg (1967) produced evidence to show that the two halves of the brain (the left and right hemispheres) become specialized for different functions around puberty, a process called lateralization. Prior to puberty, they argued, a critical period exists during which the brain is more plastic and allows, among other things, the transfer of a function from one hemisphere to the other when the former has been injured and for new patterns of behaviour to be efficiently processed. This loss of plasticity is significant in that it signals a loss of flexibility of 'neurophysiological programming of neuromuscular coordination mechanisms' (Scovel 1981, p. 37), something that would be expected to adversely affect an individual's ability to control the articulators necessary in SL pronunciation. The second approach is exemplified by Seliger (1978) (with a multiple critical periods hypothesis) and Scovel (1981, 1988), among others, who agree that SLA abilities decline with loss of neurological plasticity, but they feel that there is likely more than one neurophysiological cause of the loss of plasticity, not just lateralization. Scovel (1988) singles out six:

> hemisphere specialization, the proportionately rapid growth of the brain compared to body growth, increased production of neuro-transmitters, the process of myelinization, the proliferation of nerve pathways in the cerebral cortex, and the speeding up of synaptic transmission. (p. 62)

Walsh and Diller (1981), on the other hand, ascribe loss of plasticity to the fact that different types of neurons in the brain have different maturational rates.

As we have come to expect, there is some evidence to counter each of these explanations. With regard to the social-psychological considerations, it is probably a mistake to assume that children are not subject to some of the same inhibitions as adults. Indeed, Hatch, in writing about Young's Alma (1978, p. 12), and Kubota (1987), in reserching Japanese children's acquisition of English in the United States, point to the fact that not all children have as uniformly an easy time with SLA as folklore would lead us to believe. (See also Yumoto 1984.) Furthermore, we need more precision in the area of social-psychological factors: just which of these factors, in what combination, and to what degree are supposed to affect learning and why?

As for the cognitive explanation, there appears to be some disagreement as to when the formal operations stage is attained. Piaget claimed the stage was attained by age fourteen to fifteen; Ausubel says ten to twelve and that some individuals never do attain it. Indeed, some developmental psychologists even question whether Piaget's stages exist at all. Also, the cognitive explanation assumes that general problem-solving abilities are not involved in child language development, yet some claim they are (Karmiloff-Smith 1979).

Finally, we would expect to see evidence of different acquisition processes and sequences (e.g. different errors or stages) if children and adults were learning in different ways, but there is little evidence of this to date, at least where child/adult SLA comparisons are involved. (For discussion, see Newport 1984; Clahsen and Muysken 1986; Duplessis, Solin, Travis and White 1987; Clahsen 1988; Jordens 1988.) There is, in fact, some evidence that they are acquiring a second language the same way (Cook 1973; Fathman 1975; Ritchie 1978; Bley-Vroman, Felix and Ioup 1988). More research is needed.

Some challenge to the claim that it is the superior input that favours language learners is the observation that younger learners may receive simpler input, but older learners may obtain better (more comprehensible) input because they are more likely and better prepared to negotiate it (Scarcella and Higa 1982). In reference to the argument that children benefit by receiving more input, there are studies in which it is reported that adult second language learners receive abundant input (Schmidt 1981; Pavesi 1984) and yet still fall far short of target-level performance.

As for the first neurological explanation, since the work of Penfield and Roberts, lateralization has been shown to start prenatally and end around age five (Krashen 1973), yet most sensitive period effects appear later than this. (See Scovel 1988, however, for a different interpretation of when lateralization ends.) With regards to the case for the second neurological argument, there is currently no direct link between known neurophysiological changes and specific changes in language learning abilities (Whitaker, Bub and Leventer 1981). Thus, this position is undeniably somewhat speculative, given the current state of knowledge and instrumentation problems in neurophysiology (see Jacobs 1988a,b, however, for a review of recent progress in this area). Also, there are accounts in the anthropological literature of other societies where adults do achieve native-speaker abilities in second languages (Sorensen 1967; Hill 1970), suggesting that it might even be culturally induced expectations, more than age-bound neurological barriers, which impede older-learner SLA.

Whatever the explanation, a conclusion not reached by Krashen et al., but which we think is supported by the data, is that children ultimately win out not just quantitatively but also qualitatively: only child starters seem capable of attaining native-like SL abilities. The evidence here is clearest for phonology but also exists for accent recognition, listening comprehension and syntax, with suggestively similar tentative findings for collocation, discourse and pragmatics. The crucial findings for resolving this issue are those documenting adult starters' failure to reach native-like standards. Contrary to what several writers have recently claimed, the early rate advantage for adults no more negates the idea of sensitive periods for SLA than it does for first language development. There, older children, such as isolates and deaf children starting sign language late, also start off faster, presumably because of their greater cognitive maturity. If they begin too late, however (around age ten, according to Curtiss 1980), they stop far short of native-like abilities, a fact widely accepted as evidence of maturational constraints on child language development (see Long 1988a for review).

While various explanations of the age relationship have been proposed, the idea that there exist biological constraints on SLA currently seems the most tenable one at present. It, too, is not without problems, however, in addition to the ones mentioned above; principally the lack of any known neurological changes clearly coinciding with changes in SLA ability, a state of affairs we have to assume reflects the relative paucity of research in both areas, not the absence of such relationships. Also, if adult SLA really is different, there should be more evidence than has currently been reported of different processes at work. (For interesting initial work in this area, see Clahsen and Muysken 1986, and Bley-Vroman, Felix and Ioup 1988.) Longitudinal child–adult interlanguage comparisons will clearly be key, yet are virtually nonexistent to date.

Obviously in this area, as in many others, much work remains to
be done.

6.3 Aptitude

Regardless of the age of the learner, what is undeniable is that individuals learn languages at different rates. What is contested, however, is
just why this is the case. In this section we will consider whether at
least some of the differences can be attributed to language-specific
aptitude.

According to Carroll, a psychologist whose name is perhaps most
often associated with research on language aptitude:

> Aptitude as a concept corresponds to the notion that in approaching
> a particular learning task or program, the individual may be thought
> of as possessing some current state of capability of learning that task
> – if the individual is motivated, and has the opportunity of doing so.
> That capability is presumed to depend on some combination of more
> or less enduring characteristics of the individual. (1981, p. 84)

The plurality of the term 'enduring characteristics' suggests that
aptitude is multidimensional. After the application of a statistical
procedure called multiple regression analysis[3] to separate measures
of aptitude, Carroll proposed that foreign language aptitude consisted
of four independent abilities:

1. phonetic coding ability – an ability to identify distinct sounds, to
   form associations between those sounds and symbols representing
   them, and to retain these associations;
2. grammatical sensitivity – the ability to recognize the grammatical
   functions of words (or other linguistic entities) in sentence
   structures;
3. rote learning ability for foreign language materials – the ability
   to learn associations between sounds and meanings rapidly and
   efficiently, and to retain these associations; and
4. inductive language learning ability – the ability to infer or induce
   the rules governing a set of language materials, given samples
   of language materials that permit such inferences. (1962 in
   1981, p. 105)

Perhaps the best known test of language aptitude is Carroll and
Sapon's Modern Language Aptitude Test (MLAT). Designed to

measure foreign language aptitude in adolescents and adults, the MLAT consists of five subtests:

1. Number learning – Examinees are asked to memorize names for certain numbers in an invented language and then to write the numbers down for novel combinations they hear.
2. Phonetic script – Examinees associate graphic symbols and English speech sounds.
3. Spelling clues – Examinees must detect an English word when given a phonetic rendition of it.
4. Words in sentences – Examinees identify the word or phrase in one sentence that functions the same way as a word/phrase in another sentence.
5. Paired associates – Examinees study foreign-language translations for native-language words for a short time and then take a multiple-choice test in which they must recognize the translations.

Thus, the first three of the four proposed components of language aptitude are measured by at least one of the above subtests, with the fourth – inductive language learning ability – being reflected in the MLAT only weakly, by Carroll's own admission.

Another well-known language aptitude test, Pimsleur's Language Aptitude Battery (1966a), specifically designed for adolescents, consists of six parts:

1. grade point average
2. interest
3. vocabulary
4. language analysis
5. sound discrimination
6. sound-symbol correspondence

These six parts are designed to tap the three components of language aptitude Pimsleur alleges to exist (1966, p. 182):

1. verbal intelligence, which measures familiarity with words and an ability to reason analytically about verbal material (van Els et al. 1984)
2. motivation
3. auditory ability

An obvious difference between Carroll's and Pimsleur's views of aptitude is whether motivation is seen to be independent of aptitude (Carroll's position) or an integral part of it and therefore something which should be measured in an aptitude test, as Pimsleur has done in Part 2 of his Language Aptitude Battery (LAB).

Another difference is the degree to which verbal intelligence is seen to contribute to aptitude. Pimsleur considers it an important part of language aptitude and includes two subtests (3 and 4) whose primary purpose is to measure verbal intelligence. Carroll does not consider verbal intelligence a necessary component of aptitude although he acknowledges that the Spelling Clues subtest of the MLAT, which relies partly on verbal intelligence and vocabulary knowledge, can be a useful predictor.

Nevertheless, despite the differences which exist between the MLAT and LAB, both 'have been shown to make a consistent and substantial contribution to the prediction of student achievement in a variety of adolescent and adult language training programs' (Wesche 1981, p. 120). Gardner (1980), for instance, reports a median correlation of $r = 0.41$ between the MLAT scores of Anglophone Canadian children in different schools throughout Canada and the children's grade levels in French. Aptitude thus accounts for approximately 16 per cent of the total variance in grade levels.[4] Such a finding is not unique. Carroll himself notes that the predictive validity coefficients for aptitude tests typically range from .4 to .6 against criterion measures of foreign language achievement, thus accounting for 16–36 per cent of the variance predicted. This is a substantial amount of the variance and is possibly even more impressive since, as Carroll has pointed out, squaring the coefficients more likely underestimates the true predictable variance.

Despite the evidence that these tests are successful in predicting performance in foreign language courses, there are some who are of the opinion that the MLAT and LAB are not measuring innate aptitude for language proficiency. One of the reasons for this opinion is a perception of language proficiency which goes beyond a knowledge of the grammar and sound systems featured prominently in these aptitude tests, to include an ability to communicate, an ability not explicitly assessed in language aptitude tests (Ellis 1985). It may be, however, that the ability to communicate is not evaluated in the criterion measure either, often a final grade in a foreign language course. Indeed it is plausible that language aptitude tests work well to predict success because there is a concordance of tasks between the test and formal classroom study (Spolsky 1979; Wesche 1981), not because the test is measuring some innate linguistic ability.

To expand upon this point, it would be worthwhile to reintroduce Cummins's (1979) distinction between cognitive/academic language proficiency (CALP) and basic interpersonal communication skills (BICS). These are two quite distinct areas comprising language proficiency, Cummins believes. It may be that language aptitude tests assess CALP well but ignore BICS, a point similar to the one Krashen (1981a) makes in suggesting that aptitude relates only to learning, not acquisition, a distinction we will explore further in Chapter 7. Krashen claims that the kind of skills tested by the MLAT are those demanded by formal study of a language. The MLAT may work well to predict CALP, then, but not BICS.

The CALP/BICS distinction may also help to elucidate Genesee's (1976) finding that intelligence is related to the more academic L2 skills of reading, grammar and vocabulary, but not to native speakers' rating of learners' oral production. In other words, intelligence may relate better to CALP than to BICS. This would also explain Ekstrand's (1977) higher correlations between intelligence and reading, dictation and writing than those between intelligence and listening comprehension and oral production. It would also help to clarify Genesee and Hamayan's (1980) report that intelligence is less strongly correlated with the second language learning of young learners than it is with older learners. Presumably younger learners would be less concerned with CALP than with BICS.

Such evidence has led Neufeld (1978) to suggest that all humans are equipped to master basic language skills, but that humans vary with respect to their mastery of the higher-level skills and that the extent of the mastery of these latter skills is determined by an individual's intelligence. For Neufeld, then, there is no specific innate faculty called language aptitude. This position is essentially similar to that of Oller and Perkins (1978b), who dispute the existence of a special aptitude for language acquisition. They argue that there is a general factor which accounts for most of the variance in a wide variety of language proficiency measures and that this 'g' factor is the same as a general or 'g' factor of intelligence.

Carroll (1981) has countered that although there may be overlap between intelligence and aptitude, he is convinced they are not identical. For one thing, Carroll reminds us, foreign language aptitude measures correlate differently with foreign language achievement than does intelligence. This point is borne out in a study of foreign language aptitude by Skehan (1982) showing that aptitude is separable from verbal intelligence and that the former accounts for more of the success of foreign language learning than the latter.[5]

Skehan's study was conducted as a follow-up to the Bristol Language Project (Wells 1985), in which the first language development of 125 children was studied longitudinally. Skehan administered a test of general verbal intelligence and a battery of aptitude tests to as many of the original subjects as possible of the older cohort from the Bristol Project (*n* = 64). As the children went on to study in secondary school, Skehan found a high correlation between language aptitude and foreign language achievement, although this was not surprising given that the achievement ratings were only available for those children who had elected to continue their foreign language study (*n* = 23). More interesting findings were the positive correlations between first language development and foreign language aptitude (*n* = 53) and between the latter and certain family class indices.

Skehan (1985) attributes these findings to several factors. He feels that aptitude tests are good predictors of achievement because not only do they tap relevant linguistic skills and knowledge (and thus outperform tests of verbal intelligence in predicting language learning success), but also work well because they draw on examinees' ability to use decontextualized language. He arrives at the latter deduction through indirect evidence which suggests that there are few family class-linked differences among children's oral language ability, but there are class-linked differences among children's disembedded use of language, such as 'literacy-linked activities and the use of language as a tool to look in on itself' (Donaldson 1978). In other words, the reason for a differential effect of social class is not membership in the class itself but rather that class differences do relate to differences in children's ability to handle decontextualized language. This ability is revealed on scores of aptitude tests and is an ability which is important for later school success. Skehan concludes:

> To sum up, then, two main points are being made about foreign language aptitude. First, such aptitude, as presently conceived, is a hybrid, combining both a language processing ability as well as the capacity to handle decontextualised material. Aptitude tests are effective predictors because both these component abilities are important for language learning success. Further, the origin of both types of ability can be traced to a relatively early period in life. Second, the analysis of aptitude presented here is general enough to be relevant not simply to formal learning situations, but also to more communicatively oriented classrooms as well as 'acquisition' settings. (1985, p. 17)

Thus, Skehan has addressed two of the major criticisms of language aptitude. His definition is broad enough, as he indicates, to apply to more than formal learning situations. In fact, he documents this claim by noting that Reves (1982) has shown that aptitude measures were 'first-rank predictors' in an acquisition situation.

Second, Skehan's research and perspective could explain the findings reported earlier suggesting that intelligence is more related to the academic/literacy skills than to oral/aural proficiency. According to Skehan, it is not intelligence but aptitude that explains this. While aptitude and intelligence may overlap, it is the former which provides a more precise assessment of language processing ability and the ability to handle decontextualized language, and is therefore a more powerful predictor of language learning success than intelligence.

Aptitude is usually considered a cognitive variable. Also important in explaining variable performance among SL learners are affective variables. Indeed, as Henning (1983) has noted, meta-analyses of studies of general classroom achievement have generally attributed 25–50 per cent of the variance in achievement to cognitive factors, leaving the same 25–50 per cent of the variance to be explained by affective, personality and other non-cognitive indicators (Khan 1969). Given this fact, we are in agreement with Henning that it is reasonable to anticipate that in the case of foreign or second language learning, where perseverance is necessary for success, non-cognitive variables may even possess greater variance-explanatory power than studies of general classroom achievement.

In the next two sections, therefore, we will be exploring non-cognitive explanations for differential success. We will first consider social-psychological factors, preferring to use a hyphenated term since these factors relate both to an individual and to an individual as a member of a social group. After that we will examine personality factors. Thus, in our treatment of non-cognitive factors, we will avoid using the word 'affective'. We do this simply because the word is usually associated with feelings and emotions (McLaughlin 1985; H.D. Brown 1987), and what we will be considering does not easily bear such an appellation. Indeed, Scovel (1978) advises that feeling is 'but one ingredient in the complex and marvelous chemistry that creates a personality'. Moreover, researchers are not in total accord about the meaning of affect. For example, Leontiev (1981), unlike most other researchers, distinguishes among affect, emotion and feeling.

6.4 Social-psychological factors

As we have just seen, much of the initial research concerning individual variation centred on language aptitude. Gardner and Lambert

(1959) were pioneers in demonstrating that statistically significant and independent relationships could also be established between motivation/attitude and SLA. Although as Ellis (1985) notes, motivation and attitude are often indistinct in the literature, we will endeavour to treat them distinctly here, beginning with a review of the salient literature having to do with motivation and SLA.

6.4.1 Motivation

Gardner and Lambert's ideas about motivation were largely shaped by Mowrer's (1950) view of L1 acquisition. Mowrer attributed a child's success in acquiring an L1 to the child's quest for identity, initially with members of the child's immediate family and then later with members of the larger speech community. Borrowing the concept of identification from Mowrer, Gardner and Lambert proposed a construct they called *integrative motivation*. A learner is said to be integratively motivated when the learner wishes to identify with another ethnolinguistic group. By way of contrast to integrative motivation, Gardner and Lambert introduced the concept of *instrumental motivation*, in which the learner is motivated to learn an L2 for utilitarian purposes, such as furthering a career, improving social status or meeting an educational requirement.

According to Gardner and Lambert, an instrumentally oriented learner can be as intensively motivated as an integratively oriented one; however, they hypothesized that the latter orientation would be better in the long run for sustaining the drive necessary to master the L2. This hypothesis was borne out in their early studies in Canada and in certain contexts in the USA. Indeed, in a study of newly arrived foreign students at US universities, Spolsky (1969) discovered that the students' greater desire to be like speakers of English than like speakers of their own language was significantly correlated with the students' English proficiency. This led Spolsky to conclude that 'learning a second language is a key to possible membership of a secondary society: the desire to join that group is a major factor in learning' (1969, p. 282).

Although this is no doubt true, as Gardner and Lambert expanded the number of contexts they investigated, the perspective which held that integrative motivation was better than instrumental motivation was challenged. Students learning English as a foreign language in their Philippine study, for instance, were highly successful despite their having instrumental, not integrative motivation. Moreover, in another study they found that instrumental motivation to learn English worked very well for French-speaking children living in Maine and attending an American high school. Such findings led Gardner and Lambert to qualify their original statement about the superiority of having integrative motivation:

> It seems that in settings where there is an urgency about mastering a second language – as in the Philippines and in North America for members of linguistic minority groups – the instrumental approach to language study is extremely effective. (1972, p. 141)

Despite this qualification, reports continued to be made that suggested that even this was an understatement. Lukmani (1972) investigated the relationship between the English proficiency of Marathi-speaking high school students in India and their motivational orientation. Lukmani determined that those students with instrumental motivation outperformed those with integrative motivation on a test of English language proficiency. Research reported on by Izzo (1981 in McLaughlin 1985) also suggested that there are conditions under which instrumental motivation leads to more successful second language learning than does integrative, and Burstall (1975) found that her subjects' achievement in French was linked to both types of motivation.

Clement and Kruidenier (1983) have offered one explanation for these discrepant findings: ambiguity in the definition of integrative and instrumental motivation. They concur with Oller, Baca and Vigil (1977) that an example of the problem lies in such descriptions as 'having friends who speak English'. A subject selecting this as a reason for learning English could be said to be motivated by either type of motivation. A second cause Clement and Kruidenier advance for the discrepant findings is contextual factors. It makes sense, for example, that someone studying a target language as a foreign language would less likely aspire to integrate with the target-language community than someone for whom the target language was a second language. Thus the type of motivation and its strength are likely to be determined less by some generalized principle and more by 'who learns what in what milieu' (1983, p. 288).

Clement and Kruidenier's conclusion reminds us of Macnamara's observation ten years earlier:

> More pressing for most students than a general desire to be able to communicate at a future date is a specific desire to be able to communicate in some actual situation where what is being

communicated is of vital concern to the persons involved. (1973, pp. 64–5)

Cooper also stresses the importance of the language learning context: 'If most students had to know a given foreign language in order to accomplish some goal to them, then most would learn it' (1981, p. 133).

Genesee, Rogers and Holobow (1983) have discovered another angle to the issue of the relationship between motivation and context. These researchers asked adolescent English-speaking Canadian students why they were learning French as a second language and why they thought French-speaking Canadians wanted them to learn French. The results showed that the respondents' expectations of motivational support from the TL group emerged as significant, and in some cases, unique predictors of SL performance. Genesee, Rogers and Holobow concluded that social-psychological models of SLA need to consider the role of intergroup factors more seriously.

A final study worth mentioning in the area of motivation is Strong's (1984) research on Spanish-speaking children learning English in an American classroom. Strong found that the students' intensity of integrative motivation increased relative to their English language proficiency. A plausible explanation, Strong contends, is that motivation does not necessarily promote acquisition, but rather results from it: those who meet with success in SLA become more motivated to study. We will return to this theme later.

6.4.2 Attitude

As we stated earlier, Gardner and Lambert did not distinguish between motivation and attitudes in their early work. By factor analysing[6] responses from Anglophone students of French in Montreal on a whole battery of measures, Gardner and Lambert (1959) were able to identify two factors responsible for French proficiency. The first was aptitude and the second was a constellation of attitudes towards French Canadians, motivational intensity and an integrative motivation. It wasn't until two decades later that the relationship among the three variables in the second factor was redefined. At that time, Gardner (1979) claimed a linear relationship such that attitudes were said to affect motivation which in turn affected SLA. Thus, based on correlations, attitudes were said to have an important but indirect effect on SLA.

Of all possible attitudes which could have this indirect relationship with SLA, the one most extensively researched has been the learners' attitude towards speakers of the TL. Most of the Canadian studies demonstrated that a positive attitude towards the target language was related to SLA success in the Canadian bilingual setting (van Els et al. 1984, p. 119). Others, too, reported such relationships. For example, Scherer and Wertheimer (1964) showed that American college students' positive attitudes towards Germans and towards themselves speaking German were correlated with proficiency in German.

It may be, however, that attitudinal factors have relatively little influence on SLA by children, perhaps simply because attitudes are not fully developed in young learners. As Macnamara (1973, p. 37) put it: 'A child suddenly transported from Toronto to Berlin will learn German no matter what he thinks of Germans.' To lend empirical support for this assertion, we should point out that Genesee and Hamayan (1980) found no relationship between attitude factors and the proficiency in French of six-year-old Anglophone Canadians.

In a series of studies, Oller and his colleagues limited still further the claim that positive attitudes towards speakers of the TL correlate with successful SLA. In the first study (Oller, Hudson and Liu 1977), the results supported the prevailing view of the relationship between attitude and SLA: Chinese-speaking foreign students in the USA who had generally positive attitudes towards the target-language group were more proficient in ESL as determined by their scores on a cloze test. This was not the case, however, with a population of Mexican-American women living in Albuquerque, New Mexico (Oller, Baca and Vigil 1977). Women who rated Americans high on positive personal traits did more poorly on an English cloze test. Oller, Baca and Vigil attribute the differences in findings between the two studies to the fact that the Chinese were from a high socioeconomic class and were in the USA by choice, whereas the women were members of a lower socioeconomic stratum and might feel a 'colonized minority' and thus resent the Anglophone majority. Despite the resentment, they might be very eager to learn English 'to remove themselves from oppressive conditions brought about by their lack of English' (Gardner 1980, p. 266). Thus, in such circumstances, negative attitudes apparently do not detract from SLA.

In an attempt to see if the same sort of results would be obtained in a foreign language context, Chihara and Oller (1978) studied the attitudes of Japanese students of EFL living in Osaka. Results showed mostly weak correlations, with only two negatively significant, between factors distilled from the attitude measures and attained EFL proficiency. A similar finding was also reported by Cooper and Fishman (1977, p. 272), who found that positive attitudes towards English speakers were largely irrelevant to Israelis learning and using English.

Gardner (1980) offers as an explanation for these apparently contradictory findings that the different social contexts would appear to influence the outcomes. For example, all the studies he was involved with in the Canadian context were based on Anglophone students learning French as a second language in a bilingual context. The effect of attitudes might be much stronger in such a context where there is much more of an opportunity for contact between learners and TL speakers than in a foreign language context where the opportunities are more limited.

Thus, the conclusion we draw at this point with regards to the effect of attitudes on SLA is not unlike that of motivation. The SL versus FL context and various characteristics of the populations within those contexts appear to make a non-causal difference as to the degree of impact of attitudes on SL success.

Another finding parallel to that revealed in our discussion of the literature on motivation is attested to in a study by Hermann (1980). After studying a group of 750 German children learning EFL, she adduced evidence which suggested that those children who had been studying English for five years showed a significantly higher level of positive attitude towards the target culture than a group who had just started to study English. Moreover, the lower-proficiency learners showed significantly more prejudice than the higher-proficiency group.

Hermann formulates a 'resultative hypothesis' to explain her findings: 'The mere satisfaction [a learner] derives from his achievement of the learning task may influence his attitude to the ethnolinguistic group in question and even result in a change of such attitude' (p. 249). Hermann's hypothesis also serves as an explanation for the fact that Savignon (1972) found no correlation between early attitudes and measures of final achievement of American college students in their first semester of French study at the University of Illinois. However, as this study progressed, the correlation between their attitude and their achievement in French increased substantially. These reports suggest that success in SLA may breed positive attitudes towards the TL group, just as Strong (1984) has contended that success contributes to heightened motivation to acquire a SL.

As already mentioned, most of the research in the area of attitudes and SLA deals with the language learners' views of the TL group; however, there are other sources of and targets for attitudes which come into play when people are engaged in SLA. As Spolsky (1969) has maintained:

> In a typical language learning situation, there are a number of people whose attitudes to each other can be significant: the learner, the teacher, the learner's peers and parents, and the speakers of the language. Each relationship might well be shown to be a factor controlling the learner's motivation to acquire the language. (p. 237)

We turn our attention now to what research does exist in other areas *vis-à-vis* attitudes.

(1) *Parents.* Several studies have investigated parental role in how attitudes towards speakers of the TL are developed. Gardner (1960) showed that Anglophone students learning French as a second language in Montreal possessed attitudes which were reflective of their parents' attitudes towards French Canadians. Feenstra (1969) went a step further and produced evidence not only that Anglophone Canadian children adopted their parents' attitudes but also that these attitudes towards the French Canadian community affected the children's achievement in learning French. Similarly, Stern (1967) reported that children's success in Welsh-medium schools was directly related to parents' attitudes towards the Welsh language.

(2) *Peers.* The attitudes of peers, too, can affect learners' acquisition of a second language. Elias-Olivares (1976 in McLaughlin 1985) relates how second-generation Mexican-Americans prefer to use *calo* dialect or to code-switch rather than to use the standard Spanish they were learning in their bilingual classroom. In fact, older users of calo made fun of the schoolchildren who attempted to speak the standard variety. Shuy, Wolfram and Riley (1967) studied social dialects in Detroit and found that dialect patterns cluster according to age, sex and socioeconomic status. Such patterns are presumably due to a large extent to the influence of peers.

(3) *Learning situation.* C. Brown's (1983) research suggests that learners' attitudes towards the learning situation affected their degree

of success. Moreover, she determined that the attitudes, and therefore the consequences of the attitudes, were different for older versus younger learners. Other studies of learners' attitudes towards the course of instruction have been conducted by Mueller and Miller (1970), Gardner et al. (1976) and Bourgain (1978 cited in van Els et al. 1984).

Schumann and Schumann (1977), in a review of diary studies, contend that learners can hold negative attitudes towards the learning situation if the teacher's agenda is very different from the learners'. Sometimes this negativity becomes severe enough that learners abandon language study completely.

(4) *Teachers.* Teachers' attitudes towards learners, of course, can also affect the quality and quantity of the learning which takes place. In fact, Tucker and Lambert (1973) consider teachers' attitudes even more important than parental or community-wide attitudes in influencing the outcome of instructed SLA. Research reviewed by Brophy and Good (1974) indicates that teachers have differential expectations regarding the performance of children who vary in such characteristics as ethnicity. One study (Jackson and Costa 1974) reported on in McLaughlin (1985), for instance, revealed that teachers praised and encouraged Anglophone students more often than Chicanos and asked the former more questions than the latter. In another, teachers tended to call on non-Asian more than Asian students (Sato 1982b).

(5) *Ethnicity.* One's ethnic group membership might also determine attitudes and behaviour toward members of other groups (Giles, Bourhis and Taylor 1977), and these in turn might affect SL attainment. For example, Gatbonton (cited in Segalowitz and Gatbonton 1977, p. 82) found that French Canadians who reported strong ethnic feeling had lower proficiency in producing English ð and θ than those who were less ethnically oriented.

Beebe's (1977) work has demonstrated that the ethnicity of an L2 learner's listener will have an effect on the L2 learner's speech performance. Beebe found that the Thai spoken by ethnic Chinese sounded more Chinese when they were speaking to an ethnic Chinese interviewer than when they were speaking to an ethnic Thai interviewer. Giles's Social Accommodation Theory offers an explanation for this phenomenon. According to the theory, speech shifts occur in conversation, resulting either in convergence in which speakers modify their speech to become more similar to their listeners (Giles and Smith 1979, p. 46), or in divergence through which linguistic differences are maintained or emphasized between interlocutors (discussed in Zuengler 1982).

Shifts in performance due to attitude can take place synchronically within a particular conversational exchange or diachronically over a period of time. Eisenstein (1982) conducted a study which revealed that students developed dialect sensitivity and attitude formation in a parallel fashion. Learners of ESL were tested on their ability to discriminate between dialects of English and the extent to which they could recognize dialects of greater or lesser prestige. Using a matched guise technique, Eisenstein showed that by the time the learners had reached advanced levels of English proficiency, they could discriminate between dialects and had assimilated attitudes of native English speakers towards those dialects to an amazing extent.

Changes in attitudes can be deliberately encouraged as well. Indeed, enhancing attitudes of groups towards one another is usually an explicitly stated objective of proponents of bilingual education. Cziko, Lambert and Gutter (1979), in an investigation of the stability of attitudes, compared Anglophone students in a French immersion programme in Canada to non-immersion Anglophone students. The immersion students perceived themselves to be more similar to Francophone Canadians than did the non-immersion students. Thus, Cziko et al. conclude that the immersion programme experience has resulted in a shift of attitudes, 'reducing the dividing influences of ethnicity' (Snow with Shapira 1985, p. 8).

Snow and Shapira also discuss two other important studies on the development and change of ethnolinguistic attitudes. Genesee's (1983) research supports Cziko et al.'s earlier finding in that Anglophone students in early immersion programmes had more positive attitudes towards French Canadians than did the non-immersion students. A significant new finding, however, is that the attitudes of immersion students in later grades resemble those of the non-immersion Anglophones. Genesee feels that this attitude change takes place due to the absence of social contact between Anglophone and Francophone Canadians, something which is necessary for sustaining positive attitudes. Day (1980) lends further support to there being a developmental shift in attitudes among children. Day investigated kindergartners' and first-graders' preference for Hawaii Creole English and Standard English in two different elementary schools in urban Honolulu. Children in a higher socioeconomic neighbourhood school preferred Standard English, whereas only the first-graders in a lower socioeconomic school preferred Standard English. The kindergartners in the latter school expressed a preference for, and had positive attitudes toward, Hawaii Creole English. Day attributes this disparity to a switch in attitudes and preferences of children from the less-advantaged neighbourhood occurring between kindergarten and first grade due to the social conditioning the children receive at school, as well as to parental influence.

Thus far in our discussion of social-psychological factors which influence SLA, we have been content to consider each factor in turn. We should not fail to mention here that there are SLA theories that embrace constellations of such factors and indeed perceive social-psychological factors as being central to an understanding of SLA. Gardner's (1985) 'socio-educational model' is one of these. The model focuses on the social-psychological processes involved in learning a second language. Gardner views SLA 'as an important social phenomenon' (p. 176). Since one's identity is very much bound up with the language one speaks, the process of acquiring a second language forces a re-evaluation of one's self-image and the successful integration of new social and cultural ideas. (For a discussion of the model, see Au 1988 and Gardner 1988.) Although we will discuss his theory in much more detail in Chapter 7, we should also acknowledge Schumann's acculturation model as belonging in this category. Schumann considers the attitude of the second language learning group as one factor of many that contribute to the social distance or proximity between the two groups. Schumann posits that it is the social distance which affects the degree to which a second language learning group acquires the language of a particular TL group.

One of the difficulties with Schumann's hypothesis lies in measuring social distance. How can one determine the weight that positive or negative attitudes contribute to social distance, and how can relative distances be quantified? One solution has been offered by Acton (1979). Arguing that people act on their perceptions of social distance, not actual social distance, Acton developed the Professed Difference in Attitude Questionnaire which asks learners to respond to three dimensions of distance: (1) distance between themselves and their countrymen in general, (2) distance between themselves and the members of the target culture in general, and (3) distance between their countrymen and members of the target culture. Acton claims that the Questionnaire results are very successful at identifying the good language learners within a group.

Acton's solution reminds us of Genesee, Rogers and Holobow's (1983) conclusion that what is significant is the learner's perception of motivational support. While Acton's solution to the problem of measuring social distance may be satisfactory, it raises a very nettlesome issue in the area of social-psychological factors, namely that of measurement. Is it possible that we are not getting clear-cut results in much of the research in the area due to the inadequacy of our instrumentation? Equally worrisome is the prospect that some of the significant results we are getting might be artificial artefacts of the instrumentation. (See Oller 1982 and Gardner and Glicksman 1982 for discussions on the validity of measurement of attitudes and motivation.)

Oller (1981b) points out that unlike measuring language proficiency, the measurement of social-psychological variables is 'necessarily inferential and indirect' (p. 18). What usually transpires is that researchers administer carefully designed questionnaires to subjects. Subjects are asked to rate themselves according to certain scales or as to what extent they agree or disagree with certain statements.[7] Thus, obtaining reliable and valid measures is dependent upon learners' self-awareness and candour. Oller and Perkins (1978a) have been leading figures in questioning the validity of self-reports obtained in this way. They charge that there may be three sources of non-random variance 'which may inflate estimates of reliability and validity of those measures substantially' (1978a, p. 85). The first of these is the approval motive, or answering the questions in such a way as to win the approval of the administrator. The second source is when subjects answer the questions in a self-flattering rather than honest way, or how one wishes one was rather than how one is. The final source is response set, meaning the human tendency to give consistent, uncontradictory answers. In other words, once respondents answer a question having to do with a particular attitude one way, they are likely to strive to answer all other questions they perceive as probing the same attitude in a like manner, even if this consistency is not representative of their actual attitudes. None of these behaviours is thought to be practised as a result of intentional malice; however, it is clear that if any of them do influence the way learners respond to the questions, then serious questions about the validity of the findings are raised.

Oller and Perkins continue by suggesting that the findings concerning social-psychological measures may be due to learners' intelligence and language proficiency. Their argument is that a learner must be able to fully understand the questions in order to provide valid answers, but if the learner is able to do so, then his or her responses might be affected by one or more of the three sources of non-random variance discussed above.

Le Mahieu (1984) has schematized the two positions as follows:

Gardner:
| Variance in attitudes | cause → | Variance in motivation | cause → | Variance in L2 proficiency |

Oller and Perkins:
| Variance in L2 proficiency | cause → | Variance in attitudes |

However, as many have pointed out (Upshur, Acton, Arthur and Guiora 1978; Gardner 1980; Le Mahieu 1984), merely postulating sources of variance does not mean that they exist. In fact, Gardner has stated unequivocally that in several of his studies challenged by Oller and Perkins, he has demonstrated that social desirability has not played a role in subjects' responses. Moreover, Gardner has claimed that very few social-psychological factors, as measured by his Attitude Motivation Index, were correlated with the MLAT, indicating that language aptitude would not seem to have a bearing on the responses gathered by questionnaires. (For discussion see Gardner 1980; Gardner and Glicksman 1982; and Oller 1980, 1982.)

Ultimately, of course, one would like to have any measure of social-psychological variables validated against how people actually believe and behave. There is, however, no objective measure of these variables in existence, and self-reports are what we must rely on for now. However, even if there were an objective means for assessing social-psychological factors, correlating the assessments with language proficiency would not help us address all of our questions. This is because simple correlations are incapable of proving causal relationships. Thus, more convincing evidence of the link between social-psychological variables is unlikely to be made through the use of simple correlational analyses.

Perhaps at this point we should accept Le Mahieu's compromise schema:

| Variance in attitudes | cause → ← cause | Variance in L2 proficiency |

as at least a plausible reconciliation between the two positions detailed here on the role of social-psychological variables and SLA. What's more, if we replace the word 'attitudes' with 'social-psychological factors', such a schema seems not only to reconcile the two positions, but also offers a reasonable, if somewhat simplified, summary of the research we have reviewed in this section.

For much of the above discussion of social-psychological factors, we have been dealing with learners as members of social groups; for example, we have been addressing questions such as how the members of the language-learning group perceived the target-language group. It is convenient at this point to draw attention to the work of the Soviet psychologist Vygotsky and his colleagues, including Luria, Leontiev, Wertsch and Kohlberg. According to Lantolf and Frawley (1983), Vygotsky and his colleagues adopt the position that a human is from the outset social and then develops into an individual. Thus, rather than sharing the Piagetian view that humans are born individuals who become increasingly socialized, it is these researchers' view that humans develop from being like everyone else to being unique. In keeping with this view, we turn now to a discussion of personality traits. Instead of considering how membership in a group contributes to or impedes SLA, we will look at how certain traits individuals possess favour or disfavour SLA. The traits we will consider here are those that have been claimed by Rubin (1975), Naiman, Fröhlich, Stern and Todesco (1978) and others to be related to successful SLA.

6.5 Personality

(1) *Self-esteem.*   Shavelson, Hubner and Stanton (1976) proposed a ternary hierarchy to account for self-esteem, or the feeling of self-worth an individual possesses. At the highest level is global self-esteem, or the individual's overall self-assessment. At the medial level is specific self-esteem, or how individuals perceive themselves in various life contexts (education, work, etc.) and according to various characteristics (intelligence, attractiveness, etc.). At the lowest level is the evaluation one gives oneself on specific tasks (writing a paper, driving a car, etc.).

Heyde (1979) studied the effects of these three levels of self-esteem on performance on a French oral production task by American college students. She found that the students' performance correlated significantly with all three levels, the highest correlation existing for task self-esteem. One of the interesting sidepoints of Heyde's research was her discovery that the task self-esteem scores fluctuated from one class to the next. Assuming that the students' distribution in the classes was random, it would appear that the instructors had some effect on the students' self-evaluations.

(2) *Extroversion.*   Folk wisdom holds that extroverted learners learn at a faster rate than introverts. However, like so much of the work

in these areas, the results of empirical research are inconclusive. Naiman et al. (1978) found no significant correlation between scores on an extroversion/introversion measure and performance on listening comprehension and imitation tasks by Canadian self-professed good language learners. Likewise, Suter (1976) measured English pronunciation skills of foreign students studying in American universities and found no correlation with extroversion. Finally, in Busch's (1982) study of Japanese learners of English in Japan, a significant negative correlation was found between the subjects' English pronunciation and extroversion. In addition, introverts tended to have higher scores on the reading and grammar components of the standardized English test. Only on the oral interview task did certain of the subjects – junior college males who had 'tendencies towards extroversion' – have higher scores. Extroversion also correlated positively with the length of time students at an adult school spent studying English.

These studies are worth examining further for some of the issues they raise when researchers attempt to investigate the relationship between personality and SLA. First is the issue of measurement of the personality trait. Researchers in all three of these studies used the Eysenck Introversion–Extroversion Scale (Eysenck and Eysenck 1963). There are some very real concerns about the construct validity of this test (Naiman et al. 1978), that is, whether it is really adequately measuring the degree to which a person is extroverted. Naiman et al. noted the discrepancy between the researchers' opinions of the students and the results of the test (p. 67). We have already discussed Oller and Perkins's challenge regarding measures which purport to assess attitudes. The same concerns can be raised in this section with regard to personality measures. If they are invalid, then obviously any relation to SLA they reveal is likely spurious.

A second issue revolves around the SLA criterion measure used. As we have already indicated, Naiman et al.'s tests of SL proficiency were a listening comprehension and an imitation test. Suter correlated extroversion with a test of English pronunciation. In addition to administering an oral interview, Busch used a standardized exam with separate subtests of grammar, vocabulary, and comprehension and dictation. While all of these may be valid in their own right, none of them may provide a global measure of language proficiency; furthermore, the use of different criterion measures for each study makes comparison difficult.

Another issue we have already dealt with twice in this chapter. This pertains to differences arising from the context. While personality differences may be more impervious to contextual factors than social-psychological variables, it is conceivable that cultures value personality traits differently and this affects the way in which personality traits influence SLA. The three different groups studied – Anglophone Canadians learning French, foreign students learning English in the USA, and Japanese learning English in Japan – support all kinds of interesting speculations for why these particular correlations between extroversion and SLA were obtained.

Fourth, we have to entertain the possibility with personality variables, as we did with motivation, that they may be indirect as opposed to direct influences on SLA. We had an indication of this in Busch's study when she reported a positive correlation between the length of time spent studying English and extroversion. In other words, extroversion may not in itself lead to SL proficiency but may be a trait that encourages people to continue with their study, which in turn promotes SLA.

Having introduced these three studies for the issues they raise, we should now go on to review other studies which have addressed the link between extroversion and SLA. Certainly some studies have offered support for the common perception that extroversion leads to language-learning success. Metraux (discussed in Valette 1964) reported that the more successful English-speaking children learning French in France were talkative, outgoing and adaptable. The quiet, reserved, conformist children were slower learners. Chastain (1975), using the Marlowe–Crowne scale of reserved versus outgoing personality (Crowne and Marlowe 1974), found a positive correlation between scores on the scale for outgoing personality and course grades for language students in US universities studying German and Spanish, but not for students of French. Rossier (1976) found that extroverted Spanish-speaking adolescents became proficient in English oral fluency more rapidly than the introverted students. Strong (1983) also found a relationship between aspects of sociability or outgoingness and communication skills among kindergartners learning ESL in the United States. On the other hand, Swain and Burnaby (1976) obtained no correlation between Canadian kindergartners' traits of extroversion, sociability, and talkativeness and children's performance on French tests. Strong hypothesizes that all of the discrepancies in findings (and those not reported here but included in Strong 1983) could be due to differences in the nature of the language being assessed. When 'natural communicative language' is being assessed, a relationship is demonstrated between extroversion and performance. When 'linguistic task language' is being assessed, often no relationship is found; other times there is a relationship but only under the condition that linguistic task language is elicited in a more 'informal' way. Thus, Strong's explanation, reminiscent of Cummins' distinction between CALP and BICS, leaves intact the intuitively appealing link between extroversion and language learning, while at the same time offering a hypothesis which is eminently testable.

(3) *Anxiety.* While all humans presumably experience anxiety at one time or other, it is thought that certain people might be anxious more often than others, or have a more severe reaction to anxiety-producing situations such that language learning would be impeded. Chastain (1975) administered an anxiety scale consisting of combined items from the Sarason Text Anxiety Scale and the Taylor Manifest Anxiety Scale to American university students. He then correlated the students' scores on the scales with their final course grade in a foreign language they were studying. Although Chastain found that anxiety was a significant predictor only for those studying Spanish, the correlations were high across languages; however, the direction of correlation was not always consistent. In some cases the correlation was negative, indicating the deleterious effect of anxiety; in other cases anxiety seemed to enhance performance. Chastain's finding can be explained by Alpert and Haber's (1960) distinction between *facilitating* and *debilitating anxiety.* Scovel (1978, p. 139) comments:

> Facilitating anxiety motivates the learner to 'fight' the new learning task; it gears the learner emotionally for approval behavior. Debilitating anxiety, in contrast, motivates the learner to 'flee' the new learning task; it stimulates the individual emotionally to adopt avoidance behavior.

Kleinmann's (1977) study is a good example of the interplay between these two types of anxiety. Kleinmann found that ESL students who scored high on items designed to measure facilitative anxiety (e.g. 'Nervousness while using English helps me do better') employed certain structures in English which other members of their language group tended to avoid. In other words, those students who scored high on facilitative anxiety 'were emotionally equipped to approach (to "fight" in primitive terms) the very structures that their peers tended to avoid' (Scovel 1978, p. 137).

Another example of the schizophrenic nature of anxiety is K.M. Bailey's (1983a) diary study of her own competitiveness and anxiety while learning French as a foreign language. Bailey realized that sometimes her drive to compete with other members of the class hindered her SLA; other times it motivated her to try harder. The rationale she offered for the benefits of competitiveness was that facilitating anxiety was motivating. Bailey's experience suggests that it is not so much an individual's permanent predisposition to anxiety but rather the strength of the anxiety one is feeling at the moment which determines whether the anxiety is debilitating or facilitating. This brings to mind another useful dichotomy to emerge from the literature on anxiety, namely state anxiety, specific to a situation, versus trait anxiety, a permanent characteristic of one's personality (Spielberger, Gorusch and Lushene 1970). We will return to the *state* versus *trait* distinction later.

(4) *Risk-taking.* Perhaps closely related to a high tolerance for anxiety-inducing situations is the willingness to take risks. Rubin (1975) characterized good language learners as willing to guess, willing to appear foolish in order to communicate, and willing to use what knowledge they do have of the TL in order to create novel utterances. All of these could be termed risk-taking behaviours (Beebe 1983). However, just as too much anxiety can be debilitating, there might be an upper threshold to risk-taking beyond which further risk-taking could be detrimental. We say this in part due to the fact that people with a high motivation to achieve are moderate, not high, risk-takers (Kogan and Wallach 1967).

Beebe (1980a) has studied the risk-taking behaviour of Puerto Rican children learning ESL. Children who were experiencing difficulty with *do* insertion in WH-questions displayed significantly greater risk-taking behaviour with an English-speaking interviewer than with a bilingual English-dominant Hispanic interviewer. Risk-taking was defined by both the amount of talk by the children and the amount of information they volunteered. Beebe looks for an explanation in Giles's Accommodation Theory, discussed earlier, the central thesis of which is that people will unconsciously adjust their speech to their interlocutors. Thus, the bilingual children may have made their speech converge with that of the native speakers in order to gain the latter's approval.

Ely (1986) studied the risk-taking behaviour of university students enrolled in Spanish courses during the first two quarters of the academic year. Ely operationalized risk-taking as being evidenced by four behaviours:

> a lack of hesitancy about using a newly encountered linguistic element; a willingness to use linguistic elements perceived to

be complex or difficult; a tolerance of possible incorrectness or inexactitude in using the language; and an inclination to rehearse a new element silently before attempting to use it aloud. (p. 8)

Classroom participation was measured as the times a student said something in Spanish without being called on to do so.

Ely found that the students' risk-taking behaviour was a positive predictor of students' voluntary classroom participation. Furthermore, the students' level of classroom participation positively predicted oral correctness for the students studying Spanish during the first quarter, but not those who were at Level 2, studying in the second quarter.

(5) *Sensitivity to rejection.* The antithesis of risk-taking behaviour would appear to be a sensitivity to rejection – the subject's expectation of the 'negative reinforcing quality of others for himself' (Mehrabian 1970, p. 417). Naiman et al. (1978) hypothesized that those individuals who were sensitive to rejection might avoid active participation in language class, fearing ridicule by their classmates or teacher. This lack of participation would then translate into less successful SLA. Naiman et al. administered the Mehrabian Sensitivity to Rejection Scale (1970) to their subjects, 72 eighth-, tenth- and twelfth-grade Anglophone students of French as a SL. Subjects were asked to score items such as the following on the strength of their agreement or disagreement:

I enjoy discussing controversial topics like politics and religion.
I often visit people without being invited.

When their subjects' scores on this 24-item scale were correlated with their performance on a listening comprehension and imitation task, no significant relationship was found.

(6) *Empathy.* In order to assess their subjects' empathic capacity, Naiman et al. administered the Hogan empathy scale. Empathy relates to an individual's ability to put oneself in another's place. Naiman et al. found no correlation between their subjects' scores on Hogan's scale and their two criterion measures. However, Guiora, Lane and Bosworth (1967) reported a positive correlation between pronunciation accuracy of fourteen French teachers and their scores on the Micro-Momentary Expression (MME) test. The MME was designed to measure the frequency of subjects' perceptions of changes in facial expression in a film of a woman, a measure alleged by Guiora et al. to give an indication of the subjects' empathy. However, a subsequent

study (Taylor, Catford, Guiora and Lane 1969) found no correlation between another test of empathy (the Thematic Apperception Test) and the MME, and in another study (Guiora, Brannon and Dull 1972) scores on the MME correlated differently for different languages (positive for some, negative for others) and thus led Schumann (1975) to call into question the validity of the MME as a measure of empathy.

Guiora (1972) has given the role of empathy in SL learning a decidedly psychoanalytic interpretation. According to Guiora, just as a child develops a general ego, so the child also acquires a language ego. When the child is young, the ego boundaries are relatively flexible, but they become more rigid with age. When the language ego boundaries are flexible, a new accent is more readily adopted than when the boundaries are more fixed. Some adults, presumably those who are more empathic, are likely to have more *permeability of language ego boundaries*, since they are able to temporarily suspend the separateness of their identity, and that should in turn result in their having an advantage in FL pronunciation.

(7) *Inhibition.*   Closely aligned with the research on ego permeability and empathy were the experiments conducted by Guiora and his colleagues which were designed to induce states of lower inhibition and thus heightened empathy and permeability of ego boundaries. In one study, some subjects who had been given one and a half ounces of alcohol scored significantly better on a Thai pronunciation test (Standard Thai Procedure or STP) than those who had a non-alcoholic placebo. However, the subjects given two and three ounces of alcohol scored significantly lower than the control group. Guiora et al. (1972) attribute the one-and-a-half-ounce group's superior performance to the fact that the subjects' ego boundaries became more flexible (permeable) with a small ingestion of alcohol.

In another study (Schumann, Holroyd, Campbell and Ward 1978), subjects were hypnotized during an experiment. Earlier, Guiora had hypothesized that hypnosis would both lower inhibitions and make a person willing to modify a basic self-identification. No evidence, however, was found to indicate that hypnosis improved pronunciation, although subjects who rated themselves deeply hypnotized did perform significantly better than less well hypnotized subjects.

In 1980, Guiora, Acton, Erard and Strickland tested the effect of benzodiazepine (Valium) on subjects' performance on the STP. No direct effects on the pronunciation score were found, although as the dosage of Valium increased, the effect of having been tested by a particular experimenter also increased. The researchers interpret this finding as suggesting that Valium does affect permeability of ego boundaries, but in a different way than they had anticipated.

(8) *Tolerance of ambiguity.* The last personality variable which we will discuss is tolerance/intolerance of ambiguity. It is one of the few personality characteristics for which Naiman et al. (1978) reported significant correlations. Using Budner's (1962) scale, Naiman et al. found that tolerance of ambiguity scores were significantly correlated with scores on their listening comprehension task but not on their imitation task. Budner's test consists of a series of items to which subjects register their extent of agreement on a 7-point Likert scale ranging from strongly agree to strongly disagree. Two such statements are as follows:

An expert who doesn't come up with a definite answer probably doesn't know too much.
There really is no such thing as a problem that can't be solved.

It is not too difficult to imagine how tolerance of ambiguity relates to language learning. A language learner is confronted with new stimuli, many of which are ambiguous. Clarity is not usually immediately forthcoming, and persons with a low tolerance of ambiguity may experience frustration and diminished performance as a result. Another behavioural manifestation of a person with low tolerance of ambiguity is their making frequent appeals to authority, such as requesting a definition of every word of a passage, not being satisfied with comprehending the gist. Such people may also prefer to categorize phenomena rather than to calibrate them along a continuum (Levitt 1953). They may also tend to jump to conclusions (Frenkel-Brunswik 1949).

The previous two references were cited in Chapelle and Roberts (1986), who used the MAT-50, a 62-item Likert-type scale to measure tolerance of ambiguity (Norton 1975). Although this scale had not been used in previous SLA research, it was demonstrated to have high reliability and was found to be significantly positively correlated with Budner's scale by Chapelle and Roberts. These researchers administered the MAT-50 during the course of a semester to 61 ESL students enrolled in the Intensive English Institute at the University of Illinois. These students also took several English proficiency tests at the beginning of the semester, and again at the end. No significant correlations between tolerance of ambiguity and language proficiency scores were found at the beginning of the semester; however, significantly positive correlations were found between scores on the MAT-50 and proficiency scores from the end of the semester. Chapelle and Roberts submit that those students who are tolerant of ambiguity may be able to gain more from their L2 study than their less tolerant peers.

As we conclude our discussion of the personality variables, we have seen that the research indicates some traits, such as the last one we considered, appear to have some bearing on success in SLA. More often than not, however, the results *vis-à-vis* the other variables have been inconclusive. There are two observations we can make after our review of the literature, though. The first is that for some of the traits, the optimal setting for SLA is a point medial between two poles. Moderate anxiety can be facilitating, moderate risk-taking is linked with achievement, etc.

The second generalization which could be drawn from the personality studies is that it is difficult to predict an individual's behaviour in a particular situation based on global trait measurements. Although there no doubt exist personality traits which are fairly consistent, new research initiatives should attend to personality states as well as traits. Ely (1986) has noted that most of the research on the role of personality in second language learning has been concerned with general personality traits, not states. And as Schumann et al. (1978) suggest, 'being an alcoholic and being under the influence of alcohol could differentially relate to driving ability' (p. 148). Thus, it is now imperative that we give some attention to the interaction of person and situation.

6.6 Cognitive style

Closely aligned with personality is a variable called cognitive style, the preferred way in which individuals process information or approach a task. A number of different cognitive styles have been identified in the psychological literature, with a few of these being investigated for their SLA implications. Cognitive styles are typically discussed as if they were polarities; in reality, humans more likely show a tendency towards one pole or the other, with their scores on cognitive style tests arranged along a continuum between the poles. We use the term 'tendency' advisedly. As with the 'state' versus 'trait' distinction for personality variables, Witkin and Goodenough (1981) use the term 'mobility of functions' to refer to the fact that those usually favouring one particular cognitive style may switch to another in some circumstances.

To what extent a predilection towards a particular cognitive style or constellation of cognitive styles affects SLA is difficult to say. For one thing, the research results are mixed. Moreover, questions have been raised as to the adequacy with which a particular cognitive style is measured (Missler 1986). Finally, there is the question of the uniqueness of each cognitive style and, indeed, whether certain cognitive styles are distinct from general intelligence (Roach 1985). Perhaps the cognitive style that has received the most attention in the SLA literature, starting with Naiman et al. (1978), who did find a link between it and SL achievement, is field independence/dependence.

(1) *Field independence/dependence.* Naiman et al. administered the Hidden Figures Test, in which subjects are instructed to find simple geometric figures within complex designs. The perceptual challenge the subject faces is to be able to break up the visual field and keep part of it separate. This challenge was hypothesized to be analogous to a person learning an SL who has to isolate an element from the context in which it is presented. People are termed field dependent if they are unable to abstract an element from its context, or background field. In support of their hypothesis, Naiman et al. found that field-independent twelfth-grade students scored higher on imitation and listening comprehension tasks than did subjects who were field dependent.

Tucker, Hamayan and Genesee (1976) also reported that a trait factor which included field independence significantly predicted the French scores of Anglophone seventh-grade students on a standardized achievement test. By contrast, Bialystok and Fröhlich (1977, 1978) attributed a very minor role to field independence. However, their test involved only reading comprehension, which might account for the discrepancy.

Hansen and Stansfield (1981) administered a different measure of field independence/dependence, the Group Embedded Figures Test, to 293 college students enrolled in a first-semester Spanish course. They then correlated scores on this test with scores on linguistic, integrative (i.e. a cloze test) and communicative measures. All of the correlations were positive and significant for field independence.

When we discussed tolerance of ambiguity, we mentioned the Chapelle and Roberts (1986) study. In the same study these researchers investigated field independence by having their 61 subjects take the Group Embedded Figures Test (GEFT). The language proficiency ratings collected at the beginning and the end of the semester both correlated significantly with field independence, the latter rating being particularly strong.

Thus, most of the available evidence offers support for a relationship between field independence and second language learning success.

One disturbing consequence of this relationship is that both empathy and field independence have been linked with second language success, but the former is usually thought to be something a field-dependent person is more likely to exhibit. H.D. Brown (1977) offers an explanation that we have evoked before to explain other such conflicts. Brown suggests that field independence may be important to classroom learning and to performance on paper-and-pencil tests; however, when it comes to untutored SLA, field dependence may be more beneficial because successful SLA will be determined by how well the learner can communicate with speakers of the TL, and empathy will help in this regard. It is interesting to note that of their three measures of language proficiency, Hansen and Stansfield found the weakest link between field independence and communicative competence.

Saracho's (1981) inventory of relevant characteristics for field-independent and dependent learners would seem to add further support for Brown's claim. Saracho identifies field-dependent individuals as being strongly interested in people; they get closer to the person with whom they are interacting and have a sensitivity to others. Field-independent individuals, on the other hand, are oriented toward active striving, appear to be colder and more distant, and have strong analytic skills.

Some researchers have suggested that the tendency to field independence or dependence may be culture bound. Ramirez, Herold and Castaneda (1974) link field dependence – they term it field sensitivity – with Mexican-American culture. However, Fradd and Scarpaci (1981) found that students from Latin American countries in their study of University of Florida students were not significantly more field-dependent than their non-Latin counterparts.

By way of contrast, Hansen (1984) did find cultural differences for this cognitive style. Hansen studied 286 subjects between the ages of fifteen and nineteen in six Pacific island cultures. She found that Hawaiian subjects were more field-independent than Samoan, Tongan, Fijian, Indian-Fijian and Tahitian subjects. Hansen's finding provides some evidence for Cohen's (1969) hypothesis that the more analytic style develops in highly industrial and technological societies, whereas field dependence is more typical of agrarian societies.

(2) *Category width.* The cognitive style of category width refers to certain people's tendency to include many items in one category, even some that may not be appropriate (broad categorizers), or to other people's tendency to exclude items from categories even when they may belong (narrow categorizers).

Category width is often measured by Pettigrew's Width Scale (1958), which consists of twenty multiple-choice items for which subjects are asked to estimate some variable based on the information given. For example, subjects read:

> Ornithologists tell us that the best guess of the average speed of birds in flight would be about 17 miles per hour. What do you think is the speed in flight of the fastest bird?
>
> 1. 25   2. 105   3. 73   4. 34

Scoring of the items is based on how far the particular alternative is from the given mean of the category. Those subjects who consistently choose the alternatives farthest from the mean are considered broad categorizers.

H.D. Brown (1973) and Schumann (1978d) have hypothesized that broad categorizers would likely commit many errors of overgeneralization, whereas narrow categorizers may formulate more rules than are necessary to account for TL phenomena. One's categorizing pattern may also be related to one's degree of risk-taking. Through analogy to risk-taking, Naiman et al. (1978) hypothesized that the best learners would neither generalize too much nor too little. Naiman et al. were not able to adduce empirical support for their hypothesis based on subjects' performance on their two measures of language proficiency. Nonetheless, it is still intuitively appealing to connect this particular cognitive style and SLA. Research using different dependent variables – i.e. measures of language proficiency – is needed.

(3) *Reflectivity/impulsivity.* Individuals who have a reflective cognitive style tend to mull things over when making a decision. Conversely, an impulsive person tends to make a quick guess when faced with uncertainty. According to H.D. Brown (1980), the Matching Familiar Figures Test (MFFT) (Kagan et al. 1964) is most often used to measure reflectivity/impulsivity. Subjects are presented with a figure and then a number of facsimiles. Subjects' response time in making a match is considered a measure of this cognitive style. Subjects who take longer, but make fewer errors, are considered reflective; those with the opposite pattern are considered impulsive.

Not surprisingly, Messer (1976) reports that impulsive children make more errors in reading their mother tongue than children whose cognitive style is reflective. Equally understandable are the results of a study by Doron (1973), who found that adult ESL students who were considered reflective on the basis of their MFFT scores were more accurate readers than those who were classified as impulsive.

(4) *Aural/visual.*[8] This cognitive style refers to a person's preferred mode of presentation: aural or visual. Levin et al. (1974) observed that many learners could be considered bimodal, i.e. learning via one mode or the other does not contribute appreciably to a difference in outcome. But for a sizeable minority, approximately 25 per cent of all learners, the mode of instruction clearly does influence their success as learners.

Lepke (1977), reporting on a study of university students in the US learning German, claimed that when students were taught through their preferred modality, they performed better. In another study reported by Lepke (1977), French students at a junior college in Texas not only performed better when they had a choice of modality presentation, but also there was a substantial increase in enrolment in language courses over what there had been when students' preference did not determine the modality of instruction.

A useful tool for diagnosing this cognitive style is Edmond's Learning Style Identification Exercise (ELSIE), developed by Reinert (1976, 1977). ELSIE is designed for native English speakers studying a foreign language. Fifty words are read to each subject, who then classifies each word as to whether upon hearing the word he or she (a) has a mental image of the concept represented by the word, (b) has a mental image of the word spelled out, (c) receives meaning of the word from the sound without accompanying image, or (d) has a fleeting kinesthetic reaction. Subjects usually have high scores in two areas and low scores in the other two. Those subjects who score high in the auditory category may find speed reading difficult; conversely, students who obtain high scores in the kinesthetic area are usually compulsive note takers.

(5) *Analytic/gestalt.* In 1974, Hatch made a distinction between learners who are data-gatherers and those who are rule-formers. The former are fluent but inaccurate producers of the TL; the latter are much more halting in their use of TL but more accurate as well. Observing a similar distinction, Peters (1977) has demonstrated that children approach the SL learning task in different ways. Some children seem to take language word by word, analysing it into components; others approach language in a more holistic or gestalt-like manner. Peters' subject Minh, a young Vietnamese boy, was an example of a learner

with a gestalt style. Minh learned characteristic intonation contours for TL phrases before he learned to render all the segmentals. To be sure, Minh would articulate certain words in phrases or sentences, but he also used 'filler syllables' between those words as place-holders so that he could preserve the correct intonation contour. Peters portrays his performance as Minh's learning the tune before the words.

Ventriglia (1982) makes a three-way distinction among beaders, braiders and orchestrators. Beaders are the analytic learners who learn the meaning of each word and then string them together to make meaning. Braiders are more holistic in their approach in that they assimilate language in chunks and are more daring about using them in social contexts than their more cautious counterparts, the beaders. Orchestrators process the TL neither by words nor by chunks; rather, they attend to the sound patterns of the TL, paying particular attention to the meaning of the intonation contours initially. Orchestrators, like beaders, are likely to be slow to start producing the language but use sounds rather than words as the building blocks.

As we have noticed before, these three observers of SL learners' behaviour all seem to be alluding to the same type of phenomenon: whether the language learner approaches the task of SLA from an analytical or synthetic perspective. This same distinction of cognitive style seems parallel to research which indicates brain hemisphere specialization.

6.7 Hemisphere specialization

In our earlier discussion of age-related factors in SLA, we introduced the notion of lateralization. Lateralization is a process whereby each of the two hemispheres of the brain becomes increasingly specialized. Research on the two cerebral hemispheres indicates that each hemisphere may be responsible for a particular mode of thinking. Evidence for this differentiation comes from studying the behaviour of patients who have had their left or right hemisphere injured; patients who, for reasons of preventing further seizures, have had their corpus callosum (the bridge between the two hemispheres) severed; and normal subjects who are given tasks (e.g. dichotic listening[9]) which ostensibly tap processing by one hemisphere or the other.

In almost all right-handed individuals, and approximately two-thirds of left-handed individuals, the left hemisphere specializes in logical, analytic thought which is processed linearly, e.g. subjects can report which of two stimuli came first in a sequence. The left hemisphere is also responsible for abstraction from a field (Hartnett 1975).

Conversely, the domain of the right hemisphere is appositional thought, which means that its basic processing mode is simultaneous or 'gestalt-synthetic'. The right hemisphere is specialized for spatial relations and for tasks which involve matching some part of a schema to a whole. In fact, images – be they visual, tactile or auditory – are perceived and remembered by subjects using their right hemisphere even when they find the images hard to describe or name, special talents of the left hemisphere (Hartnett 1975).

How these observations relate to SLA is that certain individuals perform relatively better on tests using one hemisphere or the other and thus are thought to be left- or right-hemisphere dominant. If this is the case, it might offer neurophysiological basis for those individuals who are more field-independent and analytic. Such individuals may be left-hemisphere dominant. Learners who are more field-dependent and holistic in their approach may then be more right-hemisphere dominant. Indeed, evidence at least for one of these associations comes from Cohen, Berent and Silverman (1973 cited in Hartnett 1985). These researchers report that electroconvulsive shock to the right hemisphere seems to reduce field dependence, while electroconvulsive shock to the left hemisphere seems to have the same effect on field independence.

Although not exactly related to individual differences, there is none-theless a body of neurolinguistic research which has been devoted to exploring the role of the right hemisphere in bilinguals. It stands to reason that if there is increasing lateralization as the brain matures, the way in which the hemispheres enter into the L1 and L2 process would differ. In particular, since it is generally agreed that the language centre of the brain is the left hemisphere, researchers have sought to identify the role of the right hemisphere in SLA (Seliger 1982; Genesee 1982). The right hemisphere, for example, may not only account for Minh's 'tunes', but may also be responsible for older learners' use of unanalysed formulaic expressions.

Most of the work in the area of SLA has dealt with testing the stage hypothesis (Krashen and Galloway 1978; Obler 1981). The stage hypothesis contends that the right hemisphere is involved in SLA, especially during the early stages. As one might expect, there are the two inevitable positions on this hypothesis. Research by Galloway and Scarcella (1979) and Galloway (1981a) suggests little involvement for the right hemisphere, with the exception, perhaps, of when students are learning to read a different orthographic system (Galloway 1981b). Wesche and Schneiderman (1982) and Schneiderman and Wesche (1983), on the other hand, found some support for the role of the right hemisphere in the early stages of SLA by adults. As Wesche and Schneiderman (1982) note, the field would be well-served by more rigorous methodology for studying lateralization in bilinguals [and monolinguals!] and by longitudinal research of first and second language acquirers. This is all the more important as Genesee (1988) points out that what has been studied to date is only how hemisphere specialization relates to language processing, not how it relates to language learning; the two may not be the same. Furthermore, even the best techniques for studying lateralization of function are problematic (Springer and Deutsch 1981). 'Finally there arises the inexorable and vexing question of what the results mean. Do they show that a capacity is lateralized? Or merely that one hemisphere is dominant for that capacity? And what exactly does "dominant" mean?' (Churchland 1986, p. 198). We have added these last three cautionary notes because it is important to realize that the 'right brain/left brain' dichotomy is oversimplified as are most dichotomies and that there are many difficulties in researching and interpreting these lateralization phenomena (Scovel 1988) that go unmentioned in the popular press.

6.8 Learning strategies

Perhaps a product of one's personality, cognitive style or hemisphere preference, the next category we will consider has been termed 'learning strategies' (Rubin 1975; O'Malley, et al. 1985a,b,c), 'learning behaviours' (Wesche 1977; Politzer and McGroarty 1985), 'cognitive processes' (Rubin 1981), and 'tactics' (Seliger 1984). We will use the first term since it was used in perhaps the earliest study in this area and it enjoys the widest currency today. Rubin (1975) uses learning strategies to mean 'the techniques or devices which a learner may use to acquire knowledge' (p. 43). Rubin goes on to delineate strategies she asserts good language learners use. Good language learners, according to Rubin, are willing and accurate guessers who have a strong desire to communicate, and will attempt to do so even at the risk of appearing foolish. Even though they are highly motivated to communicate, they also attend to form and meaning. Moreover, good language learners practise and monitor their own speech and the speech of others. Rubin is circumspect, however, and notes that the employment of these strategies depends upon the level of TL proficiency, the learner's age, the task, individual style, the context and possible cultural differences.

Indeed, Chesterfield and Barrows Chesterfield (1985) have demonstrated that learners' strategies do change over time. Furthermore, through the use of implicational scaling techniques, they found that their subjects, fourteen Mexican-American children, followed the same general sequence in the development of learning strategies.

Wesche (1977) recruited 37 English-speaking Canadian civil servants studying beginning French intensively. She obtained information on their learning strategies through the use of an observation grid, which was applied to videotaped classes, and through the use of in-depth structured interviews with a number of the subjects. When she correlated their learning strategies with their listening comprehension, speaking skills, and teachers' ratings, she discovered significant correlations for 'role-plays when using French, having a variety of different learning behaviors, discusses lesson material with other students, total number of occurrences of strategies and voluntarily repeats French sounds, words to oneself'. Wesche concludes that 'in the classroom, both the *diversity* of observed learning activity and the relative *amount* of such activity characterized the better students' (p. 363).

In 1981, Rubin refined her earlier position on learning strategies. The distinction she introduced was between actions which permit learning and those that actually contribute directly to learning. For example, if learners realize that practising is important, they may create opportunities for practice which then may lead to practising. Both behaviours are essential, but only the latter contributes directly to the learning process. Seliger (1984) makes a similar point when he distinguishes between macro-tactics and micro-tactics. The former result in situations whereby the learner may obtain data; the latter provide direct input for learning.

In 1985, O'Malley et al. (1985a) designed a study to identify the range, type and frequency of learning strategies used by beginning and intermediate ESL students. From the data they collected, they were able to make a distinction between metacognitive strategies, such as directing attention to the learning task or evaluating one's efforts, and cognitive learning strategies such as inferencing or guessing meaning from context (Table 6.1).

Thus, their distinction seems to overlap with, but is not identical to, Rubin's and Seliger's. O'Malley et al. went on to claim that intermediate-level students tended to use proportionately more metacognitive strategies than students with beginning-level proficiency. They concluded that students who develop greater TL

Learning Strategy	Description
A. Metacognitive strategies	
Advance organizers	Making a general but comprehensive preview of the organizing concept or principle in an anticipated learning activity.
Directed attention	Deciding in advance to attend in general to a learning task and to ignore irrelevant distractors.
Selective attention	Deciding in advance to attend to specific aspects of language input or situational details that will cue the retention of language input.
Self-management	Understanding the conditions that help one learn and arranging for the presence of those conditions.
Advance preparation	Planning for and rehearsing linguistic components necessary to carry out an upcoming language task.
Self-monitoring	Correcting one's speech for accuracy in pronunciation, grammar, vocabulary, or for appropriateness related to the setting or to the people who are present.
Delayed production	Consciously deciding to postpone speaking to learn initially through listening comprehension.
Self-evaluation	Checking the outcomes of one's own language learning against an internal measure of completeness and accuracy.
Self-reinforcement	Arranging rewards for oneself when a language learning activity has been accomplished successfully.

TABLE 6.1 Learning Strategy Definitions (O'Malley et al. 1985a)

Learning Strategy	*Description*
B. Cognitive strategies	
Repetition	Imitating a language model, including overt practice and silent rehearsal.
Resourcing	Using target language reference materials.
Directed physical response	Relating new information to physical actions, as with directives.
Translation	Using the first language as a base for understanding and/or producing the second language.
Grouping	Reordering or reclassifying and perhaps labelling the material to be learned based on common attributes.
Note-taking	Writing down the main idea, important points, outline, or summary of information presented orally or in writing.
Deduction	Consciously applying rules to produce or understand the second language.
Recombination	Constructing a meaningful sentence or larger language sequence by combining known elements in a new way.
Imagery	Relating new information to visual concepts in memory via familiar, easily retrievable visualizations, phrases, or locations.
Auditory representation	Retention of the sound or similar sound for a word, phrase, or longer language sequence.
Key word	Remembering a new word in the second language by (1) identifying a familar word in the first language that sounds like or otherwise resembles the new word, and (2)

TABLE 6.1 (*continued*)

Learning Strategy	Description
Key word *(cont.)*	generating easily recalled images of some relationship between the new word.
Contextualization	Placing a word or phrase in a meaningful language sequence.
Elaboration	Relating new information to other concepts in memory.
Transfer	Using previously acquired linguistic and/or conceptual knowledge to facilitate a new language learning task.
Inferencing	Using available information to guess meanings of new items, predict outcomes, or fill in missing information.
Question for clarification	Asking a teacher or other native speaker for repetition, paraphrasing, explanation and/or examples.
C. Social mediation	
Cooperation	Working with one or more peers to obtain feedback, pool information, or model a language activity.

TABLE 6.1 *(continued)*

proficiency are more able to attend to metacognitive control of learning than are the beginners.

6.9 Other factors

A number of other factors have been claimed to affect SLA. These include:

(1) *Memory, awareness, will.* Cook (1979) maintains that short-term memory capacity develops with age and that one's memory in a second language is more limited than in one's native tongue.[10] On the other hand, Gattegno (1976) would attach no real significance to memory attenuation in an L2 as he ascribes very little role to memory in the SLA process. For Gattegno, what is central to SLA is the development of awareness, and learner differences 'are caused by

their differences in levels of awareness and how they use their will'
(de Cordoba 1985, p. 122).

Leontiev (1981) also discusses the concept of will. A volitional act,
according to Leontiev, is the conscious choice of one of several possible
options which arise as the result of a struggle between motives. It
is perhaps 'will' which Strevens (1978) has in mind when he lists
learning stamina, or the ability to maintain the learning effort for
a period of time, as one of the several crucial factors contributed
by the learner in SLA. For success to occur, learners must persist
despite obstacles they may encounter, not the least of which is an
adverse reaction to a language teaching method (F. Schumann 1980).
While some learners might abandon their study completely with such
an encounter, others find a way to make the method work for them or
they augment classroom instruction by other means.

(2) *Language disability*.　So far we have limited our discussion to learners who are endowed with normal faculties. If students suffered from
specific language disorders such as dyslexia or strephosymbolia,[11] or
had impaired hearing or vision, SLA would obviously not be precluded
but presumably would be adversely affected.

(3) *Interest*.　Henning (1983) conjectures that successful SLA may be
dependent on the interests that a language learner brings to the learning
situation. Henning surveyed the interest of Egyptian ESL students.
The students were asked to respond to a 50-item Likert-scale questionnaire in which they were asked on a scale of 1 to 5 to what extent
they would be willing to pay a small fee for information on a particular
topic. What was determined were statistically positive correlations with
the Ain Shams University [English] Proficiency Exam and adventurous
and political interests; significantly negative correlations were obtained
between the exam and materialistic interests.

(4) *Sex*.　Although we know of no study that has systematically investigated the rate of SLA in females versus males, it is a generally
accepted fact in L1 acquisition that females enjoy a rate advantage,
initially at least. We are able, however, to cite a few SLA studies that
have reported sex-related differences incidental to their main focus.
For example, Farhady (1982) found that female subjects significantly
outperformed male subjects on a listening comprehension test in his
study of 800 university students who were obliged to take a placement
test. Eisenstein (1982) also showed that females performed significantly
better than males on a dialect discrimination task and in the extent to
which they could recognize dialects of greater or lesser prestige.

In addition to differences in proficiency or dialect discrimination, other sex-linked differences which might affect SLA have been noted. Lakoff (1973) suggests the existence of a 'woman's language', which is replete with hedging devices such as question tags. It has also been noted that males tend to interrupt more than females (Zimmerman and West 1975, cited in Gass and Varonis 1986).

In one SLA study which did not investigate rate of acquisition differences between the sexes but did study the conversational behaviour of male and female second language learners, researchers Gass and Varonis (1986) found that men dominated the conversations. The researchers concluded, therefore, that men received more speaking practice in such interactions; however, since women initiated more meaning negotiations than men, women may have benefited from receiving more comprehensible input.

(5) *Birth order.* Another factor which has been shown to have an effect in first language acquisition, but which has yet to be investigated in SLA, is birth order. Rosenblum and Dorman (1978 cited in Seliger 1984) report that good imitators among their five- to six-year-old subjects were either first-born or only children. Whether such findings also hold true in SLA remains to be seen.

(6) *Prior experience.* Strevens (1978) suggests that the extent of learners' command of their mother tongue, including whether they are literate, will affect their progress in the SL. Adding empirical support to Strevens's suggestion is a study conducted by Cummins et al. (1984) which examined age difference and the influence of L1 on L2 school language development. Various English language tests were administered to Japanese and Vietnamese students living in Canada. It was found that the older students outperformed the younger students on CALP-type or school language measures, whereas the younger students did significantly better on measures designed to assess BICS. The development of L1 school language accounted for a highly significant proportion of the variance in L2 school language, a finding consonant with Cummins' (1978) interdependence hypothesis which predicts that the development of L2 school language is partially dependent upon the prior level of development of L1 school language. According to Cummins, there is a common underlying proficiency which makes possible the transfer of school skills across a student's two languages.

Not only will one's knowledge of one's native language influence SLA, but also knowledge of other languages will have an effect. Rivers (1979) reports that in learning her sixth language, Spanish, she relied heavily on her second language, French, since they shared cognates. Most people believe that at some point learning additional languages becomes increasingly easy. If this is the case, it may be that knowledge of several languages constrains the hypotheses one is likely to make about the new language, and this accelerates the process, or it may simply be that one has learned how to learn and thus the process is facilitated (Nation and McLaughlin 1986).

Of course, previous experience can also be deleterious for the current learning situation if the previous experience was unsuccessful, unpleasant in any way, or limiting. Farhady (1982), for instance, found significant relationships between examinees' nationalities and their performance on a university placement examination. Farhady attributes these to different educational policies in different countries, with the result being that students from one country may have more limited experience working with a particular skill than students from other countries.

6.10 Conclusion

We are well aware that our readers, particularly those who are more intolerant of ambiguity, might feel frustrated in reading this chapter in which few answers are furnished to questions about differential success among second language learners. It is certainly true that many of the studies reviewed here yield inconclusive or contradictory findings. Practical implications must, therefore, remain tenuous at best. Nevertheless, some of the research findings reported here have been interpreted as supporting a particular educational practice. Thus, we conclude this chapter with the implications that have been drawn. Doubtless, other implications will occur to readers in addition to these, which we have culled from the literature.

(1) *Age.*   Whatever the explanation for a critical or sensitive period turns out to be, the documented age-related decline in SLA abilities suggests that foreign language programmes should be begun in elementary school, where feasible, if eventual native-like attainment is important. The data on older versus younger children suggest, however, that the optimal timing is not the earliest possible, but may be around age nine, although being this specific is probably a little premature. Starting then should be more efficient, as suggested by evaluations of early and late immersion programmes in Canada (for review, see Genesee 1983), and yet allow the

child time to establish a firm basis in the L1, which in turn has been claimed to benefit SLA and general school achievement (Cummins 1979). Where adult beginners are concerned, appropriate instruction helps (see Chapter 8), so teachers and students still have a job to do, but there are probably biological (as well as pedagogical) arguments against a diet of 'ship-sheep' and 'slip . . . s–l–e–e–p'.

(2) *Aptitude.* As for implications concerning language aptitude, controversy exists around the issue of whether or not language aptitude can be developed. Neufeld (1978) believes that one's ability in an L2 is not innate, but rather is dependent upon prior learning experiences. Carroll (1981, p. 86), on the other hand, asserts that language aptitude is 'relatively fixed over long periods of an individual's life span, and relatively hard to modify in any significant way'. To support the latter view, Skehan (1985) cites the work of Politzer and Weiss (1969) and Carroll (1979), which demonstrates that aptitude is not particularly amenable to training. To say that aptitude is not particularly trainable, is not necessarily to accept that nothing can be done. After all, whether language aptitude is innate or not, 'there is indisputable evidence linking performance on language aptitude tests with classroom achievement in a new language' (Wesche 1981, pp. 119–20); its impact would thus seem to be too important to ignore.

One comforting prospect is that high-quality language instruction may nullify aptitude differences (Carroll 1965). With high-quality instruction, most learners' needs will be met. Conversely, when the quality is not particularly high, students may have to compensate for the lack of suitable instruction, and that is when aptitude differences may be most apparent.

In addition to striving to offer the very highest-quality instruction (a worthy objective regardless of its effect on aptitude differences), another way in which aptitude can influence educational practice follows from Wesche's (1981) work with Public Service Commission employees studying French in Canada. Wesche used students' aptitude test profiles to assign students to one of three particular methodological approaches – an audio-visual method, an analytic approach, and a functional approach. Wesche found that when students were matched with the methodological approach that suited their aptitude profiles best, positive attitudes were encouraged and students' achievement was enhanced. Thus, matching students' language aptitude profiles with particular methodological approaches might ameliorate the negative consequences of working with groups of students with heterogeneous aptitude profiles.

(3) *Social-psychological*

Motivation. Alpetkin (1981) admonishes language teachers to be sensitive to the motivation type of their students. Some teachers may be operating under the questionable assumption that students' integrative motivation brings better results than instrumental motivation. Such teachers may be tempted to use methodological approaches that encourage assimilation to the target culture in a second language context. Teachers should be discouraged from such practices, according to Alpetkin, who challenges H.D. Brown's (1980) assertion that 'even in cases of "instrumentally" motivated language learning, a person is forced to take on a new identity if he is to become competent in a second language' (p. 233 in Brown, cited on page 278 in Alpetkin). Alpetkin rejects the notion that successful learners must assume new identities, and argues instead that foreign students at American universities not be treated in the same way as immigrants to the United States. Any attempt to ascribe integrative motives to the students, Alpetkin observes, will be distasteful to the students and could intensify any anomie they are experiencing or any readjustment problems they may encounter upon their return home.

Given the research reported on earlier in this chapter, it seems that instrumental motivation can be just as powerful as integrative. As such, since the instrumental motives of foreign students in the United States are often accompanied by an urgency to master English in order to proceed with their academic studies, Alpetkin recommends an ESP (English for specific purposes) approach in which the language is taught according to the students' general academic fields. In this way, students' utilitarian motives are attended to.

Attitude. In the Montreal suburb of St Lambert, an experiment in language instruction grew out of concern that language and attitudinal barriers between English-speaking and French-speaking communities were making Montreal a divided city. In the plans for the experimental immersion programme, French was to be used exclusively for the first three years of an Anglophone child's education. English-language arts were to be added in the third grade, and later more and more instruction was to be conducted in the mother tongue. Much has been written about the French immersion programme subsequent to its inception in 1965. A pertinent finding from

Lambert and Tucker's (1972) comprehensive evaluation is that the immersion children developed positive attitudes towards French- and English-speaking Canadians. The Anglophone controls enrolled in an FSL program showed a similar tendency, although the Francophone controls did not.

Encouraged by the success of the Canadian French immersion programme, the first Spanish immersion programme in the United States was begun in 1971 in Culver City, California. Relevant to a discussion of attitude development is the corroborating research evidence adduced by Waldman (1975), related in Snow with Shapira (1985). Waldman used the Cross-Cultural Attitude Inventory to ascertain that immersion and monolingual English control students preferred the Anglo culture over Mexican-American; however, the immersion students gave the Mexican-American culture higher ratings than did the control students, a finding consistent with the results of a match guise procedure as well:

> Waldman concluded that the immersion students had developed less ethnocentric notions than had students in traditional English-only programs. In addition, they demonstrated more positive feelings toward the Mexican American culture and Spanish speakers. (Snow with Shapira 1985, p. 8)

(4) *Personality.* Earlier, when we discussed the personality variable of extroversion, we pointed out that in some cases extroversion seemed positively linked with language learning success; in other cases, the more introverted learners outperformed their extroverted counterparts. Wong Fillmore's classroom-centred research (1982) provides us with one clue as to why no clear pattern emerges. According to Wong Fillmore, the type of instruction individuals receive might make a difference as to which personality type is favoured, and therefore, more successful. For example, Wong Fillmore observed that shy children progressed more rapidly than more outgoing children in classrooms which were more teacher-oriented and structured, rather than oriented towards group activities. This observation suggests the need to investigate how personality characteristics interact with type of instruction. However, such a notion, while appealing for the practical consequences it might imply, is by no means an easy feat. McLaughlin (1985, p. 172) reiterates one of our earlier concerns about the measurement of personality traits:

> . . . in spite of the logical appeal of discovering relationships between learner characteristics and learning situations empirical evidence for

the utility of such an approach for improving educational procedures is weak (Cronbach and Snow 1977). One of the major problems is measuring individual difference variables. Interaction studies are based on human traits for which assessment technology is quite primitive.

Despite such limitations, the thought that not all personality types respond equally well to the same instructional practices seems intuitively sound. Moreover, there has been a little research to suggest different types of students do benefit from different practices. In addition to the Wong Fillmore study mentioned above, McLaughlin also cites Hamayan, Genesee and Tucker (1977), who found that the personality traits of conformity and control correlated positively with second language learning success in a French as a second language programme in Canada, but not in a French immersion programme. The researchers conjectured that such personality traits might favour learners enrolled in a more conventional language teaching programme, and make little or no difference in an innovative programme.

One final study we should mention before concluding our discussion of practical implications of research on personality characteristics of language learners is a test-anxiety study conducted by Madsen (1982) with 114 university students enrolled in ESL classes at Brigham Young University. Madsen hypothesized that students who were more anxiety-prone would not be evaluated as accurately on stressful tests as those who were less anxiety-prone. This hypothesis was borne out by evidence which demonstrated that student performance on the most anxiety-producing subtest was shown to be debilitating for the anxiety-prone students. Thus, tests that evoke a high level of anxiety are presumably less valid measures of students' performance when such students are susceptible to debilitating anxiety.

(5) *Cognitive style.* Most of the applied research in the area of cognitive style shares a motive with that of research in the personality area, i.e. determining the effects of the interaction between cognitive style and instructional practice. The principal cognitive style distinction which has received the most attention is the distinction between analytic and gestalt or holistic learning styles. Hartnett (1975) confirmed the hypothesis that analytic learners preferred and did better in a deductive method of learning Spanish (the Bull method), while holistic learners behaved likewise in the inductive Barcia method. Employing a test of Conjugal Lateral Eye Movement,[12] Hartnett also showed that the more analytic learners indicated more eye movement to the right associated with left-hemisphere preference than students in the inductive

class, who showed more eye movement to the left, associated with right-hemisphere preference. Thus, hemispheric specialization may be linked to cognitive style and which instructional method students prefer when they are given a choice. Hartnett's results seem to indicate that students learn faster if they are in a class where the methodology matches their cognitive style. This conclusion is supported in research by Abraham (1985). Abraham divided 61 subjects into two groups, each group having the same number of field-independent and field-dependent subjects, as determined by the subjects' scores on the Group Embedded Figures Test (GEFT). One group was taught a lesson on participial phrases inductively, the other deductively. Subjects with the higher GEFT scores performed better on the deductive lesson.

Most teachers will not find themselves in a situation where students can be streamed according to a particular cognitive style they employ. A reasonable alternative, therefore, might be to diversify language instruction as much as possible based upon the variety of cognitive styles represented among one's students. Teachers could presumably diagnose their students' styles through the use of self-report questionnaires such as Hill's Cognitive Style Mapping (Hill 1971), or Learning Style Inventories (Dunn, Dunn and Price 1975; Kolb 1976).

We should also acknowledge, however, that learning styles are not immutable and that individuals can change in response to unique contextual demands (Schmeck 1981). A learner may thus develop a preferred style, but may very well be able to adapt when confronted with circumstances that make cognitive demands of a different sort. Indeed, some would argue that rather than catering to students' particular cognitive styles, learners should be challenged to develop a range of styles.

Reid (1987) conducted a large survey of non-native speakers of English and found that their learning style preferences often differed significantly from those of native speakers. The conclusion Reid draws from this is that learners should be exposed to the concept of learning styles and indeed should be given the opportunity to diagnose their own preferences, and yet also should be encouraged to diversify those preferences. Reid suggests further that exposing students to different teaching styles may allow students to develop a versatility of learning styles which will aid them in meeting the demands of future academic subject teaching (Grasha 1972).

Whatever the manner in which cognitive style is addressed, Tumposky (1984. p. 306) underscores the fact that cognitive style

> is a significant factor which must be considered in instruction. In order to be successful, materials and methodologies should be able

to accommodate different dimensions of personality and cognitive style. . . . It follows that materials lacking such flexibility may contribute to poor performance and must be considered in any overall assessment of a learning program.

We would add that the term 'materials' should be interpreted broadly enough to include the assessment of language proficiency. Stansfield and Hansen (1983) allege that cloze tests, previously thought by many to be useful all-purpose tests of SL proficiency, seem to be biased so that field-independent learners are more likely to do well on them than field-dependent learners.

(6) *Learning strategies.* We turn now to implications of research on learning strategies, those unconscious or conscious activities undertaken by learners that promote learning. In fact, some well-established areas of learning strategy research have already been applied to SL learning situations. One of these is the use of mnemonic techniques for vocabulary learning (Cohen and Aphek 1980, 1981; Cohen 1987). Not all learning strategies may be so readily developed, however. In a discussion of the implications of learning strategies for language instruction, Bialystok (1985) rejects the notion that teachers should employ teaching strategies that are incongruous with the learners' usual experience. While one might argue that doing so would encourage learners to broaden their learning strategy repertoire, 'the human ability to incorporate forms of thought or ideas that are radically different from present experience seems to be severely limited' (p. 259). Invoking Piaget's (1929) principle that what is optimal for learning is some level of novelty which is only slightly beyond the child's present level of development, and Vygotsky's (1962) concept of 'zone of proximal development', Bialystok instead argues that disparities between teaching and learning strategies will greatly reduce the potential benefit of instruction. This position would seem to be worth investigating empirically. Bialystok also raises a related implication which has been investigated empirically. The question is whether or not relevant learning strategies can be taught to students in order to promote their learning or skill development. Bialystok reports that the results of strategy training demonstrate that it is effective in altering student performance only under specific conditions.

Supporting this generalization is a study by O'Malley et al. (1985b). In their study, 75 high-school ESL students received instruction in the use of certain learning strategies and then were asked to perform listening and speaking tasks. Analyses of the effects of training produced the anticipated mixed results: the listening task was apparently too difficult for the students to be able to utilize the strategy training they had received; the subjects' skills on the speaking task, however, were improved, relative to a control group which had received no learning strategy training.

Evidence that learners can benefit from explicit coaching in learning strategies has led to proposals that such instruction be incorporated into instructional programmes (Dansereau 1978). It should be noted, however, that as with any new behaviour, it takes considerable time for students to develop proficiency in using new strategies; and for some groups, particular learning strategies may be more ingrained than for others. O'Malley (1987) for example, reports that Asian experimental subjects were more reluctant than Hispanics to relinquish rote-memorization techniques of vocabulary learning. Because of its potential import to SLA, no doubt the notion of teaching learning strategies will receive increasing attention in teacher education programmes. In fact, Wenden (1985) suggests that language teachers should no longer be content to regard their subject matter simply as language. Instead:

> Learners must learn how to do for themselves what teachers typically do for them in the classroom. Our endeavors to help them improve their language skills must be complemented by an equally systematic approach to helping them develop and refine their learning skills. Learner training should be integrated with language training. (p. 7)

If we step back from our consideration of the implications of each of these areas for language instruction, we are able to discern three general patterns that seem to apply for many of the variables we have considered here:

1. Where possible, customizing instruction by grouping learners according to individual characteristics and then matching the groups with an appropriate methodology may be desirable.
2. Where this is not deemed desirable, or where it is inappropriate, teachers should become as aware as possible of the individual characteristics of their students and work towards meeting their

individual needs. This may be accomplished by teachers' using a variety of approaches in the class.
3. Students, too, should be helped to adapt to the teacher's style. Empowering language learners by having them develop learning strategies may help them to cope with the demands of class and, indeed, may help them to continue to learn on their own apart from the class.

Finally, we conclude this chapter by submitting that there are some obvious implications for researchers to be drawn from the studies presented here. In addition to the ones mentioned earlier, such as the need for more valid measures of individual learner variables, a further implication is the need to adopt more complex research designs. While on the one hand it is agreed that language learning is a complex process, on the other hand researchers sometimes continue to employ rather simple univariate analyses, such as simple correlations between a single individual variable and learner performance on some language proficiency measure. As d'Anglejan and Renaud (1985) rightly point out, learner variables inevitably overlap and interact with others, suggesting that we are not getting a true measure of a factor if we isolate it from all the others. More powerful multivariate statistical techniques do exist and can provide means for examining the relationship among learners' characteristics.

We cannot stop here, however. As Seliger (1984, p. 37) contends:

> The more variables we identify, the more we attempt to explain the recombinations of these variables through the wonders of the computer and multivariate analyses. . . . While many characteristics have been related correlationally to language achievement, we have no mechanism for deciding which of the phenomena described or reported to be carried out by the learner are in fact those that lead to language acquisition.

Seliger's point is, we think, well taken. Progress in understanding SLA will not be made simply by identifying more and more variables that are thought to influence language learners. We have certainly witnessed the lengthening of taxonomies of language-learner characteristics over the years, and we doubtless will want to continue to add to the lists. However, it is not clear that we have come any closer to unravelling the mysteries of SLA now than before. Perhaps what will serve the field best at this point is setting our sights higher: attempting to explain SLA, rather than merely describing it. We will return to this point in the next chapter.

Notes

1. Since AO and LOR may be positively correlated themselves, researchers employ statistical procedures to 'partial out' the effect of one factor on another. By using these procedures, researchers can learn what the unique relationship of each variable is.
2. Masked speech is speech which is overlaid with another sound, making the speech difficult to understand, especially for non-native speakers. Oyama used masking white noise produced by a Grason Stadler noise generator with signal-to-noise ratios ranging from 5 to 16.5 decibels.
3. Multiple regression analysis is used when one wants to know what the unique and significant predictors are of a particular criterion, in this case foreign language aptitude.
4. The figure of 16 per cent is arrived at by squaring the correlation coefficient (0.41) and expressing this as a percentage. This figure represents the proportion of the criterion variable (such as a final course grade) which can be predicted by a score on another variable, in this case an aptitude test.
5. It should be noted, however, that the test of verbal intelligence (Heim 1970) Skehan employed ranked second to, and overlapped with, the more specific language-analytic aptitude tests in the regression equation.
6. Factor analysis allows one to investigate mathematically the interrelations (given in terms of correlation coefficients) of all the measures to determine which of the measures form separate clusters (i.e. factors).
7. There are, however, different ways of getting these ratings. The direct way is to ask subjects to indicate to what extent they agree or disagree with statements like 'I should not be forced to learn English' and 'English is the mark of an educated person.' In the indirect way, attitudes are measured with a scale of stereotypes modelled on the work of Spolsky (1969). Subjects are given twenty attributes and are asked to rate (a) themselves, (b) themselves as they would like to be, (c) their ethnic group and (d) the ethnic group of the TL speakers. Pierson, Fu and Lee (1980), unlike Spolsky, found the indirect measures less successful than the direct measures in predicting English attainment.
8. Knotts (1983) is credited for bringing to our attention this body of research literature.
9. Dichotic listening tasks are tasks which affect the two ears differently, as when one sound is conveyed to the left ear at the same time as a different sound is being transmitted to the right.
10. For a detailed discussion of memory and second language learning, see Leontiev (1981) and Stevick (1976).

11. Strephosymbolia results in reversal of perception of left-right order such that a word like 'top' would be read as 'pot'.
12. The Conjugal Lateral Eye Movement test is based on the observation that people move their eyes in a characteristic way when thinking and that the direction in which they gaze is associated with the individual's hemisphere preference. Individuals who move their eyes right when engaged in thought are relying on their left hemisphere and, conversely, individuals who look to the left are thought to be right-hemisphere dominant.

Activities

Comprehension

1. Explain briefly why Krashen, Long and Scarcella, who reviewed the literature regarding age and SLA, concluded *older is faster, but younger is better*.
2. List and briefly elaborate upon the hypothesized causes of a sensitive or critical period. What is the counter-evidence to each?
3. State the arguments pro and con the existence of a specific aptitude for language.
4. Discuss why it is questionable to assume that integrative motivation is superior to instrumental motivation.
5. Discuss the 'resultative hypothesis' with regard to attitude and motivation.
6. What are some of the challenges for researchers in investigating the relationship between personality and SLA?
7. An optimal cognitive style is one that is medial between two extremes. Review the cognitive styles presented in this chapter. Is this true?
8. Discuss how hemisphere specialization relates to cognitive style.
9. How have the immersion programmes influenced attitudes towards the TL community?
10. Discuss the pros and cons of matching students with particular characteristics with particular instructional methodologies.
11. To what extent can a language learner's learning strategy repertoire be expanded?

Application

12. Almost all of the instruments used to measure the various personality traits discussed in this chapter have been borrowed from the field of psychology. Examine one of the instruments and discuss

whether it is an appropriate measure of the particular trait as the trait might influence success in SLA.

13. If you have the opportunity to study a second language, try keeping a diary on your experience. Record on a regular basis how you feel about the progress you are making: what is helping and what is hindering you in learning the SL. Later, you may choose to sift through the diary entries, looking for particular patterns or salient experiences. See what these reveal about your own social-psychological, personality, cognitive style, etc., profile.

14. Whether you have kept a diary or not, recall a former language-learning experience. Plot the changes in your motivation over time, labelling the vertical axis as the level of motivation (high, medium, low) and the horizontal axis as time calibrated at appropriate intervals, i.e. weeks, months, years, etc. What accounts for the rises and falls over time in your motivation to study the L2?

15. If you are teaching at the moment, have your students complete a learning style inventory such as the one developed by Kolb (1976). Do the results accord with your own diagnosis of each student's preferred style profile? Do they accord with the students' own self-assessment?

16. If you were asked by a local education official or board to recommend the age at which formal instruction in an L2 should begin, what would you recommend? Why?

17. Administer the Conjugal Lateral Eye Movement test to second language learners with whom you are familiar. The procedure, as reported in Hartnett (1975, 1985) is as follows:
Ask the learners the following ten questions (which would have to be culturally adjusted):
    1. How do you spell 'journey'?
    2. What is six times twelve?
    3. How many letters are there in the word 'Washington'?
    4. What is similar about salt and water?
    5. What is similar about first and last?
    6. Which way does Lincoln face on the penny?
    7. How many sides are there on a five-pointed star?
    8. Is the top stripe of the American flag red or white?
    9. Is the moon now waxing or waning?
    10. What is your favourite colour?
Notice which direction their eyes moved first. You should work with the learners one by one; i.e. the other learners should not overhear the questions nor notice that you are observing eye movement. Learners who make eight out of ten movements

to the right are thought to be left-hemisphere dominant; left movers, right-hemisphere dominant. Some learners, of course, will show no preferred direction. Do those who show different eye-movement preferences also favour different cognitive styles? For example, do you find, as Hartnett did, that individuals who appear to be left-hemisphere dominant favour an analytic learning style? Do those who appear to be right-hemisphere dominant favour a gestalt style?

18. Consult a taxonomy of learning strategies such as Oxford-Carpenter's (1988). Plan a series of lessons in which you would teach one or more of the strategies which are purported to be practised by successful SL learners.

Suggestions for further reading

Other sources which deal with many of the variables treated here are:

Au, S 1988 A critical appraisal of Gardner's social-psychological theory of second language (L2) learning. *Language Learning* 38 (1): 75–100.

Brown, H D 1987 *Principles of language learning and teaching*, second edition. Prentice-Hall, Inc., Englewood Cliffs, N.J.

Gardner, R 1988 The socio-educational model of second-language learning: assumptions, findings and issues. *Language Learning* 38 (1): 101–26

Skehan, P 1989 *Individual differences in second-language learning*. Edward Arnold

For a thorough treatment of the critical period hypothesis, see:

Ekstrand, L 1979 Replacing the critical period and optimum age theories of second language acquisition with a theory of ontogenetic development beyond puberty. *Educational and Psychological Interactions* No. 69. Department of Educational and Psychological Research, Malmo School of Education, Lund University

Scovel, T 1988 *A time to speak: a psycholinguistic inquiry into the critical period for human speech*. Newbury House/Harper & Row, New York

For a discussion of social-psychological variables, see:

Schumann, J 1978 Social and psychological factors in second language acquisition. In Richards, J (ed.) *Understanding second and foreign language learning*. Newbury House, Rowley, Mass.

For a work on cognitive styles, consult:

Willing, K 1988 *Learning styles in adult migrant education*. National Centre for English Language Teaching and Research, Macquarie University, Sydney

Learning strategies are treated in depth by:

Carpenter, R 1989 *Language learning strategies: what every teacher should know.* Newbury House/Harper & Row, New York

O'Malley, M and Chamot, A 1989 *Learning strategies in second language acquisition.* Cambridge University Press

Segal, J, Chipman, S and Glaser, R (eds.) 1985 *Thinking and learning skills,* Vols. 1 and 2. Erlbaum, Hillsdale, N.J.

Wenden, A and Rubin, J (eds.) 1987 *Learner strategies in language learning.* Prentice-Hall, Englewood Cliffs, N.J.

For a pioneering attempt to assess the importance of matching instruction and learning style, see:

Hartnett, D 1985 Cognitive style and second language learning. In Celce-Murcia, M (ed.) *Beyond basics: issues and research in TESOL.* Newbury House, Rowley, Mass.

For a discussion of learning styles, consult:

Willing, K 1988 *Learning styles in adult migrant education.* National Centre for English Language Teaching and Research, Macquarie University, Sydney

7 Theories in second language acquisition

7.1 Introduction

The words 'theory' and 'theoretical' evoke a variety of responses in language teaching and research circles, many of them, for different reasons, negative. For some, the negative response they feel is due to their having sat through conference presentations or read journal articles labelled 'theoretical' which have consisted of a good deal of rhetoric, however eloquent, and very little substance. 'Theoretical' here is mis-used, and just means 'data-free'. For others, the particular theories that have received most 'air-time' in the SLA literature until now have been uninteresting, wrong, or vacuous, leading them to be potentially hostile to any new ones. Still others have no problem with theory in general (or think they don't), but simply feel that work in SLA has not advanced far enough yet for theorizing to be productive.

Those who subscribe to the last view – and they include several prominent figures in SLA – hold that because, in their opinion, we know relatively little about SLA, any theory we come up with at this stage is likely to be wrong. Hence, it will be counter-productive, in that many people will waste their time working on a theoretical red herring instead of discovering more *facts* about acquisition. In our view, while superficially reasonable, this shows that the purpose and value of theories in (social) science are still not widely understood in our field, and that it is therefore worth devoting some time to the topic in this book.

In this chapter, we therefore begin by introducing some of the basic concepts and procedures in theory construction. Familiarity with the theory construction process is helpful in understanding the condition of a field of scientific inquiry, necessary for doing meaningful research in that field and, indeed, essential for determining whether a field is a science at all. We will argue that more rigorous theorizing would speed up progress in SLA research. Further, it might go some way towards protecting language teachers from seductive but inadequate 'theory-based' prescriptions for the classroom. In subsequent sections, we describe and critique examples of three major classes of theories in second language acquisition: nativist, environmentalist and interactionist theories.

7.2 Theory construction and social science

7.2.1 The role of theories in making research cumulative

Although there has been an explosion of data-based research activity in the field of SLA, dissatisfaction is increasingly expressed by researchers themselves and by potential consumers of some of the findings, such as language teachers, to the effect that little of that research is cumulative and/or clearly motivated. They want to know, in other words, where it is getting us.

There are various ways in which data-based work is less productive for being theoretically unmotivated. Thus, some studies are still only descriptive, with the 'issue' addressed appearing to have occurred to the investigator *after* the data were collected. This seems to be the explanation for research reports which end by saying that, 'of course', no conclusions can be drawn about X (the issue which supposedly motivated the study) because of the unfortunate lack of certain crucial data or some missing element in the design (such as a control group), and which then go on to suggest how future research on the issue should be conducted, presumably by someone else.

Correlational studies which purport to resolve issues, as opposed to providing exploratory surveys of them, are little better. Most treat only one or two variables, and if more than one, present simple correlations for each variable separately. Yet, as early as 1973, using semi-partials,[1] Oyama found that an *apparent* relationship between integrative orientation and SL proficiency 'evaporated' once age of onset was controlled for. This finding was confirmed by Purcell and Suter (1980) using multiple regression in a reanalysis of Suter's (1973) dissertation data. More recently, as noted in Chapter 6, Hermann (1980) and Strong (1984) have provided evidence for the 'resultative hypothesis', i.e. that motivation to learn an SL results from increasing proficiency rather than causes it.

Results such as these show why it is risky, even misleading, to purport to investigate relationships between attitude, motivation, or some other variable and SLA using simple correlations to compare questionnaire responses with proficiency test scores. Such studies need to address the serious measurement questions to which we referred in the previous chapter. Research in many other areas shows the same failure to build on previous work – the tendency, in other words, to reinvent the wheel.

Despite these shortcomings, progress clearly is being made. While limited, descriptive studies are very useful and still necessary, much effort is currently being wasted which could be expended more profitably both for the researchers as individuals and for the field as a whole if it were 'organized' effort. Specifically, much SLA research is less fruitful than it might be were it governed by a *theory*, which for many (but not all) is equivalent to saying, 'were it done scientifically'.

Our purpose here is not to argue for a particular theory, but rather for the value of theory in general in motivating SLA research, and for certain kinds of theories over others. In contrast to the considerable attention paid to other aspects of research methodology – the design of studies, data-collection procedures, analytic techniques, methods of displaying data, etc. – we devote insufficient time to the role of theory in our work, and some of what we do is less useful as a result. When theoretical notions *are* mentioned, on the other hand, and this is increasingly frequent, terms are sometimes used very loosely. As will become clear, we think that this low priority accorded to theory is most unfortunate.

7.2.2 Purposes and types of theory

What then, first of all, is meant by a theory? One understanding is that a theory is a more or less formal, more or less explicit, synthesis of what is 'known' at a given point in time about some natural phenomena, such as the factors involved in SLA. 'Knowledge', and hence a theory, in other words, sometimes simply refers to what has been discovered through empirical *observation*. A common form theories of this kind take, when the observations have been repeated and the patterns consistent, is that of a set of laws. On other occasions, theories are more than that, involving a claim to *explain* the phenomena, or the way they interact. In this second understanding of the term, a theory does not just represent a storehouse of information, but aims instead at an *understanding* of the phenomena. The test for whether the understanding, i.e. the explanation, is correct, is whether or not *predictions* about future events derived from the theory turn out to be correct. This kind of theory often takes a causal-process form. The relationship between these two major types and forms of theories is described below.

(1) *The set-of-laws form.* The different functions of theories are reflected in the varied forms they take. The 'storehouse' variety, for example, typically consists of a collection of (often unrelated) statements recording what is (thought to be) known about the phenomenon. Examples in SLA theory construction might include:

1. Learners of structure X (ESL negation, GSL word order, etc.) pass through N developmental stages (a, b, c. . .) before attaining the target version.
2. Adults proceed through developmental sequences faster than children in the early stages of morphological and syntactic development.
3. Learners who begin SLA after puberty do not acquire a native-like accent in the SL.
4. Developmental sequences are not altered by instruction.
5. ILs containing voiced stops will also contain voiceless stops.

Ignoring for the moment whether or not these particular statements are correct, each would represent a conclusion, based upon repeated observation, concerning relationships among variables. Each would be the product of research, preceding it only when someone seeks to disprove the claimed finding. The statements would have the status of *generalizations* or of *laws*, depending on the number and (especially) the uniformity of the observations which supported them, as well as on the degree of consensus among experts as to their truth. (Generalizations allow for exceptions, laws do not. If 'all swans are white' were a law, one black swan would disprove it, or else it would not be considered a swan.) This form of theory is known as the *set-of-laws form.*

Since the main function of set-of-laws theories is to serve as repositories of confirmed knowledge about the subject of interest, they have better than usual chances of being correct. They also suffer from several disadvantages, however. To begin with, statements in the set-of-laws form will not necessarily be related to one another, often having arisen from independent lines of inquiry, as in the examples above. The independence of the statements in turn means that each claim the theory makes must be tested separately, which is uneconomical in terms of the research costs and effort involved.

Second, it is important to note that such statements cannot contain unoperationalizable *constructs*. This is because each generalization or law began life as a *hypothesis*, a prediction about a relationship among variables which not only was testable, but repeatedly was *tested* against data, i.e. as a statement which was empirically falsifiable. As such, the statements typically do not provide an *explanation* of the processes they deal with. Rather (for those who accept the findings) they are themselves facts about SLA in need of explanation. For example, why do learners exhibit the same developmental sequences, and why do they experience a (fairly) common accuracy order in the acquisition of certain grammatical morphemes?

(2) *The causal-process form.* Other theories, however, take very different forms, of which, traditionally, at least, the most valued in the nomothetic scientific tradition[2] is the *causal-process* form (for discussion, see Cummins 1983; Harre 1987; Crookes 1988a). Causal-process theories are generally, although not necessarily absolutely, consistent with existing knowledge about the matter they treat, but, unlike theories of the set-of-laws form, also attempt to *explain* those phenomena. Causal-process theories consist of: (1) sets of definitions of theoretical concepts and constructs, together with operational definitions of some (but not necessarily all) of them; (2) sets of existence statements; and (3) sets of (deterministic and/or probabilistic) causal statements, which together specify not only *when* or *that* a process (such as SLA) will occur, but *how* or *why*.

In order to provide this sense of understanding, the *how* or *why* of the process they purport to explain, statements in causal-process theories are not independent (as they are in the set-of-laws form), but inter-related. This in turn means that hypothetical constructs are permitted – and indeed are typical – in such theories. While a statement containing such a construct cannot itself be tested directly, because the construct is unoperationalizable, and so untestable, a related statement can be tested. If this statement survives the test, the related statement containing the construct receives indirect support. Thus, whereas every hypothesis must be testable, this is not true of every statement in a theory, provided it is of the causal-process form. A theory remains falsifiable as long as parts of it are testable and all untestable parts are related to testable ones.

The last condition raises an interesting problem for post-1980 versions of Krashen's Monitor Theory, and provides a simple example of why it is necessary for SLA researchers and language teachers to take theory construction seriously. Krashen (1982a, p. 33 and elsewhere) claims that

> in order to acquire, two conditions are necessary. The first is comprehensible (or even better, comprehend*ed*) input containing *i* + 1, structures a bit beyond the acquirer's current level, and second, a low or weak affective filter to allow the input 'in'. This is equivalent

to saying that comprehensible input and the strength of the filter are the true causes of second language acquisition.

Later, Krashen (1984, p. 351) recognizes that the Input Hypothesis contains at least two constructs, *i* and *i* + 1, which pre-empt direct testing of that hypothesis. This would not be a problem (a) were the second and only other causal statement in the theory, the Affective Filter Hypothesis, related to the first; and (b) if the Affective Filter Hypothesis did not itself contain a construct. In fact, however, the Affective Filter Hypothesis is not related (except by assertion) to the Input Hypothesis, and further, not only contains a construct but is itself a construct. An affective filter moving up and down, selectively letting input in to penetrate relevant brain areas (see Krashen 1982a, p. 31) is, after all, a metaphor. Monitor Theory, that is to say, is untestable, and so unfalsifiable, in its post-1980 formulation. This may or may not rule it out as an acceptable basis for prescriptions for the classroom, depending on one's views as to the need for theories to be falsifiable at a particular point in time. Some areas of theoretical physics, after all, although in principle testable, are currently untestable, due to the lack of needed technology, such as large enough particle-colliders. This should not be allowed to inhibit theory construction in SLA any more than in theoretical physics, but it should mean that claims to have tested a theory of SLA need to be subjected to close scrutiny, especially if classroom prescriptions are to follow.

The above comments are intended to emphasize the importance, when formulating or evaluating a theory, of determining whether the claims contained in it remain falsifiable. They are not intended as arguments against basing language teaching on theory. On the contrary, we agree with Krashen (1982a and elsewhere) that sound pedagogic practice should be based on theory, especially if the applications have first been tested in the classroom. Neither are they arguments against the use of constructs in SLA theory building. Least of all are they intended to dispute the value of causal-process theories. Clearly, after all, theories in the causal-process form, which allows such constructs, lead to more efficient research. This is because a causal-process theory offers an interim explanation of a process before its true workings are discovered, although often invoking a *mechanism* (Atkinson 1982) which is not directly observable, e.g. the LAD, in order to do so. A set-of-laws theory, on the other hand, simply reports what is (thought to be) known about a process at any moment.

Because a causal-process theory is the theorist's interim explanation of the process he or she is investigating, the theory motivates and directs the research, telling the investigator which the relevant data are, which is the crucial experiment to run. For the same reason, such theories also provide researchers with a meaningful way of interpreting the results of their studies. Moreover, perhaps because they are less 'bound by data', causal-process theories and the 'theory-then-research' strategy of scientific investigation they entail, have been those associated with *paradigm shifts*, or scientific revolutions, in other fields (Reynolds 1971).

Like set-of-laws theories, however, causal-process theories have disadvantages. A serious problem is that of scientists not knowing when to abandon, rather than simply to modify, a causal-process theory they have invested time in developing. The fact that some parts of such theories may not be directly testable at any time, or, put another way, that the theory will always be 'ahead of the data', means that when the findings of a particular study seem to conflict with one of the theory's predictions, it will not always be clear which aspects of the theory need altering or even whether anything is wrong at all. It might be the case, for example, that the way the study operationalized a particular construct was inappropriate. (This can happen with research on set-of-laws theories, too, of course.) Even if this does not appear to have been a problem, however, it will not always be clear with a causal-process theory which of two or more related statements is now in jeopardy.

The two forms of theory we have described above – set-of-laws and causal-process – are by no means the only ones in the social sciences. They may also reflect a degree of idealization about the theory construction process. It is doubtful whether many researchers always adhere strictly to one approach or the other, especially in the early stages of their work, as will be obvious shortly when we consider some theories in SLA. Hatch and Hawkins (personal communication) point out that in practice, most recognize a reciprocal, cyclical, relationship between theory and data. There are basic differences between the two processes and their products, however, which distinguish at least some of the most active lines of research in SLA, and which have been argued to hold different potential for success in this as in any field of inquiry.

Theories of SLA range along a continuum from nativist through interactionist to environmentalist. They differ, in other words, in the relative importance they attach to innate mechanisms and knowledge, to interactions among innate abilities, learned abilities and environmental factors, and to experientially conditioned learner characteristics and the linguistic input. In this regard, they reflect long-standing nature–nurture debates in many other areas of behavioural sciences (see, e.g., Hinde 1974; Wilson 1975; Gould 1981; Oyama 1985; Waterhouse 1986). The explanations also vary in the kinds of variables – neurological, cognitive, affective, linguistic and situational – they claim to be causal.

By our count, at least forty 'theories' of SLA have been proposed – more if one includes theories of other kinds of language development (first language acquisition, creolization, historical language change, etc.) adopted by some SLA researchers. We will discuss a small illustrative sample grouped into three types: nativist, environmentalist and interactionist, defined in terms of the relative emphasis each type gives to biological and environmental contributions, noting the variables particular theories consider most important, and concentrating on some of the more influential and/or interesting claims. In light of the discussion of forms of theory in the previous section, we will be dealing with some theories not labelled as such by their proponents, and with some which were not originally developed to account for SLA at all, but which either have been, or are beginning to be, influential in SLA research.

7.3 Nativist theories of SLA

7.3.1 General characteristics

Nativist theories are those which purport to explain acquisition by positing an innate biological endowment that makes learning possible. In some cases (e.g. Chomsky 1965; Bickerton 1981, 1984a,b; Pinker 1984; Wode 1984; Krashen 1985), the endowment is language-specific. Thus, Chomsky (1965), for example, posits innate knowledge of substantive universals such as syntactic categories (subject, object, noun, verb) and distinctive phonological features, and of formal universals (abstract principles governing possible rules and parameters of human languages). In other (general) nativist theories (e.g. O'Grady 1987; Parker 1988a), what is held to be innate consists of general cognitive notions (dependency, adjacency, precedence, continuity, etc.) – out of which grammatical principles are built – and mechanisms used for all kinds of learning, including language learning. In still others (e.g. Dulay and Burt 1975, 1977; Felix 1985), the innate endowment involves both linguistic principles and general cognitive notions. Chomsky's various theories of child language development (e.g. Chomsky 1965, 1980, 1981a) are the best known nativist claims, and some of his ideas have been invoked (often critically) in SLA theory construction as well (see, e.g., Flynn 1983, 1984; Zobl 1983b; Felix 1984; Mazurkewich 1984; Cook 1985, 1988; Krashen 1985; Van Buren and Sharwood-Smith 1985; White 1985a, 1987a; Hilles 1986; Liceras 1986, in press; Rutherford 1986; Bley-Vroman 1988; Bley-Vroman, Felix and Ioup 1988; Lightbown and White 1988; Flynn and O'Neil, in press; Gass and Schachter, 1989; Gregg, in press).

7.3.2 Chomsky's Universal Grammar and SLA

Chomsky and those working in a broadly Chomskyan framework note various factors which they claim support the idea that humans are innately (i.e. genetically) endowed with universal language-specific knowledge, or what Chomsky calls Universal Grammar (UG). The main argument, often referred to as the 'logical problem' of language acquisition (Hornstein and Lightfoot 1981; Bley-Vroman 1988), is that without some such endowment (first or second) language learning would be impossible because the input data are insufficiently 'rich' to allow acquisition ever to occur, much less to occur (so uniformly and so quickly) in about five years for child language, and especially not if the child (or adult) were only equipped with general inductive learning procedures with which to attempt to make sense of that input.

According to the Chomskyan view, the input is deficient, or 'poor', in two ways. First, it is claimed to be 'degenerate' (Chomsky 1965; Fodor 1966) in the sense that it is marred by performance features, such as false starts, slips, fragments, and ungrammaticality resulting from these and other pressures inherent in real-time oral communication, and is therefore an inadequate data base for language learning. As we saw in Chapter 5, this is not, in fact, true. Both caretaker speech and language addressed to non-native speakers have been found to be predominantly well formed.

Second, and more serious, however, the input is 'degenerate' in the sense that it is inadequate in various ways. Thus, it does not usually contain 'negative evidence', information from which the learner could work out what is *not* possible in a given language. Overt negative evidence is unavailable because caretakers react to the truth value, not the form, of children's utterances, and rarely correct ungram-matical speech (Brown and Hanlon 1970; Hirsh-Pasek, Treiman and Schneiderman 1984).[3] The same is true of native speakers in non-instructional NS-NNS conversation (Chun, Day, Chenoweth and Luppescu 1982). Although many teachers do explicitly 'correct' classroom learners' errors, research has shown that the corrective feedback they provide is apparently erratic, ambiguous if perceived at all, ill-timed and ineffective in the short run (Allwright 1975; Long 1977; Chaudron 1986b, 1988). Covert negative evidence is also unavailable, since all that learners hear is grammatical utterances. (If they *did* occasionally hear ungrammatical ones, it would make matters worse since, given the lack of correction, there would still be no way of knowing that some were unacceptable, and more reason for thinking all were correct.) Hence, the grammars that learners in fact evolve are said to be 'underdetermined' by the input.

White (1985b) provides several examples of the problem created by hearing only 'positive' evidence in the input, i.e. how do learners find out which sentences are ungrammatical? Thus, in the absence of overt or covert negative evidence, White asks, how does a SL learner who hears (1a), (1b) and (1c) know that (1d) is wrong and (1e) right?

1(a) The car is expensive.
  (b) Is the car expensive?
  (c) The car which is advertised in the paper is expensive.
  (d) *Is the car which – advertised in the paper is
      expensive?
  (e) Is the car which is advertised in the paper – expensive?

The fact that children do not make errors like (1d) suggests, Chomskyans claim, that they already 'know' that rules are 'structure dependent'.

Similarly, Lightbown and White (1987) ask how, without negative evidence, a learner finds out (again, it seems, without ever making errors of the kinds in the asterisked sentences) that (2) through (4) are correct, but that the (b) sentences in (5) through (8) are not.

2(a) Peter stole something.
  (b) What did Peter steal – ?
3(a) The policeman believes that Peter stole something.
  (b) What does the policeman believe that Peter stole – ?
4(a) The lawyer says that the policeman believes that
      Peter stole a watch.
  (b) What does the lawyer say that the policeman believes that
      Peter stole – ?
5(a) Mary likes the children in her morning class.
  (b) *Which class does Mary like the children in – ?
6(a) His love of weapons frightened her.
  (b) *What did his love of – frighten her?
7(a) The workers believed the story that the owner would

close their factory.
(b) *What did the workers believe the story that the
owner would close – ?
8(a) They wondered whether he would declare bankruptcy.
(b) *What did they wonder whether he would declare – ?

The rule of WH-movement formed on the basis of (2b) works in more complex cases like (3b) and (4b), but not in the others. Yet the learner does not make errors like (5b) through (8b), Lightbown and White report, which rules out a hypothesis-testing/error-correction explanation. Other potential explanations can also be discounted, White (1985d) argues. Non-occurrence of the ungrammatical examples cannot handle the data, since forms like (4b) are equally unlikely to have been heard, yet are grammatical, and learners are also well known to make numerous errors in constructions they do hear. The grammatical sentences here are often longer than the ungrammatical ones, eliminating sentence length as a possible factor. Unintelligibility cannot be how learners determine ungrammaticality, since the corresponding statements (and even some of the ungrammatical questions) are perfectly comprehensible. Situational or discourse context, likewise, would never be subtle enough to distinguish the grammatical items. Finally, (first or second) language learners dealing with complex structures like these would be past the stage of receiving well-formed, 'simplified' input, ruling that out as a potential explanation.

The Chomskyan answer to the problem is to posit innate knowledge of constraints on WH-movement, currently dealt with in UG by the 'subjacency' principle (Chomsky 1981a; van Reimsdijk and Williams 1986, Chapter 4). This principle states that a constituent, such as a WH-word, may only be moved out of one bounding category. What constitutes bounding categories varies across languages. S and NP are bounding categories in English. Sentences (5b) through (8b) are ungrammatical, therefore, because in each case the WH-word has been moved out of more than one NP or S. Thus, the principle of subjacency has been violated. What appear to be violations of subjacency in (3b) and (4b) are not, according to Chomsky, because they are products of successive applications of WH-movement, known as the 'comp to comp' analysis of WH-movement. UG consists of a set of such innate, abstract, linguistic principles, which govern what is possible in human languages, thereby helping to alleviate the learning problem created by 'poverty of the stimulus'.

In addition, in order to deal with some of the general (as opposed to idiosyncratic) ways in which languages differ from one another, the principles are held to be able to vary in certain restricted ways, along so-called 'parameters'. Each parameter governs a set of properties of a language, and has an initial (unmarked) 'setting'. To handle the fact, discussed earlier, that learners must be able to learn a language from positive evidence only, the unmarked parameter settings in UG are always the most conservative, or restrictive, i.e. those which accurately represent the properties of some of the world's languages in the areas of grammar they concern, but which are able to be modified to reflect the grammar of other languages simply through the learner experiencing utterances (positive input) which trigger different (more marked) settings of a particular parameter (Baker 1979; Berwick 1985). The principles and the parameters, once their correct settings are triggered by the input, constitute 'core grammar'. There are also more marked, language-specific, rules, which must be learned purely by experience (since they are not parameterized), and which make up the 'peripheral grammar'.

Learnability by positive input alone is illustrated by the differential distribution of pied-piping and preposition-stranding in languages, some allowing only one (pied-piping), and some both. The conservative, unmarked hypothesis must be the restrictive one, that only pied-piping is possible (White 1987a):

9(a) *From where* did you get that fish?
  (b) *With which friend* does Dorothy live?

and that preposition-stranding is not:

9(c) Where did you get that fish *from?*
  (d) *Which friend* does Dorothy live *with?*

A child learning Spanish, which disallows preposition-stranding, will adopt the conservative stance, and hear nothing in the input which does not conform to that rule. A child learning English, on the other hand, will also start by assuming pied-piping is required, but then hear examples of preposition-stranding as well (positive evidence of what is possible in a language), and learn to use both structures. Note that a child who started by assuming either that preposition-stranding (only) or that both pied-piping and preposition-stranding were possible would have no problem with learning English. If he or she were exposed to Spanish, however, the acceptability of pied-piping would be confirmed by the input, but that input would never provide the needed negative evidence, information that preposition-stranding was ungrammatical. The child would consequently make errors by using it. That children supposedly do not actually make such errors is said to show that the initial, unmarked, hypothesis is in fact the conservative one (pied-piping only).

Another illustration of learnability by positive input alone concerns the supposed 'pro-drop', or 'null subject', parameter (Chomsky 1981b; Jaeggli 1982; Rizzi 1982) – 'supposed' because the identity, scope and initial settings of this and other parameters are still much debated. Some languages (+ pro-drop [henceforth, +PD] languages), such as Spanish and Italian, permit empty subjects (except where overt expression of subject is required, e.g. to show a switch in topic):

10(a) – Es mi hermano
   (b) *– Is my brother (He is my brother)

Such sentences are ungrammatical in other (–PD) languages, such as German, French and English, which do not allow the subject pronoun to be 'dropped' in this way.[4] The same languages also do not allow free subject-verb inversion in declaratives:

11(a) Se rio Pepe
   (b) *Laughed Pepe (Pepe laughed)

and do not allow subject extraction from clauses containing a complementizer ('*that*-trace violations'):

12(a) Quien dijo que – se rio?
   (b) *Who did he say that – laughed? (Who did he say laughed?)

Chomsky (1981b) assumes the PD parameter is initially 'set' neutrally, and claims that noticing relevant features in the input will trigger the correct (+PD or –PD) setting for the language concerned for all structures governed by it, even if the child has not yet heard all of those structures – another way in which the language-learning problem is made feasible. Hyams (1983) posits +PD as the initial (unmarked) setting. She notes that English-speaking children go through a stage when some utterances have empty subjects, and others do not. (Their suppliance of subjects in some sentences, incidentally, rules out processing constraints due to length of utterance as an explanation of the empty subject examples.) Their speech at this stage, however, is also marked by a lack of non-referential *it* ('Wet in garden' instead of 'It's wet in the garden') or existential *there* ('Dog in road' instead of 'There's a dog in the road'), and by the absence of lexical material (i.e. modal auxiliaries) in AUX. Hearing expletives in English L1 (*it* and *there* as dummy subjects), Hyams claims, will trigger resetting of the initial +PD setting of the parameter to −PD. Since other internal aspects of the structure of Chomsky's Government and Binding theory (see Hilles 1986, pp. 36–8, for a brief summary) lead to the claim that all natural languages opt for one of two mutually exclusive sets of features (+/−PD), noticing the expletives and consequent fixing of the parameter as −PD will also trigger a variety of other changes in the child's grammar, according to Hyams, including the emergence of modal auxiliaries and the switch to suppliance of overt subject pronouns.

As indicated earlier, work in UG has been motivating a growing amount of SLA research (see Rutherford 1986; Gass and Schachter, 1989). In an early study, White (1986) had 34 speakers of +PD languages (Spanish and Italian) and 37 speakers of a −PD language (French), all studying English in Canada, complete two English tasks: a grammaticality judgement task probing areas supposed to be governed by the PD parameter – missing subjects, free inversion in statements and *that*-trace violations – and a question formation task also testing for *that*-trace violations. On the grammaticality judgement task, the +PD L1 group performed significantly poorer than the (−PD) French speakers on judgements of sentences with missing pronouns. There was no difference between the two groups on free inversion, all subjects rejecting VS word order as ungrammatical in English. (White interpreted this finding as support for arguments by Chao 1981 that VS word order is not in fact part of the pro-drop parameter.) The (−PD) French speakers were only slightly better at recognizing *that*-trace violations. This part of the test proved very difficult for all subjects, however, so any possible difference between groups may have been masked. The predicted effect did materialize on the question-formation task, where the French speakers made significantly fewer errors than subjects in the +PD group.

In a related study, Hilles (1986) set out to test whether Hyams's claims regarding the triggering potential of one structure for others on the PD parameter applied to SLA, too. By examining longitudinal data on the naturalistic acquisition of English by one of the adolescent subjects, Jorge, in the Harvard Project (Cazden, Cancino, Rosansky and Schumann 1975), Hilles was simultaneously able to address the issue of whether older learners have access to UG. She interpreted Jorge's data as generally consistent with Hyams's predictions (see Figure 7.1). PD was present in his early IL, as would be expected in a speaker of a +PD L1 (Spanish) learning a −PD L2 (English). The incidence of PD decreased over time in rough tandem with a corresponding increase in lexical material in AUX. The first appearance of expletives (Tape 6) coincided with a marked decline in the frequency of PD (from Tapes 5 to 7, continuing to Tape 15). Hilles cautions that the number of tokens was small, which can create large swings in percentages, and that the study also involved just one learner. As she claims, however, the results are encouraging enough to warrant testing on a broader data base. Teaching the use of *it* and *there* subjects, Hilles also suggests, *might* prove an effective indirect way of getting classroom learners with +PD L1s to use subject pronouns in other contexts, too. This idea would have implications for syllabus design, if true, and merits testing in a classroom study.

Other studies have utilized Chomsky's ideas to address the role of transfer in SLA in a theoretically coherent manner. White (1987a) points out that UG and theories of language learnability provide a principled way of determining markedness values *a priori*. As noted above, they do this by taking as the unmarked (core grammar) value of a parameter or member of a pair of structures that value or structure which can if necessary be modified by positive input alone to conform to the grammar of a particular target language (Baker 1979; Berwick

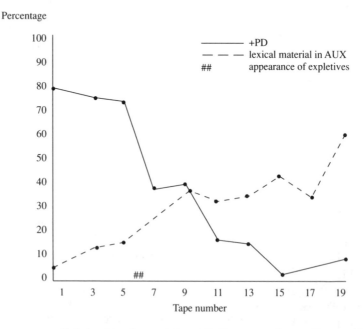

FIGURE 7.1   Relationships Among Three PD Features in Jorge's IL
(based on Hilles 1986)

1985). White then reports on two studies in which learners of French were tested via grammaticality judgements to see whether they would transfer marked structures from the L1 into their L2, i.e. whether those in whose L1 marked (preposition-stranding and double object) constructions were grammatical would accept them as grammatical in the L2. She found that the English speakers did not accept preposition-stranding as grammatical in French, interpreting this as evidence that they still had access to UG, specifically, to the initial unmarked (pied-piping only) setting. The same subjects did transfer marked English double-object constructions to French, however, accepting ungrammatical dative structures as grammatical at all proficiency levels. White called for more research to explain these conflicting findings.

7.3.3 A critique of language-specific nativist theories

While valuable in their own right, studies like that of Hilles (1986) do have a potentially serious interpretation problem as tests of claims about parameter-(re)setting, due to the vagueness of the original idea that settings are triggered 'instantaneously' (once the appropriate input is 'noticed'). Chomsky (1981b) calls this a 'simplifying assumption', a view Hyams apparently shares:

> It is well known that children's language behavior does not change over night. That is to say that the various 'stages' of acquisition . . . are idealizations. . . . In our discussion of grammatical development we have also idealized to a model in which parameters shift in an instant. It is clear, however, from the 'fuzzy' data that there is a period during which the parameters may waver between two values. If this is the case, the 'precocious' expletives may mark the beginning of the shift. (Hyams 1983, p. 234)

Instantaneous setting or resetting would seem to imply categorical change in the IL, e.g. suppliance of *all* subject pronouns. This would be a strong, interesting – and testable – claim, but one which Hilles' (1986) study would then be seen as falsifying rather than supporting. Figure 7.1 shows that Jorge supplied subject pronouns approximately 20 per cent of the time (80 per cent PD) *before* the first appearance of expletives, and only 65 per cent soon after that, followed by a gradual improvement to target-like suppliance over the next several taping sessions. The initial steep decline in PD after expletives appeared is, of course, the potentially supportive finding. The question that remains, however, is how great a change must occur for the data to be accepted as consistent with the model, or conversely, how much 'error' arising from non-instantaneous setting is tolerable before the parameter-setting claim must be rejected. There will eventually come a point at which the (relative frequency) changes observed will be sufficiently slight to render the growth curves of some IL phenomena supposedly governed by triggered parameter-setting indistinguishable from those of traditional developmental sequences.

In addition to some problems concerning empirical falsifiability, Chomsky's explanation of language acquisition involves at least three questionable assumptions. The first is that learning occurs quickly and is mostly complete by age five. In fact, a good deal of complex syntax is not mastered until much later (as shown, among others, by C. Chomsky 1969). English dative movement, for example, is not fully learned until about age sixteen. Mazurkewich and White (1984) found that nine-year-olds overgeneralized the rule, which is lexically conditioned, to verbs to which it does not apply, as in (13d):

13(a) Toshi gave the letter to Kate.
  (b) Toshi gave Kate the letter.
  (c) Ted donated the money to the charity.
  (d) *Ted donated the charity the money.

Between nine and sixteen, learners gradually master first the semantic (new possessor) constraint on movement, and then the phonological (native verbs) constraint (for details, see Mazurkewich and White 1984). As Mazurkewich and White point out, this is an example of a late-acquired, lexically conditioned syntactic rule, which is initially overgeneralized, must be learnable without negative evidence, and is too language-specific to be innately determined. Other examples of 'late' acquisition include some WH-questions not learned until age ten (Hildebrand 1987), and then, as with most syntax, after the learner has passed through a sequence of stages of gradually increasing complexity (see discussion below); and many other constructions not acquired until after age five (see Karmiloff-Smith 1986 for review). Some of the transitional structures in developmental sequences, it should also be noted, are not predicted by UG, e.g. '*is* + S' yes/no questions (Crain and Nakayama 1987; and see Chapter 4, Question 12, for child second language examples).

A second crucial assumption is that certain syntactic principles are unlearnable, and therefore innate. This is increasingly being challenged. General cognitive strategies and notions, such as conservative hypothesis-formation, developmental sequences based on cumulative complexity, and avoidance of discontinuity, are being used to reanalyse such UG icons as structure-dependence, PD phenomena, subjacency and binding principles (O'Grady 1987, to appear; Parker 1989).

In the case of structure dependence, Parker (1989) argues that the fact that learners do not produce utterances like (1d):

1(d) *Is the car which – advertised in the paper is expensive?

is not necessarily evidence for innate linguistic knowledge. In English, movement in question formation takes place only in main, not embedded, clauses. (We do not invert in sentences like 'I don't know where *she is*'.) This, Parker notes, reflects the typological tendency for main clauses to permit greater word-order variation than embedded clauses (Mallinson and Blake 1982). Since learners only hear inversion in main clauses, she continues, they have no reason to suppose it is possible elsewhere, and so do not produce utterances with movement from an embedded relative clause like (1d). All that is necessary for a learning explanation is to assume that a learner makes conservative hypotheses (O'Grady 1987) and can distinguish main and embedded clauses. The structural knowledge that relative clauses are embedded is a necessary part of having learned that a relative clause modifies a noun phrase, and does not require innate knowledge of structure-dependence. In addition, Parker notes, while Crain and Nakayama (1987) did not find children making errors like that in (1d), they did observe utterances like (14):

14. *Is the boy who can see Mickey Mouse is happy?

Verb-copying in initial position as a strategy for question-formation prior to attaining the target construction, she suggests, is impossible to explain within a UG framework without recourse to a learning theory.

Subjacency effects, illustrated in (2) through (8), can also be accounted for without recourse to innate linguistic knowledge, through the assumption in a theory of learning of a preference for continuity (O'Grady 1987; Parker, 1989). Discontinuity arises in WH-questions like those in (2) through (8), when a constituent is moved to initial position, because there is then an element missing elsewhere in the sentence. The moved element has left a discontinuous VP in the grammatical examples, (2) through (4). The ungrammatical sentences, (5b) through (8b), all involve simultaneous discontinuities in more than one type of phrase, e.g. in (5b), the moved element has left a discontinuous PP embedded in an NP embedded in a VP. If a learner is assumed to make conservative hypotheses, Parker points out (following O'Grady

1987), then he or she should expect on the basis of (1) through (3) that English allows discontinuity only in VP, not in any structures embedded within VP, and so does not produce sentences like (5b) through (7b), and similarly does not allow discontinuity in dependent clauses, and so does not produce sentences like (8b). The grammaticality of sentences like (8b) in some languages, e.g. Swedish, from this perspective, would be the result of positive evidence in those languages, but would pose a problem for a UG account.

White's (1987a) finding that English learners did not transfer marked preposition-stranding into French, Parker suggests, can also be explained more parsimoniously as adoption of the conservative position, i.e. as the result of learners not accepting greater discontinuity than is exhibited in (this time, the L2) input. The finding in the same study, on the other hand, that some ungrammatical (marked) L2 dative constructions were accepted is consistent, she notes, with the first language tendency for learners to be conservative in the syntax, but to overgeneralize in the lexicon (Pinker 1984), the dative rule being different in that it is lexically conditioned, as shown, e.g. by the use of *give* and *donate* in (13b) and (13d).

A third assumption is that the input available to learners is inadequate, specifically that it lacks essential negative evidence with which to remedy excessive complexity and overgeneralization. While obviously true as far as the absence of negative input is concerned, this need not imply innate linguistic knowledge. Rather, as indicated above, learning may be a process involving initial adoption of conservative hypotheses (not maximum complexity), followed by movement along a developmental continuum (of gradually increasing complexity), governed by a learning theory and guided by positive evidence.

In its treatment of lexical rules, which it says are part of the marked periphery, and so not regulated by innate principles, even UG implicitly recognizes that lack of negative evidence does not necessarily prevent acquisition. Bowerman (1987) points out that, since lexical rules are language- and culture-specific, and so cannot be regulated innately, lexical overgeneralization is a problem which has to be dealt with through linguistic experience in any theory, including a nativist theory. The cure for lexical overgeneralizations, which all learners, first or second language, child or adult, make, has to be a theory of learning which constrains the initial hypotheses in some way, and then modifies them via positive evidence (e.g. Pinker 1984), or else perhaps a processing model, such as Parallel Distributed Processing (Rumelhart and McClelland 1986 – see Section 7.4.1), which views learning as the gradual strengthening or weakening of associations (yielding what looks like rule-governed behaviour), based upon the frequency with which the learner encounters various form–meaning pairs. UG's recognition that overgeneralization of lexical rules is remediable by experience of positive evidence alone weakens its claim that basic syntactic rules cannot be learned this way, but only by use of a heavy language-specific innate endowment.

The existence of well-attested developmental sequences (see Chapter 4) in first and second languages lends further support to the idea that the lack of negative evidence is less significant for learning than Chomskyans claim. Thus, in a cross-sectional study of children aged four through ten learning English as L1, Hildebrand (1987) found three stages in the acquisition of WH-questions. O'Grady (1987) points out that those stages were progressively more complex, as measured by the degree of discontinuity each involved:

15(a)   What did the little girl hit – with the block today?
           (Disc. VP)
    (b)   What did the little boy play with – behind his mother?
           (Disc. PP, VP)
    (c)   What did the boy read a story about – this morning?
           (Disc. PP, NP, VP)

Parker (1989) notes that a learning theory account can explain this sequence as the product of an initially conservative learner hypothesis (preference for continuity), followed by gradual acceptance of progressively more serious and complex cases of discontinuity. The data are problematic for a parameter-setting model, on the other hand, she points out. Given that positive evidence of all three constructions is available in the input, there is nothing in the theory to explain why sentences like (15c), which illustrate the most radical, most marked, level of discontinuity, do not trigger simultaneous emergence of sentences like (15a) through (15c).

Parker goes on to make an interesting suggestion as to why cross-sectional grammaticality judgement studies of whether adult SL learners have access to UG obtain the mixed results they do. Some researchers find SL learners performing significantly better than chance (Bley-Vroman, Felix and Ioup 1988), and others worse than would be expected (Schachter 1989) if UG were still available to them. Parker suggests that the ambiguous findings are caused by treating continued access in a binary fashion, thereby obscuring the possibility that, rather than having/not having access to UG, learners are progressing through the developmental sequences which learning theories elucidate. In this respect, one might add, the parameter-setting model is following tradition (described in Chapter 3) where linguistics and SLA research are concerned: while attractive because they offer precise, testable, theoretically motivated predictions, UG-inspired analyses suffer from the same static, target-language orientation that has plagued other approaches to IL development based upon theories of language rather than theories of language learning.

7.3.4 Krashen's Monitor Theory

One of the best known and most influential theories of SLA in the 1970s and early 1980s was Krashen's Monitor Theory (MT). MT began life not as a theory of SL acquisition, but as a model of SL performance (Krashen 1976). In its earliest incarnation, it was an attempt to capture and reconcile two phenomena. First, a generalization was emerging from the 'morpheme studies' (see Chapter 4) that there existed statistically significant associations (although not invariance) between the orders of appearance of certain English grammatical morphemes, accurately supplied in obligatory contexts, in the speech and writing of SL learners of different ages, L1 backgrounds and (formal and informal) conditions of exposure. Second, disturbances were observed in this 'natural order' (Krashen 1977) on certain performance tasks, specifically the reading and writing tasks, as compared with three other listening and speaking tasks, in Larsen-Freeman's (1975a) study.

Krashen (1976) claimed that two separate knowledge systems under-lay SL performance. The first and most important, the *acquired system*, was the product of application by learners of the same (unspecified) language-learning abilities children used for first language acquisition, and consisted of subconscious knowledge of the SL grammar, like the subconscious knowledge NSs have of their first language. The second and less important knowledge system, the *learned system*, was the product of formal instruction (typically classroom language teaching), and comprised conscious knowledge of 'easy' SL grammatical rules, such as those for subject–verb agreement or for pluralizing NPs in English. The acquired system was typically the only knowledge source speakers could use in real-time communication, when they were attending to meaning, not form; the learned system served only as a planner and editor with which to inspect, or monitor, the output of the acquired system. The learned system was only accessible when three conditions were met: there was time (i.e. a task was unspeeded), the learner was focused on form (usually, during a discrete-point grammar test), and (obviously) when the learner knew the rule. The 'natural order',

Krashen held, was the surface manifestation of the acquired system; disturbed orders were caused by ('big M') Monitoring, intrusion of the learned system on performance tasks which encouraged its use, with the result that certain morphemes governed by low-level grammar rules, like third-person singular -*s*, regular past -*ed* and plural -*s*, were supplied more accurately, and consequently rose in rank.

Krashen claimed that ('small m') monitoring, self-correcting using conscious or subconscious general awareness of language, could be done by 'feel' judgements, using the acquired system. Learners might pause to see whether a word or construction looked or sounded right, in the same way that NSs sometimes compare mental images of two possible spellings of a word they are unsure of, say, 'ceiling' and 'cieling', or even write out both versions to see which looks correct. (Monitoring with the learned system – 'big M' Monitoring – on the other hand, would be equivalent to accessing a rule of English spelling the NS happens to know, like 'i before e, except after c'.) Knowledge from one system could not pass into the other, however (Krashen and Scarcella 1978; Krashen 1985, pp. 38–43). The two systems, like the processes which produced them, *acquisition* and *learning*, operated separately; there was no 'cross-over' or 'interface', e.g. through some 'consciousness-raising' process (Sharwood-Smith 1981; Rutherford 1987; Schmidt 1988b). Finally, learners varied in their use of the Monitor, some being under-users, some optimal users (those who used the learned system to improve accuracy without too great a loss of fluency), and some over-users (Krashen 1978).

In a series of books and papers appearing between 1978 and 1985, the Monitor Model underwent a number of modifications. It became a 'theory' – Monitor Theory (MT) – of (child and adult, naturalistic and instructed) SLA, its scope broadening to include a wide array of SL phenomena, with a 'hypothesis' summarizing Krashen's conclusions in each area of literature he surveyed.[5] There were as many as ten 'hypotheses' in the early 1980s (see Krashen 1981b, 1982a), reduced to five major claims in more recent formulations (e.g. Krashen 1985). These are the Acquisition-Learning, Natural Order, and Monitor Hypotheses, which handle the issues focused on in the original Monitor Model, and the Input and Affective Filter Hypotheses, which, on the surface, at least, are the central claims of 'Extended Standard' MT. There follows a brief explanation of each.

The *Acquisition-Learning Hypothesis* states that there are two independent ways of learning an SL: acquisition and learning, both technical terms in MT. As indicated earlier, 'acquisition' refers to the subconscious process used by children developing their first language;

'learning' is a conscious process, which results in a separate system of simple grammar rules, or knowledge about the SL.

The *Natural Order Hypothesis* says that SL rules are acquired in a predictable order, one apparently not determined solely by linguistic complexity, and certainly not by the order in which the items appear in teaching syllabuses. Acquisition orders, that is, do not reflect instructional sequences. Krashen's 'natural order' is his synthesis of the findings of the 'morpheme studies' (see Chapter 4), studies which actually addressed accuracy, or difficulty, orders, not acquisition orders, it should be noted.

The *Monitor Hypothesis* encapsulates the relationship posited between the acquired and learned systems during SL performance. As in the earlier Monitor Model, the acquired system is the utterance initiator, with the learned system acting in a planning, editing and correcting function when three conditions are met.

The *Input Hypothesis* attempts to explain how a learner acquires an SL. Krashen calls it the central claim of MT.[6] It maintains that an SL is acquired through processing *comprehensible input* (CI), i.e. language that is heard or read and *understood*. Language that is not understood does not help; it is too advanced, just noise in the system. Not all CI helps, either. Understanding messages in an SL because they are encoded in target-language samples less complex than the learner is already capable of dealing with may help the ego, but will not lead to IL improvement. Progress along the 'natural order' is achieved when a learner at some stage, *i*, of IL development receives CI that contains structures (lexis, sounds, morphology, syntax, etc.) one step beyond the current stage, or structures at '*i* + 1' (see Krashen 1983 for a more detailed formulation). The unknown structures are *understood*, the necessary precursor for acquisition in Krashen's model, through the help of linguistic and extra-linguistic context, knowledge of the world, previously acquired linguistic knowledge, and in a classroom, by these means and such devices as pictures, translation and explanation. Linguistic and conversational adjustments also play a role here (see Chapter 5). A corollary of the primacy attributed to comprehension is that speaking is a result, not a cause of acquisition; it emerges as a product of growth in competence, achieved through understanding target-language samples.

This part of the Input Hypothesis makes claims about what are potentially usable data for SLA, but, as Larsen-Freeman (1983c) points out, says nothing about how the data are actually used (for a testable proposal, see Chaudron 1985a, 1985b). This is because Krashen assumes a heavy innate endowment to handle acquisition. This, in fact, is really Krashen's and MT's central claim. Recent formulations of the Input Hypothesis make MT's nativist, and specifically, Chomskyan, allegiances explicit. Krashen (1985, pp. 2–3) writes:

> If input is understood, and there is enough of it, the necessary grammar is automatically provided . . . input is the essential environmental ingredient . . . [but] there is a significant contribution of the internal language processor (Chomsky's Language Acquisition Device: LAD).

He suggests (1985, p. 3) that what he considers to be the extensive evidence for the Input Hypothesis 'supports Chomsky's position, and extends it to second-language acquisition'. Like Chomsky, Krashen further assumes (p. 3) that the endowment is language-specific: 'deep down, the "mental organ" for language (Chomsky, 1975) produces one basic product, a human language, in one fundamental way'. While the overt importance attached to the Input Hypothesis might lead one to assume MT to be an interactionist or even an environmentalist theory, Krashen ultimately adopts a strict nativist position, a point, it would seem, crucial enough to merit its own hypothesis in future formulations.

Following Dulay and Burt (1977), the *Affective Filter Hypothesis* embodies Krashen's view that various affective factors, including motivation, self-confidence and anxiety, play a facilitative, but non-causal, role in SLA (for review, see Krashen 1981a). Lack of motivation, low self-esteem, debilitating anxiety, and so on, Krashen claims, can combine to 'raise the filter', to form a 'mental block', which prevents CI from reaching the LAD (Krashen 1982a, p. 31), and thereby from being used for acquisition. A negative affective disposition (a filter that is 'up'), that is, constitutes a constraint on the successful workings of CI. Put another way, positive affect is necessary, but not sufficient, for SLA.

Krashen (1981b, 1985) states explicitly that the five 'hypotheses' can be summarized as follows:

> People acquire second languages only if they obtain comprehensible input and if their affective filters are low enough to allow the input 'in'. When the filter is 'down' and appropriate comprehensible input is presented (and comprehended), acquisition is inevitable. It is, in fact, unavoidable and cannot be prevented – the language 'mental organ' will function just as automatically as any other organ. (Krashen 1985, p. 4)

Omission of any reference to three of the five 'hypotheses' in the 'summary' shows that MT consists *de facto* of just one causal statement involving two variables (making it, after Schumann's Acculturation Model – see below – the second strongest claim in the SLA literature to date): 'CI, plus a "low affective filter", is necessary and sufficient for SLA.' Krashen recognizes this when he asserts (1985, p. 4) that 'comprehensible input is the essential ingredient for second-language acquisition. All other factors thought to encourage or cause SLA work only when they contribute to comprehensible input and/or a low filter.' As indicated above, however, MT is really much more powerful than this statement would suggest, since an even more 'essential ingredient' in MT is actually a *language-specific innate endowment*: *Chomsky's UG*. It is this, not CI, which Krashen says makes SLA possible.

Krashen has been quite willing to apply MT to the SL classroom (see especially Krashen 1981b, 1982a, 1985, Chapter 3), taking a forthright stance (e.g. 1982a, pp. 1–8) on the relevance of theory to classroom practice when this was not fashionable. His ideas have been influential in designing various kinds of teaching programmes. In addition, while recognizing, of course, that it pre-dated MT, Krashen claims (1985, p. 16) that 'immersion "works" because, like other good methods, it provides students with a great deal of comprehensible input', as in the case of the Canadian French-immersion programmes, by teaching content curricula through the SL, which is adjusted appropriately (something impossible in *sub*mersion situations) since teachers are dealing with linguistically homogeneous classes of students.

Partly inspired by the Canadian French immersion model, Krashen was instrumental in pioneering so-called 'sheltered subject matter' courses. These are special sections of basic university courses (Psych. 101, etc.) for foreign students, in which, once again, the instructors can, as needed, adjust the English they use (roughly, at least) for the advanced but still non-native language ability of the students. This idea has also been adopted in a number of school systems in the USA as (supposedly) one way of catering to the language needs of minority-language children, such as recent immigrants. Finally, in collaboration with Terrell, author of the Natural Approach (originally developed as a method of teaching foreign languages), Krashen has applied his ideas to classroom foreign and second language instruction for adults (Krashen and Terrell 1983). Common to all these applications are advocacy of: (1) a focus on meaning, not form, by teacher and students at all times (communication which will ensure the provision of CI); (2) proscription of structural grading and error correction (either of which would lead to a focus on language as object); and (3) creation of a positive affective classroom climate in order to 'lower the filter'.

7.3.5 A critique of Monitor Theory

MT has received a great deal of criticism in the SLA literature, perhaps more than its fair share. There are probably several reasons for this, over and above any defects it may have. It was one of the first 'theories' developed specifically to explain SLA, and so was for some time *a*, and for many, *the* major position to be subjected to empirical test (or armchair polemic). It made a large number of claims about a wide array of SLA phenomena, many of which seemed empirically falsifiable, and so attracted researchers. It was closely tied to recommendations for classroom practice, and therefore again seemed important to test. Furthermore, many of those recommendations challenged basic assumptions about language teaching, rousing the ire of some with vested interests to protect. Being clearly presented by Krashen both in writing and at conferences, and not requiring of the consumer any daunting technical expertise in linguistics or psychology, it was easily understood, even by the non-specialist, a virtue which had the side-effect, however, of creating instant experts who had not actually read the related research, much less conducted any themselves, but who now asserted their own views. Finally, MT was one of the first explicit attempts to harvest SLA research findings for language teachers.

In general, however, most of the published criticism was scientifically motivated and, not surprisingly, given MT's wide scope, aimed at a variety of targets. Serious concerns were first expressed by McLaughlin (1978) about the learning/acquisition distinction. He noted that this rested on another distinction, that between conscious and subconscious processes. Krashen claimed to distinguish those via introspection, i.e. by whether subjects reported making grammaticality judgements based on 'rule' or 'feel', respectively. McLaughlin questioned the reliability (and thus the validity) of this methodology. (See, further, Rivers 1980; Morrison and Low 1983.) He also criticized other aspects of studies using the methodology. For example, asking subjects to state the rules if they thought they had been monitoring by rule on a grammaticality judgement task (Krashen, Butler, Birnbaum and Robertson 1978), he pointed out, might have biased them towards saying they were monitoring by 'feel', because this was an easier option than trying to articulate the rules. A cognitive psychologist, McLaughlin was in general suspicious of the use of subjective, introspective and anecdotal evidence to support (or attack) the conscious–subconscious distinction itself or the primacy of 'learning' or 'acquisition'.[7]

In response, Krashen (1979, pp. 152–3), a mentalist linguist by train-ing, admitted that 'at this moment, we have no physiological measure that shows an acquisition–learning difference', but noted (1979, p. 152) that 'in this way, second language acquisition research is identical to research in cognitive psychology, in which researchers posit an abstract hypothesis and then see if it predicts measurable phenomena'. This is, of course, to confuse hypothesis and theory, as discussed earlier (see fn. 5). Krashen further accepted that there would be some ambiguous cases, but suggested that this, too, often happened in psychology, and was not grounds for rejecting a distinction that usually could be verified – a point with which most would agree.

Turning his attention to other aspects of MT, McLaughlin made two criticisms of Krashen's explanation of variation in morpheme accuracy orders. First, he claimed it was 'circular' to say that a 'natural order' was obtained under Monitor-free conditions, the product of 'acquisition', but that when the Monitor operated, the order was disrupted, the product of learning. Second, he objected to Krashen modifying his initial claim as to when the Monitor could be accessed, with resulting disturbances in the 'natural order', after viewing the results of studies. Krashen, Butler, Birnbaum and Robertson (1978), for example, had predicted the 'natural order' on speeded compositions, and a disturbed order on unspeeded compositions written by the same students when told to concentrate on the accuracy, not the quantity, of what they wrote. Finding the 'natural order' under both conditions, Krashen et al. concluded not that the study disconfirmed the hypothesis, but that it showed that writers focused on meaning, not form, when writing compositions, i.e. as indicating a mis-classification of the second writing task. Similarly, contrary to their prediction, Krashen, Sferlazza, Feldman and Fathman (1976), like Fuller (1978), obtained a natural order on an oral administration of the Fathman's SLOPE test, a series of picture-cued, open-completion grammar items ('The boy has two ——' [dogs]). The researchers again maintained their original hypothesis, claiming the study showed that the SLOPE was not, after all, one that elicited Monitor use.

Krashen's response to this objection of McLaughlin's was to note that, within reason, modifying a claim in the light of new evidence (here by recognizing that the domain of the conscious monitor, apparently restricted to extreme discrete-point test items, was even more limited than originally believed) was perfectly normal in science, indeed, that it signified progress:

> My view of scientific method is simple. We look for generalizations, abstractions, that predict real world phenomena. We can arrive at these generalizations any way we like (intuitions, data, etc.), but our

generalizations need to be able to predict [new data]. . . . If they do, we are still in business, but if they do not, we have to change the hypothesis, alter it. If these alterations cause major changes in the fundamental assumptions in the original generalizations, make it too *ad hoc*, too cumbersome, we may have to abandon the hypothesis. (Krashen 1979, pp. 158–9)

Ignoring for the moment the unfortunate uses of terminology in this statement ('intuitions, data, etc.', 'generalizations predicting', and so on), Krashen's general position is defensible. Up to a point, modification is an acceptable alternative to wholesale abandonment of general theoretical claims (although not hypotheses), a community of scholars judging when the modifications are becoming 'too *ad hoc*'. It must also be noted, however, that the revision option does have the short-term side-effect, intended or not, of immunizing a claim against falsification.

MT had several other shortcomings *qua* 'theory', and even worse problems if viewed as a set of empirically testable hypotheses. The incestuous nature of the original three (Learning-Acquisition, Natural Order and Monitor) Hypotheses was problematic, with resulting difficulties in interpreting empirical tests of each.[8] The lack of any independent measure of whether someone was an 'under-, optimal or over-user' of the Monitor constituted a further obstacle to falsification. A task might be 'mis-classified' as one eliciting Monitor use; alternatively, the task might be fine, but a particular subject 'mis-classified' as a Monitor user.

The Input Hypothesis and Affective Filter Hypothesis were also untestable. The former contains vital constructs, i and $i + 1$, which Krashen (1984) himself recognized are unoperationalizable, given the state of knowledge in IL studies. The latter is a metaphor; to provide it with empirical content, Krashen would need to specify which affect variables, singly or in what combinations, and at what levels, serve to 'raise the filter'. For example, is it sufficient for one aspect of a learner's affective state, such as attitude, to be negative, or do all aspects have to be negative, and if so, to what degree? Can one positive aspect, e.g. high motivation, offset a negative one, e.g. low self-esteem? Finally, what are (cross-linguistically, cross-culturally) acceptable measures of those affect variables, and thereby, of the filter?[9]

Answers to these questions determine whether cases like Wes (Schmidt 1981, 1983) do or do not constitute a falsification of MT. Schmidt's subject, a highly successful Japanese artist living in Honolulu, with access to massive amounts of CI over many years, seemed to have stabilized far short of native-like norms in most areas of grammatical morphology Schmidt studied, despite the fact that his affective profile was for the most part extremely positive, although not perfectly so. Krashen seems ambivalent about Wes:

> His grammatical problems cannot be blamed on the quantity of input he received. . . . Wes seems to have a 'low filter' type of personality – high self-esteem, low anxiety, and motivated to communicate. Schmidt does point out, however, that Wes's motivations for moving to Hawaii were only in a small way integrative. . . . Wes retained a strong sense of being Japanese. (Krashen 1985, p. 50)

Interestingly, Schumann (1986), unlike Krashen, does accept Wes as a counter-example to the Acculturation Model (see Section 7.4.2).
    Additional problems for MT include the following:

1. There is no explanation for why the 'filter' does not exist in children, and only comes into play at puberty, thereby, according to Krashen, accounting for the low success of adults, like Wes, with plenty of CI (Gregg 1984).
2. A simple binary distinction, $+/-$ Monitor mode, is inadequate to handle the highly complex, but systematic, variability observed in ILs (see Chapter 4). Researchers have shown that a variety of lects can be elicited, even if not wholly predictably, on a range of tasks, all of which are supposedly non-Monitorable (Tarone 1985).
3. The limited content ('easy' grammar rules) and domain (discrete-point tests) of the learned system, cannot account for the data on the effects of instruction on IL development (Long 1983d, 1988b; and see Chapter 8).
4. MT offers no *explanation* for the morpheme orders on which many of its claims are based and (supposedly) tested, nor for any other developmental sequences (Gregg 1984; Pienemann and Johnston 1987). Indeed, following Bahns and Wode (1980) and Meisel, Clahsen and Pienemann (1981), its criteria for acquisition (80 or 90 per cent accuracy) could be said to preclude statements about acquisition and/or the acquisition process altogether by looking only at the end point, or product, of acquisition, not at the process by which that product is achieved.
5. The appeal to Chomskyan UG to explain acquisition must mean that MT suffers from the same theoretical and empirical troubles that afflict other UG positions, issues and studies not mentioned

at all by Krashen, who, as noted, has yet to include in MT a 'UG Hypothesis'.

6. White (1987b) brings 'poverty of the stimulus' arguments to bear on the Input Hypothesis, arguing for the value of *in*comprehensible input as a crucial source of negative evidence in SLA.

7. Gregg (1988, in press) provides rigorous critiques of the vague linguistic content both of MT and of attempted defences of Krashen's views, such as that by Schwartz (1986).

8. Critical reviews of the teaching applications have focused on the lack of classroom evaluation studies,[10] the absence of much specificity as to the syllabus content of MT-inspired language teaching programmes, and what is seen by some to be unwarranted rejection of advantages to be gained by various kinds of focus on language form in language teaching. Counter-proposals, it should be noted, however, often differ as much from each other as from Krashen's ideas on the subject (see, e.g., Sharwood-Smith 1981; Long 1985a, 1988b; Pica 1985; Pienemann 1985b; Long and Crookes 1986; Nicholas 1986; Schmidt and Frota 1986; Candlin 1987; Pienemann and Johnston 1987; Rutherford 1987; Crookes 1988a; Nunan 1988; Schmidt 1988a).

In conclusion, the Monitor Model and its successor, MT, served SLA researchers well by offering an early attempt to make sense of a wide array of disparate research findings. In addition, Krashen's ideas themselves initially stimulated a good deal of data-based research, and forced some fresh thinking in language teaching circles. While some of the original claims no longer excite much interest among researchers and/or have been superseded by other developments, they served a valuable purpose by identifying some of the relevant issues and, where apparently wrong, by obliging critics to seek out and substantiate alternatives.

7.4 Environmentalist theories of SLA

7.4.1 General characteristics

Environmentalist theories of learning hold that an organism's nurture, or experience, are of more importance to development than its nature, or innate contributions. Indeed, they will typically deny that innate contributions play any role at all other than that of providing the animal with the internal structure which environmental forces can proceed to shape. The best known examples are the various forms of behaviourist and neo-behaviourist stimulus–response learning theories, such as those of Skinner (1957), but such positions have had little impact since Chomsky's (1959) famous review of Skinner's *Verbal Behavior*, and subsequent writings by Chomsky and his followers, despite attempted rebuttals (e.g. MacCorquodale 1970) and serious problems with nativist alternatives. Neo-behaviourist learning theory was influential in language teaching circles, chiefly through the underpinnings it provided the Audio-Lingual Method (ALM) in the work of Fries, Lado, Politzer, Prator and others. The ALM and related classroom practices fell into disfavour soon after Chomsky's early work appeared, however, the explicit demolition coming in *The Psychologist and the Foreign-Language Teacher* (Rivers 1964).

While S–R models show little promise as explanations of SLA, except for perhaps pronunciation and the rote-learning of formulae, a related family of *connectionist* models have excited considerable interest in some circles as potential sources of insight into more general properties of learning and development in diverse areas, including motor control, visual perception, and memory. Of particular interest for language learning theory is the work on *Parallel Distributed Processing* (PDP) (McClelland, Rumelhart and the PDP Research Group 1986). PDP is a theory of cognition which assumes no innate endowment. PDP theorists hold that learning is based on the processing of input, but do not believe that the input processing results in the accrual of rules. Rather, learning is held to consist of the strengthening and weakening of connections in complex neural networks as a function of the frequency of stimuli in the input. The networks control what looks like rule-governed behaviour, but which is simply a reflection of the connections formed on the basis of the relative strengths of various patterns in the input. Thus, Rumelhart and McClelland (1986) demonstrated that computers can be programmed to simulate typical developmental patterns in English past tense formation, complete with (mostly) typical production errors, based on input consisting of average frequencies, changing over time in the ways documented in empirical studies, of strong and weak verb forms marked for past time reference in caretaker speech to children.

Reception of PDP has bordered on ecstatic in some quarters, Sampson (1987), for example, foreseeing a greater impact for it on linguistics than publication of Chomsky's *Syntactic Structures*. Others have been predictably less enthusiastic, Chomsky (1987, p. 27) dismissing 'connectionism' as 'immediately refuted, in some cases refuted in principle', a programme whose 'prospects . . . seem very dim' and which offers 'nothing substantive to discuss'. More significantly, among those psycholinguists who have given PDP serious attention, important problems are identified by Lachter and Bever (1988), Pinker and Prince (1988) and others. The interested reader is referred to a 1988 issue of *Cognition* devoted to critical examination of the PDP paradigm. Schmidt (1988) and Gasser (1990) outline some potential implications of PDP for SLA theory and research.

While it is arguable that no pure environmentalist theories of language learning other than connectionism have been advanced in recent years, several theories currently fall into the environmentalist camp by default because they try to explain acquisition by invoking learner external variables, without saying anything about cognitive processing. Among the strongest such claims is Schumann's attempt to account for naturalistic SLA as a by-product of acculturation.

7.4.2 Schumann's Pidginization Hypothesis and Acculturation Model

As part of a larger study, the Harvard Project (Cazden, Cancino, Rosansky and Schumann 1975), Schumann (1975, 1978a) conducted a ten-month observation of the untutored acquisition of ESL by Alberto, a 33-year-old working-class Costa Rican. Alberto lived with a Costa Rican couple in a mostly Portuguese section of Cambridge, Massachusetts, worked as a frame polisher in a factory staffed mostly by NNSs of English, and socialized mostly in Spanish. Alberto was the least successful of the six learners studied by Cazden et al. He was, for example, the only one still at the *No V* negation stage at the end of the study; there were few *don't V* tokens in his speech, and only four instances of *aux-neg* and analysed *don't* during the entire ten-month period. For seven months after the ten months of the study proper, Schumann attempted to improve Alberto's negation through formal instruction (transformation drills), but with little effect. Before the teaching, Alberto's negatives were 22 per cent (23/105) correct in spontaneous speech, chiefly due to the occasional appropriate use of *don't*, and 10 per cent (7/71) correct in elicited utterances, when Alberto was asked to negate affirmative sentences presented by Schumann. After instruction, elicited negatives, where Alberto was monitoring his output, improved to 64 per cent (216/335) correct, but spontaneous negatives were slightly worse, at 20 per cent (56/278) correct.

Other aspects of Alberto's IL were equally poorly developed after ten months. He remained at Stage 1 of question formation throughout the study, failing to invert in the vast majority of both yes/no and

WH-questions. Only twelve WH-questions and only 5 per cent (11/213) of his yes/no questions were inverted over ten months, and of the combined total of twenty-three inverted questions, nine were with *like*, five with *say*, four with *want*, and one each with *see* and *are* (Schumann, 1978a, pp. 29–30). His development of inflectional morphology (possessive, regular and irregular past, plural and progressive *-ing*) was also erratic, generally poor, and much slower than that of the other subjects.

In light of these findings, Schumann's study gradually became an attempt to explain why Alberto's acquisition of ESL was so limited. Cognitive ability was ruled out as a cause, since Alberto performed normally on a Piagetian test of adaptive intelligence. Age was rejected on the grounds that many older learners do far better than Alberto. Rather, Alberto's social and psychological distance from speakers of the target language appeared to Schumann to constitute a more likely explanation.

Social distance, a group-level phenomenon, consists of eight factors in Schumann's Model, the values of most of which seemed negative, i.e. likely to mitigate against successful SLA, or were at best neutral where Alberto was concerned:

(1) *Social dominance* (dominance, non-dominance, subordination). Alberto was a member of a social group (working-class Latin American migrants) which was politically, culturally, technically and economically subordinate to (hence, distant from) the target-language group.

(2) *Integration pattern* (assimilation, acculturation, preservation). He was a member of a group whose integration pattern typically lay somewhere between (for SLA, supposedly negative) preservation of cultural identity and (for SLA, supposedly positive) assimilation into the target-language culture.

(3) *Enclosure*. He was a member of a group with many of its own churches, clubs, newspapers, and so on, i.e. a group with relatively high enclosure. (In some cases, Schumann states, high enclosure can involve a group having its own trades, crafts, professions and schools, as well.)

(4) *Cohesiveness*. He was a member of a fairly cohesive group, which tends to mitigate against contact with the TL group.

(5) *Size*. He was a member of a fairly large group, which tends to facilitate intra-group contact rather than inter-group contact.

(6) *Cultural congruence*. His group and the TL group were culturally not very congruent, mitigating against inter-group contact.

(7) *Attitude*. While hard to assess in this case, inter-group attitudes were often neutral to hostile.

(8) *Intended length of residence*. Anticipated duration of stay in the TL environment was relatively short, making it less likely for extensive contacts with the TL group to be developed.

While social distance is a group phenomenon, *psychological distance* is a construct involving four affective factors at the level of the individual: *language shock, culture shock, motivation* and *ego permeability*. Schumann (1978a, p. 86) asserts that these individual (affective) psychological variables become important in cases where an individual is a member of a group which is neither particularly favourably nor especially negatively situated for SLA, as defined by social distance factors.

Alberto's responses on an attitude and motivation questionnaire indicated both positive attitude and positive motivation. Schumann suggests, however, that a halo effect (a respondent attempting to look good in the researcher's eyes by answering in ways he or she guesses accord with the researcher's own beliefs) was probably operating, since most features of Alberto's personal life contradicted his answers. He held a night job, made little effort to meet speakers of English, socialized with Spanish speakers, listened to Spanish music, and never went to ESL classes.

Noting, however, (a) that the ILs of all the learners in the Harvard study, including the ultimately more successful ones, were linguistically similar in the early stages, and (b) that (in his view) similarities existed between the social and psychological dimensions of Alberto's learning context and the conditions associated with pidginization, Schumann went on to claim that the processes underlying pidginization and the early stages of naturalistic SLA were analogous and universal:

> The social and psychological forces that cause the persistence of pidginization have been discussed. The term *persistence* is used because pidginization appears to be characteristic of early second language acquisition in general. (Schumann 1978a, p. 110)

Both pidginization and early naturalistic SLA, he proposed, involved development in an SL of the means necessary to satisfy one only of what Smith (1972) identified as the three basic functions of language: the referential, or *communicative function*, i.e. that dealing simply with getting and giving information in inter-group communication. Neither pidgins nor early SLs developed forms to handle the other two functions of a native language according to Smith, i.e. the *integrative function*, used to mark one's identity in society, or the *expressive function*, used to fulfil certain psychological needs, such as one's attitude towards what one is saying, since these were handled by the speaker's L1 in intra-group communication. The course of later stages of the SLA process was similarly determined, Schumann argued, with development being an artefact of the degree to which an individual *acculturated* into the target-language community.

Schumann (1978a) claimed that early SLs and pidgins shared several linguistic features because each was governed by the same underlying simplification processes, themselves the product of their restricted function: 'As a result of this functional restriction [to satisfying only basic referential communicative needs], pidginization produces an interlanguage which is simplified . . . and reduced' (p. 76). Examples of the kinds of linguistic 'simplicity' observed in pidgins included the following:

(a) The use of free morphemes to replace inflectional morphemes,[11] as illustrated by West African Pidgin English (data from Smith 1972):

i cop	He eats, is eating, etc. (unmarked)
i bin cop	He eats
i don cop	He has eaten
i go cop	He will eat
i bi don cop	He had eaten
i go don cop	He will have eaten

(b) The elimination of redundant morphology, as in Hawaiian Pidgin English (HPE):

tu mach ka	a lot of cars
tri haus	three houses

(c) The lack of some kinds of movement rules (transformations), such as passive, and the use of intonation rather than subject–verb inversion to form questions in Neo-Melanesian pidgins (data from Smith 1972):

Mi wokim haus	(1 2 3)	I am building a house	(1 2 3)
Yu wokim haus?	(1 2 3)	Are you building a house?	(2 1 2 3)
Yu mekim wanem?	(1 2 3)	What are you doing?	(3 2 1 2)

(d) A reduced lexicon, as shown by the lower total number of words (types, not tokens) in pidgins, by cases of reduced differentiation, e.g. HPE:

haus	house, home
brok	break, tear, rip

and by the use of lexical paraphrase, or decomposition, for 'standard' languages' monomorphemic items, e.g. HPE:

wat pleis?	where?
wat wei?	how?

(e) Reduplication, as in an English–Japanese pidgin created by US Air Force personnel and Japanese counterparts in Hamamatsu in the mid-1950s (data from Goodman 1967):

testo-testo	to examine
saymo-saymo	similar, alike
hubba-hubba	to hurry
dammey-dammey	not good

(f) The absence of tense markers, definite article and copula, with adverbials or context substituting for time reference, as in HPE:

tsumaro mi Honoruru go	I'm going to Honolulu tomorrow
bifo draiba no mo	There didn't use to be a driver

(g) A preference for topic-comment order (cf. Givon 1984)
(h) Pre-verbal negation (*No have*)
(i) Possession by juxtaposition (*John pig*, instead of *John's pig*).

Most of these features occurred in Alberto's IL, Schumann claimed. Alberto maintained a pre-verbal negation system, failed to invert questions, and omitted most auxiliaries, subject pronouns, and verbal and possessive inflections. The pidginization analogy was endorsed by Andersen (1981a), based on an exclusively linguistic comparison of Alberto's speech and Hawaiian Pidgin English as described by Bickerton and Odo (1976) and Bickerton (1977).

Theories vary as to the conditions necessary for pidginogenesis. Representing the stricter view, Whinnom (1971) distinguished three forms of language hybridization, only the last of which sufficed for the emergence of a true pidgin. Primary hybridization is seen when languages break up into different dialects. Secondary hybridization is exemplified by SLA in a bilingual contact situation, where an

IL is developed through its use with NSs of the SL, i.e. with access to, and development towards, the target language. Tertiary hybridization, on the other hand, occurs in cases where different L1 groups develop a functionally reduced SL, based on limited access to a superstrate language, for certain restricted kinds of referential inter-group communication, e.g. Japanese, Portuguese, Chinese and Filipino workers developing an English-based pidgin for use among them on the sugar plantations of Hawaii. The SLA counterpart would be migrant workers from different countries communicating in German or English pidgins on the factory floor (Clyne 1968, 1977; Meisel 1975; Heidelberger Forschungsprojekt 1978; Dittmar 1982) or other cases of SLA with restricted access to the target, as when an NS of Spanish and an NS of German use their English ILs to communicate with one another. It is tertiary hybridization, with *restricted access to the target language*, which Whinnom, Bickerton and others claim is necessary for the development of a true pidgin.

Schumann, on the other hand, followed scholars such as Samarin (1971) and Hall (1966) in choosing a more flexible definition, claiming that *pidginization* (the process, not necessarily resulting in the development of the product, a pidgin) can be observed in a wider range of settings, including those described by Whinnom as secondary hybridization (see Hymes 1971, for review and discussion):

> The position taken in this book is essentially that of Samarin and Hall. No claim is made that Alberto spoke a pidgin, but since the simplifications and reductions in his English are characteristics of pidginization, we simply observe that his English shows evidence of pidginization. (Schumann 1978a, p. 71)

Schumann was not claiming, in other words, that pidgins and early SLs are the same, but rather that the same simplification processes are at work in producing each, the extent of the simplification and reduction being a function of the social and psychological distance between the learner, both as a member of a group and as an individual, respectively, and speakers of the target language.

Schumann went on to claim that, as a learner later attempted to use his or her SL for integrative and expressive purposes, the IL would complexify structurally. That is, expansion of the *functions* of the IL would lead to a corresponding growth in linguistic form. Redundancy would increase, obligatory tense markers and other grammatical functors would emerge, and the lexicon would expand. This process Schumann (1978a) initially viewed as analogous to *creolization*, which is what happens when the first-generation children of pidgin speakers learn the parents' (restricted) pidgin as their first language. The pidgin gradually expands linguistically to satisfy a full range of functions and will serve the children as their native language. Thus, Bickerton (1977) refers to pidginization as SLA with restricted input, and to creolization as first language acquisition with restricted input.

Schumann (1978b) later abandoned the comparison between SLA and creolization, reasoning that the complication and expansion that takes place in SLA is motivated by the learner's goal of increasingly conforming to the TL. Bickerton (1975) suggested that the developing stages of SLA may parallel the decreolization continuum since in decreolization, a creole evolves in the direction of the standard language which served as its base. Thus, both SLA and decreolization have a standard language target. Stauble (1977, 1978) tested this hypothesis by studying the acquisition of ESL negation by three adult NSs of Spanish. She reported finding evidence supporting the claim, and viewed both SLA and decreolization as involving rule changes accomplished by 'the replacement of forms and the restructuring of underlying units' (1977, p. 16), where each stage of development is closer than its antecedent to the target.

Andersen (1983a) attempts to reconcile the various views regarding pidgins/creoles and SLA by adopting a broader perspective. He believes creolization, pidginization and early SLA are processes involving the creation of independent linguistic systems, at least partly autonomous from the input language. This process he calls 'nativization'. 'Denativization' is his cover term for decreolization, depidginization and later SLA, in which circumstances cause the learner to reconstruct his or her linguistic system to conform more closely to that of the target language.

As indicated, Schumann holds that the degree of elaboration observed in later stages of IL development will be a function of the same social and psychological variables that initially produce pidginization, although the values of the variables, of course, need to change to positive ones. Collectively, they make up one large causal factor in SLA, *acculturation*, roughly translatable as 'the process of becoming adapted to a new culture' (H.D. Brown 1980, p. 129). In the strongest claim in the SLA literature to date, Schumann (1978b, p. 34) maintains: '[SLA] is just one aspect of acculturation and the degree to which a learner acculturates to the target language group will control the degree to which he acquires the second language'.

According to Schumann (1986), there are two types of acculturation. In Type One acculturation, learners are both socially integrated into the target-language group and psychologically open to the target language. The first factor means that they have enough contacts with speakers for them to acquire the L2; the second means that the input to which these contacts expose them becomes intake. In Type Two acculturation, learners are socially integrated and psychologically open, but also consciously or unconsciously wish to adopt the lifestyle and values of the target-language group. Either type of acculturation is sufficient to ensure SLA, according to Schumann, but he stresses that social and psychological contact with the target-language group alone (i.e. Type One acculturation) are the essential conditions for SLA; a wish to become like the L2 speakers is not necessary.

7.4.3 A critique of the Pidginization Hypothesis and Acculturation Model

The analogy between pidginization and early naturalistic SLA has been very productive, in that it has generated a good deal of empirical research and theoretical debate. Not all critics have been as sympathetic as Andersen (1981a), however. The following are some of the objections that have been raised to the analogy:

1. Pidgins develop when groups of speakers of several different L1s are in contact, whereas SLA is a situation of bilingual contact (Flick and Gilbert 1976).

2. The admixture (merging of two or more languages into one) characteristic of pidgins is not seen in ILs (Meisel 1975).

3. SLA generally involves monolinguals, whereas speakers of pidgins generally know several other languages, with correspondingly greater 'access' at some level to general properties of human languages, and consequently higher tendencies to simplify towards those more general properties (Bickerton 1975; Flick and Gilbert 1976).

4. Pidginization is a group phenomenon, SLA an individual phenomenon, meaning that SL use for intra-group communication is unusual. Pidgin speakers, on the other hand, form a closed community, with greater stability inherent in pidgins than in ILs, and stronger notions of grammaticality in the pidgin-speaking community (Meisel 1975; Flick and Gilbert 1976). (Pidgins are often extremely variable, too, however, as shown for Hawaiian Pidgin English by Bickerton 1977.)

5. SLA, with access to the target language, allows for correction and consequent gradual approximation to that target; pidginization,

with restricted access, does not provide this option (Flick and Gilbert 1976). Pidginization, that is, is not targeted language change, but more independent linguistic development.

6. For socioeconomic and political reasons (colonialism, with imported slave or contract labour), the factors underlying social distance between superstrate language and pidginizing language groups are different from those determining social distance in most SLA situations, with attendant differences in the amount of contact with the target language that is available (Meisel 1975; Flick and Gilbert 1976).

7. However remote due to high social distance, the target language is always the model for ILs, whereas the often very restricted access to the target in pidginization means that the superstrate language is the model only to a limited extent. Thus, pidgins often show incorporation of features from diverse source languages by way of compensation (Flick and Gilbert 1976).

8. Alberto's IL contains some features it should not, or in frequencies that are very high, if it is an example of pidginization. Both Schumann (1978a) and Andersen (1981a) recognize this, e.g. when discussing Alberto's 85 per cent suppliance of plural, and offer transfer from Spanish as the explanation. Transfer from Spanish is not considered when other potential cases, e.g. *No V* negation is at issue (Hartford 1981). Instead, *No V* negation is assumed to result from natural simplification processes.

9. Schumann draws selectively from a variety of pidgins in producing a rather arbitrary list of features found in one or more of them, six of which he then notes occur in Alberto's speech. There is no weighting of features, such that some can be identified as more central than others, e.g. universal, pervasive, frequent, and rare, with the result that there is no means of evaluating the significance of features which are present in Alberto's IL but rare in pidgins (like plural and auxiliaries) or frequent in (either English-based or all) pidgins but rare or non-existent in Alberto's IL (like reduplication and admixture) (Hartford 1981).

Schumann (1978b, pp. 368–73) responds to almost all of these criticisms in the same way, by arguing (1) that most simply reflect his critics' narrower view of true pidginization, i.e. as a process occurring in situations of tertiary hybridization only, as opposed to his view that pidginization occurs in situations of secondary hybridization, too; and/or (2) from failure to distinguish the claim that the *processes* of pidginization and early SLA are analogous from the claim (which he does not make) that the end-products (SLs and pidgins) are the same.

(For further extensive debate on these and other points, see Andersen 1983a; Romaine 1988). A study by Stauble (1984) retrospectively deals with the possibility that *No V* negation was really due to transfer, rather than simplification, by showing that naturalistic Japanese acquirers (with post-verbal L1 negation) also pass through a *No V* stage in English (see also Gillis and Weber 1976), some Japanese–English ILs appearing to fossilize at that stage.

Schumann's Acculturation Model has served to turn what have otherwise often been rather vague notions about the role of social and psychological factors in SLA into coherent predictions. The Model arguably suffers from three problems, however. First, it has been claimed to be empirically untestable (H.D. Brown 1980) on the grounds that no reliable and valid measures of psychological and social distance exist, a point Schumann (1986) concedes (cf. Acton 1979) when he states that he thinks the Model may be testable in theory but not in fact. Equally serious problems exist in the measurement of affective variables in general, of course, and in SL populations in particular (Oller 1981b), where cross-cultural validation concerns are especially acute.

Second, if concerns about instrumentation are temporarily set aside, then empirical findings have been mixed. Using self-report data, Stauble (1978) found a rough correlation between (perceived) psychological distance and the ESL proficiency of three adult NSs of Spanish in Los Angeles, with psychological distance appearing to predict better than social distance. This result was supported by Kitch (1982) in a case study of another adult Spanish speaker, whose psychological distance was low and whose ESL development after nine years' residence in the USA was quite advanced despite apparently high social distance. Kelley (1982) studied six more adult Spanish speakers and found no relationship between acculturation and SL proficiency, the most acculturated subject actually being the least proficient and one of the least acculturated the most proficient in English. As part of a larger study, Stauble (1981) found no linear relationship between acculturation (using Kelley's questionnaire as the measure) and the ESL development of six Spanish and six Japanese naturalistic adult acquirers, also long-term residents in the USA, although she did find a slightly higher number of reported English-speaking associates and amount of target language use among the eight mesolang (mid-stage of development) and upper mesolang speakers compared with the four basilang (stage of development furthest from TL) speakers. (The latter is a result consistent with a hypothesized effect for input and/or practice opportunity, rather than social and psychological variables, of course.)

A study which does report finding evidence consistent with Schumann's predictions is that of Maple (1982). Maple looked at 190 Spanish-speaking students in an ESL programme at the University of Texas, and found a strong negative correlation between seven out of eight components of social distance proposed by Schumann (all but cultural congruence) and several measures of English proficiency (pre-semester and gain scores on the CELT [Comprehensive English Language Test for Speakers of English as a Second Language], composition and TOEFL scores and final course grades). Maple's research is interesting because his sample was of respectable size, he attempted to validate his social distance measure (a questionnaire) by interviews with a sub-sample of thirty subjects, and he used more sophisticated statistical procedures to assess relationships between the various independent variables and SL proficiency. Maple found social distance accounted for from 15–29 per cent of the variance on some measures (the CELT scores) and consisted of the following component variables in descending order of importance: attitudes, social class, cohesiveness, intended length of residence, size of L1 group, enclosure, and perceived status. (Social class and marital status, not part of the original Acculturation Model, were both found to predict some variance.)

Kelley (1982, 1983), Stauble (1981) and Schumann (1986) all note some of the methodological problems encountered in research of this kind, apart from the basic one of producing a reliable and valid measure of acculturation. They draw attention to the lack of any principled means of weighting the various sub-components of acculturation, i.e. the numerous social and psychological variables that go to make up the construct, recognizing the possibility that the influence of each factor may vary both from individual to individual and over time – and, one might add, at different proficiency levels and for different types of linguistic abilities. (Variables, definitions and instrumentation also tend to change from one study to the next, one notes, making comparison of findings hazardous.) They also emphasize another measurement problem arising from the fact that social and psychological distance may change over time, namely, that cross-sectional studies correlate SL proficiency with *current* orientation, which may be very different from that during the period when the proficiency was acquired, giving misleading results. (Note that the design used by Strong 1984 provides a plausible solution to this problem.) Finally, Schumann notes that studies like those by Maple on instructed 'foreign language' populations (who learned much of their L2 in their own countries) are strictly irrelevant as tests of his ideas (although valuable for other purposes), since the Acculturation Model is intended to apply only to immigrant groups acquiring a SL naturalistically in the target-language environment.

When examining SLA by members of groups whose social distance does not appear to be either positive or negative, which is when Schumann claims psychological factors will determine SL attainment, a number of researchers have found little or no relationship between those psychological factors and achievement. Studies include Oyama (1976, 1978), Purcell and Suter (1980), Klein and Dittmar (1979), d'Anglejan and Renaud (1985) and Schmidt (1981, 1983). As noted in Chapter 6, the *reverse* ('resultative') relationship has even been reported for SL achievement and integrative motivation (Hermann, 1980; Strong, 1984), and *anti*-integrative motivation has been found to correlate with proficiency in some samples, e.g. working-class Spanish speakers in the American Southwest (Oller, Baca and Vigil 1977) and foreign students at the University of Illinois (England 1982). Schumann (1986) points out, however, that most of these are studies which, because they are large-scale, tend to employ (less satisfactory) achievement test scores rather than detailed linguistic IL analyses, this in order to handle the *n*-sizes needed for use of the more powerful statistical procedures the researchers favour.

Schmidt's longitudinal study of Wes, introduced in Chapter 3 and in this chapter, above, in many ways provides a better test of the Model in Schumann's view. Schmidt's list of the relevant affect factors for Wes (Table 7.1) shows that Schumann's model would predict successful acquisition for Wes. In fact, however, as described earlier, while Wes did achieve a certain communicative ability, his IL showed many signs of slow development and premature stabilization, and Schumann (1986) accepts the case as providing counter-evidence to the causal claim for acculturation.[12]

The third problem with the Acculturation Model concerns two conceptual aspects of the Model which make falsification impossible. First, while Schumann repeatedly claims that individual psychological factors are important in cases where group-level social factors under-determine the prognosis for success, he actually allows for other possibilities which predict every possible learning outcome, holding that psychological factors can override social ones and lead an individual to:

> violate the modal tendency of his group. Thus an individual might learn the target language where he is expected not to, and not learn the language where successful acquisition is expected. In these cases it is psychological distance or proximity between the learner and the

Social and psychological factors	Wes	Predicted influence on SLA
Age	33	Neutral if other factors positive
Formal study of L2	Insignificant	Not relevant
Language aptitude	Possibly low	Not relevant
Communicative need	High, increasing	Facilitative
Interaction, type and amount	Varied, increasing	Facilitative
Social dominance pattern	Equal	Facilitative
Social interaction pattern	Adaptive	Facilitative
Enclosure, cohesiveness	Low	Facilitative
Similarity of cultures	Different	Negative
Attitudes toward L2 group	Positive	Facilitative
Intended length of residence	Indefinite/permanent	Facilitative
Culture shock	Low	Facilitative
Language shock	Low	Facilitative
Empathy, social outreach	High	Facilitative
Inhibition, fear of appearing foolish	Low	Facilitative
Motivation type	Integrative	Facilitative
Motivation, drive for communication	Very high	Facilitative
Motivation for formal language study	Very low	Possibly negative
Preferred learning style	Natural acquisition	Facilitative

TABLE 7.1 Wes's Affective Profile (from Schmidt 1983, p. 143)

TL group that accounts for successful versus unsuccessful second
language acquisition. (Schumann 1978a, p. 86)

Since there is no *a priori* specification of the conditions necessary for
psychological factors to override social ones, every possible combination of (positive, neutral and negative) social factors, psychological
factors and level of SL attainment is 'predicted' by the model. Second,
Schumann provides no indication of the combinations and/or levels
of social and psychological factors he claims predict learning. Is it
enough, for example, for one social distance factor (say, group size)
or one psychological factor (say, ego permeability) to be negative in
order for SLA to be affected? Alternatively, is it necessary for most or
all dimensions of social and/or psychological distance to be negative?
And as all the dimensions are relative, not absolute, as Schumann
recognizes, how positive or negative need they be before predictions
are made? Also, can a positive value on one dimension cancel out the
effects of a negative value on another?

Lastly, Schumann provides no explanation of *how* social or psychological factors might determine the linguistic shape of an IL in terms
of simplification of linguistic features, i.e. of how learners internalize
knowledge of the L2. Why do social and psychological variables affect
the grammatical structures they (supposedly) do in the ways they
do, and why not others? Why does the Model discount the proven
effects of L1 or learner age (see Chapters 4 and 6) in this regard?
(Meisel, Clahsen and Pienemann 1981 make more precise claims about
relationships between these variables and simplification processes, as
we discuss below.) Nor is it clear how social and psychological factors
might affect either the ultimate level of SLA or the rate of attainment.
If the argument is that social and psychological factors determine
communicative needs, and that those needs in turn determine how far
an IL needs to be elaborated to satisfy them, then there are numerous
obvious counter-examples, including learners who acquire far more of
the target language than they need and learners who acquire far less
than they need (despite favourable affective profiles and unlimited
access to input). If a *direct* connection between social and psychological
factors and SLA is what is being claimed, the Model says nothing about
how the effect is achieved, or even about why. If the claim is that high
social distance and a negative affective disposition lead to low contact
with NSs, and so to restricted input, and that it is the restricted input
(not the social and psychological factors *per se*) that determines SLA,
this needs to be made explicit, and further, some explanation suggested
as to how restricted input leads to qualitatively different (as opposed,

say, simply to slower) SLA. Schumann seems to be moving away from his original claim towards this last position in his 1986 paper, where, after reasserting his causal claim for acculturation, he writes that

> there may be a chain of causality in natural SLA that perhaps operates in the following way. Acculturation as a remote cause brings the learner into contact with TL-speakers. Verbal interaction with those speakers as a proximate cause brings about the negotiation of appropriate input which then operates as the immediate cause of language acquisition. Acculturation then is of particular importance because it initiates the chain of causality.

Andersen (1979, 1983b) attempts to address the question of the learner's internal processing mechanisms in his Nativization Model. He proposes that development is a function of two processes. *Nativization* guides pidginization and early stages of both first and second language acquisition, Andersen claims. It refers to the learner's tendency to make new input conform to his or her 'internal norm', or mental picture, of what the L2 grammar is like. It involves *assimilation* of new knowledge to old (in the shape of knowledge of the L1 and pragmatics) through hypothesis formation and application of cognitive processing principles like Slobin's (1973) 'operating principles' ('pay attention to the ends of words', 'avoid exceptions', etc.). *Denativization*, on the other hand, guides depidginization and later stages of first and second language acquisition. It refers to the learner's adjustment of his or her IL system in the direction of his or her mental picture of the target, or 'external norm'. It involves *accommodation* of new input by altering the IL grammar to match it. As Ellis (1985, pp. 254–5) has noted, however, Andersen, like Schumann, is vague as to how the operation of nativizing and denativizing strategies on the input is reflected in the learner's output.

In conclusion, Schumann's Pidginization Hypothesis and Acculturation Model have been useful in that they have focused researchers' attention, respectively, on some important linguistic simplification processes in early IL development and on a possible causal role for a large body of social and psychological factors in SLA. Both claims concern potential SLA universals, which would, therefore, be generalizable cross-linguistically if verified. Each has been criticized on a variety of formal, conceptual and empirical grounds, but each has made a contribution. To attempt to predict *individual* attainment on the basis of *group*-level phenomena is obviously to flirt with the ecological fallacy, and likely to be doomed. It may turn out, however, that Schumann has identified several of the contextual factors relevant in predicting group-level success in acculturating to a new society; the social-psychological variables he discusses may constitute the raw material for a viable model of acculturation, that is, rather than one of SLA.

Further, both group and individual social and psychological factors must surely have some role in a comprehensive theory of SLA, perhaps most obviously as variables conditioning the amount and type of target-language exposure the learner experiences. Equally clearly, on the other hand, it should come as no surprise if a *mental* process, (second) *language learning*, is not successfully explicable by any theory which ignores *linguistic* and *cognitive* variables.

7.5   Interactionist theories of SLA

7.5.1   General characteristics

Interactionist theories are more powerful, all other things being equal, than either nativist or environmentalist theories, because they invoke both innate and environmental factors to explain language learning. (Greater power, it should be remembered, is a negative characteristic where theories are concerned, meaning that more factors, variables, causes, processes, etc., are needed by the researcher to handle the data of interest. Power, that is, here contrasts with a desirable attribute of theories, parsimony.) Greater power does not make interactionist theories uninteresting, of course; it simply reflects what interactionists have decided is the material needed to do the job, explaining (S)LA, which they think too complex to be handled by less powerful nativist or environmentalist factors alone.

Beyond this general characteristic, interactionist theories of SLA differ greatly from one another. Some, such as Givon's (1979a, 1979b, 1984) Functional–Typological Theory originate in work in functional–typological syntax and diachronic language change. Others, such as those of Clahsen, Meisel and Pienemann (1983), Pienemann and Johnston (1987), McLaughlin, Rossman and McLeod (1983), McLeod and McLaughlin (1986), and McLaughlin (1987, 1990) were partly inspired by work in experimental psycholinguistics and cognitive psychology. Still others, such as Hatch's Experience Model (Hatch 1978; Hatch, Peck and Wagner-Gough 1979; Hatch, Flashner and Hunt 1986), draw on social, cognitive and linguistic theory and on findings from discourse analyses of first and second language acquisition for their framework for studying and explaining SLA. We will here consider work conducted within the framework of

Givon's Functional-Typological Theory and that of the ZISA group and associates' Multidimensional Model.

7.5.2 Givon's Functional–Typological Theory and SLA

A substantial body of functionalist IL research has drawn, explicitly or implicitly, upon the work of Givon (1979a, 1979b, 1981, 1983a, 1983b, 1984, 1985). Examples include Huebner (1985), Kelley (1983), Kumpf (1984), Sato (1985b, 1988), Schumann (1986, 1987a, 1987b), Stauble and Schumann (1983), and Stauble (1984). Givon's goal is a unified theory of all kinds of language change, including language acquisition. To this end, he has developed an approach called 'functional–typological syntactic analysis' (FTSA), which is functionalist in its view that syntax 'emanate[s] from properties of human discourse' (Givon 1979b, p. 49), and typological in its consideration of a diverse body of languages, not simply a single language or language family. Givon claims that syntactic change is driven primarily by psycholinguistic and pragmatic principles relating to speech perception and production in face-to-face interaction. These principles are themselves derived from more basic ones underlying human perception and information processing.

Although FTSA was first developed in the study of historical language change, specifically, diachronic syntax, Givon now claims that it can be applied to all situations of language variation and change, including synchronic register variation in adult speech, the development of pidgins and creoles, child language acquisition and second language acquisition. In all of these situations, Givon (1979b) claims, speakers and linguistic systems move from a discourse-based, *pragmatic mode* of communication to a more *syntactic mode*. This process of 'syntacticization' operates over a number of features which are contrasted across the pragmatic and syntactic modes of communication (Table 7.2).

Early IL should be marked by all of the features of the pragmatic mode. Thus far, research on IL development has investigated features (a), (b), (d), (e) and (f), with the following mixed results.

Topic–comment structure feature (a) has been the subject of a number of studies to date (see Schumann 1982, 1986, 1987a; Stauble and Schumann 1983; Givon 1984), with researchers looking for structures like:

* Los Angeles, it big city.

as opposed to a subject–predicate version of the same utterance:

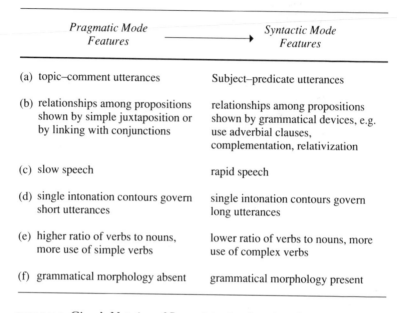

Pragmatic Mode Features ⟶	Syntactic Mode Features
(a) topic–comment utterances	Subject–predicate utterances
(b) relationships among propositions shown by simple juxtaposition or by linking with conjunctions	relationships among propositions shown by grammatical devices, e.g. use adverbial clauses, complementation, relativization
(c) slow speech	rapid speech
(d) single intonation contours govern short utterances	single intonation contours govern long utterances
(e) higher ratio of verbs to nouns, more use of simple verbs	lower ratio of verbs to nouns, more use of complex verbs
(f) grammatical morphology absent	grammatical morphology present

TABLE 7.2 Givon's Notation of Syntacticization (based on Givon 1985)

Los Angeles is a big city.

Although the general conclusion is that early IL is indeed characterized by topic–comment structuring, this feature has been very difficult to analyse. Many early IL utterances are as difficult to disambiguate in this regard as in other ways, the length of a pause often being the only (unusable) clue, for example:

* My family . . . come New York.

In fact, the available results cannot be interpreted as strong evidence of the existence of topic–comment *as opposed to* subject–predicate structure in early IL, due to the inappropriate conflation of syntactic, semantic and pragmatic dimensions in the analyses undertaken (for detailed discussion, see Sato 1985b, 1988).

Features (b) and (d) in Table 7.2, which have to do with information 'packaging' in discourse, were examined in a longitudinal study by Sato (1985a, 1986, 1988, to appear) of two Vietnamese learners of English. Sato found the following evidence of syntacticization: (1) the learners tended to produce propositions in single utterances, i.e. they did not spread parts of a single proposition over more than one utterance (cf. Scollon's 1976 description of 'vertical constructions' in child language);

and (2) they did not rely on interlocutor collaboration ('scaffolding') to produce propositions.

Other aspects of the learners' ILs did not appear to be highly syntacticized, however. Throughout the ten-month study, very few multipropositional utterances (in surface structure, complex sentences) were produced. In Givon's terms, the learners tended to produce small chunks (single propositions) under one intonation contour. Finally, with respect to Givon's feature (b), only preliminary evidence was found of a movement from loose coordination to tight subordination. Both learners used *and* and *or* to connect propositions by the second month of the study, but they did not produce infinitival complements until the end of the study. They also used few relative clauses and no gerundive complements.

A low noun/verb ratio in early IL (feature (e) in Givon's pragmatic and syntactic modes of communication) has not been confirmed by studies conducted to date (Kelley 1983; Stauble and Schumann 1983). In contrast, a lack of grammatical morphology (feature (f)) in basilang IL has been amply documented (e.g. by Stauble 1978, 1984; Stauble and Schumann 1983). Feature (c) has yet to be examined in functionalist research on IL development.

7.5.3 A critique of Givon's theory in SLA research

With respect to Givon's opposition of pragmatic and syntactic modes of communication, the mixed results obtained thus far in SLA research suggest that it is too early to judge how well the distinction serves researchers as a point of departure for the functionalist analysis of language change. Perhaps because of its very scope and generality, FTSA cannot be expected to capture accurately the differences among types of language-change situations. One kind of difference concerns the level of generalization achieved through FTSA as applied to acquisition contexts. Whereas linguists are primarily concerned with language as a group phenomenon, (first and second) language acquisition researchers tend to focus on the level of the individual learner. Further, acquisition researchers cannot take as given, as FTSA does, the presence of a wide array of linguistic devices (e.g. morphology and syntax) whose division of labour shifts through syntactization of a particular language over time. Rather, in acquisition research, it is necessary and desirable to document the emergence of the devices themselves.

Sato (1985a, 1988) has argued that Givon's application of FTSA to conversational data is biased toward the syntax of written language and toward the sentence (rather than the 'utterance' or 'conversational turn') as the basic unit of analysis. This bias has led to difficulties in the quantification of natural speech data in a number of the above studies. As a result, the testing of Givon's various claims regarding pragmatic and syntactic modes of communication remains incomplete.

7.5.4 The ZISA group's Multidimensional Model

One of the most important bodies of SLA research to date is that emanating from the Zweitsprachenwerb Italienischer und Spanischer Arbeiter (ZISA) project, conducted chiefly at the University of Hamburg in the late 1970s under the direction of Jurgen Meisel. The ZISA project consisted of a cross-sectional study of 45 adults, and a two-year longitudinal study of 12 adults, both using interview data, of the naturalistic acquisition of German as an SL (GSL) by speakers of Spanish and Italian. In addition to furnishing a range of findings on the acquisition of GSL, the project prompted several methodological reorientations in SLA research in Europe and North America, and produced a theory of SLA which, while continuing to be refined by the original researchers and their subsequent associates, has motivated new studies of naturalistic and instructed SLA on GSL, ESL and Japanese as an SL (JSL) with potentially important implications for language teaching and testing.

One major focus of the original research was GSL word-order rules, where it was found that, after an initial period during which learner production consisted of isolated words and formulae, both children and adults adhered to the five-stage developmental sequence shown in Figure 7.2 (Clahsen 1980; Pienemann 1980, 1981; Meisel, Clahsen and Pienemann 1981; Clahsen, Meisel and Pienemann 1983). Learners did not abandon one IL rule for the next as they traversed the sequence, it should be noted; they accumulated rules, adding new ones while retaining the old. However, the five rules constituted an implicational scale:

$$SVO < ADV < SEP < INV < V\text{-}END$$

presence of one rule in an IL implying presence of earlier rules in the sequence, but not later ones.

As noted in Chapter 4, accuracy orders and developmental sequences have been established empirically for various grammatical domains in several SLs. However, although some progress has been made using typological markedness (Rutherford 1982; Hyltenstam 1987), less has been done to identify factors determining the sequences

Stage *X* – Canonical order (SVO)

> *die kinder spielen mim ball*
> the children play with the ball

(Romance learners' initial SVO hypothesis for GSL WO is correct in most German sentences with simple verbs.)

Stage *X* + 1 – Adverb preposing (ADV)

> *da kinder spielen*
> *there* children play

(Since German has a verb-second rule, requiring subject–verb inversion following a preposed adverb (*there play children*), all sentences of this form are deviant. The verb-second (or 'inversion') rule is only acquired at stage *X* + 3, however. The adverb-preposing rule itself is optional).

Stage *X* + 2 – Verb separation (SEP)

> *alle kinder muss die pause machen*
> all children *must* the break *have*

(Verb separation is obligatory in standard German.)

Stage *X* + 3 – Inversion (INV)

> *dann hat sie wieder die knoch gebringt*
> then *has she* again the bone brought

(Subject and inflected verb forms must be inverted after preposing of elements.)

Stage *X* + 4 – Verb-end (V-END)

> *er sagte, dass er nach hause kommt*
> he said that he home *comes*

(In subordinate clauses, the finite verb moves to final position.)

FIGURE 7.2   Developmental Sequence for GSL Word Order Rules (based on Pienemann 1987)

(for discussion, see Rutherford 1984; Berman 1987). What makes the ZISA group's work on word order especially interesting is that it included a proposed *explanation* for the GSL word-order data, and one which had potential generalizabilty to other developmental sequences and to other languages.

The explanation was cognitive, namely that the five structures and the rules that account for them are manifestations of five (or more) underlying stages in IL development, each stage in turn reflecting the learner's use of varying combinations of three *speech-processing strategies* (Clahsen 1981, 1984, 1987; Pienemann 1985a). Since, as described below, processing is supposedly *constrained* by the set of strategies available to the learner at any one time, 'development' viewed from this perspective really consists of the *shedding of strategies*, or of the gradual removal of the constraints they impose on what is processable. This in turn subsequently motivates an important claim for language teachers by Pienemann (1984) to the effect that the strategies constrain what is comprehensible, and so *learnable* at any time, and hence, what is *teachable*, implying that attempts to teach structures will be futile if they involve permutations and analysis beyond a learner's current processing level.

Drawing on research findings on L1 speech processing and memory by Bever, Forster, and others, the three strategies Clahsen (1981, 1984) identified were as follows:

(1) Canonical Order Strategy (COS) – surface strings reflect direct mapping of underlying meaning onto syntactic form, as in the postulated NVN strategy (Bever 1970), with movement into or out of the fixed meaning-bearing sequences blocked.
(2) Initialization-Finalization Strategy (IFS) – movements of elements to internal positions in underlying sequences are blocked, so that [XYZ] can be rearranged to become either [ZXY] or [YZX], but not [YXZ] or [XZY].
(3) Subordinate Clause Strategy (SCS) – permutations of elements in subordinate clauses are avoided.

Figure 7.3 shows how the three strategies can be used to explain the five developmental stages in the word-order data. As can be seen, the strategy combinations are hierarchically related, such that each new one entails and adds to the sophistication of the previous one, thereby gradually allowing the processing of psycholinguistically more complex structures. The complexity of a structure is determined by the type of reordering and rearrangement of constituents necessary to map underlying meaning onto surface form. The strategies available to

	GSL Word Order Stage	Permissible Permutations	Controlling Strategies
X	(SVO)	canonical order	[W X Y Z]	[+COS, +SCS]
X + 1	(ADV)	initialization/finalization	[W X Y Z]	[+COS, +IFS, +SCS]
X + 2	(SEP)	disruption and movement into salient position	[W X Y Z]	[−COS, +IFS, +SCS]
X + 3	(INV)	internal movement	[W X Y Z]	[−COS, −IFS, +SCS]
X + 4	(V-END)	sub-categorization	[W X Y Z] [A B C]	[−COS, −IFS, −SCS]

FIGURE 7.3 Processing Strategies Underlying the GSL Word Order Stages (based on Pienemann and Johnston, in progress)

the learner determine what they are currently capable of processing, thereby acting as constraints on development.

The strategies at work in determining how GSL word order is acquired are as follows. Stage X reflects the general finding from research into sentence processing that the simplest way to mark underlying grammatical and semantic relations within a clause is canonical order (Slobin and Bever 1982; Clahsen 1984). Learners sequence words and phrases at this stage simply according to meaning or information focus, not on the basis of any knowledge of the grammatical status of the elements concerned.

Each subsequent stage in the sequence involves a qualitative change in the difficulty of processing structures at that stage. Thus, Stage $X +$ 1 involves moving elements from one salient (easier to recognize and recall) position in a string to another salient position (+IFS), i.e. either from initial to final or from final to initial position (the latter in the case of adverb-preposing in German or topicalization in English), while leaving the canonical order intact (+COS). The learner still does not need any knowledge of the grammatical categories to which the moved elements belong, so this stage is still 'pre-syntactic' (Pienemann and Johnston 1987).

Whereas adverb-preposing (ADV) does not disturb the canonical order for the rest of the string, the next two rules, SEP and INV, both do, making them more complex than SVO and ADV. They are also more complex in that they require grammatical knowledge, thereby marking the advent of true syntax. Stage $X + 2$ involves disruption of associated elements (such as aux + V) inside a string (−COS) and movement of one of those internal elements to a salient (either initial or final) position (+IFS), as in the case of SEP in GSL or inversion in English yes/no questions ('Can you play?'). This means that the simple SVO strategy is no longer adequate for comprehending sentences of this type. Grammatical knowledge is involved because the learner must recognize the element that is moved from inside the string as belonging to a particular category, such as auxiliary, which qualifies for the move.

The same is true of structures at stage $X + 3$, but these are still more complex because they involve disruption (−COS) and movement of an internal element not to a salient position, but to another internal position (−IFS), as exemplified by INV in GSL and inversion in English WH-questions ('When did you arrive?'). Thus, whereas learners can rely on a general perceptual processing strategy (utilizing salience) at stage $X + 2$, they are forced to depend on language-specific processing prerequisites at $X + 3$, involving recognition of elements in a string as being members of different grammatical categories.

Finally, stage $X + 4$, illustrated by V-END in the GSL word-order sequence and by indirect object/direct object word order ('I gave him my pen') in English, is held to come last in the sequence because it requires the ability to process or produce a hierarchical structure, which involves identifying sub-strings within a string ($-$SCS) and moving elements out of those sub-strings to other positions. Another example would be the processing of subordinate clauses, which are more marked than main clauses; Clahsen (1984) claims that learners have to recognize that normal main clause processing strategies will not work here, and that subordinate clauses are processed differently.

As indicated, the constraints are supposedly universal; they are claimed to control all developmental sequences in ILs, not just word order, and to work for any SL, not just GSL. Thus, any structures (in any language) meeting the description of those processable by a particular strategy should be acquired at roughly the same time. In ESL, for example, Pienemann and Johnston (1987) propose that a learner should master the apparently unrelated horizontal sets of constructions listed in Figure 7.4 at the same time because they involve the same kinds of movement and rearrangement, and therefore, the same strategies.

An initial problem with applying the model to English is that, whereas German has several word-order rules that are obligatory with use of quite a wide range of high-frequency items (including all past-tense forms and modals), word-order changes in English chiefly occur in a more restricted set of contexts, such as subject–auxiliary inversion (only) in questions and after fronted 'negative' adverbs ('Never had he seen. . .'). Several of those contexts, moreover, tend to arise less frequently in typical IL speech samples, given, for example, that researchers usually ask most of the questions in interviews. The problem was ameliorated, however, when Pienemann and Johnston (1985) showed that some morphological items could also be analysed in terms of the same strategies.

An example is classification of third-person singular -*s* as a stage $X + 3$ structure, requiring learners to be able to handle string-internal movement. Pienemann and Johnston's rationale is as follows. Given that the -*s* morpheme contains information whose source is a noun phrase or pronoun, the easiest, most natural place to put the -*s* in linear production is immediately following that source, yielding (ungrammatical) source–marker–verb strings. (The psychological plausibility of this is suggested by the fact that many learners often do produce utterances like 'He's go' and 'They's want'.) In order to produce the correct English version, however, learners have to

Stage *X:*

> *You are student?* (SVO?)
> *I no like* (*no* + X)
> *I like Sydney* (SVO)

(Structures at Stage *X* conform to the canonical SVO order.)

Stage *X* +1

> *In Vietnam, I am teacher* (ADV-FRONTING)
> *Do you have apartment?* (*Do*-FRONTING)
> *Why you no eat?* (WH-FRONTING)

(Note that the canonical SVO order is undisturbed by the fronted items.)

Stage *X* +2

> *Have you job?* (YES/NO INVERSION)
> *I like to eat my friend house*
> (COMPLEMENTIZER INSERTION)
> *You can take your coat off* (PARTICLE SEPARATION)

(The canonical order is now disturbed by movement of string-internal elements to initial or final position. Grammatical knowledge is also required for identification of movable elements, marking the beginning of true syntax.)

Stage *X* + 3

> *Why did you go?* (AUX SECOND, with agreement)
> *She does not know* ('DO' SECOND, with agreement)
> *I wrote it myself* (REFLEXIVE PRONOUN)
> *He gave the money to the police* (DATIVE 'to')
> *She eats too much* (3RD SINGULAR '-s')

(Movement at this stage requires recognition that the elements moved are members of certain grammatical categories, and is string-internal.)

Stage *X* + 4

> *She makes me work hard* (CAUSATIVE)
> *He has never met her* (ADVERB VP)
> *He didn't leave, did he?* (QUESTION TAG, with agreement)

(Grammatical sub-strings must be recognized, and operations conducted within and across those substrings.)

FIGURE 7.4 Developmental Stages and Sample ESL Structures (based on Pienemann and Johnston 1987)

move -*s* to the end of the finite verb following the source NP or pronoun (or, as some might prefer to conceive of the operation, to hold -*s* in short-term memory until the verb to which it is attached is produced). In other words, they have to recognize the grammatical status of two string-internal elements (the -*s* marker and the finite verb in source–marker–verb strings) and permute them to produce source–verb–marker strings, an operation analogous to that involved in producing utterance-internal subject–auxiliary inversion ('Where did you go?'). This analysis was supported by the findings on developmental sequences, for this and other morphological and syntactic structures, from Johnston's Syntactic and Morphological Progressions in Learner English (SAMPLE) project (Johnston 1985), using interview data on twelve Polish and twelve Vietnamese naturalistic acquirers of Australian English. Similar reasoning places the adverbial -*ly*, comparative -*er* and superlative -*est* suffixes at stage $X + 3$, and also allows classification of a variety of other structures by stage before an empirical study is undertaken (see Table 7.3).

If, as claimed, the processing constraints are universal, acquisition context should not affect developmental sequences. This prediction has been borne out by several studies of instructed IL development involving students from a range of typologically different L1 backgrounds. Thus, classroom learners of German as a foreign and second language have been shown to adhere to the same word-order sequence, regardless of the order in which the rules are presented in textbooks or of the relative emphasis given them by GFL or GSL teachers (Pienemann 1984, 1987; Eubank 1986, 1987; Jansen 1987; Ellis 1989; cf. Westmoreland 1983), and instructed learners of English and Japanese have been found to develop various syntactic and morphological constructions in those languages in the sequences predictable by the processing strategies hypothesized to govern them (Doi and Yoshioka 1987; Pienemann 1987; Yoshioka and Doi 1988).

A further prediction derivable from the framework is that, despite receiving instruction aimed at achieving this, learners should not be able to skip a stage in a developmental sequence, given that each stage depends upon the availability of processing strategies at previous stages, plus a new one. That prediction has also been borne out, this time by the results of a particularly interesting classroom study (Pienemann 1984, 1989). Pienemann looked at the differential effects on GSL word-order development in ten Italian children, ages seven to nine, of two weeks of both linguistically focused and communicatively oriented instruction in a structure at stage $X + 3$ (INV). As revealed by analyses

STAGE	VERB	NOUN	PN	Q
	'WORDS'	or	FORMULAE	
X	" IL-ing IRREG	" " "	1st 2nd 3rd	SVO? " "
X+1	-ed "	REG_PL IRREG_PL	POSSESS	DO_FRONT WHX_FRONT
X+2	AUX_EN AUX_ING	(POSSESS) "	" "	PSEUDO_INV Y/N_INV
X+3	3SG_S +"	(PL_CONCD) "	CASE(3rd) RFLX(ADV)	AUX_2ND SUPPLET
X+4	(GERUND) " " "	" " " "	RFLX(PN) " " "	Q_TAG " " "

KEY: (Round brackets indicate tentative assignment only.)
IL-ing = non-standard 'ing'; PP = in prepositional phase.
DO_FRONT = yes/no questions with initial 'do'.
WHX_FRONT = fronting of wh-word and possible cliticized element (e.g. 'what do').
TOPIC = topicalization of initial or final elements.
ADV_FRONT = fronting of final adverbs or adverbial PPs.
AUX_EN = [be/have] + V-ed, not necessarily with standard semantics.
PSEUDO_INV = simple fronting of wh-word across verb (e.g. 'where is the summer?').
COMP_TO = insertion of 'to' as a complementizer as in 'want to go'.
PART_MOV = verb-particle separation, as in 'turn the light on'.
AUX_ING = [be] + V-ing, not necessarily with standard semantics.
Y/N_INV = yes/no questions with subject-verb/aux inversion.

TABLE 7.3 Tentative Developmental Stages in ESL (Pienemann and Johnston 1987, pp. 82–3)

NEG	AD	ADJ	PREP	W_ORDER
no no+X "	– – –	– –	PP " "	SVO " "
don't+V "	(ADV) –	– (more)	" "	TOPIC ADV_FRONT
" "	" "	(better) (best)	COMP_TO "	PART_MOV PREP_STRNDG
DO_2ND SUPPLET	-ly "	-er -erst	" "	(DAT_TO) "
" " " "	" " " "	" " " "	" " " "	ADV VP (DAT MVMT) (CAUSATIVE) (2_SUB_COMP)

PREP_STRNDG = stranding of prepositions in relative clauses.

3SG_S = third person singular '-s' marking.

PL_CONCD = plural marking of NP after number or quantifier (e.g. 'many factories').

CASE (3rd) = case marking of third person singular pronouns.

AUX_2ND = placement of 'do' or 'have' in second position;
    DO_2ND = as above, in negation.

SUPPLET = suppletion of 'some' into 'any' in the scope of negation.

DAT_TO = indirect object marking with 'to'.

RFLX (ADV) = adverbial or emphatic usages of reflexive pronouns;
    RFLX (PN) = true reflexivization.

Q_TAG = question tags; ADV_VP = sentence internal adverb location.

DAT_MVMT = dative movement (e.g. 'I gave John a gift').

CAUSATIVE = structures with 'make' and 'let'.

2_SUB_COMP = different subject complements with verbs like 'want'.

TABLE 7.3 *(Continued)*

of pre- and post-test data consisting of transcribed samples of the children's free speech, learners who began the period of instruction at stages X or $X + 1$ were no better at INV when the instruction ended. Conversely, learners at stage $X + 2$ when the instruction began applied (the stage $X + 3$) INV after instruction, and did so, furthermore, at a higher frequency and in a wider range of linguistic contexts than would be normal during the initial period of $X + 3$ mastery in the IL of a naturalistic acquirer. (When combined with the ZISA project data, these results also give some idea of the potential effects of instruction on rate of SL development, since naturalistic adult acquirers had been found to take at least six months to move from stage $X + 2$ to $X + 3$ in GSL word order.) Since the learners, all members of the same class, received the same lessons together, the differential effects of the instruction can presumably be attributed to the differences in the stages of development the learners had attained when the instruction began. The instruction at $X + 3$ was learnable by children at $X + 2$; children at earlier stages could not skip stages to take advantage of it. The Teachability Hypothesis (Pienemann 1984) predicts that the *teachability* of an item, and indeed the effects of any external factors, such as natural exposure to a target structure, will always be constrained by its *learnability* in this way. In other words, since the underlying speech-processing prerequisites constitute an implicational hierarchy, the devices at one stage being part of what is required for operations at the next stage, none of the abstract stages of processing complexity can be bypassed. Items will only be successfully taught when learners are psycholinguistically 'ready' to learn them.

Thus far, we have mentioned only one dimension, the *developmental* axis, of the ZISA model. It is called the 'multidimensional' model, however, because the original ZISA data revealed a second dimension to SLA, along which learners differed, the *variational* axis (see Figure 7.5). Thus, while developmental IL sequences are held to be invariant (because they are subject to universal processing constraints), it is recognized that individual learners nevertheless follow different paths, or routes, in SLA, principally in terms of the degree to which they display either a predominantly 'standard' orientation, favouring accuracy, or a predominantly 'simplifying' one, favouring communicative effectiveness. A learner's orientation may vary over time, and is independent of developmental stage, some more advanced learners (with proficiency being defined developmentally), whether naturalistic or instructed, being less accurate, less norm-oriented, than some less advanced learners (Meisel, Clahsen and Pienemann 1981; Clahsen, Meisel and Pienemann 1983; Nicholas 1984, 1985).

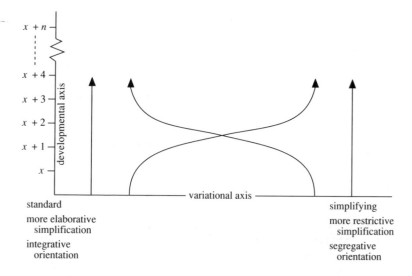

FIGURE 7.5 Two Dimensions of Language Development and Some Potential Routes to Acquisition

The original evidence for the variational dimension in the ZISA data consisted of an observed tendency of learners to differ from one another in the degree to which they supplied approximately twelve German grammatical functors, including articles, prepositions in certain linguistic environments, and the copula (Clahsen, Meisel and Pienemann 1983). Thus, some learners produced the copula as soon as they began using equational or attributive utterances ('He is brother', 'He is good'). Others either initially or permanently omitted the copula in those contexts. The latter group tended to produce their deviant equational and attributive utterances earlier than the former group's standard versions emerged, however, meaning that, while less accurate, they became communicatively effective speakers of German more quickly in those domains. It was further noted that neither the absolute nor the proportional frequency of copula suppliance necessarily increased in some learners' ILs as they advanced developmentally. Linguistic features exhibiting these characteristics are termed *variational features*. They seem often to include grammatically important but communicatively redundant linguistic items in a language, although no definition of this category is provided by the ZISA group.

The same tension between accuracy and communicative effective-ness was also observed in standard-oriented and simplifying learners' differential application of ADV and INV. Acquisition of German adverb-fronting (ADV, stage $X + 1$ – see Figure 7.3) increases the communicative options available to a learner, primarily through providing another means of attention-focusing – *'*In Mexico* I met her' instead of 'I met her in Mexico'. However, the fact that the subject–verb inversion (INV, stage $X + 3$) that is in turn required in such sentences in German ('In Mexico *met I* her') is still well beyond the learner, means that each of the communicatively more effective utterances will automatically be ungrammatical for a lengthy period (for details, see Pienemann 1986). It was found that, while simplifying learners tended to exploit ADV early, standard-oriented learners tended to avoid it, thereby preserving accuracy at the cost of communicative effectiveness.

Pienemann (1988) claims that recognition of the two classes of (developmental and variational) linguistic features can help teachers better predict and understand the source(s) of learner errors, as well as provide useful input to certain types of syllabus design. In this regard, another interesting finding with respect to variational features is that, whereas the effects of instruction are subject to processing constraints where developmental features are concerned, this is not the case with variational features. On the basis of other results from teaching experiments, it is claimed that instruction is capable of achieving considerable reductions in the omission rate of items like the copula, and that this can be done as soon as they can be produced. (Pienemann 1984, 1988; Pienemann and Johnston 1987).

While the ZISA group identified 'standard' and 'simplifying' learner types, both groups exhibited two kinds of simplification in their ILs: (1) *restrictive simplification*, involving omission of various grammatically obligatory but communicatively redundant items ('Julia happy', 'She eat sandwich'), and (2) *elaborative simplification*, involving over-suppliance of such items ('He wented', 'Theys go') (Meisel, Clahsen and Pienemann 1981; Meisel 1983c). It was found, however, that the relative frequencies of the two kinds of simplification differed between certain groups of learners (learner 'types') at one time, and within learners over time. The groups were distinguishable in the ZISA study by informants' profiles on clusters of social and psychological variables, assessed using interviews and questionnaires. Restrictive simplification tended to be more common among *segregatively oriented* learners, i.e. those with less leisure-time contact with Germans, lower intended length of residence in Germany, and so on; elaborative simplification was more frequent among *integratively oriented* learners, i.e. those with more leisure-time contact, higher intended length of residence, more positive attitudes towards Germans, etc. (Clahsen, Meisel and Pienemann 1983).

7.5.5 A critique of the Multidimensional Model

Whatever the ultimate validity of the Multidimensional Model may turn out to be, both the Model itself and the ZISA project from which it sprang have already made several important contributions to the study of SLA. To begin with, the ZISA project was one of the first to relinquish the prevailing target-language orientation of the 1970s, thereby avoiding what Bley-Vroman (1983) has called the 'comparative fallacy in IL studies'. As noted in Chapter 3, in most North American and European SLA research of the 1960s and 1970s, the focus was either on errors defined in terms of the mature L2 system, or alternatively, on items held to be acquired when they were supplied 80 or 90 per cent accurately in obligatory contexts (or some variant thereof). Studying 'acquisition', in other words, mostly meant assessing how far learners were from the finishing line or studying them as they crossed it. The ZISA group explicitly rejected this approach, redefining acquisition (of a form) as the first appearance of a form in an IL, this and the subsequent evolution of form–function relationships being treated from the same learner-oriented perspective that had long been taken for granted by creolists, for whom a target-oriented viewpoint is, of course, not an option. By studying the learning *process* in this way, researchers can seek to *explain* SLA, to understand how it happens. Looking primarily or even exclusively at the product, on the other hand, researchers can, at most, hope to identify which variables predict that SLA will occur, but not understand how or why.

A second improvement on much existing work of the period (and some current efforts) is the attempt, whether successful or not, to tie contextual factors, including a range of social and psychological variables, to internal psycholinguistic processes, in the form of simplification and processing strategies, and these in turn to precisely defined exponents in the IL data. Thus, instead of the often rather vague claims in some theories for general effects of social and/or psychological factors on the SLA *product*, typically defined by global proficiency test scores, the Multidimensional Model seeks to explain how such factors interact with cognitive mechanisms to produce precisely specified microlinguistic features. One example is the mediating effect of standard and simplifying orientations, predictable from learners' affective profiles, leading to differing degrees of attention to accuracy or communicative effectiveness, and finally to differing rates of suppliance of the so-called variational features.

The degree of accountability to data this example simultaneously illustrates is another positive characteristic of most work inspired by the Model to date. Indeed, research within the predictive framework has generally maintained a welcome degree of linguistic precision. Hence, Pienemann's prediction that learners will only benefit from appropriately timed instruction is testable, since learners' current abilities, as well as both appropriate and inappropriate structures for them, can be defined linguistically in terms of the developmental stages in the Multidimensional Model. In contrast, as noted earlier, what on the surface looks like a similar claim by Krashen for the relevance of i and $i + 1$ in Monitor Theory cannot. Whether or not the stages turn out to be correct, the important point is that they are empirically testable, and the framework in turn falsifiable.

Perhaps the single most important strength of the Multidimensional Model itself is its *independent motivation* of the observed developmental stages through use of the speech-processing constraints. That is, the sequence of developmental stages comes with an *explanation* (itself an advance on much other work on such sequences), and moreover, one derived from another source (experimental psycholinguistics), rather than from the data themselves. This is always preferable because its independence from these particular data means it has greater potential for predicting and explaining new data. This is really another way of saying that the data are made interesting by their combination with a causal-process *theory*, an explanation with predictive power, and so with generalizability, in this case, not only to other sequences and linguistic domains, but also to other languages, since the speech-processing constraints are supposedly universal. This is a tremendous improvement on a claim to have discovered empirically that WXYZ is the developmental sequence for such-and-such a grammatical sub-domain in English, that ABCDEF is the sequence in another, or that a particular set of grammatical morphemes exhibit an accuracy order 1 through 15. These are useful findings, but themselves merely facts about SLA in need of an explanation, not such an explanation. Even their usefulness as facts is rather limited since they are language-specific, and so at most concern ESL, GSL, JSL, etc., whereas the ultimate purpose of the enterprise is an understanding, i.e. an explanatory theory, of SLA – any SL.

Despite these positive characteristics, as might be expected, the Multidimensional Model is not without problems. Of these, potentially the most serious is the possibility that the Model may turn out to be quite revealing about *constraints* on acquisition, among other things, without saying much about how learners actually learn whatever they do, constrained as they are. Put another way, identifying the nature of the processing strategies governing some aspects of acquisition (assuming this is achieved) will be an especially important advance due to their universal status and consequent cross-linguistic generalizability, but it would still not in itself specify how it is that learners learn whatever they manage to produce despite the constraints. What kinds of grammatical rules, for example, underlie the structures that are produced in conformity with the processing constraints, and how are they acquired, or are they or some other kind of knowledge innate?[13]

A second problem concerns the falsifiability of certain aspects of the Model and predictive framework, of which we will briefly mention three. First, Pienemann and Johnston's (1985, 1987) extension of the analysis to morphology explicitly assumes (following Selkirk 1983) that morphemes have the psychological status of words, with a syntax of their own. As Pienemann and Johnston are, of course, aware, however, this is not always the case with early 'chunked' morphology, since SL learners, like children acquiring their L1, frequently produce their first tokens of such items as English irregular past, plural *s*, and even third-person singular *-s* as parts of unanalysed forms, such as *went* and *stairs* and *breaks* (for discussion, see, e.g., Pica 1982; Young 1988). This means that some tokens of such items will occur in the speech of learners well before they reach the stages (see Figure 7.5) at which they are predicted to attain productive use of them. Johnston (1985) explicitly recognizes and attempts to deal with this problem empirically by flagging commonly observed 'chunked' items in his ESL data-base, e.g. high-frequency 'chunked' *-ly* adverbs, like *really* and *especially*, which he found did not indicate productive stage $X + 4$ processing of the structure. While such information is very useful for practical applications of the model, e.g. to oral language testing, the falsification problem remains, nevertheless, in two forms: apparent violations due to the premature appearance of some items in chunks, but chunks not recognized as such, and the unavailability of the empirical option each time the predictive framework is applied to new languages.

A second falsifiability problem is due to the lack of clarity over identifying variational features *a priori*. It is currently impossible to distinguish between two interpretations of the potential outcome of some teaching experiments, namely, when a grammatical item is learned by students whose current stage of development predicted that it would not be learnable: (1) the result is a disconfirmation of the model (assuming there was nothing wrong with the way the structure was classified in terms of the processing constraints), and (2) it is a (newly discovered) variational feature of the language concerned (hence, teachable at any stage), and so not a disconfirmation. A further complication where variational features are concerned is that they, too, have developmental sequences, e.g. different contexts for article use (Yamada and Matsura 1982; Huebner 1983a; Pica 1983b; Master 1987), not all of which, therefore, can be teachable at any stage.

A third falsifiability problem arises from vagueness as to what would constitute violations of the processing constraints among mainstream developmental features. For instance, in an unpublished pilot study of ESL and JSL at the University of Hawaii in 1984 testing the predictive framework, it was found that the general IL profile for some learners might place them, say, at stage $X + 4$ in ESL (see Figure 7.5), but still show them producing stage $X + 3$ structures in one or more domains and $X + 5$ structures in one or more domains. While some 'trailing' and 'scouting' in particular structural domains is to be expected, the question arises as to how many developmental levels can separate the least and most advanced structures before the model can be said to have been falsified. One would, of course, also have to be careful that such cases were not simply the result of using inadequate IL samples, i.e. finding 'gaps' due to using free speech data which show what some learners did and did not produce instead of data from targeted elicitation procedures showing what they could and could not produce.

Each of these three problems concerning falsifiability could be rectified: the first by some laborious empirical work and/or careful searches for chunked items in particular IL samples, the second by defining variational features *a priori* or, at least, specifying the status of particular items before a study is undertaken, and the third by setting limits on 'gaps'. Further, while all three do appear to be loopholes in the current model, this is by no means to claim that the Model or predictive framework are unfalsifiable. On the contrary, as detailed earlier, most aspects of both are empirically testable in fairly straightforward ways, including some of the problems. Thus, the current vagueness about what constitute variational features does not mean, e.g., that the Teachability Hypothesis cannot be tested. It clearly can (and has been) by concentrating on structures known to be reliable developmental features.

In conclusion, while it is too early to assess its validity, the Multidimensional Model has clearly already made several valuable theoretical and methodological contributions to SLA. There are some current problems with the falsifiability of the predictive framework, and a major question looming concerning just what the Model will explain about acquisition, as opposed to constraints on acquisition. These are mostly limitations rather than flaws, however.

One of the Model's greatest strengths *qua* theory is its *predictive* power, a quality which also promises several potentially exciting practical applications. One is the use of the developmental stages as a principled means of sequencing items in a syllabus (for any SL), given that the stages are by definition statements about what a learner can be taught at a given stage of development. Pienemann (1985b) has illustrated this with respect to both structural and notional-functional syllabus design. Another application is to teaching methodology, where knowledge of developmental stages and variational features can serve as a useful diagnostic resource for teachers, allowing them to identify different kinds of errors and to assess their 'remediability'. A third application is to placement and achievement testing. Language testing in general has too long focused on accuracy – which the learner orientation component of the Multidimensional Model and numerous other SLA studies have shown to be a highly suspect candidate for measurement in any case – or, more recently, on equally problematic notions of 'proficiency' (for extensive discussion, see Brindley and Singh 1982; Crystal 1982; Clahsen 1985; Brindley 1986b; Pienemann and Johnston 1987). What has clearly been needed for a long time is 'IL-sensitive' tests – instruments or procedures which capitalize on research findings about developmental sequences in SLA, e.g. utilizing the stages defined in the predictive framework. (It should be noted, however, that these currently only extend to roughly 'intermediate' levels.) Since the early 1980s, several research projects have begun exploring relationships among sets of IL features and between traditional proficiency measures and developmental features (see, e.g., Stauble 1981; Hinofotis et al. 1982; Lamotte, Pearson-Joseph and Zupko 1982; Brindley 1986b). For an early application of the developmental stages in the predictive framework to a teacher-rating procedure for assessing spoken language, see Pienemann and Johnston (1986) and Pienemann, Johnston and Brindley (1988).

7.6 Conclusion: the state of SLA theories

7.6.1 Comparing and evaluating theories

Knowing when to modify and when to abandon a leaky theory is a pervasive problem in the sciences. (See Wagner 1984 for a lucid analysis of the evolution of theories in sociology, for example.) It seems to be particularly acute in SLA research, however, for several reasons. As noted earlier, there are at least forty 'theories', 'models', 'perspectives', 'metaphors', 'hypotheses' and 'theoretical claims' in the SLA literature. (The terms are generally used in free variation.) There is often overlap among them, but equally often, areas of uniqueness. What makes them difficult to evaluate is the fact that they sometimes differ greatly in (1) *scope*, or the range of SLA phenomena they treat; (2) the type of *data* to which they are (implicitly or explicitly) held accountable; and (3) the degree of *abstraction* of the statements they contain.

Differences in scope are easily documented. Krashen's Monitor Theory, for example, though changing considerably over time, has always been supposed to account for all SL acquisitional types, as have Wode's (1981) linguo-cognitive strategies, whereas Schumann's Acculturation Model is explicitly limited to naturalistic SLA, and the Multidimensional Model (currently) just to morphology and syntax. Leaving aside for the moment the evidence in fact available to support either position, which would be the better theory in the event that one decided that something was wrong with *parts* of Krashen's theory, but that Schumann's model was in good shape? Would an empirically sounder theory of admittedly narrower scope be preferable to one which set out to handle a wider range of SLA phenomena and had mixed empirical support?

Differences in the types of data to which theories are held accountable often result in one theory being tested more precisely and so more stringently than another. Meisel, Clahsen and Pienemann (1981 and elsewhere), for example, test predictions against established developmental sequences in IL syntax, identifiable linguistic exponents of various types of simplification strategies, and the relationship between these and learner types (as defined by clusters of affect variables). McLaughlin, Rossman and McLeod's (1983) 'information-processing perspective' and Bialystok's (1978) 'theoretical model of second language learning', on the other hand, like many others, say little or nothing about IL development at all, focusing instead on SL performance, attainment or proficiency factors. Supporting or disconfirmatory data usually take the form of global test scores, reaction-time measures, and the like, not linguistic features in ILs.

Lastly, with regard to differences in degree of abstraction, compare two apparently similar claims (in otherwise radically different theories) concerning the potential for acquisition of new forms in a learner's input. Krashen's Input Hypothesis holds that structures acquired (from comprehensible input) will be 'one step ahead of', or 'a bit beyond the acquirer's current level' of development, *i*. Pienemann's Learnability and Teachability Hypotheses predict which learners, grouped by acquisitional stage, in turn defined by suppliance of particular developmental structures, will benefit from instruction in the next interlingual structure in a previously established developmental sequence, and which groups will not – predictions tested, as we have seen, by Pienemann and others in classroom studies.

Differences like these present serious problems when one attempts to evaluate the relative merits of such positions. Is a more general theory, part of which appears to have been falsified, in better or worse shape than a less general one which has some, albeit limited, data to support it? Are differences in the types of data, and hence, the aspects of SLA a theory speaks to, relevant in evaluating competing explanations supposedly of the same process? And does the high degree of explicitness and precision of one claim, which inevitably makes it easier to falsify, at least in detail, make it less worthy of attention than a more loosely defined one, whose more general predictions make it harder to disprove or necessitates testing it in a wider range of contexts before its true worth is known?

Well-established criteria exist to resolve some of these problems, of course. Thus, it is generally held that a theory must be falsifiable (subject to the previously mentioned caveats concerning the availability of relevant technology). Obviously, it must not yet have been falsified, though, which is to say that it must be able to account for existing data, i.e. be 'observationally adequate'. All other things being equal, a theory of wider scope is better than one of narrower scope because it can be used to address a wider range of problems, or is more generalizable. If two theories are equally good explanations of existing data, the better theory is the simpler one, the one that makes fewer distinctions and uses fewer caveats (less power) to handle the data. And so on. But the current state of SLA means one is often having to weigh the results of applying two or more evaluation criteria simultaneously, and criteria applied to different *types* of theory at that, at which time the picture becomes very murky indeed.

Now, it would be a truism to say that all this simply reflects the current state of development of a what is, after all, a relatively new field. The point is, will more research of the 'fishing expedition' variety help? Or is what is needed a good theory?

7.6.2 A note of caution

We alluded earlier to the fact that not all SLA researchers share our view that SLA research will best be served by advancing a theory or theories to account for what is known about SLA. The reservations those researchers have are essentially two. We have already stated the first: a theory at this point in the nascency of SLA research is likely to be, at best, an oversimplification, if not a downright erroneous description of the actual SLA process. Thus, a theory may mislead or obfuscate, rather than elucidate and be helpful in motivating additional fact-finding.

The second reservation stems from the observation of the effect of a monolithic theory in related fields, e.g. linguistics and psychology. It can sometimes be the case that a single theory can be so 'politically' powerful that it has the effect of stifling alternative points of view. Investigators who do not embrace the prevailing theory find it difficult to get published or to find a forum for alternative interpretations of the facts as they see them. It would be unacceptable in our view if this were to happen in our field. The rise of a single dominant theory which discourages competing points of view, given our present limited state of understanding, would be counter-productive. We must guard against overzealousness on the part of theorists or their devotees who feel that they have a monopoly on the truth. While SLA research and language teaching will benefit from the advantages of theoretically motivated research which we have spelled out in this chapter, it would be dangerous at this stage for one theory to become omnipotent.

With these notes of caution in mind, what, then, is our own view of the role of theory in SLA? As stated in Chapter 1, we see SLA research as anything but an 'ivory tower' activity. Its findings, for example, often affect the life chances of 'at risk' populations, such as adult refugees needing an SL in order to hold down a job in a new country, minority-language children seeking an education through an SL, and so on. Our view is that researchers working in SLA who are serious about their work and about such issues will want to proceed as swiftly, as efficiently and as *scientifically* as possible, and so will value the unifying (not stultifying) effect which a good theory can have on their own research and the work of others. They will appreciate the clear direction a theory can give them when designing and executing studies, the interim solution it provides practitioners until SLA is better understood.

Notes

1. 'Semi-partials' (semi-partial correlation coefficients) is one name for a statistical procedure which allows a researcher interested in the

relationship between two variables (e.g. age and motivation) and SLA to assess how strongly each is related to acquisition when the other is held constant, and so 'controlled out' of the study. For example, instead of simply comparing the learning achieved by students of *different ages* with (say) 40, 45, 50...90 point scores on an (0–100 point) index of 'motivation to learn' an SL, the researcher can hold age constant in the sample of learners and look at the relationship (uncontaminated by age differences) between motivation and SLA, by comparing the differential effects of same age but differently motivated learners, and vice versa. A variety of more powerful statistical analyses exist for this kind of study, some of which, e.g. multiple regression, factor analysis and path analysis, permit the researcher to assess the relative contribution of a much larger number of variables.

2. See Ochsner (1979) for a history of the nomothetic and hermeneutic traditions and their roles in modern SLA research.

3. Hirsch-Pasek et al. found that mothers repeated about 21 per cent of their two-year-olds' ungrammatical utterances, as compared with 12 per cent of their grammatical ones. The repetitions often took the form of an expansion, i.e. contained an implicit correction of the error by supplying the missing item. However, since the children had no way of knowing which of their utterances were grammatical, and since their parents repeated some grammatical as well as some ungrammatical utterances, the children would have no way of knowing whether a maternal repetition or expansion was intended as a correction or a simple paraphrase, or even whether it was more likely to be one rather than the other. Hence, there is no way in principle that they could use this information as evidence about grammaticality. (It is instructive to consider these issues in the context of intended and perceived 'correction' in the adult SL classroom.) The difference in the kinds of utterances that were repeated disappeared with older children.

4. Michael Montgomery (personal communication) has pointed out that some varieties of English, e.g. varieties of Southern American English, do in fact allow dropping of subject pronouns, especially in informal registers.

5. 'Hypothesis' appears in quotation marks because Krashen consistently means something else when he uses the term. Some of the so-called 'hypotheses' in (Extended Standard) MT, e.g. the Natural Order Hypothesis, are *generalizations* based on reviews of empirical studies. Some, e.g. the Acquisition-Learning, Monitor, and Input Hypotheses, are *claims* about putative SLA processes. One, the Affective Filter Hypothesis, is a metaphor. Most involve *constructs*, e.g. 'acquisition', 'learning', '*i*', and '*i* + 1', which, as Krashen (1984) acknowledges, is fine in (certain types of) theories, but not possible in hypotheses, which differ from theories, among other ways, in that they must be *empirically testable*, usually taking the form of predictions about some observable natural phenomena. Constructs cannot be subjected to empirical test, because they are not operationalized,

and in some cases (like '*i*' and '*i* + 1'), are not operationalizable, and so are unmeasurable.

6. Given the minor role assigned to the Monitor and the decline of interest in its workings, 'MT' is now really a misnomer, a vestige of its modest beginnings and original focus.

7. For treatments of the role of introspection in SLA research, see Chaudron (1983c); Cohen and Hosenfeld (1981); Faerch and Kasper (1987); Seliger (1983); Singh, d'Anglejan and Carroll (1982); Birdsong (1986).

8. To which of three 'hypotheses' did a morpheme study which produced an 'unnatural' order constitute counter-evidence – the Natural Order, Learning/Acquisition, or Monitor Hypotheses? Recall that the 'natural order' was held by Krashen to be evidence for the construct *acquisition*, but simultaneously evidence that *learning* either could not be or had not been applied via monitoring. Did a disturbed order mean, therefore, that subjects had used their learned systems to monitor their output or that one or more of the original notions *monitoring, natural order* or *acquisition* was faulty?

9. These are questions in need of answers from anyone advancing an SLA theory claiming a role for affect variables, of course, not just Krashen. (See, e.g., Schumann 1978, 1986; Acton 1979; H.D. Brown 1980; Gardner 1985; and our discussion in Chapter 6.)

10. Krashen and Terrell (1983, p. i) speak enthusiastically of a conference paper by Voge (1981) as reporting a crucial classroom validation of the Natural Approach, but to our knowledge this study has never been published, and is apparently unavailable even in manuscript form. A non-equivalent control group design is reported by Edwards et al. (1984), in which students in special sheltered ESL and French SL sections of a basic psychology course at the University of Ottawa did as well in psychology as students in sections taught through their L1, and achieved comparable gains in SL proficiency to students in regular ESL and FSL classes.

11. Schumann (1978a, pp. 71–2) cites these data as examples of the use of word order to replace inflectional morphology.

12. Schmidt's findings are based on a single-shot case study of one individual, as were Schumann's original claims. There are probably a lot of learners like both Wes and Alberto, however. Theorizing will undoubtedly continue based on limited samples until more (labour-intensive) longitudinal studies of adult SLA are conducted – currently one of the greatest needs in the field.

13. Pienemann and Johnston (in progress) indicate awareness of this problem, and adopt a variant of Lexical–Functional Grammar (Kaplan and Bresnan 1978; Bresnan 1982). White (1989) raises a related issue, namely, whether the same processing constraints are supposed to or can apply to both comprehension and production.

Activities

Comprehension

1. Define and distinguish *hypothesis* and *theory*. Give an example of each.
2. Distinguish *hypothesis*, *generalization* and *law*. Can you illustrate each of them from the SLA literature?
3. What are the strengths and limitations of (a) the *set-of-laws* form, and (b) the *causal-process* form of theory? How do they differ in the kind of 'understanding' each can provide of SLA?
4. In what sense are interactionist theories more powerful than nativist or environmentalist theories?
5. What is meant by 'negative evidence' and by the claim that natural languages are unlearnable from the input?
6. What do the terms 'marked' and 'unmarked' mean in Chomsky's Universal Grammar? How do these definitions differ from typological notions of markedness?
7. How does Krashen explain the 'natural order'? What does he use the 'natural order' to explain?
8. Which parts of comprehensible input does Krashen claim are usable for IL development? Is his claim testable?
9. What is the difference between 'learning' and 'acquisition' in Monitor Theory? What was McLaughlin's (1978) objection to the distinction, and what was Krashen's (1979) response?
10. Is Schumann's claim that ILs are like pidgins or that early naturalistic SLA is like pidginization?
11. Give two examples of linguistic features in Alberto's IL that you think best support the Pidginization Hypothesis, and two features that you think provide the greatest challenge to the analogy.
12. Summarize two studies that support Schumann's claim for acculturation as the causal variable in SLA, and two studies which provide counter-evidence.
13. Are Givon's pragmatic and syntactic modes a dichotomy or two poles on a continuum? What evidence decides this?
14. What is meant by 'syntacticization' in Givon's work? Give two examples of linguistic changes in an IL which would constitute evidence of the syntacticization process, and two which would not.
15. What about the developmental stages in the Multidimensional Model makes them generalizable, but (say) the stages for ESL negation not?
16. What are variational features in the Multidimensional Model, and what do they supposedly indicate?

17. If developmental stages are fixed, how can there be different routes to development?
18. Define and illustrate restrictive and elaborative simplification. Is either strategy unique to standard or simplifying learners?
19. What is the relationship between Pienemann's Learnability and Teachability Hypotheses? Are they hypotheses in the technical sense of the term? Does your answer affect your opinion as to the validity of basing teaching recommendations on them?
20. How does the specificity of Pienemann's Learnability and Teachability Hypotheses make the claims vulnerable? Does the generality of a claim make it more or less vulnerable to falsification?
21. Can you explain why -*ly* adverbs in English are classified as stage $X + 3$ structures in Pienemann and Johnston's predictive framework?

Application

22. Which (if any) of the five examples of potential 'laws' of SLA do you think actually merit the status of hypotheses, generalizations or laws, and why? What other findings of SLA research do you consider strong enough and widely enough attested to merit the status of generalization or law? Would ascription of the status of generalization or law be easier if you recast any of the statements in probabilistic form?
23. Give an example of how a supposedly innate grammatical principle might in fact be learnable from positive evidence alone.
24. What (if any) modifications could be made to the Affective Filter Hypothesis to make it testable?
25. Can you see a greater potential role for connectionism in first or second language learning than Chomsky is willing to imagine? If not, why not? If so, what role might connectionist learning play in SLA?
26. Compare the different 'simplification' processes and strategies identified by Schumann and by Meisel, Clahsen and Pienemann. What similarities and differences do you find? Could either set be subsumed by the other?
27. How could instrumentation problems be solved for the measurement of affective factors in SL populations?
28. Which (if any) modifications observed in foreigner talk discourse could be analysed as examples of a shift to a pragmatic mode of communication?

29. Take a simple syntactic structure in another language and classify it according to Pienemann and Johnston's framework. Do the same with another structure in that language which should be acquired at the same time. How could you test your analysis?

30. Do you think the Multidimensional Model is a theory of SLA or of SL performance?

31. The role of theory discussed in this chapter reflects the fairly conventional view of nomothetic science, which assumes that there indeed are laws and causal relationships governing natural phenomena, including SLA, which are, as it were, 'waiting to be discovered'. These views are no longer as widely accepted as they once were, even in the physical sciences which first gave rise to them. They have been challenged by hermeneuticists of various persuasions, such as ethnomethodologists (see, e.g., Garfinkel 1967; Mehan and Wood 1975; Turner 1978; Leiter 1980) who dispute the assumptions, and argue that the stable, replicable 'rules' of human behaviour 'discovered' by nomothetic scientists are simply an artefact of the contrived laboratory experiments, supposedly designed to test them, which they conduct. Even among scientists working within the nomothetic, or nomological, paradigm, the traditional shapes and purposes of theories have been challenged, as by proponents of Rene Thom's Catastrophe Theory (see, e.g., Zeeman 1977; Woodcock and Davis 1978). The validity of the assumptions of nomothetic science for SLA research in particular has been criticized by several writers (see, e.g., Ochsner 1979; Candlin 1983; Guiora 1983; Schumann 1983; van Lier 1988).

Given the findings of SLA research reviewed in previous chapters, which of those findings (if any) do you suspect may be an artefact of the research methodology employed, and why? If you reject the role or types of theory argued for in this chapter, how would you suggest that researchers proceed in their (supposed) accumulation of understanding of the SLA process? What would you tell a school district or language teaching programme director who asks you for recommendations, based upon your knowledge of the SLA literature, as to the type of SL programme they should design and implement for their students? In other words, how would you fill in the admitted gaps in current knowledge when making suggestions for practitioners who have programmes to run on Monday morning and who cannot wait until the final answers are in?

Suggestions for further reading

For introductions to theory-construction in social science, consult:

Cummins, R 1983 *Psychological explanation*. MIT Press, Cambridge, Mass.

Feyerabend, P 1978 *Against method*. Verso

Greenwald, A, Pratkanis, A, Leippe, M and Baumgardner, M 1986 Under what conditions does theory obstruct research progress? *Psychological Review* 93 (2): 216–29

Harre, R 1987 *Varieties of realism*. Basil Blackwell, New York

Mehan, H and Wood, H 1975 *The reality of ethnomethodology*. Wiley, New York

Mitroff, I and Kilmann, R 1978 *Methodological approaches to social science*. Jossey-Bass, San Francisco

Reynolds, P 1971 *A primer in theory construction*. Bobbs-Merrill, Indianapolis

Wagner, D 1984 *The growth of sociological theories*. Sage Publications, Beverly Hills

Woodcock, A and Davis, M 1978 *Catastrophe theory*. Pelican

For theory construction in first and second language acquisition, see:

Atkinson, M 1982 *Explanations in the study of child language development*. Cambridge University Press

Ellis, R 1985 *Understanding second language acquisition*, Chapter 10: Theories of second language acquisition. Oxford University Press

Gregg, K (In press) Krashen's theory, acquisition theory, and theory. In Barasch, R (ed.) *Responses to Krashen*. Newbury House, Cambridge, Mass.

Larsen-Freeman, D 1983c Second language acquisition: getting the whole picture. In Bailey, K, Long, M and Peck, S (eds.) *Second language acquisition studies*, pp. 3–22. Newbury House, Rowley, Mass.

Long, M 1985 Input and second language acquisition theory. In Gass, S and Madden, C (eds.) *Input and second language acquisition*, pp. 377–93. Newbury House, Rowley, Mass.

McLaughlin, B 1987 *Theories of second language learning*. Edward Arnold

Ochsner, R 1979 A poetics of second language acquisition. *Language Learning* 29 (1): 53–80

Schumann, J 1983 Art and science in second language acquisition research. In Clark, M and Handscombe, J (eds.) *On TESOL '82*. TESOL, Washington, D.C.

Spolsky, B 1989 *Conditions for second language learning*. Oxford University Press

For Chomsky's Universal Grammar and SLA, see:

Cook, V 1985 Chomsky's universal grammar and second language acquisition. *Applied Linguistics* 6: 2–18

Cook, V 1988 *Chomsky's universal grammar*. Basil Blackwell, New York

Gregg, K 1989 Linguistic perspectives on second language acquisition: what could they be, and where can we get some? In Gass, S and Schachter, J (eds.) *Linguistic perspectives on second language acquisition*. Cambridge University Press

Pankhurst, J, Sharwood-Smith, M and van Buren, P (eds.) 1988 *Learnability and second languages*. Foris, Dordrecht

Ritchie, W 1983 Universal grammar and second language acquisition. In Rogers, D and Sloboda, J (eds.) *The acquisition of symbolic skills*. Plenum Press, New York

Rutherford, W 1986 Grammatical theory and L2 acquisition: a brief overview. *Second Language Research* 2: 1–15

White, L 1986 Implications of parametric variation for adult second language acquisition: an investigation of the pro-drop parameter. In Cook, V (ed.) *Experimental approaches to second language acquisition*. Pergamon

And see back issues of *Second Language Research* (Edward Arnold), a journal which regularly publishes SLA research conducted within the UG framework.

For Krashen's Monitor theory, see:

Barasch, R (ed.) (to appear) *Responses to Krashen*. Newbury House/Harper and Row, New York

Gregg, K 1984 Krashen's monitor and Occam's razor. *Applied Linguistics* 5: 79–100

Krashen, S 1982 *Principles and practice in second language acquisition*. Pergamon Press

Krashen, S 1985 *The input hypothesis: issues and implications*. Longman, New York

McLaughlin, B 1978 The monitor model: some methodological considerations. *Language Learning* 28: 309–32

For Schumann's Pidginization Hypothesis and Acculturation Model, see:

Andersen, R (ed.) 1983 *Pidginization and creolization as language acquisition*. Newbury House, Rowley, Mass.

Romaine, S 1988 *Pidgin and creole languages*. Longman

Schumann, J 1978 The acculturation model for second language acquisition. In Gingras, R (ed.) *Second-language acquisition and foreign language teaching*. Center for Applied Linguistics, Washington, D.C.

Schumann, J 1978 *The pidginization process: a model for second language acquisition*. Newbury House, Rowley, Mass.

For Givon's Functional–Typological theory and SLA, see:

Givon, T 1979 *On understanding grammar*. Academic Press, New York

Sato, C 1988 Origins of complex syntax in interlanguage development. *Studies in Second Language Acquisition* 10 (3): 371–95

Sato, C (to appear) *The syntax of conversation in interlanguage development*. Gunter Narr, Tubingen

Schumann, J 1987 Utterance structure in basilang speech. In Gilbert, G (ed.) *Pidgin and creole languages: essays in memory of John E. Reinecke*. University of Hawaii Press, Honolulu

For the ZISA group's Multidimensional Model, see:

Clahsen, H, Meisel, J and Pienemann, M 1983 *Deutsch als Zweitsprache: Der Spracherwerb ausländischer Arbeiter*. Gunter Narr, Tubingen

Hyltenstam, K and Pienemann, M (eds.) 1985 *Modelling and assessing second language acquisition*. Multilingual Matters

Meisel, J, Clahsen, H and Pienemann, M 1981 On determining developmental stages in second language acquisition. *Studies in Second Language Acquisition* **3** (2): 109–35

Pienemann, M and Johnston, M 1987 Factors influencing the development of language proficiency. In D Nunan (ed.) *Applying second language acquisition research*, pp. 45–141. National Curriculum Resource Centre, Adelaide, NSW

8 Instructed second language acquisition

8.1 Introduction

As explained in Chapter 1, a major goal for many SLA researchers is to provide a sound psycholinguistic basis for SL *teaching*. While much of the research we have examined thus far has implications for teachers, syllabus designers and developers of language tests, there is a growing body of work within SLA which focuses directly on these issues. In particular, a considerable number of studies have been carried out whose explicit focus has been to determine the effects (if any) of formal instruction on interlanguage development.

Several theorists have claimed that interlanguage development in instructed (classroom) learners does not differ significantly from that in learners acquiring an SL naturalistically. The processes and/or sequences in SL development are held to be the same in both acquisitional contexts. Accordingly, some writers on language teaching have advocated provision of 'natural' language learning experiences for classroom learners, and the elimination of structural grading, a focus on form and error correction, even for adults.

In this chapter we will examine the evidence offered in support of the claims concerning instructed IL development. Some studies of the potential of formal instruction in four areas are summarized: (1) accuracy orders/developmental sequences, (2) acquisition processes, (3) rate of acquisition, and (4) the level of ultimate SL attainment. We will see that while, on the basis of the evidence currently available, developmental sequences indeed seem impervious to instruction, a focus on form, or language as object, does appear to have beneficial effects in the other three areas, the effect on rate of acquisition being especially evident.

8.2 Early research on the effect of instruction, and some claimed implications

The rapid increase in the quantity of SLA research in the late 1960s and early 1970s took place during a generally conservative era in language teaching. In most quarters, teaching materials and classroom methodology were still based largely on a combination of structuralist contrastive analyses of the L1 and L2 and neo-behaviourist learning theory. Mentalism was in the ascendent in linguistics, however, inspired by Chomsky's strong claims for innate, universal linguistic properties of the mind. Hence, it was perhaps not surprising that since many early SLA researchers were trained in linguistics departments dominated by Chomsky's ideas, most began by looking for, finding, and stressing some of the inescapable similarities between naturalistic and instructed SLA. Not infrequently, they went on to claim that, therefore, teaching could have little or no effect on the acquisition process – a logical possibility, given the findings, but not necessarily true, as will become apparent.

An example of this type of research and argumentation is the work of some North American investigators (described in Chapter 4) who, in the 1970s, produced evidence that the order in which accurate suppliance of certain grammatical morphemes in obligatory contexts attained criterion (80 or 90 per cent) was *similar* across learners from different first language backgrounds (see Krashen 1977 and Burt and Dulay 1980 for review), and in naturalistic and instructed learner groups (see, e.g., Krashen, Sferlazza, Feldman and Fathman 1976). The first finding was interpreted by Dulay and Burt (1977) as evidence of a common underlying acquisition process, *creative construction*. Because it seemed that this process would operate automatically in child SL learners if they were exposed to natural samples of the target language, Dulay and Burt (1973) concluded that children *should not be taught syntax*.

Krashen (1982a and elsewhere), too, claimed that the similarities reflected a common underlying process, which he called *acquisition*, responsible for the bulk of SLA in any context, including the classroom. Krashen also claimed that unconscious, 'acquired' knowledge of the

TL was responsible for normal SL performance. Conscious knowledge of simple TL grammar rules, *learning*, was rarely accessible in natural communication, when the language user is focused on meaning, not form. Further, it could not later become acquisition (Krashen and Scarcella 1978). Hence, the instruction which produced *learning* was also relatively unimportant. *Most of an SL cannot be taught*, Krashen claimed; it must be acquired.

Some related claims were made by European researchers. Felix and Simmet (1981) studied the acquisition of English pronouns by German high-school students over an eleven-month period. The researchers showed that the children (ages ten to twelve) acquired ESL pronominalization in a highly systematic manner, with the errors resulting from substitutions of one pronoun for another falling into only eight of a mathematically far larger number of potential error types. The children followed a process of gradually adding grammatical and semantic features (person, possession, number, gender, etc.) to their interim pronoun grammars.[1] Needless to say, this was not the way their instructors were attempting to teach them English pronouns. Rather, new pronouns were being presented and drilled as distinct morphemes, with unanalysed clusters of features 'ready packaged', as it were. The acquisition strategies observed paralleled those noted in naturalistic acquirers, leading Felix and Simmet to conclude that:

> the students' instruction-independent learning strategies demonstrate . . . that the learning process can only be manipulated within narrow limits and that the principles and regularities of natural language acquisition must also be considered in foreign language instruction. (Felix and Simmet 1981, p. 26)

In another publication based on the same study, Felix (1981a) reported finding structural parallels between the IL negation, interrogation, pronouns and sentence types of German high-school EFL students and naturalistic acquirers of ESL. Felix (1981a, p. 109) concluded:

> . . . foreign language learning under classroom conditions seems to partially follow the same set of natural processes that characterize other types of language acquisition. . . . there seems to be a universal and common set of principles which are flexible enough and adaptable to the large number of conditions under which language learning may take place. *These observations furthermore suggest that the*

possibility of manipulating and controlling the students' verbal behavior in the classroom is in fact quite limited [emphasis added].

In a similar vein, Wode (1981) compared findings on the acquisition of English negation in different types of language learning: child language development, foreign language learning, naturalistic second language learning and relearning, pidginization and creolization. While recognizing that differences did exist, the similarities he found in the developmental structures and developmental sequences across acquisitional types, Wode claimed, reflected universal processing abilities and (innate) language-learning strategies (e.g. the initial preference for free over bound forms), and the availability of these abilities and strategies in any language-learning context and at any period in a learner's life. The results further indicated, according to Wode, that teachers 'should not devise their teaching materials and teaching procedures to go counter to natural learner abilities' (Wode 1981, p. 231). Wode did not elaborate as to what kinds of teaching would constitute 'going counter to' (or facilitating) the working of these natural abilities. Neither Wode's nor Felix's research, it should be noted, had *studied* alternatives in language teaching.

The European and North American research was certainly useful in drawing attention to the unarguable similarities between naturalistic and instructed SLA. At the very least, it emphasized the importance of the learner's contribution to language learning, and serves as a healthy reminder to teachers that they are partners, not masters, in a joint enterprise. Unfortunately, however, many of the conclusions about the limitations or inefficacy of instruction are *non sequiturs* or, at best, *inferences* from studies which have looked not at the *effects* of instruction, but at similarities in the interlanguages of naturalistic and classroom learners. Yet it has been the inferences, not research, which have in turn formed a large part of the basis for prescriptions for language teaching.

There have been methodological realizations of these ideas (as the innovators see them). One is the Natural Approach, originally formulated by Terrell as a method of teaching Spanish as a foreign language to university students in the USA. Generalizing his ideas and motivating them *post hoc* with Monitor Theory, Krashen and Terrell (1983) advocate provision of comprehensible input in the form of the roughly tuned teacher and peer speech that arise naturally from *communication*, delivered in a positive affective classroom climate, as the essential ingredient of any successful language teaching programme. Proscribed are structural grading, a focus on form, grammar and vocabulary explanations, error correction, and other traditional language teaching activities, except where those activities could help with the learning of a few low-level target-language rules, help satisfy learner expectations, or serve as an indirect way of providing more comprehensible input. The goal of the classroom, Krashen writes (1981b, p. 61):

> is not to produce native speakers or even error-free second language performance. It is, rather, to develop 'intermediate' second language competence, to bring the student to the point where he can begin to understand the language he hears and reads outside the class and thus improve on his own.

Another possible implementation suggested elsewhere by Krashen (1981b, pp. 66–7) is for foreign university students to receive ESL at the 'beginning' level (with the main purpose of instruction being the provision of comprehensible input), to take 'sheltered subject matter' courses at the 'intermediate' level, (e.g. Psychology 101 for foreign students, along the lines of Canadian immersion programmes), but with *optional* ESL work as a supplement, and to be mainstreamed into regular subject matter courses at the 'advanced' level, with no accompanying ESL at all at this level.[2] Sheltered subject-matter teaching has more recently been seized upon in many parts of the USA as a (supposedly) viable alternative to bilingual education for minority-language children. In point of fact, its superiority over traditional bilingual education programmes has not been established.

Such prescriptions may yet turn out to be justified, but until the evidence is in, e.g. from SL classroom research, they need to be treated with great caution, a point which Krashen (1981b, p. 67) himself stresses. Opinions about the Natural Approach, sheltered subject-matter classes, etc. will obviously vary depending on one's training and field experience in applied linguistics and language teaching. An experienced SL programme designer, for example, might be impressed by the Natural Approach's psycholinguistic credentials and/or by its methodological innovations, but would flinch at its disregard for learner needs identification or, indeed, for any kind of syllabus, or content, at all (see Long 1985a for discussion).

Regardless of one's language teaching background, however, there is a serious flaw in the reasoning behind these proposals: it is assumed that a programme with (what Krashen and Terrell believe to be) the necessary and sufficient characteristics for successful language learning is automatically the most efficient/effective programme possible. Yet this is patently untrue. It is equivalent to claiming that because some plants will grow in a desert, watering the ones in your garden is a waste of time. In fact, of course, while the desert may provide the minimum conditions for a plant to grow, watering it may help it grow faster, bigger and stronger, that is, to realize its full potential. So with language learning: while comprehensible input may be necessary and sufficient for SLA,[3] instruction may simplify the learning task, alter the processes and sequences of acquisition, speed up the rate of acquisition and improve the quality and level of SL ultimate attainment. In other words, while identifying the simplest, least powerful, theory is the goal of SLA research, that theory (alone) will not necessarily constitute the soundest basis for SL teaching, precisely because it is the simplest, *minimal* solution.

Whatever one's view of the necessity and sufficiency of comprehensible input for SLA, just how strong, in fact, is the evidence for the inefficacy of conventional SL instruction (with a focus on form) which is further assumed by several SLA theorists? The following review will attempt to show that (1) SLA research to date has barely begun to probe the effects of instruction on IL development, but that (2) studies conducted thus far have already revealed some potentially very positive contributions instruction can make. If either of these statements is correct, it follows that prescriptions from theorists at this juncture are premature if they effectively involve the abandonment of instruction.

8.3 The effect of instruction on accuracy orders and developmental sequences

Several early investigations of instructed accuracy orders were morpheme studies conducted in the 1970s, some in second and some in foreign language environments. (See Pica 1983c for a detailed review of these and other studies.) Thus, Perkins and Larsen-Freeman (1975) tested twelve Spanish-speaking university students studying in the USA, using a translation test and a question-and-answer task in which subjects described a silent film. Pre/post comparisons of the subjects' morpheme accuracy orders before and after two months of intensive ESL instruction showed that the subjects improved on their suppliance of the morphemes in obligatory contexts; however, the accuracy orders on the film-description task (although not the translation task) were very similar. The investigators interpreted this as showing that formal language instruction does not change the *order* in which morphemes are supplied accurately. Similar results were obtained by Fathman (1975a), who found statistically significant correlations between the morpheme orders on oral production tests of 260 six- to fifteen-year-old children from diverse L1 backgrounds, some of whom were mainstreamed and some of whom were receiving ESL instruction. Similar research conducted in foreign language settings generally produced the same findings. Fathman (1978) reported a significant correlation between the morpheme difficulty orders of German secondary-school students receiving EFL instruction and naturalistic adolescent acquirers in the U.S. Makino (1979, 1980) obtained a significant correlation between the difficulty order of nine morphemes on a written short answer test for 777 Japanese secondary school EFL students and various difficulty orders reported for naturalistic child ESL acquirers in the USA. Pica (1983a) obtained significant correlations between the difficulty orders in free conversation of six EFL learners in Mexico, six naturalistic, and six mixed (instruction and exposure) acquirers in the USA, all eighteen subjects being native speakers of Spanish. (See Section 8.4 for further details of this study.) In a single unexplained counter-finding, Sajavaara (1981) found a disturbed difficulty order in the elicited speech of secondary-school age Finnish EFL students, articles being notably lower. (Finnish differs significantly from English in this area, but so does Japanese, which, as reported, did not lead to a disturbed order in the Makino study.)

In a nine-month longitudinal study of the communicative classroom speech of three children aged ten to thirteen, native speakers of Punjabi and Portuguese in a predominantly audiolingual ESL programme in Britain, Ellis (1984a) found that the developmental sequences for all structures he investigated, including negation, interrogatives and some verb phrase morphology, were virtually identical to those reported for naturalistic learners. The few minor differences Ellis encountered concerned the slightly slower traversal by his subjects of some developmental stages, as illustrated by the more protracted use of uninverted yes/no questions and the slow appearance of inflected past-tense forms. These differences, he reports, could be attributed to such features of classroom discourse as the frequent use of intonation questions for procedural purposes, e.g. confirmation checks and clarification requests to establish the nature of tasks the children were required to perform, and the relatively low need for past-time reference in classroom talk. Similar results are reported by Felix (1981a) from an eight-month study of 34 German secondary students' EFL negation, interrogatives, sentence types and pronouns.

A particularly interesting body of work on the effect of instruction on acquisition sequences is that by Lightbown and her colleagues in Montreal (Lightbown and Barkman 1978; Lightbown and Spada

1978; Lightbown, Spada and Wallace 1980; Lightbown 1983). Using a panel design,[4] Lightbown et al. conducted both longitudinal and cross-sectional studies of Francophone children, aged eleven to seventeen, learning ESL in Quebec, few of whom had much contact with English outside the classroom. There were 175 children in grades six, eight and ten in the first year of the study, and 100 of the same children in grades seven, nine and eleven in the second year. All had started English in grade four or five.

Early studies, using a variety of speech-elicitation devices (verbally cued picture descriptions, communication games, etc.), found differences from previously established orders in the accuracy with which the French speakers produced various -*s* morphemes (copula, auxiliary, third-person singular, plural and possessive) and -*ing*. Several of these differences appeared attributable to influences from French, which uses the periphrastic possessive, and in which final /s/ is silent. The children were also observed to make large numbers of what Pica calls *overuse* errors, e.g. 'The girl*s* want a cookie' when describing a picture of only one girl.

Additional motivations for the error patterns were sought in various aspects of the instruction the learners received. No direct relationship was found between the frequency of the items in teacher speech or in their textbooks and either the frequency or accuracy of students' use of those forms at the same point in time. However, Lightbown (1983, p. 239) reports a 'delayed' frequency effect.

Intensive practice of -*ing* early in grade six appeared to be what led to that item remaining in sixth-grade students' speech throughout the year, even though it was relatively infrequent in classroom language after its initial presentation. Students' suppliance of -*ing* during this period included both accurate suppliance in obligatory contexts and overuse. Later, however, after uninflected verbs, such as simple present forms and imperatives, had been taught, both students' overuse and accurate use of -*ing* declined in favour of uninflected verbs, the forms favoured by naturalistic acquirers from the outset. Lightbown wonders whether the kind of intensive drill work used in the audiolingual method to produce 'overlearning' may not create artificial barriers to natural interlanguage development, obstacles which learners later have to overcome before they can construct their own productive interlanguage systems.

As reported earlier, after intensive practice of various -*s* morphemes, there was a parallel tendency for students to overuse those items, especially by adding -*s* to clause-initial NPs, errors which then decreased over time. An important difference between what subsequently occurred with -*ing* and with certain -*s* morphemes, however, was that, unlike the -*ing* form, *appropriate* use of -*s* in obligatory contexts for copula and auxiliary did not decrease in tandem with the decrease in overuse errors with -*s* morphology. With some of the -*s* morphemes, that is, instruction appeared to accelerate attempts to use the forms, but with some negative side-effects (overuse errors). The side-effects wore off with time, however, leaving the benefits intact.

While providing evidence of possibly beneficial effects of instruction on acquisition processes (see Section 8.4), Lightbown's findings suggest overall that formal SL instruction is only successful in altering accuracy *orders* in a trivial manner. On the basis of the Quebec findings, the effects on sequences seem to be temporary, and possibly harmful in that they may delay the start of a learner's inevitable passage through the normal sequences. Lightbown's interpretation is supported by Pienemann's (1984) observation of the occasional unintended side-effects of instruction in the German copula (a variational feature). Instruction can increase the frequency with which learners supply copula in *X cop Y* strings, but copula suppliance inhibits learners' attempts to apply a new syntactic rule (subject–verb inversion), which must take place over copula to produce *Y cop X* strings. (Learners in fact tend temporarily to start omitting copula again in order to facilitate early application of the new inversion rule.) While some studies reported below (Section 8.4) might superficially appear to show an alteration of sequences, too, this is probably not the case, as will become clear. Acquisition orders may well be immutable.

Further support for the idea that acquisition orders are impervious to instruction is to be found in the same study by Pienemann (1984) discussed in more detail in Chapter 7. It will be recalled that ten Italian children, aged seven to nine, received two weeks of classroom instruction (including both linguistically focused and communicative exercises) in subject–verb inversion in German. At the end of this period, the children's spontaneous speech was analysed to determine whether they had progressed to the next stage in word-order development by mastering inversion. It was found that those children who had begun at stage $X + 2$ (SEP) had progressed to stage $X + 3$ (INV), a process normally taking several months in untutored development, whereas children who had begun the study at stage $X + 1$ (ADV) were still at that stage. As noted earlier, Pienemann's interpretation of these findings is that students can only learn from instruction when they are psycholinguistically 'ready' for it – the *learnability hypothesis*. The learnability of a structure in turn constrains the effectiveness of instruction – the *teachability hypothesis*. Instruction in something for which learners are not ready cannot make them skip a stage in a developmental sequence. Instruction for which they are ready can speed up the rate of progress through the sequence, however. Additional findings confirming the same word-order sequence for instructed GSL and/or the inability of instruction to alter the sequence are reported by Daniel (1983), Westmoreland (1983), Eubank (1986), Jansen (1987), Ellis (1989) and Pienemann (1989).

The learnability/teachability hypotheses provide a potential *post hoc* explanation for the results of several other studies which have shown either no effect or no lasting effect for instruction in particular structures. Thus, Lightbown, Spada and Wallace (1980) found that instruction in the copula in equational sentences, locative prepositions and some -*s* morphology resulted in an average 11 per cent improvement in accuracy on those items on a grammaticality judgement test, compared with a control group's average improvement of 3 per cent. The gain was temporary, however, with the experimental group's scores declining to the norm on a readministration of the same test six months later. (These findings appear to conflict with claims as to the supposed teachability of 'variational' features in the Multidimensional Model, discussed in Chapter 7.) Schumann's efforts to raise Alberto's performance of ESL negation directly from stage 1, *No V* ('No like hamburger'), to stage 4, analysed *don't* ('He doesn't like hamburgers') through intensive practice in the target forms had no effect on Alberto's spontaneous speech, although brief improvements were obtained during the drills themselves (Schumann 1978; Adamson and Kovac 1981). Similarly, Ellis (1984b) found no improvement in the spontaneously produced WH-questions of thirteen children following three hours of instruction in both the meaning of WH-pronouns (*what*, *where*, *when* and *who*) and inversion in WH-questions. The children's spontaneous speech prior to this part of Ellis's study showed that they were beginning to use uninverted WH-questions (of any kind) when the instruction was provided.

It should be noted, however, that while a lack of effect for instruction in studies like these is probably due to the researchers' choice of items which were developmentally beyond the reach of the learners involved, i.e. to poor *timing* of instruction, at least two alternative or additional explanations are also possible. First, the findings in some studies (e.g. Bruzzeze 1977; Schumann 1978) could be the result of targeted grammatical sub-systems having fossilized before the instruction was provided. Second, if the claims of the Multidimensional Model are correct, instruction can be expected to have differential effects according to whether the targeted structures are 'developmental' or 'variational' (see Chapter 7).

Further research in this area is clearly a high priority, but investigators will need to select subjects and targeted structures very carefully. In addition, if the aim is to establish a causal relationship between instruction and SL development/performance, more researchers than have done so to date must be prepared to adhere to such principles of experimental design as the inclusion of a control group in their studies and random assignment of subjects to groups. More longitudinal studies would be particularly useful.

8.4 The effect of instruction on acquisition processes

Exploratory work on the effect of instruction on acquisition processes by Wode (1981), Felix (1981a), and Felix and Simmet (1981) was outlined earlier. The researchers' focus, it was noted, was the similarities which exist in the acquisition processes of classroom and naturalistic acquirers. There has been very little work to date which looks for differences as well as similarities in this aspect of interlanguage development, with the major study being that by Pica (1983a). As with so much of the research on the effect of instruction on IL development to date, however, Pica's findings are highly suggestive, and encouraging for teachers.

Pica distinguished three acquisition contexts in her work: naturalistic, instructed and mixed, the last being a combination of classroom instruction plus natural exposure in the target-language environment. After some initial screening interviews, eighteen adult native speakers of Spanish learning ESL were identified whose learning histories placed them uniquely in one context. There was a total of six subjects per context, with the subjects in each cell in the criterion group design representing a fairly wide range of SL proficiency, as defined by the stage each had reached in his or her acquisition of ESL negation (*No* V, *don't* V, aux-neg, and analysed *don't*). Each speaker was interviewed informally (the six instruction-only subjects in Mexico City), with each conversation covering the same range of topics. Approximately one hour of free speech was transcribed and analysed in a variety of ways.

Pica first performed a supplied in obligatory contexts (SOC) analysis of nine grammatical morphemes in the speech of learners from the three language-learning contexts. This revealed morpheme orders which correlated highly with each other and with a 'natural order' previously established by Krashen (1977), suggesting some basic similarities in SLA, regardless of context, and providing additional support for the claims made by previous researchers to this effect.

While the SOC morpheme rank orders for all groups correlated strongly with one another, Pica noted that there were considerable differences among the groups in the case of certain morphemes in terms both of the ranks they occupied and the SOC percentage scores on which the ranks were based. For example, the instruction-only group scored 19 percentage points and one or two ranks higher on plural -*s* than the mixed and naturalistic groups, respectively, and 38 per cent and 41 per cent higher than the naturalistic and mixed groups on third-person singular -*s*. Pica notes that both these morphemes have transparent form–function relationships ('easy grammar' in Krashen's terms), and suggests that it may be precisely in this area that instruction has its greatest effect.

Aware of the many limitations of SOC analysis (for review, see Long and Sato 1984), Pica next conducted a target-like use (TLU) analysis of the same morphemes. The way researchers perform TLU analysis varies somewhat (see Pica 1984 for a detailed account), but always involves looking not just at accurate suppliance of elements in obligatory contexts, but also at target-like and non-target-like suppliance of the elements in non-obligatory contexts. TLU analysis, therefore, captures such important distinctions as that between the following two (hypothetical) learners. As measured by SOC analysis, both supply definite articles with over 90 per cent accuracy. However, while one scores that high by differentiating between contexts for definite and indefinite articles, the other uses definite articles in all contexts for articles of both types (thereby scoring well for definite but zero for indefinite), and has not really grasped the use of definite articles at all. (See Andersen 1984a for a real example of this sort.)

Pica's rank orders for TLU of the same morphemes correlated well across the three groups and with the natural order. What the TLU analysis also revealed, however, was a number of fascinating differences between the three groups, with the greatest differences obtaining between the instruction-only group and the other two.

Controlling for proficiency level as measured by negation stage, Pica looked at the kinds of errors made by the learners in all three groups, and compared the acquisition strategies and processes revealed by those errors. Pica found that learners who had never received formal SL instruction tended to omit grammatical morphemes, such as -*ing* and plural -*s*, whereas classroom learners (and to a lesser degree, and in later stages, mixed learners) showed a strong tendency to overapply morphological marking of this kind.

Overapplication errors consisted of two types: (1) a small number (2 per cent of the total errors for classroom learners, and 1 per cent for naturalistic learners) of *overgeneralization* errors, involving suppliance of regularized irregular morphemes in obligatory contexts (e.g. 'He buy*ed* a car yesterday'); and (2) frequent errors of *overuse* of morphemes in *non*-obligatory contexts (e.g. 'He liv*ed* in London now', 'I don't understand*ing* these people'). While both naturalistic and instructed learners made errors of these kinds, the frequency of such errors in instructed over uninstructed learners was significantly higher at almost all proficiency levels. Mixed learners performed like naturalistic learners at lower proficiency levels, but became more like instructed learners at higher levels of proficiency. Further, while instruction-only subjects used the plural -*s* form significantly more often than subjects in the other two groups, the naturalistic group tended to omit target-like noun endings and to use a free form quantifier instead (*two book, many town*), a production strategy observed in many of the world's pidgins and creoles.

On the basis of these results, Pica draws the following conclusions: (1) similarities (e.g. common morpheme difficulty orders) across the three learner types support the idea that a great deal of SLA depends upon learner, not environmental, or contextual, factors; and (2) instruction affects SL production/performance (a) by triggering oversuppliance of grammatical morphology and (b) by *inhibiting* (not preventing altogether) the use of ungrammatical, even if communicatively effective, constructions found in pidgins. The last point (b) appears to hold for any learners receiving formal instruction, i.e. mixed as well as instruction-only learners. Mixed learners show a greater inclination to pidginize in the early stages, but appear to 'shake off' this tendency later. In sum, Pica notes that, as evidenced by the error profiles of her subjects, 'differing conditions of L2 exposure appear to affect acquirers' hypotheses about the target language and their strategies for using it' (Pica 1983a, p. 495).

Pica cautions that no conclusions can be drawn about rate of acquisition or level of ultimate SL attainment from her findings, only about SL production. It is noteworthy, however, that the tendencies to overapply grammatical morphology and to avoid pidginization strategies distinguished instructed from totally uninstructed learners at nearly all proficiency levels in her (cross-sectional) study. This could signal long-term, even permanent, differences between the two types of learners.

More likely, such differences mean differing *probabilities* of eventual target-like attainment for the groups. One hypothesis would be that the instructed learners will eventually relinquish what appears to be something akin to 'psycholinguistic hypercorrection'. In the study of Francophone children learning English at school in what was effectively an EFL setting in Quebec, Lightbown (1983, p. 239) found that the learners oversupplied -*s* on clause-initial NPs, but that this tendency gradually decreased over time. Naturalistic acquirers, on the other hand, may be less likely to begin supplying what are often, after all, communicatively redundant and probably still non-salient forms, especially after prolonged periods of communicatively successful TL use of their grammatically reduced codes.

This is to enter the realm of speculation, however. What is needed is some research on the *long-term effects* (if any) of these initial differences in preferred acquisition processes. To our knowledge, not one study has addressed this basic issue. It goes without saying that until such work is done, it is premature to recommend that teachers give up on conventional SL instruction.

8.5 The effect of instruction on rate of acquisition

As noted above, Pienemann's 1984 study suggests that it is impossible to alter developmental sequences, but simultaneously provides evidence of instruction's facilitating effect on the rate of SL learning. It is in the latter area, in fact, that instruction is most clearly beneficial, with empirical support for the claim strong and diverse. A rate advantage is, of course, theoretically less interesting than the possibility of altering developmental sequences, since it demonstrates that instruction has an effect, but does not explain how. Nonetheless, speeding up acquisition is extremely important for teachers and learners and so is worthy of consideration.

Long (1983d) reviewed eleven studies of the achievement of learners after comparable periods of classroom instruction, natural exposure, or combinations of the two. He found six which clearly showed faster development in children and adults receiving formal SL teaching, two (Fathman 1976; Hale and Budar 1970) whose findings, while ambiguous, were arguably in the same direction, and three which showed minor or no effects for instruction. A summary of the studies and their results appears in Table 8.1. The findings present four problems for Krashen's interpretations of the same research within the framework of Monitor Theory (see, e.g., Krashen 1982a). It seems that instruction is beneficial (1) for children (who lack the cognitive maturity to develop metalinguistic awareness and, hence, a monitor)

Study	SLA Type	Subjects	Proficiency (B, I or A)	Acquisition Environment	Test Type (DP or I)	Instruction helps?	Exposure helps?	I>E or E>I?
Studies showing that instruction helps								
1. Carroll (1967)	FLL in USA & SLA abroad	adults	B I A	mixed	I	yes	yes	E>I
2. Chihara & Oller (1978)	EFL (Japan)	adults	B I A	poor	DP I	yes	no	I>E
3. Brière (1978)	SpSL (Mexico)	children	B	mixed	DP	yes	yes	I>E
4. Krashen, Seliger, & Hartnett (1974)	ESL in USA	adults	B I	rich	DP	yes	no	I>E
5. Krashen & Seliger (1976)	ESL in USA	adults	I A	rich	I	yes	no	I>E
6. Krashen, Jones, Zelinski, & Usprich (1978)	ESL in USA	adults	B I A	rich	DP I	yes	yes	I>E
Ambiguous cases								
7. Hale & Budar (1970)	ESL in USA	adolescents	B I A	rich	DP I	?	yes	E>I?
8. Fathman (1976)	ESL in USA	children	B I A	rich	I	?	yes	E>I?
Studies showing that instruction does not help								
9. Upshur (1968; Experiment I)	ESL in USA	adults	I A	rich	DP	no	—	—
10. Mason (1971)	ESL in USA	adults	I A	rich	DP	no	—	—
11. Fathman (1975)	ESL in USA	children	B I A	rich	I	no	—	—
Additional study showing that exposure helps								
12. St Martin (1980)	ESL in USA	adults	I A	mixed	DP I	—	yes	—

Note: B = beginning, I = intermediate, A = advanced, DP = discrete-point, I = integrative

TABLE 8.1 Relationships Between Instruction (I), Exposure (E), and Second Language Acquisition (from Long 1983d)

as well as for adults, (2) for intermediate and advanced learners, (3) on (supposedly unmonitorable) integrative as well as discrete-point tests, and (4) in acquisition-rich as well as acquisition-poor environments. All four findings further suggest that it is premature to discount instruction as ineffective.

Krashen (1985) maintains that the findings showing instructed learners outperforming naturalistic acquirers in most studies simply reflect the utility of the classroom as a source of comprehensible input (CI) for 'beginners', who find it difficult to engage native speakers in conversation outside classrooms, and not an effect for instruction *per se*. This explanation is problematic, however, in light of the findings of beneficial effects of instruction for intermediate and advanced learners, learners whose higher SL proficiency means they no longer depend on the classroom as a source of comprehensible input (H.D. Brown 1980 and several studies in Table 8.1). It also underlines the need for *a priori* definitions of terms like 'beginners' if they are crucial to the validity of a claim. (For more detailed discussion of these issues, see Krashen 1985, pp. 28–31; Long 1988b.)[5]

Several additional findings appearing since the original review, support the conclusion that instruction speeds up learning. The study by Pienemann (1984) has already been described. In another, Weslander and Stephany (1983) report a large-scale evaluation of 'pull-out' ESL for 577 limited English-speaking children (grades two through ten) in public schools in Des Moines, Iowa. Results showed that children receiving more ESL instruction outperformed those receiving less on the Bilingual Syntax Measure (BSM), with effects being strongest at lower levels (BSM levels 2.2–2.8) in the first year of schooling, and then diminishing in importance in the second and third years.

In a further case relevant to the rate issue, Gass (1982) describes an experiment at the University of Michigan showing the effectiveness of instruction in accelerating the learning of relative clause formation ('hard grammar' in Krashen's terms, and so supposedly unteachable). Gass taught one group of adult ESL students relativization on the object of a preposition for three days' classes. Object of a preposition is the fourth lowest in Keenan and Comrie's (1977) proposed universal accessibility hierarchy of relative clause formation.[6] A control group received the same amount of instruction in relativization, but starting from the highest (subject and object) positions in the hierarchy. Subjects' knowledge of any kind of relativization was minimal at the outset, as shown by their performance on pre-tests consisting of both grammaticality judgement and sentence-combining measures.

Post-tests using the same measures produced two main findings of interest here: (1) overall scores (all relativization positions) of the experimental group had improved significantly on the grammaticality task, and (2) on the sentence-combining task, both groups' post-test scores were significantly improved, the experimental group's scores being better not just on object of a preposition relatives, but also for relatives in all the higher positions in the accessibility hierarchy, i.e. those on which they had not received instruction, but which would be implied as known by subjects who knew object of a preposition relativization. As in the Pienemann (1984) study, in other words, here is more evidence not only of the effect of instruction on the rate of acquisition of particular structures, but also of the generalizability of the effect to other constructions, at least where these are the implied terms in a markedness relationship. Similar findings have since been obtained by Zobl (1985), Doughty (1988) and Eckman, Bell and Nelson (1988) (as discussed in Section 8.6 below).

8.6 The effect of instruction on the level of ultimate SL attainment

Even less research has been conducted in this fourth area, the long-term effects of instruction on SL proficiency, than in the three areas discussed thus far. This is clearly a sad reflection on the state of knowledge concerning language teaching, but equally clearly a fact which should (but has failed to) pre-empt hasty conclusions about the inefficacy of instruction by some SLA researchers and theorists.

The major study to date is that by Pavesi (1984), who compared relative clause formation in instructed and naturalistic acquirers. The instructed learners were 48 Italian high-school students, aged fourteen to eighteen, who had received from two to seven years (an average of four years) of grammar-based EFL teaching, and who, with the exception of three who had spent two months or less in Britain, had had no informal exposure to English. The naturalistic acquirers were 38 Italian workers (mostly restaurant waiters), aged nineteen to fifty, in Edinburgh, who had received only minimal or (usually) no formal English instruction. They had been in Britain for from three months to twenty-five years (an average of six years), during which time they had been exposed to English in a variety of home, work and recreational settings.

This is, then, a non-equivalent control-groups design, pre-empting the testing of any causal relationships. In addition to the difference in age between the two groups, Pavesi notes that the overall educational level of the naturalistic acquirers was generally quite low, and their socioeconomic background also lower than that of the school students. The latter, she reports, had also been exposed to a substantial amount of British literature and other written English. On the other hand, while the exact amount of informal SL exposure for the naturalistic group was difficult to determine, the balance was clearly in their favour, i.e. they had had many more hours of exposure than the students had had of instruction. Hence, finding that the school students outperformed the naturalistic acquirers, as Pavesi did, provides further evidence of the positive effect of instruction – or a factor associated with it – on rate of SL development, assuming one discounts the inter-group differences. Rate of development was not the focus of Pavesi's study, however.

Relative clause constructions were elicited by asking subjects about the identity of characters in a set of pictures ('Number seven is the girl who is running', etc.), with relativization off all NP positions in the Keenan and Comrie Accessibility Hierarchy being elicited. Using implicational scaling (see Question 16 in Chapter 4), the developmental sequences for each group were then plotted, and each found to correlate statistically significantly with the order in the accessibility hierarchy, with a progression from least to most marked constructions. The learning context, that is, had not influenced the developmental sequence (another result consistent with those of the studies reviewed in Section 8.3). This, as we have seen, is the kind of finding which has led some researchers to conclude that instruction does not affect acquisition at all. As Pica (1983a) had done, however, Pavesi looked further before discounting instruction, and like Pica, found that her subsequent analyses revealed interesting differences between the two groups.

The differences were of two kinds. First, more instructed learners reached the 80 per cent criterion on all of the five lowest NP categories in the accessibility hierarchy, with differences between the groups attaining statistical significance at the second lowest (genitive, 'whose') position, and falling just short ($p < .06$) at the lowest (object of comparative) level. More instructed learners, that is (and in absolute terms, very few naturalistic acquirers), were able to relativize off NPs at the more marked end of the implicational hierarchy. In gross terms, instructed learners had 'gone further', or reached higher levels of SL attainment.

A second difference to emerge between the groups concerned the kinds of errors each made with regard to resumptive nominal and pronominal copies. Naturalistic acquirers exhibited statistically significantly more frequent noun retention than instructed learners ('Number four is the woman who the cat is looking at *the woman*'). Instructed learners, on the other hand, produced statistically significantly more resumptive pronoun copies than naturalistic acquirers ('Number four is the woman who the cat is looking at *her*'). (The fact that neither Italian nor English allows copies of either kind, coupled with the finding that the developmental sequence for all learners followed the accessibility hierarchy, is further evidence of the need to treat interlanguage syntax as an emergent autonomous system.)

While Pavesi's results have been presented here in terms of the differences they suggest can result from formal SL instruction, Pavesi herself does not in fact interpret them this way. Instead, following Ellis (1984c), she suggests that the instructed group's superior performance derived not from formal SL instruction *per se*, but from the instructed learners' exposure to the more elaborated, more complex input of language used as the *medium* of instruction, i.e. from their exposure to what Ochs (1979) terms 'planned discourse'. Planned discourse has been documented as containing, among other things, a higher degree of grammaticalization (Givon 1979a,b), including a higher frequency of linguistically more marked constructions. If an explicit focus on form – i.e. the object, not the medium of SL instruction – was producing the observed effects, Pavesi argues, how could one account for the failure of such instruction to alter developmental *sequences* which, as has so often been shown, do not reflect teaching syllabuses?

Our own view is that the well-attested failure of interlanguage developmental sequences to mirror instructional sequences, for which Pavesi's study provides further evidence (see also Doughty 1988; Ellis 1989), is due to the powerful influence of universals, themselves the product of internal learner contributions, and/or to the failure of instruction to respect principles of learnability/teachability such as those outlined by Pienemann. Further, in Pavesi's study, it is presumably those same universal tendencies which account for both instructed and naturalistic groups' use of resumptive nominal/pronominal copies, since these are disallowed in English and in Italian and would not have been present (let alone salient) in either simple/unplanned or complex/planned discourse modes. A simpler explanation for the acquisition of the more marked relativized constructions by the schoolchildren is that they were acquired as a result of the SL instruction, not necessarily (probably not, in fact) because of explicit discussion of rules or examples (there is no information about the kind of instruction given in the Pavesi study), but through being made *salient* as a result of a focus on form, this leading the learners to notice and begin to process them.

While an interesting idea, the 'planned discourse mode' explanation also seems unlikely for the simple reason that so many of the marked/language-specific features that the elaborated mode undoubtedly contains and provides exposure to will nevertheless not be perceptually salient to the learner. A focus on form which (some) second language instruction provides, on the other hand, would draw the learner's attention to such items.

Strong impressionistic evidence for this view can be found in a recent diary study, supplemented by subsequent analyses of recorded interlanguage speech samples, of the acquisition of Brazilian Portuguese by a trained linguist and SLA researcher (Schmidt and Frota 1986). Schmidt kept detailed notes of his interlanguage development over a six-month period, including records of linguistic items (1) which he was taught in a formal Portuguese as a SL class in Rio de Janeiro, (2) which he noticed/failed to notice in the Portuguese to which he was exposed outside the classroom, and (3) which he produced (not necessarily accurately) or ignored or avoided in his own speech.

After much detailed discussion of these and other data sources and of relationships among them, Schmidt and Frota conclude (1986, p. 281):

> It seems, then, that if [R] was to learn and use a particular type of verbal form, it was not enough for it to have been taught and drilled in class. It was also not enough for the form to occur in input, but [R] had to notice the form in the input . . . [R] subjectively felt as [he] was going through the learning process that conscious awareness of what was present in the input was causal.

Schmidt and Frota also note that several items, such as reflexive *se*, though frequent in the input, had little or delayed effect on Schmidt's production because of their lack of saliency.

Finally, his retrospective analyses convinced Schmidt that he usually noticed forms in the out-of-class input *after they were taught*. One excerpt from the diary must suffice to illustrate the process here:

> *Journal entry, Week 6*
> This week we were introduced to and drilled on the imperfect. Very useful! The basic contrast seems straightforward enough: *ontem eu fui ao clube* ['yesterday I went to the club'] vs. *antigamente eu ia ao clube* ['formerly I used to go to the club']. L [the teacher] gave us

a third model: *ontem eu ia ao clube*, 'yesterday I was going to the club
. . . but didn't', which L says is a common way of making excuses.
The paradigm is also straightforward . . . though maybe not as easy
as I first thought . . . Wednesday night A came over to play cards,
and the first thing he said was: *eu ia telefonar para voce* ['I was going
to call you'], exactly the kind of excuse L had said we could expect.
I noticed that his speech is full of the imperfect, which I never
heard (or understood) before, and during the evening I managed to
produce quite a few myself, without hesitating much. Very satisfying!
(Schmidt and Frota 1986, p. 279)

Rather than 'voting' on the discourse mode/formal SL instruction
issue, however, one way of resolving it empirically would be to compare
advanced non-native speakers who received SL instruction with a focus
on form with the graduates of immersion or submersion programmes.
The latter receive massive exposure to elaborated/planned SL discourse through being educated *through* an SL, but (in theory, at least)
with no focus on form. An indication of the way such a comparison
might result can perhaps be seen in the findings of a study of the
product of French immersion programmes in Canada by Swain (1985).
Swain's study shows that the results of SL learning through immersion
education are impressive, but also documents the failure of immersion
students to have mastered even a wide range of unmarked morphology
and syntax after seven years. Similar findings were obtained in an
earlier evaluation of a Spanish immersion programme in Culver City,
California (Plann 1977).

Further evidence for the interpretation that it is the formal
instruction which helps may lie in the findings of a series of three
studies reported by Zobl (1985) on the teaching of English possessive
adjectives to French-speaking university students in Canada. Zobl's
first study of the difficulty orders of 162 French-speaking learners
of English, using implicational scaling, was devoted to studying
markedness in masculine/feminine and human/nonhuman pairs of
possessive adjectives. The findings corroborated linguistic arguments
concerning markedness in the two domains. The study showed (1) that
his is the unmarked member of the *his/her* pair, and (2) that categorical
control of the rule governing gender marking of possessed animate
or human entities (*his* mother, *her* father, etc.) implies categorical
control of the rule governing possessed inanimate, or nonhuman,
entities (*her* hand, *his* car, etc.), but not vice versa, i.e. that *nonhuman*
is the unmarked member of the *human/nonhuman* pair.

Zobl next ran a study in which two randomly formed groups of
approximately twenty low-level adult speakers of French each received

fifteen minutes of instruction in the use of the possessive forms in English. One group was exposed only to examples with human-possessed entities; the other group exclusively experienced examples with nonhuman-possessed entities. Controlling for input frequency, the instruction consisted of intensive oral question-and-answer practice, based on pictures, with no overt explanations or rules, but with corrections from the teacher where necessary through rephrasings of incorrect student responses, i.e. some focus on form. Pre- and post-tests consisted of responses to questions written as quickly and unreflectingly as possible. A year later, a third (replication) study was run on a new sample of students.

The findings of the two experimental studies were (1) that students who had experienced the input containing marked (human) examples improved in both the human and nonhuman domains (confirmed in both studies), while (2) students who had received exposure only to unmarked (nonhuman) input slightly deteriorated in that domain (first study) or improved in that domain, but less than the human data group in that domain (replication study), and showed no improvement in the marked (human) domain (both studies). In other words, students who had been exposed only to marked data improved more than students who had been exposed only to unmarked data in both the marked domain and the unmarked (nonhuman) domain.

Zobl employed various measures of the students' test performance. Among other features he noted was a tendency for the groups receiving unmarked input to show a higher incidence of rule simplifications following the treatment (e.g. overuse of the unmarked determiner, *his*). Conversely, the group receiving marked input supplied more gender-marked, third-person forms in new contexts, including overgeneralizations of the marked form, *her*, showed less use of articles (which the first, descriptive study had revealed as a transitional form in acquiring the possessive adjectives), and also less avoidance (through use of immature forms like the gender-neutral *your* or determiner omission).

Zobl concludes by offering a very interesting explanation for the finding that exposure to unmarked data appeared to lead to rule simplification (overgeneralization of the unmarked *his*), while exposure to marked data produced rule complexification (overgeneralization of the marked *her*). He suggests that 'once grammars reach a certain level of complexity such that their rules begin to predict to unmarked structures with some regularity, marked data become necessary if progress on unmarked structures is not to stagnate' (Zobl 1985, p. 343). Further, he notes that both experiments showed that exposure to the marked (human) domain led to overgeneralization of the marked *her*, whereas exposure to the unmarked (nonhuman) domain produced overgeneralization of the unmarked *his*. That is, exposure to the unmarked *nonhuman* triggers the correlated markedness value, unmarked *his*; conversely, exposure to the marked *human* triggers the correlated markedness value, marked *her*. If this explanation is correct, and if it translates from the experimental to the naturalistic acquisition context, Zobl hypothesizes, it would mean that acquisition along one parameter entails acquisition along another related parameter, which would in turn mean a significant reduction in the amount of input a learner requires to reach the same level as a learner who experiences mostly or exclusively unmarked data.

To the extent that instruction focuses on marked elements in the SL, here, then, is a potential explanation for its positive effect on the rate of acquisition. Note, too, that Zobl's findings on the benefits of exposure to marked data are consistent with those of Pavesi in two respects. They help explain the rate advantage for the Italian high-school students, and potentially explain the higher level of ultimate attainment. It could be that the preponderance of unmarked data that naturalistic acquirers encounter not only slows them down, but also leads to simplifications in the grammars before full target competence is attained, i.e. to premature fossilization.

8.7 Conclusion

The review of research on the effect of instruction on SL development suggests the following conclusions. First, formal SL instruction does not seem able to alter acquisition sequences, except temporarily and in trivial ways which may even hinder subsequent development. On the other hand, instruction has what are possibly positive effects on SLA *processes*, clearly positive effects on the *rate* at which learners acquire the language, and probably beneficial effects on their *ultimate level of attainment*.

Second, there has clearly been insufficient research to warrant firm conclusions in any area we have considered except rate of acquisition, and no research at all in other important ones, such as the kinds of competence (e.g. collocational and sociolinguistic abilities) achievable with and without instruction.

Third, and following from the first two, the position taken by some theorists and methodologists that formal instruction in an SL is of limited use (e.g. that it is good for beginners only, or for 'simple' grammar only), is obviously premature and almost certainly wrong.

While of little theoretical interest, the findings regarding rate alone are obviously very important for teachers and learners.

Fourth, future experimental research on this issue must be conducted with greater rigour than has typically been the case to date. Reference has already been made to the need to choose subjects carefully, to follow standard procedures in their (random) assignment to treatments, to employ control groups, and to select for teaching experiments those aspects of the SL which are 'learnable' at the time instruction is provided. It is also important, however, for investigators to record and report precisely what 'instruction' consisted of in their studies. This would have two effects. First, it would disambiguate potential confoundings between such factors as a focus on the SL itself and exposure to linguistic features through the SL (as claimed, e.g. by proponents of the comprehensible input and planned discourse positions). Second, should instruction prove to be beneficial, as currently seems likely, it might help pre-empt misuse of such a finding as a justification for resuscitating some of the teaching practices which SLA research first helped to discredit.

One example may help clarify the last point. Suppose that a focus on *form* turns out to be a key feature of SL instruction, because of the saliency it brings to targeted features in classroom input, and also to those features in input outside the classroom, where this is available. Such a finding would not make an instructional programme built around a series (or even a sequence) of decontextualized forms any more supportable now, either theoretically, empirically or logically, than when Krashen and others attacked it several years ago. It is not hard to imagine, however, that a return to teaching discrete decontextualized grammar points, plus or minus overt grammar explanations, is just what some would see vindicated by any finding that formal SL instruction was beneficial. Clearly, we want to avoid an unwarranted inference of that kind. Were researchers to specify just what kind of instruction was involved in their studies, regarding a focus on form and other parameters, it might help avoid another pendulum swing in the field (Larsen-Freeman, in press), and would certainly save a lot of time on subsequent research on the relative effectiveness of different types of instruction, time that all too few language teachers (or learners) can afford.

8.8 Explanations

In addition to the need for a great deal of further study of the effects of instruction on processes, sequences and, especially, ultimate attainment, a further major question remains unresolved and in need of serious attention: *How* does instruction affect SLA? Most obviously, how is it that instruction appears not to alter developmental sequences, yet, if the review of studies presented here is correct, still to have a major impact on rate of development, and (possibly) on processes and levels of ultimate attainment?

A number of interesting proposals have been made on this topic, but very little empirical research has been conducted as yet. One solution to the puzzle, advanced by Krashen (1982a and elsewhere), is sometimes referred to as the *non-interface position*. This is based on the dichotomy assumed in Monitor Theory between conscious and unconscious knowledge ('learning' and 'acquisition'), described in Section 7.3.4, and the claim that learning cannot become acquisition (Krashen and Scarcella 1978). Krashen argues that any 'learning' induced by classroom work on language form only shows up on certain (monitorable) tasks, and is unusable on communicative ones. Common developmental sequences, meanwhile, are a reflection of language universals and universal acquisition processes, i.e. 'acquisition'. Any rate advantages claimed for the classroom, according to Krashen, are due to the kind of input provided in classrooms, i.e. comprehensible input, being better for acquisition ('intake'), especially for beginners, than the untuned mix of comprehensible and (unusable) incomprehensible input available through natural exposure (street learning) alone.

The non-interface position has the potential to account for the data showing that developmental sequences are not altered by instruction through positing that 'acquisition' underlies such sequences, any effect for instruction being 'trapped' in the 'learned' system. There are several problems with this position, however, as an explanation for the data on rate advantages, including (as discussed in Section 8.5) the fact that the differential predictions it makes for classroom instruction favouring adults over children, beginners over non-beginners, and discrete-point over integrative tests are all generally unsupported (Long 1983d). Further, Ellis (1985, pp. 232–3) points out that the instruction that occurred in most classrooms in the studies showing rate advantages would presumably have been of the structurally focused (input-poor) variety, with little negotiation for meaning, and so must have produced the advantages it did without providing much comprehensible input for acquisition, which the non-interface claims to be instruction's true value. To help resolve this problem, experiments are needed which compare the performance of three groups: students receiving equal amounts of (1) natural exposure, (2) comprehensible input-rich classroom instruction (e.g. via the Natural Approach), and (3) classroom instruction with a focus on form.

A second explanation is known as the *interface position*, of which there are several variants. As the name suggests, the idea here is the opposite of the previous one, namely, that a 'cross-over' of some kind does occur. It is also usually held that the two kinds of knowledge between which movement takes place are end-points on a continuum rather than discrete systems. Thus, while most adherents to this position claim that new TL forms can be and are acquired directly in something like the way children acquire a first language, they also posit a process whereby forms are initially learned with some kind of awareness of the learning, and then transformed, e.g. from 'learning' to 'acquisition' (Stevick 1980), from 'explicit' to 'implicit' knowledge (Bialystok 1982), or from 'controlled processing' and short-term memory to 'automatic processing' and long-term memory (McLaughlin 1978). This transformation is achieved via 'use' (Stevick), 'practice' (Bialystok), 'routinization' (McLaughlin), 'consciousness-raising' (Sharwood-Smith 1981; Rutherford 1987; Rutherford and Sharwood-Smith 1988) or some combination thereof. Arguments for the cross-over effect itself are usually based on L1 studies showing movement from controlled to automatic processing (Schneider and Shiffrin 1977), a few related SL experiments (Bialystok 1981; McLaughlin, Rossman and McLeod 1983; McLeod and McLaughlin 1986), and L1 studies showing that learning of patterned strings of symbols is facilitated when learners are told that patterns exist, instructed to look for them, and the patterns themselves are made salient through initial explicit presentation, followed by implicit presentation through examples, rather than through implicit presentation alone (Reber, Kassin, Lewis and Cantor 1980). (For further relevant L2 work, see Seliger 1975; McLaughlin 1987, Chapter 6, and 1990.)

The advantage of the interface position is that it can potentially explain the rate advantage through its claim that form-focused instruction facilitates development. The disadvantage of most variants of the position, however, is that they offer no principled way of explaining the lack of any effect of the same successful instruction on acquisition sequences, i.e. the reverse problem of the non-interface position. One of the few to attempt to deal with the issue is Seliger (1979), who recognizes the need for learner 'readiness' for pedagogic grammar rules to be useful, but does not explain what being 'ready' might mean. As stated, most interface theories would predict disruption of the developmental sequences seen in untutored learning, yet reports of such disturbances to date (Lightbown 1983; Ellis 1984a; Pienemann 1984) are rare, small-scale and temporary (see Section 8.3), really consisting of delays in traversing the sequences, not changes in the sequences themselves.

One way of improving the interface position in order to account for the lack of effect for instruction on acquisition sequences would be to introduce the notion of processing constraints, either as formulated in the Multidimensional Model or in some other version, governing when and how instruction is effective. Pienemann's Teachability Hypothesis (see Section 7.5.4) is particularly relevant here. It predicts that instruction will speed up development, but does so constrained by the learner's current processing capacity, thereby preventing acquisition-sequence violations. In broad brush terms, a rate advantage for instructed learners who nevertheless follow universal developmental sequences is what the Hypothesis predicts and what the data confirm.

8.9 Researching instructional design features

As indicated, such a solution, if satisfactory, would still only account for relationships among instruction, sequences and rate of development, and then only in gross terms. Besides continuing our research efforts to enhance our understanding of the SLA process, then, there is a need for a complementary applied research agenda to identify and assess the outcomes of psycholinguistically relevant instructional design features such as a focus on form. One category of features, for example, might have to do with *options in the way linguistic input to learners is manipulated.* Choices here exist in such matters as (1) the *sequence* in which learners will encounter linguistic units of various kinds (e.g. functions, notions, structures, etc.), along with (2) the *frequency/intensity* and (3) the *saliency* of those encounters brought about by linguistic/interactional modifications.

Another category might be *options in the types of production tasks classroom learners are set.* It is reasonable to expect that formal instruction may trigger such processes as transfer, transfer of training and (over)generalization, depending on the choices teachers and materials writers make in this area. For example, are students allowed or encouraged to avoid error, or are they set tasks which lead them to take linguistic risks, e.g. by using generalization in applying a new linguistic item in a context in which they have not yet encountered its use? Do the pedagogic tasks teachers set allow planning and/or more or less attention to speech, with resulting differences in the quantity and linguistic complexity of IL production and higher or lower rates of target-like use (Tarone 1984, 1988; Sato 1985a; Ellis 1987a; Crookes 1988b)?

Two things should be clear from the examples we have provided. First, what we are calling instructional design features cut across current language teaching methodologies (Larsen-Freeman 1986). We are not advocating comparing one entire method with another; significant differences between and among methods are concealed by such wholesale comparisons (see Larsen-Freeman 1988 for discussion). On the other hand, neither are we stating that every option a language teacher has available (Stevick 1986) is a candidate for research. The issues being investigated should be of optimal scope.

Optimal scope is in part defined by our second qualification. We have specified *psycholinguistically relevant* features (Long and Crookes 1986). By this we mean that the choice of features and the hypotheses generated about them should be informed by SLA research, what research/theory predicts will benefit SLA. For example, an investigation of sequencing in the input could be conducted in a theoretical vacuum with the language items (structures, functions, vocabulary, etc.) sequenced arbitrarily. Alternatively, were the sequences based on a prior classification of the items according to some (psycholinguistically) theoretically motivated predictions about their (non-)learnability, the results would potentially generalize beyond the study.[7]

There has been surprisingly little research of this type conducted to date. Some important work has recently been reported, however, including studies of the effects of planning and focus on form on IL performance by Crookes (1988b) and Doughty (1988), respectively. In general, two interesting possibilities exist, neither of them mutually exclusive. They might usefully include (1) psycholinguistically motivated qualitative micro-analyses of SL classroom processes of the kinds reviewed by Allwright (1988), Chaudron (1988) and van Lier (1988), as well as (2) quantitative research on instructional design features of the sort we have qualified above. Research of this sort would be greatly aided by using Il-sensitive indices of development. Some specific proposals for the second type of research are set out by Larsen-Freeman and Long (to appear).

Questions of the sort posed above having to do with the effect on students' learning of varying the ways linguistic input is manipulated or production tasks are set, are questions that language teachers should be asking themselves, of course. Indeed, it is in researching instructional design features where teaching and researching most apparently coincide. There is a growing amount of attention these days being given to teacher-initiated *action research* whose intent is to help teachers gain new understanding of and, hence, enhance their teaching. 'Action research usually involves a cycle of self-observation or reflection, identification of an aspect of classroom behavior to be investigated, and selection of appropriate procedures to investigate and interpret behavior' (*Teacher Education Newsletter* 4 (2), Fall 1988). By applying these steps, teachers are encouraged to take *action* to improve their teaching and, hence, enhance their students' learning (Nixon 1981; Strickland 1988).

The attention action research is receiving gives us cause for optimism. We hope that someday all language teacher preparation programmes will implement a 'train-the-teacher-as-a-classroom-researcher' component (Long 1983e). If such a development were to ensue, eventually we might find language teachers less vulnerable to the vicissitudes of language teaching fashion and more willing to rely on the power of their own research.

Notes

1. It is not clear to us why Felix and Simmet collapse the longitudinal data from this study, and then resort to implicational scaling of (ostensibly) cross-sectional findings to establish acquisition orders.

2. 'Beginning', 'intermediate' and 'advanced' appear in quotation marks here since Krashen defines them vaguely and variably, although the meaning they have is often crucial for him in interpreting the outcome of studies (see, e.g., Krashen 1985, pp. 28–31) and could presumably be equally crucial for the success of his proposals for language teaching described above.

3. Another view is that there is evidence of the *necessity* of comprehensible input (evidence reviewed in Long 1981a), that it is, as Krashen says, a causal variable in SLA. On the other hand, there is almost no research on whether comprehensible input is *sufficient* for acquisition, but suggestive evidence that it is not (see, e.g., Plann 1977; Schmidt 1981; Higgs and Clifford 1982; Swain 1985), unless one can tolerate sometimes (1) quite limited levels, and (2) slow rates, of attainment. Evidence for the beneficial effects of instruction on the *efficiency* of SLA is the subject of this chapter.

4. A panel design is one in which the same variable is investigated recurrently over an extended period of time, for the purpose of studying change in response.

5. It is interesting to note that the interpretation Krashen et al. (1978) put on their findings was more like the one suggested here. They then claimed

(1978, p. 260) that the advantages for instructed learners 'replicate and extends previous findings' (Krashen, Seliger and Hartnett 1974; Krashen and Seliger 1976). In our opinion, theirs was and still is the correct interpretation: 'What may be inferred from these results is that formal instruction is a more efficient way of learning English for adults than trying to learn it "on the streets" ' (Krashen et al. 1978, p. 260).

6. Keenan and Comrie posit a hierarchy of noun phrases, from least to most marked, for relativization: subject, direct object, indirect object, oblique (in English this means object of the preposition), genitive, object of the comparative. This markedness hierarchy was ascertained typologically by cross-linguistic comparisons. Surveys showed that a language which allows relativization off direct-object NPs will also allow relativization off subject NPs. One that allows relativization off indirect-object NPs will also allow relativization off subject and direct-object NPs, etc. Conversely, if a language only allows relativization off one position, it will be subject position, not (say) indirect-object position, and so on.

7. Of course, any research on instructional design features would have to take into consideration the uniqueness of the teacher (Woods 1988), the educational context and the students so that unequal comparisons across studies will not be made (Van Patten 1988).

Activities

Comprehension

1. Why was it premature to conclude that instruction did not affect IL development on the basis of similarities in instructed and naturalistic developmental sequences?

2. What is meant by the claim that acquisition orders do not reflect instructional sequences?

3. It has often been suggested that, if developmental sequences are impervious to instruction, language teaching syllabuses should be redesigned to mirror the 'natural' sequences. What arguments for and against that proposal can you offer?

4. What factors could explain the apparent ineffectiveness of instruction in so many classroom studies?

5. Define the non-interface and interface positions on the role of instruction in SLA. Provide two arguments or pieces of evidence in favour of and against each.

6. What is generally meant by 'instruction' in the research studies reviewed in this chapter? What improvements are needed in the way instruction is defined and monitored in such research in future?

7. What is meant by 'action research'?

Application

8. What implications could there be for syllabus design of findings, like those of Gass (1982), Zobl (1985), Eckman et al. (1988) and Doughty (1988) that an instructional focus on linguistically marked items has beneficial effects on unmarked ones? Outline a fragment of a syllabus designed to exploit this possibility. How could the effectiveness of your proposal be tested?

9. How would you operationalize 'formal instruction' in a study designed to assess the effect of instruction on IL development? What features might you monitor, and how, in order to determine whether 'instruction' had been delivered?

10. In light of the discussion (Chapter 6) of age differences in SLA, how might formal SL teaching differentially benefit child and adult SL learners? What evidence is there on the topic? Design a study to address this issue.

11. As reported in this chapter, Zobl (1985) offers an interpretation of his findings which we suggested could also serve as a partial explanation of the *rate* advantages for instructed over naturalistic learners shown by other researchers. Do you think this suggestion plausible? What other potential explanations can you think of for the rate advantages?

12. What other examples of implicational markedness relationships might show the same 'domino' effect for instruction as the relative-clause studies, whereby instruction in a more marked construction generalizes to less marked ones? Design a study to test your ideas.

13. We have discussed SL 'instruction' in rather global terms in this chapter, and as noted in our concluding section, there is a need for researchers to specify exactly what instruction consisted of in their studies in order to make their findings interpretable. Which options in the *type* of instruction learners receive (a focus on form, error correction, grammar explanations, structural grading, etc.) do you think could turn out (1) to have an effect, and (2) to have no effect on IL development, and why? Can you cite any research findings to support your views? (See Chaudron 1988 for a review of classroom-centred research of this kind.)

14. If true, what implications do you think the non-interface and interface positions, respectively, would have for materials design and classroom methodology? What might 'consciousness-raising'

activities look like, and how might they differ from traditional grammar exercises?

15. How might instruction affect SLA in ways other than those discussed in this chapter? What evidence can you provide for such additional effects? How might evidence be obtained in areas in which you think it is currently lacking?

Suggestions for further reading

For general treatments regarding the effect of instruction on SLA, see:

Chaudron, C 1988 *Second language classrooms: research on teaching and learning.* Cambridge University Press

Ellis, R 1984 *Classroom second language development.* Pergamon

Long, M 1983d Does second language instruction make a difference? A review of research. *TESOL Quarterly* **17** (1): 359–82

For a discussion of the effect of instruction on developmental sequences, consult:

Lightbown, P 1983 Exploring relationships between developmental and instructional sequences. In Seliger, H and Long, M (eds.) *Classroom-oriented research on second language acquisition.* Newbury House, Rowley, Mass.

For ways in which acquisition processes differ for instructed learners, see:

Pica, T 1983a Adult acquisition of English as a second language under different conditions of exposure. *Language Learning* **33** (4): 465–97

For a discussion of how the rate of acquisition is influenced by instruction, see:

Gass, S 1982 From theory to practice. In Hines, M and Rutherford, W (eds.) *On TESOL '81.* TESOL, Washington, D.C.

Pienemann, M 1984 Psychological constraints on the teachability of languages. *Studies in Second Language Acquisition* **6** (2): 186–214

For how instruction may affect ultimate levels of achievement, look at:

Pavesi, M 1986 Markedness, discourse modes, and relative clause formation in a formal and an informal context. *Studies in Second Language Acquisition* **8**: 38–55

For specific contributions of instruction to SLA, see:

Rutherford, W and Sharwood-Smith, M (eds.) 1988 *Grammar and second language teaching: a book of readings*. Newbury House/Harper and Row, New York

Schmidt, R 1990 The role of consciousness in second language learning. *Applied Linguistics* 11 (2): 129–58

Zobl, H 1985 Grammars in search of input and intake. In Gass, S and Madden, C (eds.) *Input and second language acquisition*, pp. 329–44. Newbury House, Rowley, Mass.

Epilogue

We have said that the purpose of this book was to take stock of twenty years of research in the SLA field. We have attempted to do this by sifting through the research findings of these two decades, distilling generalizations whenever possible. Doubtless not all of our generalizations will hold up under the scrutiny of further investigation. Nevertheless, it is to such investigation that we are committed.

More specifically, we have called for two research agendas. The first is for basic research which continues to address the many areas and issues treated within this book, but seeks to do so in a way which includes a greater variety of L1s and L2s, systems of language in addition to morphology and syntax, and a greater cognizance of the role of learner factors. We recognize that as we broaden our investigations to embrace the complexity of language and of learners, there is no reason to expect that the SLA process will prove to be any less complex. The second research agenda should be constructed of theory-driven qualitative and quantitative applied research studies which concentrate on improving our understanding of the effect of choosing from among particular instructional design features. Finally, we have suggested a role for both teachers and researchers in these investigations. After all, both SLA research and teaching begin with learning.

In 1980, the field of SLA was described in a *Language Learning* editorial as being in transition from infancy to adolescence (Larsen-Freeman 1980a). This observation was based on certain signs: a restlessness in the field, a search for self-identity, a growing awareness of the need for self-governance. A 1985 editorial portrayed the signs in the SLA field as ones more characteristic of older adolescence: the vigour of youth persisted, but the field seemed surer of itself as a separate and unique discipline than it ever had before (Larsen-Freeman 1985a).

Now, as we move into a new decade, we feel confident that adolescence is behind us. For one thing, we note a certain sobriety in the field following the heady days of youth when the challenges seemed less formidable and the issues less complicated. But learning there are no easy answers has spurred us on in our resolve to increase our collective understanding of SLA by constructing a theory which is empirically defensible and which allows us to proceed while asking better questions. We have learned a great deal in the last twenty years, but much work remains to be done.

Bibliography

Abraham, R 1985 Field independence-dependence and the teaching of grammar. *TESOL Quarterly* **20**: 689–707

Acton, W 1979 Second language learning and perception of differences in attitude. Unpublished Ph.D. dissertation, University of Michigan

Adams, M 1978 Methodology for examining second language acquisition. In Hatch, E (ed.) *Second language acquisition: a book of readings*, pp. 278–96. Newbury House, Rowley, Mass.

Adamson, H D 1988 *Variation theory and second language acquisition.* Georgetown University Press, Washington, D.C.

Adamson, H D and Kovak, C 1981 Variation theory and second language acquisition: an analysis of Schumann's data. In Sankoff, D and Cedergren, H (eds.) *Variation omnibus.* Linguistic Research, Edmonton, Alberta

Adjemian, C 1976 On the nature of interlanguage systems. *Language Learning* **26**: 297–320

Agard, F and Di Pietro, R 1965a *The grammatical structures of English and Italian.* University of Chicago Press

Agard, F and Di Pietro, R 1965b *The sounds of English and Italian.* University of Chicago Press

Alatis, J (ed.) 1968 *Contrastive linguistics and its pedagogical implications.* Georgetown University Press, Washington, D.C.

Allen, J, Fröhlich, M and Spada, N 1984 The communicative orientation of second language teaching. In Handscombe, J, Orem, R and Taylor, B (eds.) *On TESOL '83*, pp. 231–52. TESOL, Washington, D.C.

Allwright, R 1975 Problems in the study of the language teacher's treatment of learner error. In Burt, M and Dulay, H (eds.) *On TESOL '75*, pp. 96–109. TESOL, Washington, D.C.

Allwright, R 1980 Turns, topics, and tasks: patterns of participation in language learning and teaching. In Larsen-Freeman, D (ed.) *Discourse analysis in second language research*, pp. 165–87. Newbury House, Rowley, Mass.

Allwright, R 1983a Classroom-centered research on language teaching and learning: a brief historical overview. *TESOL Quarterly* **17**: 191–204

Allwright, R 1983b TESOL researchers: what do they read? what do they recommend? *TESOL Newsletter* **17**: 3, 27

Allwright, R 1988 *Observation in the language classroom.* Longman

Alpert, R and Haber, R 1960 Anxiety in academic achievement situations. *Journal of Abnormal and Social Psychology* **61**: 207–15

Alpetkin, C 1981 Sociopsychological and pedagogic considerations in L2 acquisition. *TESOL Quarterly* **15**: 275–84

Anastasi, A 1968 *Psychological testing*, 3rd edition. Macmillan, New York

Andersen, R 1976 A functor acquisition study in Puerto Rico. Paper presented at the 10th Annual TESOL Convention, New York

Andersen, R 1977 The impoverished state of cross-sectional morphology acquisition/accuracy methodology. *Working Papers on Bilingualism* 14: 49–82

Andersen, R 1978 An implicational model for second language research. *Language Learning* 28: 221–82

Andersen, R 1979a The relationship between first language transfer and second language overgeneralization: data from the English of Spanish speakers. In Andersen, R (ed.) *The acquisition and use of Spanish and English as first and second languages*, pp. 43–58. TESOL, Washington, D.C.

Andersen, R (ed.) 1979b *The acquisition and use of Spanish and English as first and second languages*. TESOL, Washington, D.C.

Andersen, R 1981a Two perspectives on pidginization as second language acquisition. In Andersen, R (ed.) *New dimensions in second language acquisition research*, pp. 165–95. Newbury House, Rowley, Mass.

Andersen, R (ed.) 1981b *New dimensions in second language acquisition research*. Newbury House, Rowley, Mass.

Andersen, R (ed.) 1983a *Pidginization and creolization as language acquisition*. Newbury House, Rowley, Mass.

Andersen, R 1983b Transfer to somewhere. In Gass, S and Selinker, L (eds.) *Language transfer in language learning*, pp. 177–201. Newbury House, Rowley, Mass.

Andersen, R 1984a What's gender good for, anyway? In Andersen, R (ed.) *Second language: a crosslinguistic perspective*, pp. 77–99. Newbury House, Rowley, Mass.

Andersen, R 1984b (ed.) *Second language: a crosslinguistic perspective*. Newbury House, Rowley, Mass.

Andersen, R 1984c The one to one principle of interlanguage construction. *Language Learning* 34: 77–95

d'Anglejan, A and Renaud, C 1985 Learner characteristics and second language acquisition: a multivariate study of adult immigrants and some thoughts on methodology. *Language Learning* 35 (1): 1–19

d'Anglejan-Chatillon, A 1975 Dynamics of second language development: a search for linguistic regularity. Ph.D. dissertation, McGill University, Montreal

Arabski, J 1979 *Errors as indications of the development of interlanguage*. Uniwersytet Slaski, Katowice

Arthur, B 1980 Gauging the boundaries of second language competence: a study of learner judgments. *Language Learning* 30: 177–94

Arthur, B, Weiner, M, Culver, J, Young, L and Thomas, D 1980 The register of impersonal discourse to foreigners: verbal adjustments to foreign accent. In Larsen-Freeman, D (ed.) *Discourse analysis in second language research*, pp. 111–24. Newbury House, Rowley, Mass.

Asher, J and Garcia, R 1969 The optimal age to learn a foreign language. *Modern Language Journal* 53 (5): 334–41

Asher, J and Price, B 1967 The learning strategy of total physical response: some age differences. *Child Development* 38: 1219–27

Aston, G 1986 Trouble-shooting in interaction with learners: the more the merrier? *Applied Linguistics* 7 (2): 128–43

Atkinson, M 1979 Prerequisites for reference. In Ochs, E and Schieffelin, B (eds.) *Developmental pragmatics*, pp. 229–49. Academic Press, New York

Atkinson, M 1982 *Explanations in the study of child language development*. Cambridge University Press

Au, S 1988 A critical appraisal of Gardner's social-psychological theory of second-language (L2) learning. *Language Learning* 38 (1): 75–100

Avery, P, Ehrlich, S and Yorio, C 1985 Prosodic domains in foreigner talk discourse. In Gass, S and Madden, C (eds.) *Input in second language acquisition*, pp. 214–29. Newbury House, Rowley, Mass.

Bachman, L 1989 *Fundamental considerations in language testing*. Oxford University Press

Bachman, L and Palmer, A 1985 *Basic concerns in language test validation*. Addison-Wesley, Reading, Mass.

Bahns, J 1981 On acquisitional criteria. *International Review of Applied Linguistics* 21: 57–68

Bahns, J and Wode, H 1980 Form and function in L2 acquisition: the case of do-support in negation. In Felix, S (ed.) *Second language development*, pp. 81–92. Gunter Narr, Tubingen

Bailey, K D 1981 *Methods of social research*, 2nd edition. Macmillan, New York

Bailey, K M 1980 An introspective analysis of an individual's language learning experience. In Krashen, S and Scarcella, R (eds.) *Research in second language acquisition*. Newbury House, Rowley, Mass.

Bailey, K M 1983a Competitiveness and anxiety in adult second language learning: looking *at* and *through* the diary studies. In Seliger, H and Long, M (eds.) *Classroom oriented research in second language acquisition*, pp. 67–103. Newbury House, Rowley, Mass.

Bailey, K M 1983b Illustrations of Murphy's Law abound in classroom research on language use. *TESOL Newsletter* 17: 1, 4-5, 22, 31

Bailey, K M, Long, M and Peck, S (eds.) 1983 *Second language acquisition studies*. Newbury House, Rowley, Mass.

Bailey, K M and Ochsner, R 1983 A methodological review of the diary studies: windmill tilting or social science? In Bailey, K M, Long, M and Peck, S (eds.) *Second Language Acquisition Studies*, pp. 188–198. Newbury House, Rowley, Mass.

Bailey, N, Madden, C and Krashen, S 1974 Is there a 'natural sequence' in adult second language learning? *Language Learning* 21 (2): 235–43

Bailey, R and Gorlach, M (eds.) 1984 *English as a world language*. Cambridge University Press

Baker, C 1979 Syntactic theory and the projection problem. *Linguistic Inquiry* 10: 533–82

Bates, E and MacWhinney, B 1981 Second language acquisition from a functionalist perspective: pragmatic, semantic, and perceptual strategies. In Winitz, H (ed.) *Native language and foreign language acquisition*, pp. 190–214. *Annals of the New York Academy of Sciences* 379

Bausch, K 1977 Kontrastive linguistik und fehleranalyse. In Kühlwein, W and

Barrera-Vidal, A (eds.) *Kritische Bibliographie zur Angewandten Linguistik*, Fachbereich Englisch, Dortmund

Beebe, L 1977 The influence of the listener on code-switching. *Language Learning* 27: 331–9

Beebe, L 1980a Measuring the use of communication strategies. In Scarcella, R and Krashen, S (eds.) *Research in second language acquisition*, pp. 173–81. Newbury House, Rowley, Mass.

Beebe, L 1980b Sociolinguistic variation and style shifting in second language acquisition. *Language Learning* 30 (2) 433–47

Beebe, L 1983 Risk-taking and the language learner. In Seliger, H and Long, M (eds.) *Classroom-oriented research in second language acquisition*, pp. 39–66. Newbury House, Rowley, Mass.

Beebe, L 1985 Input: choosing the right stuff. In Gass, S and Madden, C (eds.) *Input in second language acquisition*, pp. 404–14. Newbury House, Rowley, Mass.

Beebe, L (ed.) 1988 *Issues in second language acquisition: multiple perspectives*. Newbury House, New York

Beebe, L and Zuengler, J 1983 Accommodation theory: an explanation for style shifting in second language dialects. In Wolfson, N and Judd, E (eds.) *Sociolinguistics and second language acquisition*, pp. 195–213. Newbury House, Rowley, Mass.

Bennett-Kastor, T 1988 *Analyzing children's language*. Basil Blackwell

Berko, J 1958 The child's learning of English morphology. *Word* 14: 150–77

Berman, R 1987 Cognitive principles and language acquisition. In Pfaff, C (ed.) *First and second language acquisition processes*, pp. 3–27. Newbury House, Cambridge, Mass.

Berwick, R 1985 *The acquisition of syntactic knowledge*. MIT Press, Cambridge, Mass.

Bever, T 1970 The cognitive basis for linguistic structures. In Hayes, J (ed.) *Cognition and the growth of language*, pp. 279–352. John Wiley, New York

Bialystok, E 1978 A theoretical model of second language learning. *Language Learning* 28: 69–84

Bialystok, E 1981 Some evidence for the integrity and interaction of two knowledge sources. In Andersen, R (ed.) *New dimensions in second language acquisition research*, pp. 62–74. Newbury House, Rowley, Mass.

Bialystok, E 1982 On the relationship between knowing and using linguistic forms. *Applied Linguistics* 3 (3): 181–206

Bialystok, E 1985 The compatibility of teaching and learning strategies. *Applied Linguistics* 6: 255–62

Bialystok, E and Fröhlich, M 1977 Aspects of second language learning in classroom settings. *Working Papers on Bilingualism* 13: 1–26

Bialystok, E and Fröhlich, M 1978 Variables of classroom achievement in second language learning. *Modern Language Journal* 62: 327–35

Bickerton, D 1975 *Dynamics of a creole system*. Cambridge University Press

Bickerton, D 1977 *Change and variation in Hawaiian English*, Vol. 2: *Creole syntax*. Social Sciences and Linguistic Institute, University of Hawaii at Manoa, Honolulu

Bickerton, D 1979 Beginnings. In Hill, K (ed.) *The genesis of language*, pp. 1–22. Karoma, Ann Arbor

Bickerton, D 1981 *Roots of language*. Karoma, Ann Arbor

Bickerton, D 1983 Comments on Valdman's 'Creolization and second language acquisition.' In Andersen, R (ed.) *Pidginization and creolization as language acquisition*, pp. 235–40. Newbury House, Rowley, Mass.

Bickerton, D 1984a The language bioprogram hypothesis. *The Behavioral and Brain Sciences* 7: 173–88

Bickerton, D 1984b The language bioprogram hypothesis and second language acquisition. In Rutherford, W (ed.) *Language universals and second language acquisition*, pp. 141–61. John Benjamins, Amsterdam

Bickerton, D 1986 Pidgin and creole studies. *Annual Review of Anthropology* 5: 169–93

Bickerton, D and Odo, C 1976 *Change and variation in Hawaiian English*, Vol. 1: *General phonology and pidgin syntax*. Social Science and Linguistics Institute, University of Hawaii at Manoa, Honolulu

Birdsong, D 1986 Empirical impediments to theories of second language acquisition. Paper presented at the Kentucky Foreign Language Conference, University of Kentucky, Lexington, April 24–25

Blank, M, Gessner, M, and Esposito, A 1979 Language without communication: a case study. *Child Language* 6 (2): 329–52

Blatchford, C and Schachter, J (eds.) 1978 *On TESOL '78*. TESOL, Washington, D.C.

Blau, E 1982 The effect of syntax on readability for ESL students in Puerto Rico. *TESOL Quarterly* 16 (4): 517–28

Bley-Vroman, R 1983 The comparative fallacy in interlanguage studies: the case of systematicity. *Language Learning* 33: 1–17

Bley-Vroman, R 1986 Hypothesis testing in second language acquisition. *Language Learning* 36: 353–76

Bley-Vroman, R 1988 The fundamental character of foreign language learning. In Rutherford, W and Sharwood-Smith, M (eds.) *Grammar and second language teaching: a book of readings*, pp. 19–30. Newbury House/Harper and Row, New York

Bley-Vroman, R (in press) The logical problem of foreign language learning. *Linguistic Analysis*

Bley-Vroman, R and Chaudron, C 1988 Review essay: a critique of Flynn's parameter-setting model of second language acquisition. *UHWPESL* 7 (1): 67–107

Bley-Vroman, R, Felix, S and Ioup, G 1988 The accessibility of universal grammar in adult language learning. *Second Language Research* 4 (1): 1–32

Blum-Kulka, S and Olshtain, E 1984a Requests and apologies: a cross-cultural study of speech act realization patterns. *Applied Linguistics* 5 (3): 176–213

Blum-Kulka, S and Olshtain, E (eds.) 1984b Pragmatics and second language learning. *Applied Linguistics* 5 (3), Special Issue

Blum-Kulka, S and Olshtain, E 1986 Too many words: length of utterance and pragmatic failure. *Studies in Second Language Acquisition* 8: 165–79

Bohn, O 1986 Formulas, frame structures and stereotypes in early syntactic development: some new evidence from L2 acquisition. *Linguistics* 24: 185–202

Bourgain, E 1978 Attitudes et apprentissage. In Ferenczi, V (ed.) *Psychologie, langage et apprentissage*, pp. 67–84. Paris

Bowerman, M 1973 *Early syntactic development: a cross-linguistic study with special reference to Finnish*. Cambridge University Press

Bowerman, M 1987 Commentary: mechanisms of language acquisition. In MacWhinney, B (ed.) *Mechanisms of language acquisition*. Lawrence Erlbaum Associates, Hillsdale, N.J.

Bresnan, J (ed.) 1982 *The mental representation of grammatical relations*. MIT Press, Cambridge, Mass.

Briere, E 1978 Variables affecting native Mexican children's learning Spanish as a second language. *Language Learning* 28 (1): 159–74

Brindley, G 1986a Semantic approaches to learner language. *Australian Review of Applied Linguistics* 3: 1–43

Brindley, G 1986b *The assessment of second language proficiency: issues and approaches*. National Curriculum Resource Centre, Adelaide

Brindley, G and Singh, K 1982 The use of second language learning research in ESL proficiency assessment. *Australian Review of Applied Linguistics* 5 (1): 84–111

Broen, P 1972 The verbal environment of the language learning child. *American Speech and Hearing Monographs* 17

Brophy, J and Good, T 1974 *Teacher-student relationships: causes and consequences*. Holt, Rinehart and Winston, New York

Brown, C 1983 The view of the learner: does perception of language learning factors relate to success? Paper presented at Rocky Mountain TESOL

Brown, C 1985 Requests for specific language input: differences between older and younger adult language learners. In Gass, S and Madden C (eds.) *Input in second language acquisition*. Newbury House, Rowley, Mass.

Brown, H D 1973 Affective variables in second language acquisition. *Language Learning* 23: 231–44

Brown, H D 1977 Cognitive and affective characteristics of good language learners. In Henning, C (ed.) *Proceedings of the Los Angeles Second Language Research Forum*, pp. 349–54. Department of English, University of California at Los Angeles

Brown, H D 1980 The optimal distance model of second language acquisition. *TESOL Quarterly* 14: 157–64

Brown, H D 1987 *Principles of language learning and teaching*. Prentice-Hall, Englewood Cliffs, N.J.

Brown, H D, Yorio, C and Crymes, R (eds.) 1977 *On TESOL '77*. TESOL, Washington, D.C.

Brown, J D 1983 An exploration of morpheme-group interactions. In Bailey, K M, Long, M and Peck, S (eds.) *Second language acquisition studies*, pp. 25–40. Newbury House, Rowley, Mass.

Brown, J D 1988 *Understanding research in second language learning*. Cambridge University Press, New York

Brown, Roger 1973 *A first language*. Harvard University Press, Cambridge, Mass.

Brown, Roger and Hanlon, C 1970 Derivational complexity and the order of acquisition in child speech. In Hayes, J (ed.) *Cognition and the development of language*, pp. 155–207. Wiley, New York

Brown, Ron 1987 A comparison of the comprehensibility of modified and unmodified reading materials for ESL. *UHWPESL* 6 (1): 49–79

Bruzzese, G 1977 English/Italian secondary hybridization: a case study in the pidginization of a second language learner's speech. In Henning, C (ed.)

Proceedings of the Los Angeles Second Language Research Forum, pp. 235–45. University of California at Los Angeles

Buckley, D 1988 First language attrition in additive bilinguals. MA thesis, Department of English as a Second Language, University of Hawaii at Manoa, Honolulu

Budner, S 1962 Intolerance of ambiguity as a personality variable. *Journal of Personality* **30**: 29–50

Burmeister, H and Ufert, D 1980 Strategy switching. In Felix, S (ed.) *Second language development*, pp. 109–22. Gunter Narr, Tubingen

Burstall, C 1975 Factors affecting foreign-language learning: a consideration of some recent research findings. *Language Teaching and Linguistics: Abstracts* **8**: 5–25

Burt, M and Dulay, H (eds.) 1975 *On TESOL '75*. TESOL, Washington, D.C.

Burt, M and Dulay, H 1980 On acquisition orders. In Felix, S (ed.) *Second language development*, pp. 265–327. Gunter Narr, Tubingen

Burt, M, Dulay, H and Hernandez-Chavez, E 1975 *Bilingual syntax measure*. Harcourt Brace Jovanovich, New York

Busch, D 1982 Introversion-extroversion and the EFL proficiency of Japanese students. *Language Learning* **32**: 109–32

Buteau, M 1970 Students' errors and the learning of French as a second language. *International Review of Applied Linguistics* **8**: 133–45

Butler-Wall, B 1983 Optional syntax in oral discourse: evidence from native speakers of English. In Campbell, C, Flashner, V, Hudson, T and Lubin, J (eds.) *Proceedings of the Los Angeles Second Language Research Forum*, Vol. II. University of California at Los Angeles

Butoyi, C 1978 The accuracy order of sentential compliments by ESL learners. MA TESL thesis, University of California at Los Angeles

Butterworth, G 1972 A Spanish-speaking adolescent's acquisition of English syntax. MA TESL thesis, University of California at Los Angeles

Bye, C 1980 The acquisition of grammatical morphemes in Quiche Mayan. Unpublished Ph.D. dissertation, University of Pittsburgh

Bygate, M 1988 Units of oral expression and language learning in small group interaction. *Applied Linguistics* **9** (1): 59–82

Campbell, C, Flashner, V, Hudson, T, and Lubin, J (eds.) 1983 *Proceedings of the Los Angeles Research Forum*, Vol. II. Department of English, University of California at Los Angeles

Campbell, D and Stanley, J 1972 *Experimental and quasi-experimental designs for research*. Harcourt Brace Jovanovich, New York

Canale, M 1983 Program evaluation: where do we go from here? Plenary address at the TESOL Summer Meeting, Toronto

Canale, M and Swain, M 1980 Theoretical bases of communicative approaches to second language teaching and testing. *Applied Linguistics* **1**: 1–47

Candlin, C 1983 Plenary address delivered at the Second Language Research Forum, Los Angeles

Candlin, C 1987 Towards task-based language learning. In Candlin, C and Murphy, D (eds.) *Language learning tasks*. Prentice-Hall, Englewood Cliffs, N.J.

Carpenter, R 1989 *Language learning strategies: what every teacher should know*. Newbury House/Harper & Row, New York

Carrell, P and Konneker, B 1981 Politeness: comparing native and nonnative judgments. *Language Learning* 31: 17–30

Carroll, J 1963 Research on teaching foreign languages. In Gage, N (ed.) *Handbook of research on teaching*. Rand-McNally, Chicago

Carroll, J 1965 The prediction of success in intensive foreign language training. In Glaser, R (ed.) *Training, research and education*, pp. 87–136. Wiley, New York

Carroll, J 1967 Foreign language proficiency levels attained by language majors near graduation from college. *Foreign Language Annals* 1: 131–51

Carroll, J 1979 Psychometric approaches to the study of language abilities. In Fillmore, C, Kempler, D and Wang, W (eds.) *Individual differences in language ability and language behavior*. Academic Press, New York

Carroll, J 1981 Twenty-five years of research on foreign language aptitude. In Diller, K (ed.) *Individual differences and universals in language learning aptitude*, pp. 83–118. Newbury House, Rowley, Mass.

Carroll, J and Sapon, S 1959 Modern language aptitude test. The Psychological Corporation, New York

Cathcart-Strong, R 1986 Input generation by young second language learners. *TESOL Quarterly* 20: 515–30

Cazden, C 1968 The acquisition of noun and verb inflections. *Child Development* 39: 433–48

Cazden, C, Cancino, E, Rosansky, E and Schumann, J 1975 *Second language acquisition sequences in children, adolescents and adults*. Final report submitted to the National Institute of Education, Washington, D.C.

Celce-Murcia, M 1972 The universalist hypothesis: some implications for contrastive syntax and language teaching. In *Workpapers in TESL* 6. University of California at Los Angeles

Celce-Murcia, M 1980 Contextual analysis of English: application to TESL. In Larsen-Freeman, D (ed.) *Discourse analysis in second language research*. Newbury House, Rowley, Mass.

Celce-Murcia, M (ed.) 1985 *Beyond basics: issues and research in TESOL*. Newbury House, Rowley, Mass.

Celce-Murcia, M and Hawkins, B 1985 Contrastive analysis, error analysis and interlanguage analysis. In Celce-Murcia, M (ed.) *Beyond basics: issues and research in TESOL*, pp. 60–77. Newbury House, Rowley, Mass.

Cervantes, R 1983 'Say it again Sam': the effect of repetition on dictation scores. Term paper, ESL 670, University of Hawaii at Manoa, Honolulu

Chamot, A U 1978 Grammatical problems in learning English as a third language. In Hatch, E (ed.) *Second language acquisition: a book of readings*, pp. 176–89. Newbury House, Rowley, Mass.

Chao, W 1981 PRO drop languages and nonobligatory control. *Occasional Papers in Linguistics* 7: 46–74. University of Massachusetts, Amherst

Chapelle, C and Roberts, C 1986 Ambiguity tolerance and field independence as predictors of proficiency in English as a second language. *Language Learning* 36: 27–45

Chastain, K 1975 Affective and ability factors in second language acquisition. *Language Learning* 25: 153–61

Chaudron, C 1977 A descriptive model of discourse in the corrective treatment of learners' errors. *Language Learning* 27: 29–46

Chaudron, C 1982 Vocabulary elaboration in teachers' speech to L2 learners. *Studies in Second Language Acquisition* **4**: 170–80

Chaudron, C 1983a Foreigner talk in the classroom - an aid to learning? In Seliger, H and Long, M (eds.) *Classroom-oriented research in second language acquisition*, pp. 127–43. Newbury House, Rowley, Mass.

Chaudron, C 1983b Simplification of input: topic reinstatements and their effects on L2 learners' recognition and recall. *TESOL Quarterly* **17**: 437–58

Chaudron, C 1983c Research on metalinguistic judgments: a review of theory, methods, and results. *Language Learning* **33**: 343–77

Chaudron, C 1985a Intake: on models and methods for discovering learners' processing of input. *Studies in Second Language Acquisition* **7**: 1–14

Chaudron, C 1985b Comprehension, comprehensibility, and learning in the second language classroom. *Studies in Second Language Acquisition* **7**: 216–32

Chaudron, C 1986a The interaction of quantitative and qualitative approaches to research: a view of the second language classroom. *TESOL Quarterly* **20**: 709–17

Chaudron, C 1986b Teachers' priorities in correcting learners' errors in French immersion classes. In Day, R (ed.) *'Talking to learn': conversation in second language acquisition*, pp. 64–84. Newbury House, Rowley, Mass.

Chaudron, C 1987 The role of error correction in second language teaching. In Das, B (ed.) *Patterns of classroom interaction in Southeast Asia*, pp. 17–50. Regional Language Centre, Singapore

Chaudron, C 1988 *Second language classrooms: research on teaching and learning.* Cambridge University Press

Chaudron, C and Richards, J 1986 The effect of discourse markers on the comprehension of lectures. *Applied Linguistics* **7**: 113–27

Chesterfield, R and Barrows Chesterfield, K 1985 Natural order in children's use of second language learning strategies. *Applied Linguistics* **6**: 45–59

Chihara, T and Oller, J 1978 Attitudes and attained proficiency in EFL: a sociolinguistic study of adult Japanese speakers. *Language Learning* **28**: 55–68

Chomsky, C 1969 Linguistics and philosophy. In Hook, S (ed.) *Language and philosophy*. New York University Press, New York

Chomsky, N 1959 Review of *Verbal behavior* by B F Skinner. *Language* **35**: 26–58

Chomsky, N 1965 *Aspects of the theory of syntax.* MIT Press, Cambridge, Mass.

Chomsky, N 1975 *Reflections on language.* Pantheon Books, New York

Chomsky, N 1980 *Rules and representations.* Columbia University Press, New York

Chomsky, N 1981a Principles and parameters in syntactic theory. In Hornstein, N and Lightfoot, D (eds.) *Explanations in linguistics: the logical problem of language acquisition*. Longman

Chomsky, N 1981b *Lectures on government and binding.* Foris, Dordrecht

Chomsky, N 1987 *Generative grammar: its basis, development and prospects.* Kyoto University of Foreign Studies, Kyoto

Chun, A, Day, R, Chenoweth, A and Luppescu, S 1982 Errors, interaction, and correction: a study of native-nonnative conversations. *TESOL Quarterly* **16**: 537–47

Chun, J (1978) A survey of research in second language acquisition. In Croft, W (ed.) *Readings on ESL: for teachers and teacher trainees*, pp. 181–198. Winthrop Publishers Inc., Cambridge, Mass.

Churchland, P 1986 *Neurophilosophy: toward a unified science of the mind-brain.* MIT Press, Cambridge, Mass.

Clahsen, H 1980 Psycholinguistic aspects of L2 acquisition. In Felix, S (ed.) *Second language development*, pp. 57–79. Gunter Narr, Tubingen

Clahsen, H 1981 *Spracherwerb in der Kindheit.* Gunter Narr, Tubingen

Clahsen, H 1984 The acquisition of German word order: a test case for cognitive approaches to L2 development. In Andersen, R (ed.) *Second language: a crosslinguistic perspective*, pp. 219–42. Newbury House, Rowley, Mass.

Clahsen, H 1985 Profiling second language development: a procedure for assessing L2 proficiency. In Hyltenstam, K and Pienemann, M (eds.) *Modelling and assessing second language development*, pp. 283–332. Multilingual Matters

Clahsen, H 1987 Connecting theories of language processing and (second) language acquisition. In Pfaff, C (ed.) *First and second language acquisition processes*: 103–16. Newbury House, Cambridge, Mass.

Clahsen, H 1988 Critical phases of grammar development: a study of the acquisition of negation in children and adults. In Jordens, P and Lalleman, J (eds.) *Language development*, pp. 123–48. Foris, Dordrecht

Clahsen, H, Meisel J and Pienemann, M 1983 *Deutsch als Zweitsprache: der Spracherwerb auslandischer Arbeiter.* Gunter Narr, Tubingen

Clahsen, H and Muysken, P 1986 The availability of universal grammar to adult and child learners: a study of the acquisition of German word order. *Second Language Research* **2** (2): 93–119

Clark, H and Clark, E 1977 *Psychology and language: an introduction to psycholinguistics.* Harcourt Brace Jovanovich, New York

Clarke, M and Handscombe, J 1983 *On TESOL '82.* TESOL, Washington, D.C.

Clement, R and Kruidenier, B 1983 Orientations in second language acquisition: I. The effects of ethnicity, milieu, and target language on their emergence. *Language Learning* **33**: 273–91

Clyne, M 1968 Zum Pidgin-Deutsch der Gastarbeiter. *Zeitschrift für Mundartforschung* **35**: 130–9

Clyne, M 1977 Multilingualism and pidginization in Australian industry. *Ethnic Studies* **1**: 40–55

Clyne, M 1978 Some remarks on foreigner talk. In Dittmar, N, Haberland, H, Skutnabb-Kangas, T and Teleman, U (eds.) *Papers from the first Scandinavian-German symposium on the language of immigrant workers and their children*, pp. 155–69. Linguistgruppen, Roskilde UniversiteitsCenter

Cohen, A 1987 The use of verbal and imagery mnemonics in second-language vocabulary learning. *Studies in Second Language Acquisition* **9**: 43–62

Cohen, A and Aphek, E 1980 Retention of second-language vocabulary over time: investigating the role of mnemonic associations. *System* **8**: 221–235

Cohen, A and Aphek, E 1981 Easifying second language learning. *Studies in Second Language Acquisition* **3**: 221–236

Cohen, A and Hosenfeld, C 1981 Some uses of mentalistic data in second language research. *Language Learning* **31**: 285–313

Cohen, A and Olshtain, E 1981 Developing a measure of sociocultural competence: the case of apology. *Language Learning* 31: 113–34

Cohen, A and Robbins, M 1976 Toward assessing interlanguage performance: the relationship between selected errors, learners' characteristics, and learners' expectations. *Language Learning* 26: 45–66

Cohen, B, Berent, S and Silverman, A 1973 Field-dependence and lateralization of function in the human brain. *Archives of General Psychiatry* 28: 165–7

Cohen, R 1969 Conceptual styles, culture conflict, and non-verbal tests of intelligence. *American Anthropologist* 71: 826–56

Collier, V 1987 Age and rate of acquisition of second language for academic purposes. *TESOL Quarterly* 21: 617–41

Connor, V and Kaplan, R (eds.) 1987 *Writing across languages: analysis of L2 text.* Addison-Wesley. Reading, Mass.

Connor, U and McCagg, P 1983 Cross-cultural differences and perceived quality in written paraphrases of English expository prose. *Applied Linguistics* 4: 259–68

Cook, D 1965 *A guide to educational research.* Allyn and Bacon, Boston

Cook, T and Reichardt, C (eds.) 1979 *Qualitative and quantitative methods in education research.* Sage Publications, Beverly Hills, California

Cook, V 1973 The comparison of language development in native children and foreign adults. *International Review of Applied Linguistics* 11: 13–28

Cook, V 1979 Aspects of memory in secondary school learners. *Interlanguage Studies Bulletin* 4: 161–72

Cook, V 1985 Universal grammar and second language learning. *Applied Linguistics* 6 (1): 2–18

Cook, V (ed.) 1986 *Experimental approaches to second language learning.* Pergamon Press, New York

Cook, V 1988 *Chomsky's universal grammar: an introduction.* Basil Blackwell

Cooper, R 1981 Language spread as a perspective for the study of second language acquisition. In Andersen, R (ed.) *New dimensions in second language acquisition research*, pp. 130–45. Newbury House, Rowley, Mass.

Cooper, R and Fishman, J 1977 A study of language attitudes. In Fishman, J, Cooper, R and Conrad, A (eds.) *The spread of English: the sociology of English as an additional language*, pp. 239–76. Newbury House, Rowley, Mass.

Coppieters, R 1987 Competence differences between native and fluent non-native speakers. *Language* 63: 544–73

Corder, S 1967 The significance of learner's errors. *International Review of Applied Linguistics* 5: 161–70

Corder, S 1971 Idiosyncratic dialects and error analysis. *International Review of Applied Linguistics* 9: 147–59

Corder, S 1975 'Simple codes' and the source of the second language learner's initial heuristic hypothesis. Paper presented at the Colloque 'Theoretical Linguistics Models in Applied Linguistics' IV, Université de Neuchâtel. In *Studies in Second Language Acquisition* 1 (1), 1977: 1–10

Corder, S 1978 Language distance and the magnitude of the language learning task. *Studies in Second Language Acquisition* 2: 27–36

Corder, S 1981 *Error analysis and interlanguage.* Oxford University Press

Corder, S 1983 A role for the mother tongue. In Gass, S and Selinker, L (eds.) *Language transfer in language learning*, pp. 85–97. Newbury House, Rowley, Mass.

Corder, S and Roulet, E (eds.) *The notions of simplification, interlanguages and pidgins, and their relation to second language pedagogy*. Droz, Geneve

de Cordoba, C 1985 A proposal for the improvement of current teacher education programs for teachers of second and foreign languages. Unpublished Ph.D. dissertation, International College

Crain, S and Nakayama, M 1987 Structure dependence in grammar formation. *Language* 63 (3): 522–43

Crookes, G 1988a Planning, monitoring and second language development: a review. Technical Report No. 6. Center for Second Language Classroom Research, Social Science Research Institute, University of Hawaii at Manoa, Honolulu

Crookes, G 1988b Planning and interlanguage variation. Unpublished Ph.D. dissertation, University of Hawaii at Manoa, Honolulu

Crookes, G (1989) Planning and interlanguage variation. *Studies in Second Language Acquisition* 11 (4): 367–83

Crookes, G 1990 The utterance, and other basic units for second language discourse analysis. *Applied Linguistics* 11 (2): 183–99

Cross, T 1977 Mothers' speech adjustments: the contribution of selected child listener variables. In Snow, C and Ferguson, C (eds.) *Talking to children: language input and acquisition*, pp. 151–88. Cambridge University Press

Cross, T 1978 Mothers' speech and its association with rate of linguistic development in young children. In Waterson, N and Snow, C (eds.) *The development of communication*, pp. 199–216. Wiley, New York

Crowne, D and Marlowe, D 1964 *The approval motive*. Wiley, New York

Crystal, D 1982 *Profiling linguistic disability*. Edward Arnold

Crystal, D 1985 How many millions? The statistics of English today. *English Today* 1: 7–9

Cummins, J 1978 Educational implications of mother tongue maintenance in minority-language groups. *The Canadian Modern Language Review* 34: 395–416

Cummins, J 1979 Cognitive/academic language proficiency, linguistic interdependence, the optimal age question and some other matters. *Working Papers on Bilingualism* 19: 197–205

Cummins, J 1980 The cross-lingual dimensions of language proficiency: implications for bilingual education and the optimal age issue. *TESOL Quarterly* 14: 175–88

Cummins, J 1981a Age on arrival and immigrant second language learning in Canada: a reassessment. *Applied Linguistics* 2: 132–49

Cummins, J 1981b The role of primary language development in promoting educational success for language minority students. In *Schooling and language minority students: a theoretical framework*, pp. 3–49. National Evaluation, Dissemination and Assessment Center, California State University

Cummins, J 1984 *Bilingualism and special education: issues on assessment and pedagogy*. Multilingual Matters

Cummins, J and Swain, M 1986 *Bilingualism in education*. Longman

Cummins, J, Swain, M, Nakajima, K, Handscombe, J, Green, D, and Tran, C 1984 Linguistic interdependence among Japanese and Vietnamese immigrant students. In Rivera, C (ed.) *Communicative competence approaches to language proficiency assessment: research and application*, pp. 60–81. Multilingual Matters

Cummins, R 1983 *Psychological explanation*. MIT Press, Cambridge, Mass.

Curtiss, S 1980 The critical period and feral children. *UCLA Working Papers in Cognitive Linguistics* 2: 21–36

Curtiss, S 1982 Developmental dissociation of language and cognition. In Obler, L and Menn, L (eds.) *Exceptional languages and linguistics*, pp. 285–312. Academic Press, New York

Cziko, G, Lambert, W and Gutter, R 1979 French immersion programs and students' social attitudes: a multidimensional investigation. *Working Papers on Bilingualism* 19: 13–28

Dagut, M and Laufer, B 1985 Avoidance of phrasal verbs: a case for contrastive analysis. *Studies in Second Language Acquisition* 7: 73–9

Dakin, J 1973 *The language laboratory and modern language teaching*. Longman.

Daniel, I 1983 On first-year German foreign language learning: a comparison of language behavior in response to two instructional methods. Unpublished Ph.D. dissertation, University of Southern California

Dansereau, D 1978 The development of a learning strategies curriculum. In O'Neil, H (ed.) *Learning strategies*, pp. 1–29. Academic Press, New York

Dato, D 1970 *American children's acquisition of Spanish syntax in the Madrid environment: a preliminary edition*. Final Report, Project No. 3036, Contract No. O.E.C. 2–7–002 637, USHEW

Davies, A, Criper, C, and Howatt, A (eds.) 1984 *Interlanguage*. Edinburgh University Press

Davies, E 1987 A contrastive approach to the analysis of politeness formulas. *Applied Linguistics* 8: 75–88

Davis, Z T 1986 Input frequency and developmental sequence in ESL: should it drive curricula and instruction? *NABE Journal*, Spring: 199–212

Day, R 1980 The development of linguistic attitudes and preferences. *TESOL Quarterly* 14: 27–37

Day, R 1984 Student participation in the ESL classroom, or some imperfections in practice. *Language Learning* 34 (3): 69–102

Day, R (ed.) 1986 *'Talking to learn': conversation in second language acquisition*. Newbury House, Rowley, Mass.

Day, R and Iida, M 1988 Use, attitude, and motivation in foreign language acquisition. *UHWPESL* 7 (1): 109–18

Dechert, H, Bruggemeier, M and Fütterer, D 1984 *Transfer and interference: a selected bibliography*. John Benjamins, Amsterdam and Philadelphia

Dechert, H and Raupach, M 1980 *Towards a crosslinguistic assessment of speech production*. Peter D. Lang, Frankfurt

Devenney, R 1986 Intertextuality and the critical age hypothesis in second language acquisition. Term paper, ESL 650, University of Hawaii at Manoa, Honolulu

de Villiers, J and de Villiers, P 1973 A cross-sectional study of the acquisition of grammatical morphemes in child speech. *Journal of Psycholinguistic Research* 2: 267–78

de Villiers P and de Villiers J 1978 *Language acquisition.* Harvard University Press, Cambridge, Mass.

Dickerson, L 1975 The learner's interlanguage as a system of variable rules. *TESOL Quarterly* 9: 401–7

Dickerson, L and Dickerson, W 1977 Interlanguage phonology: current research and future directions. In Corder, S and Roulet, E (eds.) *The notions of simplification, interlanguages and pidgins.* Actes du 5ème Colloque de Linguistique Appliqué de Neufchâtel. AIMAV/Didier, Paris

Diller, K (ed.) 1981 *Individual differences and universals in language learning aptitude.* Newbury House, Rowley, Mass.

Dinnsen, D and Eckman, F 1975 A functional explanation of some phonological typologies. In Grossman, R et al. (eds.) *Functionalism.* Chicago Linguistic Society

Di Pietro, R 1971 *Language structures in contrast.* Newbury House, Rowley, Mass.

Dittmar, N 1980 Ordering adult learners according to language abilities. In Felix, S (ed.) *Second language development.* Gunter Narr, Tübingen

Dittmar, N 1981 On the verbal organization of L2 tense marking in an elicited translation task by Spanish immigrants in Germany. *Studies in Second Language Acquisition* 3 (2): 136–64

Dittmar, N 1982 'Ich fertig arbeite - nicht mehr spreche Deutsch': semantische Eigenschaften pidginisierter Lernervarietaten des Deutschen. *Zeitschrift fur Literaturwissenschaft und Linguistik* 45: 9–34

Doi, T and Yoshioka, K 1987 Which grammatical structures should be taught when? Implications of the Pienemann–Johnston model for teaching Japanese as a foreign language. Paper presented at the 9th Hawaii Association of Teachers of Japanese Language and Language Teaching

Donaldson, M 1978 *Children's minds.* Penguin

Doron, S 1973 Reflectivity-impulsivity and their influence on reading for inference for adult students of ESL. Unpublished report, University of Michigan, Ann Arbor

Doughty, C 1988 The effect of instruction on the acquisition on relativization in ESL. Unpublished Ph.D. dissertation, University of Pennsylvania

Dulay, H and Burt, M 1972 Goofing, an indicator of children's second language strategies. *Language Learning* 22: 234–52

Dulay, H and Burt, M 1973 Should we teach children syntax? *Language Learning* 23: 245–58

Dulay, H and Burt, M 1974 Natural sequences in child second language acquisition. *Language Learning* 24: 37–53

Dulay, M and Burt, M 1975 Creative construction in second language learning and teaching. In Burt, M and Dulay, H (eds.) *On TESOL '75*, pp. 21–32. TESOL, Washington, D.C.

Dulay, H and Burt, M 1977 Remarks on creativity in language acquisition. In Burt, M, Dulay, H and Finocchiaro, M (eds.) *Viewpoints on English as a Second Language.* Regents, New York

Dulay, H, Burt, M and Krashen, S 1982 *Language two.* Oxford University Press, New York

Dunkel, H 1948 *Second-language learning.* Ginn & Co., Boston

Dunn, R, Dunn, K and Price, G 1975 *The learning style inventory.* Price Systems, Lawrence, Kansas

Duplessis, J, Solin, D, Travis, L and White, L 1987 UG or not UG, that's the question: a reply to Clahsen and Muysken. *Second Language Research* 3 (1): 56–75

Duran, R, Canale, M, Penfield, J, Stansfield, C and Liskin-Gasparro, J 1985 *TOEFL from a communicative viewpoint on language proficiency: a working paper* (TOEFL Research Report 17). Educational Testing Service, Princeton, N.J.

Duskova, L 1969 On sources of errors in foreign language learning. *International Review of Applied Linguistics* 7: 11–36

Early, M 1985 Input and interaction in content classrooms: foreigner talk and teacher talk in classroom discourse. Unpublished Ph.D. dissertation, University of California at Los Angeles

Eckman, F 1977 Markedness and the contrastive analysis hypothesis. *Language Learning* 27: 315–30

Eckman, F 1981 On the naturalness of interlanguage phonological rules. *Language Learning* 31: 195–216

Eckman, F 1985 The markedness differential hypothesis: theory and applications. In Wheatley, B, Hastings, A, Eckman, F, Bell, L, Krukar, G and Rutkowski, R (eds.) *Current approaches to second language acquisition: proceedings of the 1984 University of Wisconsin-Milwaukee Linguistics Symposium*, pp. 3–21. Indiana University Linguistics Club, Bloomington, Ind.

Eckman, F, Bell, L and Nelson, D (eds.) 1984 *Universals of second language acquisition.* Newbury House, Rowley, Mass.

Eckman, F, Bell, L and Nelson, D 1988 On the generalization of relative clause instruction in the acquisition of English as a second language. *Applied Linguistics* 9 (1): 1–20

Edmondson, W, House, J, Kasper, G and Stemmer, B 1984 Learning the pragmatics of discourse: a project report. *Applied Linguistics* 5: 113–27

Edwards, H, Wesche, M, Krashen, S, Clement, R and Kruidenier, B 1984 Second language acquisition through subject-matter learning: a study of sheltered psychology classes at the University of Ottawa. *Canadian Modern Language Review* 41 (2): 268–82

Eisenstein, M 1982 A study of social variation in adult second language acquisition. *Language Learning* 32: 367–91

Eisenstein, M 1986 Alternatives in second language research: three articles on the state of the art. *TESOL Quarterly* 20: 683–7

Eisenstein, M, Bailey, N and Madden, C 1982 It takes two: contrasting tasks and contrasting structures. *TESOL Quarterly* 16: 381–93

Eisenstein, M and Berkowitz, D 1981 The effect of phonological variation on adult learner comprehension. *Studies in Second Language Acquisition* 14: 75–80

Eisenstein, M and Bodman, J 1986 'I very appreciate': expressions of gratitude by native and non-native speakers of American English. *Applied Lingustics* 7: 167–85

Ekstrand, L H 1976 Age and length of residence as variables related to the adjustment of migrant children, with special reference to second language learning. In Nickel, G (ed.) *Proceedings of the fourth International Congress of*

Applied Linguistics, **3**: 179–97. Hochschulverlag, Stuttgart

Ekstrand, L H 1977 Social and individual frame factors in second language learning: comparative aspects. In Skutnabb-Kangas (ed.) *Papers from the first Nordic Conference on Bilingualism*. Helsingsfors Universitat

Ekstrand, L H 1978 English without a book revisited: the effect of age on second language acquisition in a formal setting. *Didakometry* 60. Department of Educational and Psychological Research, School of Education, Malmö, Sweden

Ekstrand, L H 1979 Replacing the critical period and optimum age theories of second language with a theory of ontogenetic development beyond puberty. *Educational and Psychological Interactions* No. 69. Department of Educational and Psychological Research, Malmö School of Education, Lund University

Elias-Olivares, L 1976 Ways of speaking in a Chicano community: a sociolinguistic approach. Unpublished Ph.D. dissertation, University of Texas at Austin

Ellis, R 1984a *Classroom second language development*. Pergamon

Ellis, R 1984b Can syntax be taught? A study of the effects of formal instruction on the acquisition of WH-questions in children. *Applied Linguistics* **5** (2): 138–55

Ellis, R 1984c The role of instruction in second language acquisition. Paper presented at the IRAAL-BAAL Seminar on the Formal and Informal Contexts of Language Learning, Dublin, 11–13 September. In Singleton, D and Little, D (eds.) *Language learning in formal and informal contexts*, pp. 19–37. IRAAL, Dublin

Ellis, R 1985 *Understanding second language acquisition*. Oxford University Press

Ellis, R 1987a Contextual variability in second language acquisition and the relevancy of language teaching. In Ellis, R (ed.) *Second language acquisition in context*, pp. 179–94. Prentice-Hall, Englewood Cliffs, N.J.

Ellis, R (ed.) 1987b *Second language acquisition in context*. Prentice-Hall, Englewood Cliffs, N.J.

Ellis, R 1989 Are classroom and naturalistic acquisition the same? A study of the classroom acquisition of German word order rules. *Studies in Second Language Acquisition* **11** (in press)

Ely, C 1986 An analysis of discomfort, risktaking, sociability, and motivation in the L2 classroom. *Language Learning* **36**: 1–25

England, E 1982 The role of integrative motivation in English as a second language learning among a group of foreign students in the United States. Paper presented at the TESOL Convention, Honolulu, Hawaii

Ervin-Tripp, S 1974 Is second language learning like the first? *TESOL Quarterly* **8**: 111–27

Eubank, L 1986 Formal models of language learning and the acquisition of German word order and negation by primary and non-primary language learners. Unpublished Ph.D. dissertation, University of Texas at Austin

Eubank, L 1987 The acquisition of German negation by formal language learners. In van Patten, B, Dvorack, T and Lee, J (eds.) *Foreign language learning: a research perspective*. Newbury House/Harper and Row, New York

Eysenck, H and Eysenck, S 1963 Eysenck personality inventory, form A. Educational and Industrial Testing Service, San Diego

Faerch, C and Kasper, G (eds.) 1983 *Strategies in interlanguage communication.* Longman

Faerch, C and Kasper, G 1984 Two ways of defining communication strategies. *Language Learning* 34: 45–63

Faerch, C and Kasper, G (eds.) 1987 *Introspection in second language research.* Multilingual Matters

Fanselow, J 1977 Beyond Rashomon – conceptualizing and describing the teaching act. *TESOL Quarterly* 11: 17–39

Fanselow, J and Crymes, R (eds.) 1976 *On TESOL '76.* TESOL, Washington, D.C.

Farhady, H 1980 Justification, development, and validation of functional language testing. Ph.D. dissertation, University of California at Los Angeles

Farhady, H 1982 Measures of language proficiency from the learner's perspective. *TESOL Quarterly* 16: 43–59

Farwell, C 1973 The language spoken to children. *Papers and Reports in Child Language Development*, 5: 31–62. Stanford University

Fathman, A 1975a Language background, age and the order of acquisition of English structures. In Burt, M and Dulay, H (eds.) *On TESOL '75.* TESOL, Washington, D.C.

Fathman, A 1975b The relationship between age and second language productive ability. *Language Learning* 25: 245–66

Fathman, A 1976 Variables affecting the successful learning of English as a second language. *TESOL Quarterly* 10 (4): 433–41

Fathman, A 1978 ESL and EFL learning: similar or dissimilar? In Blatchford, C and Schachter, J (eds.) *On TESOL '78*, pp. 213–23. TESOL, Washington, D.C.

Feenstra, H 1969 Parent and teacher attitudes: their role in second-language acquisition. *Canadian Modern Language Review* 26: 5–13

Felix, S 1980a Interference, interlanguage and related issues. In Felix, S (ed.) *Second language development*, pp. 93–107. Gunter Narr, Tubingen

Felix, S (ed.) 1980b *Second language development.* Gunter Narr, Tubingen

Felix, S 1981a The effect of formal instruction on second language acquisition. *Language Learning* 31 (1): 87–112

Felix, S 1981b On the (in)applicability of Piagetian thought to language learning. *Studies in Second Language Acquisition* 3 (2): 201–20

Felix, S 1984 Two problems of language acquisition: the relevance of grammatical studies to the theory of interlanguage. In Davies, A, Criper, C and Howatt, A (eds.) *Interlanguage*, pp. 133–61. Edinburgh University Press

Felix, S 1985 More evidence on competing cognitive systems. *Second Language Research* 1 (1): 47–72

Felix, S and Simmet, A 1981 Natural processes in classroom L2 learning. Revised version of a paper presented at the IIIème Colloque Groupe de Recherche sur l'Acquisition des Langues, Paris, May 15–17

Felix, S and Wode, H (eds.) 1983 *Language development at the crossroads.* Gunter Narr, Tubingen

Ferguson, C 1971 Absence of copula and the notion of simplicity: a study of normal speech, baby talk, foreigner talk and pidgins. In Hymes, D (ed.) *Pidginization and creolization of languages*, pp. 141–50. Cambridge University Press

Ferguson, C 1975 Towards a characterization of English foreigner talk. *Anthropological Linguistics* 17: 1–14

Ferguson, C 1977 Baby talk as a simplified register. In Snow, C and Ferguson, C (eds.) *Talking to children: language input and acquisition*, pp. 219–35. Cambridge University Press

Ferguson, C and DeBose, C 1976 Simplified registers, broken languages and pidginization. In Valdman, A (ed.) *Pidgin and creole*. Indiana University Press, Bloomington

Feyerabend, P 1978 *Against method*. Verso

Fisher, J, Clarke, M and Schachter, J (eds.) 1980 *On TESOL '80*. TESOL, Washington, D.C.

Flege, J 1980 Phonetic approximation in second language acquisition. *Language Learning* 30: 117–34

Flege, J 1987 A critical period for learning to pronounce foreign languages? *Applied Linguistics* 8 (2): 162–77

Flick, W and Gilbert, G 1976 Untutored second language learning vs. pidginization. Paper presented at the 1976 TESOL Convention, New York

Flynn, K 1983 The acquisition of form and function in interlanguage: a preliminary study. Paper presented at the Second Language Research Forum, University of Southern California

Flynn, S 1983 Similarities and differences between first and second language acquisition: setting the parameters of universal grammar. In Rogers, D and Slovboda, J (eds.) *Acquisition of symbolic skills*. Plenum Press, New York

Flynn, S 1984 A universal in L2 acquisition based on a PBB typology. In Eckman, F, Bell, L and Nelson, D (eds.) *Universals of second language acquisition*, pp. 75–87. Newbury House, Rowley, Mass.

Flynn, S and O'Neil, W (eds.) (in press) *Linguistic theory in second language acquisition*. Reidel Press, Dordrecht

Fodor, J 1966 How to learn to talk: some simple ways. In Smith, F and Miller, G (eds.) *The genesis of language*. MIT Press, Cambridge, Mass.

Fourcin, A 1975 Language development in the absence of expressive speech. In Lenneberg, E and Lenneberg, E (eds.) *Foundations of language development*, pp. 263–8. Academic Press, New York

Fradd, S and Scarpaci, J 1981 Cognitive styles. *Gulf Area TESOL Newsletter* 1: 17–24

Fraser, B, Rintell, E and Walters, J 1980 An approach to conducting research on the acquisition of pragmatic competence in a second language. In Larsen-Freeman, D (ed.) *Discourse analysis in second language research*. Newbury House, Rowley, Mass.

Freed, B 1978 Foreigner talk: a study of speech adjustments made by native speakers of English in conversation with non-native speakers. Unpublished Ph.D. dissertation, University of Pennsylvania

Freed, B 1980 Talking to foreigners versus talking to children: similarities and differences. In Scarcella, R and Krashen, S (eds.) *Research in second language acquisition*, pp. 19–27. Newbury House, Rowley, Mass.

Frenkel-Brunswik, E 1949 Intolerance of ambiguity as an emotional and perceptual personality variable. *Journal of Personality* 18: 108–43

Fries, C 1945 *Teaching and learning English as a foreign language*. University of Michigan Press, Ann Arbor

Fujimoto, D, Lubin, J, Sasaki, Y and Long, M 1986 The effect of linguistic and conversational adjustments on the comprehensibility of spoken second language discourse. Unpublished manuscript, Department of ESL, University of Hawaii at Manoa, Honolulu

Fuller, J 1978 Natural and monitored sequences by adult learners of English as a second language. Unpublished Ph.D. dissertation, Florida State University

Fuller, J and Gundel, J 1987 Topic-prominence in interlanguage. *Language Learning* 37: 1–18

Gage, W 1961 *Contrastive studies in linguistics: a bibliographic checklist*. Center for Applied Linguistics, Washington, D.C.

Gagne, R 1965 *The conditions of learning*. Holt, Rinehart and Winston, New York

Gaies, S 1977 The nature of linguistic input in formal second language learning. In Brown, H, Yorio, C and Crymes, R (eds.) *On TESOL '77*, pp. 204–12. TESOL, Washington, D.C.

Gaies, S 1981 Experimental vs. non-experimental research on classroom second language learning. *Bilingual Education Paper Series* 5, 4. Evaluation, Dissemination and Assessment Center, California State University, Los Angeles

Gaies, S 1983 The investigation of language classroom processes. *TESOL Quarterly* 17: 205–17

Gallimore, R and Tharp, R 1981 The interpretation of elicited sentence imitation in a standardized context. *Language Learning* 31: 369–92

Galloway, L 1981a Contributions of the right cerebral hemisphere to language and communication: issues in cerebral dominance with special emphasis on bilingualism, second language acquisition, sex differences and certain ethnic groups. Ph.D. dissertation, Department of Linguistics, University of California at Los Angeles

Galloway, L 1981b The convolutions of second language: a theoretical article with a critical review and some new hypotheses towards a neuropsychological model of bilingualism and second language performance. *Language Learning* 31: 439–64

Galloway, L and Scarcella, R 1979 Cerebral organization in adult second language acquisition. Paper presented at the Winter Meeting of the Linguistics Society of America, Los Angeles

Gardner, R 1960 Motivational variables in second language acquisition. Unpublished doctoral dissertation, McGill University

Gardner, R 1979 Social psychological aspects of second language acquisition. In Giles, H and St Clair, R (eds.) *Language and Social Psychology*, pp. 193–220. Basil Blackwell

Gardner, R 1980 On the validity of affective variables in second language acquisition: conceptual, contextual and statistical considerations. *Language Learning* 30: 255–70

Gardner, R 1985 *Social psychology and second language learning: the role of attitudes and motivation*. Edward Arnold

Gardner, R 1988 The socio-educational model of second-language learning: assumptions, findings, and issues. *Language Learning* 38: 101–26

Gardner, R, Ginsberg, R and Smythe, P 1976 Attitudes and motivation in second language learning: course related changes. *The Canadian Modern Language Review* 32: 243–66

Gardner, R and Gliksman, L 1982 On 'Gardner on affect': a discussion of validity as it relates to the attitude/motivation test battery: a response from Gardner. *Language Learning* 32: 191–200

Gardner, R and Lambert, W 1959 Motivational variables in second language acquisition. *Canadian Journal of Psychology* 13: 266–72

Gardner, R and Lambert, W 1972 *Attitudes and motivation in second-language learning.* Newbury House, Rowley, Mass.

Gardner, R, Smythe, P and Brunet, G 1977 Intensive second language study: effects on attitudes, motivation and French achievement. *Language Learning* 27: 243–62

Garfinkel, H 1967 *Studies in ethnomethodology.* Prentice-Hall, Englewood Cliffs, N.J.

Gaskill, W 1980 Correction in native speaker–nonnative speaker conversation. In Larsen-Freeman, D (ed.) *Discourse analysis in second language research,* pp. 125–37. Newbury House, Rowley, Mass.

Gass, S 1979 Language transfer and universal grammatical relations. *Language Learning* 29: 327–44

Gass, S 1982 From theory to practice. In Hines, M and Rutherford, W (eds.) *On TESOL '81,* pp. 129–39. TESOL, Washington, D.C.

Gass, S 1983 The development of L1 intuitions. *TESOL Quarterly* 17: 273–91

Gass, S 1984 A review of interlanguage syntax: language transfer and language universals. *Language Learning* 34: 115–32

Gass, S and Ard, J 1984 Second language acquisition and the ontogeny of language universals. In Rutherford, W (ed.) *Language universals and second language acquisition,* pp. 33–68. John Benjamins, Amsterdam

Gass, S and Madden, C (eds.) 1985 *Input in second language acquisition.* Newbury House, Rowley, Mass.

Gass, S and Schachter, J (eds.) 1989 *Linguistic perspectives on second language acquisition.* Cambridge University Press, New York

Gass, S and Selinker, L (eds.) 1983 *Language transfer in language learning.* Newbury House, Rowley, Mass.

Gass, S and Varonis, E 1986 Sex differences in NNS/NNS interactions. In Day, R (ed.) *Talking to learn: conversation in second language acquisition,* pp. 327–51. Newbury House, Rowley, Mass.

Gasser, M (1990) Connectionism and universals in second language acquisition. *Studies in Second Language Acquisition* 12 (2): 179–99

Gatbonton, E 1978 Patterned phonetic variability in second language speech: a gradual diffusion model. *Canadian Modern Language Review* 34: 335–47

Gattegno, C 1976 *The common sense of teaching foreign languages.* Educational Solutions, New York

Gattegno, C 1985 The learning and teaching of foreign languages. Chapter 13 from an unpublished book, *The science of education.* Educational Solutions, New York

Genesee, F 1976 The role of intelligence in second language learning. *Language Learning* 26: 267–80

Genesee, F 1982 Experimental neuropsychological research on second language processing. *TESOL Quarterly* 16: 315–22

Genesee, F 1983 Bilingual education of majority-language children: the immersion experiments in review. *Applied Psycholinguistics* 4 (1): 1–46

Genesee, F 1987 *Learning through two languages*. Newbury House, Rowley, Mass.

Genesee, F 1988 Neuropsychology and second language acquisition. In Beebe, L (ed.) *Issues in second language acquisition: multiple perspectives*, pp. 81–112. Newbury House, Cambridge, Mass.

Genesee, F and Hamayan, E 1980 Individual differences in second language learning. *Applied Psycholinguistics* 1: 95–110

Genesee, F, Rogers, P and Holobow, N 1983 The social psychology of second language learning: another point of view. *Language Learning* 33: 209–24

George, H 1972 *Common errors in language learning*. Newbury House, Rowley, Mass.

Gerbault, J 1978 The acquisition of English by a five-year-old French speaker. Unpublished MA TESL thesis, University of California at Los Angeles

Gibbons, J 1985 The silent period: an examination. *Language Learning* 35 (2): 255–67

Gilbert, G and Orlovic, M 1975 Pidgin German spoken by foreign workers in West Germany: the definite article. Paper presented at the International Congress on Pidgins and Creoles, University of Hawaii at Manoa, Honolulu

Giles, H (ed.) 1977 *Language, ethnicity and intergroup relations*. Academic Press, New York

Giles, H, Bourhis, R and Taylor, D 1977 Towards a theory of language in ethnic group relations. In Giles, H (ed.) *Language, ethnicity and intergroup relations*. Academic Press, New York

Giles, H and Smith, P 1979 Accommodation theory: optimal levels of convergence. In Giles, H and St Clair, R (eds.) *Language and social psychology*, pp. 45–65. Basil Blackwell

Giles, H and St Clair, R (eds.) 1979 *Language and social psychology*. Basil Blackwell

Gillis, M and Weber, R 1976 The emergence of sentence modalities in the English of Japanese-speaking children. *Language Learning* 26: 77–94

Gingras, R (ed.) 1978 *Second language acquisition and foreign language teaching*. Center for Applied Linguistics, Arlington, Va.

Givon, T 1979a *On understanding grammar*. Academic Press, New York

Givon, T 1979b From discourse to syntax: grammar as a processing strategy. In Givon, T (ed.) *Syntax and semantics*, Vol. 12: *Discourse and syntax*. Academic Press, New York

Givon, T 1981 Typology and functional domains. *Studies in Language* 5: 163–93

Givon, T 1983a Topic continuity in discourse: an introduction. In Givon, T (ed.) *Topic continuity in discourse: a quantitative cross-language study*, pp. 1–42. John Benjamins, Amsterdam

Givon, T (ed.) 1983b *Topic continuity in discourse: a quantitative cross-language study*. John Benjamins, Amsterdam

Givon, T 1984 Universals of discourse structure and second language acquisition. In Rutherford, W (ed.) *Language universals and second language acquisition*, pp. 109–36. John Benjamins, Amsterdam

Givon, T 1985 Function, structure and language acquisition. In Slobin, D (ed.) *The cross-linguistic study of language acquisition*, pp. 1005–28. Lawrence Erlbaum, Hillsdale, N.J.

Glahn, E 1980 Introspection as a method of elicitation in interlanguage studies. *Interlanguage Studies Bulletin* 5: 119–28

Gleitman, L, Newport, E and Gleitman, H 1984 The current status of the motherese hypothesis. *Journal of Child Language* 11: 43–79

Godfrey, D 1980 A discourse analysis of tense in adult ESL monologues. In Larsen-Freeman, D (ed.) *Discourse analysis in second language research.* Newbury House, Rowley, Mass.

Goldstein, L 1987 Standard English: the only target for nonnative speakers of English? *TESOL Quarterly* 21: 417–36

Goodman, M 1967 The development of a dialect of English-Japanese Pidgin. *Anthropological Linguistics* 9: 43–55

Gould, S 1981 *The mismeasure of man.* W W Norton, New York

Gradman, H 1971 The limitations of contrastive analysis predictions. *PCCLLU Papers*: 11–16. University of Hawaii

Granfors, T and Palmberg, R 1976 Errors made by Finns and Swedish-speaking Finns learning English at a commercial college level. In Ringbom, H and Palmberg, R (eds.) *Errors made by Finns and Swedish-speaking Finns in the learning of English.* AFTIL, Vol. 5. Abo Akademi, Abo

Grasha, A 1972 Observations on relating teaching goals to student response styles and classroom methods. *American Psychologist* 27: 144–7

Greenwald, A, Pratkanis, A, Leippe, M and Baumgardner, M 1986 Under what conditions does theory obstruct research progress? *Psychological Review* 93 (2): 216–29

Gregg, K 1984 Krashen's Monitor and Occam's razor. *Applied Linguistics* 5: 79–100

Gregg, K 1988 Epistemology without knowledge: Schwartz on Chomsky, Fodor and Krashen. *Second Language Research* 4 (1): 66–80

Gregg, K 1989 Linguistic perspectives on second language acquisition: what could they be, and where can we get some? In Gass, S and Schachter, J (eds.) *Adult second language acquisition: linguistic perspectives.* Cambridge University Press, New York

Gregg, K (in press) Krashen's theory, acquisition theory, and theory. In Barasch, R (ed.) *Responses to Krashen.* Newbury House, Cambridge, Mass.

Grotjahn, R 1983 On the use of quantitative methods in the study of interlanguage. *Applied Linguistics* 4: 235–41

Guiora, A 1972 Construct validity and transpositional research: toward an empirical study of psychoanalytic concepts. *Comprehensive Psychiatry* 13: 139–50

Guiora, A 1983 The dialect of language acquisition. *Language Learning* Special Issue, 33: 2–12

Guiora, A, Acton, W, Erard, R and Strickland, F 1980 The effects of benzodiazepine (valium) on permeability of language ego boundaries. *Language Learning* 30: 351–63

Guiora, A, Beit-Hallahmi, B, Brannon, R, Dull, C and Scovel, T 1972 The effects of experimentally induced changes in ego states on pronunciation ability in a second language: an exploratory study. *Comprehensive Psychiatry* 13: 421–8

Guiora, A, Beit-Hallahmi, B, Fried, R and Yoder, C 1982 Language environment and gender identity attainment. *Language Learning* 32: 289–304

Guiora, A, Brannon, R and Dull, C 1972 Empathy and second language learning. *Language Learning* 22: 111–30

Guiora, A, Lane, H and Bosworth, L 1967 An exploration of some personality variables in authentic pronunciation of a second language. In Lane, H and Zale, E (eds.) *Studies in language and language behavior* 4: 261–6

Gundel, J and Tarone, E 1983 Language transfer and the acquisition of pronominal anaphora. In Gass, S and Selinker, L (eds.) *Language transfer in language learning*, pp. 281–96. Newbury House, Rowley, Mass.

Haegerman, L 1985 Scope phenomena in English and Dutch and L2 acquisition: a case study. *Second Language Research* 1 (2): 118–40

Hakuta, K 1974 A preliminary report on the development of grammatical morphemes in a Japanese girl learning English as a second language. *Working Papers on Bilingualism* 3: 18–43

Hakuta, K 1975 Becoming bilingual at age five: the story of Uguisu. Unpublished BA thesis, Harvard College

Hakuta, K 1976 A case study of a Japanese child learning English as a second language. *Language Learning* 26 (2): 321–51

Hakuta, K 1978 A report on the development of grammatical morphemes in a Japanese girl learning English as a second language. In Hatch, E (ed.) *Second language acquisition: a book of readings*, pp. 132–47. Newbury House, Rowley, Mass.

Hakuta, K and Cancino, E 1977 Trends in second language acquisition research. *Harvard Educational Review* 47: 294–316

Hale, T and Budar, E 1970 Are TESOL classes the only answer? *Modern Language Journal* 54: 487–92

Hall, R 1966 *Pidgin and creole languages*. Cornell University Press, Ithaca, New York

Hamayan, E, Genesee, F and Tucker, G 1977 Affective factors and language. *Language Learning* 27: 225–41

Hammer, J (in consultation with Rice, F) 1965 *A bibiliography of contrastive linguistics*. Center for Applied Linguistics, Washington, D.C.

Hammerly, H 1982 Contrastive phonology and error analysis. *International Review of Applied Linguistics* 20: 17–32

Hanania, E and Gradman, H 1977 Acquisition of English structures: a case study of an adult native speaker of Arabic in an English-speaking environment. *Language Learning* 27: 75–91

Handscombe, J, Orem, R and Taylor, B (eds.) 1983 *On TESOL '83*. TESOL, Washington, D.C.

Hansen, J and Stansfield, C 1981 The relationship of field dependent–independent cognitive styles to foreign language achievement. *Language Learning* 31: 349–67

Hansen, L 1984 Field dependence–independence and language testing: evidence from six Pacific island cultures. *TESOL Quarterly* 18: 311–24

Harkness, S 1977 Aspects of social environment and first language acquisition in rural Africa. In Snow, C and Ferguson, C (eds.) *Talking to children: language input and acquisition*, pp. 309–16. Cambridge University Press

Harley, B 1980 Interlanguage units and their relations. *Interlanguage Studies Bulletin* 5: 3–30

Harley, B 1986 *Age in second language acquisition*. Multilingual Matters

Harley, B and Swain, M 1978 An analysis of the verb system by young learners of French. *Interlanguage Studies Bulletin* 3 (1): 35–79

Harley, B, Allen, P, Cummins, J and Swain, M 1987 *The development of bilingual proficiency: final report*, Vol. II: *Classroom treatment*. The Ontario Institute for Studies in Education, Toronto

Harre, R 1987 *Varieties of realism*. Basil Blackwell, New York

Harrington, M 1986 The T-unit as a measure of JSL oral proficiency. *Descriptive and Applied Linguistics* 19: 49–56. International Christian University, Tokyo

Harrington, M 1987 Processing strategy transfer and interlanguage variation. *UHWPESL* 6 (1). Also in *Applied Psycholinguistics*, 1988

Hartford, B 1981 Review of J H Schumann, *The pidginization process*. *Studies in Second Language Acquisition* 3 (2)

Hartnett, D 1975 The relation of cognitive style and hemisphere preference to deductive and inductive second language learning. Unpublished MA thesis, University of California at Los Angeles

Hartnett, D 1985 Cognitive style and second language learning. In Celce-Murcia, M (ed.) *Beyond basics: issues and research in TESOL*, pp. 16–33. Newbury House, Rowley, Mass.

Hatch, E 1974 Second language learning – universals? *Working Papers on Bilingualism* 3: 1–17

Hatch, E 1976 Optimal age or optimal learners? *Workpapers in TESL* 11: 45–56

Hatch, E 1978a Discourse analysis and second language acquisition. In Hatch, E (ed.) *Second language acquisition: a book of readings*, pp. 402–35. Newbury House, Rowley, Mass.

Hatch, E 1978b Discourse analysis, speech acts and second language acquisition. In Ritchie, W (ed.) *Second language acquisition research*, pp. 137–55. Academic Press, New York

Hatch, E (ed.) 1978c *Second language acquisition: a book of readings*. Newbury House, Rowley, Mass.

Hatch, E 1979 Apply with caution. *Studies in Second Language Acquisition* 2 (1): 123–43

Hatch, E 1983 *Psycholinguistics: a second language perspective*. Newbury House, Rowley, Mass.

Hatch, E 1984 Theoretical review of discourse and interlanguage. In Davies, A, Criper, C and Howatt, A (eds.) *Interlanguage*, pp. 190–203. Edinburgh University Press

Hatch, E and Farhady, H 1982 *Research design and statistics for applied linguistics*. Newbury House, Rowley, Mass.

Hatch, E, Flashner, V and Hunt, L 1986 The experience model and language teaching. In Day, R (ed.) *'Talking to learn': conversation in second language acquisition*, pp. 5–22. Newbury House, Rowley, Mass.

Hatch, E, Peck, S and Wagner-Gough, J 1979 A look at process in child second language acquisition. In Ochs, E and Schieffelin, B (eds.) *Developmental pragmatics*. Academic Press, New York

Hatch, E, Shapira, R, and Wagner-Gough, J 1978 Foreigner talk discourse. *ITL Review of Applied Linguistics* 39/40: 39–60

Hatch, E and Wagner-Gough, J 1976 Explaining sequence and variation in second language acquisition. *Language Learning*, Special Issue No. 4: 39–57

Hawkins, B 1985 Is an 'appropriate response' always so appropriate? In Gass, S and Madden, C (eds.) *Input in second language acquisition.* Newbury House, Rowley, Mass.

Heidelberger Forschungsprojekt 1978 The acquisition of German syntax by foreign migrant workers. In Sankoff, D (ed.) *Linguistic variation: model and methods,* pp. 1–22. Academic Press, New York

Heim, A 1970 *Intelligence and personality: their assessment and relationship.* Penguin

Henkes, T 1974 Early stages in the non-native acquisition of English syntax: a study of three children from Zaire, Venezuela and Saudi Arabia. Unpublished Ph.D. dissertation, Indiana University

Henning, C (ed.) 1977 *Proceedings of the first Los Angeles Second Language Research Forum.* University of California at Los Angeles

Henning, G 1983 Interest factors in second language acquisition. In Campbell, C, Flashner, V, Hudson, T and Lubin, J (eds.) *Proceedings of the Los Angeles Second Language Research Forum,* Vol II. University of California at Los Angeles

Henning, G 1986 Quantitative methods in language acquisition research. *TESOL Quarterly* **20**: 701–8

Henrichsen, L 1984 Sandhi-variation: a filter of input for learners of ESL. *Language Learning* **34**: 103–26

Henzl, V 1973 Linguistic register of foreign language instruction. *Language Learning* **23** (2): 207–27

Henzl, V 1975 Speech of foreign language teachers: a sociolinguistic register analysis. Paper presented at the 4th International AILA Congress, Stuttgart

Henzl, V 1979 Foreign (sic) talk in the classroom. *International Review of Applied Linguistics* **17**: 159–67

Hermann, G 1980 Attitudes and success in children's learning of English as a second language: the motivational versus the resultative hypothesis. *English Language Teaching Journal* **34**: 247–54

Hernandez-Chavez, E 1977 The acquisition of grammatical structures by a Mexican-American child learning English. Unpublished Ph.D. dissertation, University of California, Berkeley

Heyde, A 1979 The relationship between self-esteem and the oral production of a second language. Unpublished Ph.D. dissertation, University of Michigan, Ann Arbor

Higgs, T and Clifford, R 1982 The push toward communication. In Higgs, T (ed.) *Curriculum, competence, and the foreign language teacher,* pp. 57–79. National Textbook Co., Skokie, Ill.

Hildebrand, J 1987 The acquisition of preposition stranding. *Canadian Journal of Linguistics* **32** (1)

Hill, J 1970 Foreign accents, language acquisition and cerebral dominance revisited. *Language Learning* **20**: 237–48

Hill, J 1971 Personalized education programs utilizing cognitive style mapping. Oakland Community College, Bloomfield Hills, Mich.

Hilles, S 1986 Interlanguage and the pro-drop parameter. *Second Language Research* **2** (1): 33–52

Hinde, R 1974 *Biological bases of human social behavior.* McGraw-Hill, New York

Hines, M and Rutherford, W (eds.) 1982 *On TESOL '81*. TESOL, Washington, D.C.

Hinnenkamp, V 1982 *Foreigner talk und Tarzanisch*. H Buske, Hamburg

Hinofotis, F, Schumann, J, McGroarty, M, Erickson, M, Hudson, T, Kimbell, L and Scott, M 1982 Relating FSI oral interview scores to grammatical analyses of the learner's speech. Unpublished manuscript, University of California at Los Angeles

Hirsh-Pasek, K, Treiman, R and Schneiderman, M 1984 Brown and Hanlon revisited: mothers' sensitivity to ungrammatical forms. *Journal of Child Language* 11: 81–8

Hoff-Ginsberg, E and Shatz, M 1982 Linguistic input and the child's acquisition of language: a critical review. *Psychological Bulletin* 92: 3–26

Hornstein, N and Lightfoot, D (eds.) 1981 *Explanations in linguistics: the logical problem of language acquisition*. Longman

Houck, N, Robertson, J and Krashen, S 1978 On the domain of the conscious grammar: morpheme orders for corrected and uncorrected ESL student transcriptions. *TESOL Quarterly* 12: 335–9

Houng, C and Bley-Vroman, R 1988 Why do Chinese use few relative clauses in English? Unpublished manuscript, University of Hawaii at Manoa, Honolulu

Huang, J 1970 A Chinese child's acquisition of English syntax. Unpublished MA TESL thesis, University of California at Los Angeles

Huebner, T 1980 Creative construction and the case of the misguided pattern. In Fisher, J, Clarke, M and Schachter, J (eds.) *On TESOL '80*, pp. 101–10. TESOL, Washington, D.C.

Huebner, T 1983a *A longitudinal analysis of the acquisition of English*. Karoma, Ann Arbor

Huebner, T 1983b Linguistic system and linguistic change in an interlanguage. *Studies in Second Language Acquisition* 6: 33–53

Huebner, T 1985 System and variability in interlanguage syntax. *Language Learning* 35 (2): 141–63

Hulstijn, J (in press) Implicit and incidental second language learning: experiments in the processing of natural and partly artificial input. In Dechert, H (ed.) *Interlingual processing*. Gunter Narr, Tubingen

Hulstijn, J and Hulstijn, W 1984 Grammatical errors as a function of processing constraints and explicit knowledge. *Language Learning* 34: 23–43

Hunt, K 1965 *Grammatical structures written at three grade levels*. NCTE Research Report No. 3. National Council of Teachers of English, Champaign, Ill.

Hyams, N 1983 The pro-drop parameter in child grammars. In Barlow, M, Flickinger, D and Westcoat, M (eds.) *Proceedings of the West Coast Conference on Formal Linguistics*. Department of Linguistics, Stanford University

Hyltenstam, K 1977 Implicational patterns in interlanguage syntax variation. *Language Learning* 27 (2): 383–411

Hyltenstam, K 1983 Data types and second language variability. In Ringbom, H (ed.) *Psycholinguistics and foreign language learning*, pp. 57–74. Abo Akademi, Abo

Hyltenstam, K 1984 The use of typological markedness conditions as predictors in second language acquisition: the case of pronominal copies in relative clauses. In Andersen, R (ed.) *Second language: a crosslinguistic perspective*, pp. 39–58. Newbury House, Rowley, Mass.

Hyltenstam, K 1987 Markedness, language universals, language typology, and second language acquisition. In Pfaff, C (ed.) *First and second language acquisition processes*, pp. 55–78. Newbury House, Cambridge, Mass.

Hyltenstam, K and Pienemann, M (eds.) 1985 *Modelling and assessing second language development.* Multilingual Matters

Hymes, D (ed.) 1971 *Pidginization and creolization of languages.* Cambridge University Press

Ioup, G 1977 Interference versus structural complexity as a predictor of second language relative clause acquisition. In Henning, C (ed.) *Proceedings of the Los Angeles Second Language Research Forum.* University of California at Los Angeles

Ioup, G 1984a Is there a structural foreign accent? A comparison of syntactic and phonological errors in second language acquisition. *Language Learning* 34 (2): 1–17

Ioup, G 1984b Testing the relationship of formal instruction to the Input Hypothesis. *TESOL Quarterly* 18: 345–50

Ioup, G and Weinberger, S (eds.) 1987 *Interlanguage phonology: the acquisition of a second language sound system.* Newbury House, New York

Isaac, S and Michael, B 1971 *Handbook in research and evaluation.* EDITS Publishers, San Diego

Jackson, P and Costa, C 1974 The inequality of educational opportunity in the Southwest: an observational study of ethnically mixed classrooms. *American Educational Research Journal* 11: 219–29

Jacobs, B 1988a Establishing a neurobiological perspective of primary and secondary language acquisition. Paper presented at the 7th Second Language Research Forum, University of Southern California, Los Angeles, February 20–22

Jacobs, B 1988b Neurobiological differentiation of primary and secondary language acquisition. *Studies in Second Language Acquisition* 10 (3): 303–37

Jaeggli, O 1982 *Topics in romance syntax.* Foris, Dordrecht

Jakobovits, L 1970 *Foreign language learning: a psycholinguistic analysis of the issues.* Newbury House, Rowley, Mass.

James, C 1974 Linguistic measures for error gravity. *AILA Journal* 12: 3–9

James, C 1980 *Contrastive analysis.* Longman

Janda, R 1985 Note-taking as a simplified register. *Discourse Processes* 8: 437–54

Jansen, B, Lalleman, J and Muysken, P 1981 The alternation hypothesis: acquisition of Dutch word order by Turkish and Moroccan foreign workers. *Language Learning* 31: 315–36

Jansen, L 1987 The development of word order in formal German second language acquisition. Paper presented at the workshop on Explaining Interlanguage Development, LaTrobe University, Melbourne, August

Johnson, D 1981 Effects on reading comprehension of language complexity and cultural background. *TESOL Quarterly* 15: 169–81

Johnson, D 1983 Natural language by design: a classroom experiment in social interaction and second language acquisition. *TESOL Quarterly* 17: 55–68

Johnson, J and Newport E 1989 Critical period effects in second language learning: the influence of maturational state on the acquisition of ESL. *Cognitive Psychology* 21: 60–99

Johnston, M 1985 *Syntactic and morphological progressions in learner English.* Research report, Department of Immigration and Ethnic Affairs, Commonwealth of Australia

Jordens, P 1977 Roles, grammatical intuitions and strategies in foreign language learning. *Interlanguage Studies Bulletin* 2: 5–76

Jordens, P 1978 Sprachspezifisch oder sprachneutral?: zur Anwendung einer Strategie im Fremdsprachenerwerb. *Deutsch als Fremdsprachenwerb.* Gunter Narr, Tubingen

Jordens, P 1983 Discourse functions in interlanguage morphology. In Gass, S and Selinker, L (eds.) *Language transfer in language learning*, pp. 327–57. Newbury House, Rowley, Mass.

Jordens, P 1986 The cognitive function of case marking in German as a native and a foreign language. In Kellerman, E and Sharwood-Smith, M (eds.) *Cross-linguistic influence in second language acquisition*, pp. 91–109. Pergamon Press

Jordens, P 1988 The acquisition of word order in L2 Dutch and German. In Jordens, P and Lalleman, J (eds.) *Language development*, pp. 149–80. Foris, Dordrecht

Kachru, B (ed.) 1982 *The other tongue: English across cultures.* University of Illinois Press, Urbana, Ill.

Kagan, J, Rosman, B, Day, D, Albert, J and Phillips, W 1964 Information processing in the child: significance of analytic and reflective attitudes. *Psychological Monographs* 78: whole issue

Kaplan, R and Bresnan, J 1978 Lexical-functional grammar: a formal system for grammatical representation. Reprinted in Bresnan, J (ed.) 1982 *The mental representation of grammatical relations*, pp. 173–281. MIT Press, Cambridge, Mass.

Karmiloff-Smith, A 1979 *A functional approach to child language: a study of determiner and reference.* Cambridge University Press

Karmiloff-Smith, A 1986 Some fundamental aspects of language development after age 5. In Fletcher, P and Garman, M (eds.) *Language acquisition.* Cambridge University Press

Kasper, G 1982 Teaching-induced aspects of interlanguage discourse. *Studies in Second Language Acquisition* 4: 99–113

Kasper, G 1984 Pragmatic comprehension in learner–native speaker discourse. *Language Learning* 34: 1–20

Katz, J 1977 Foreigner talk input in child second language acquisition: its form and function over time. In Henning, C (ed.) *Proceedings of the first Second Language Research Forum.* University of California at Los Angeles

Kean, M 1986 Core issues in transfer. In Kellerman, E and Sharwood-Smith, M (eds.) *Cross-linguistic influence in second language acquisition*, pp. 80–90. Pergamon Press

Keenan, E 1974 Conversational competence in children. *Journal of Child Language* 1: 163–83

Keenan, E and Comrie, B 1977 Noun phrase accessibility and universal grammar. *Linguistic Inquiry* 8: 63–99

Kelch, K 1985 Modified input as an aid to comprehension. *Studies in Second Language Acquisition* 7 (1): 81–90

Keller-Cohen, D 1979 Systematicity and variation in the non-native child's acquisition of conversational skills. *Language Learning* 29 (1): 27–44

Kellerman, E 1974 Elicitation, lateralisation and error analysis. *York Papers in Linguistics* 4. Reprinted in Interlanguage Studies Bulletin 1: 79–114, 1976

Kellerman, E 1977 Towards a characterization of the strategies of transfer in second language learning. *Interlanguage Studies Bulletin* 2: 58–145

Kellerman, E 1978 Giving learners a break: native language intuitions as a source of predictions about transferability. *Working Papers on Bilingualism* 15: 59–92

Kellerman, E 1979a Transfer and non-transfer: where are we now? *Studies in Second Language Acquisition* 2 (1): 37–57

Kellerman, E 1979b The problem with difficulty. *Interlanguage Studies Bulletin* 4: 27–48

Kellerman, E 1984 The empirical evidence for the influence of the L1 in interlanguage. In Davies, A, Criper, C and Howatt, A (eds.) *Interlanguage*, pp. 98–122 Edinburgh University Press

Kellerman, E 1985. If at first you do succeed... In Gass, S and Madden, C (eds.) *Input in second language acquisition*. Newbury House, Rowley, Mass.

Kellerman, E and Sharwood Smith, M (eds.) 1986 *Cross-linguistic influence in second language acquisition*. Pergamon Press

Kelley, P 1982 Interlanguage variation and social/psychological influences within a developmental stage. MA in TESL thesis, University of California at Los Angeles

Kelley, P 1983 The question of uniformity in interlanguage development. In Bailey, K M, Long, M and Peck, S (eds.) *Second language acquisition studies*, pp. 83–92. Newbury House, Rowley, Mass.

Khan, S 1969 Affective correlates of academic achievement. *Journal of Educational Psychology* 60: 216–22

Kitch, K 1982 Social distance of a Mexican-American's interlanguage and his socio-psychological profile. MA thesis, San Diego State University

Klein, W 1981 Some rules of regular ellipsis in German. In Klein, W and Levelt, W (eds.) *Crossing the boundaries in linguistics: studies presented to Manfred Bierswisch*, pp. 51–78. Reidel, Dordrecht

Klein, W and Dittmar, N 1979 *Developing grammars*. Springer, Berlin

Kleinmann, H 1977 Avoidance behavior in adult second language acquisition. *Language Learning* 27: 93–107

Knotts, B 1983 Aural and visual language learning styles. In Campbell, C, Flashner, V, Hudson, T and Lubin, J (eds.) *Proceedings of the Los Angeles Second Language Research Forum*, Vol. II. Department of English, University of California at Los Angeles

Kogan, N and Wallach, M 1967 Risk taking as a function of the situation, the person and the group. *New Directions in Psychology* III. Holt, Rinehart and Winston, New York

Kohn, K 1986 The analysis of transfer. In Kellerman, E and Sharwood-Smith, M (eds.) *Cross-linguistic influence in second language acquisition*, pp. 21–34. Pergamon Press

Kolb, D 1976 *The learning style inventory*. McBer, Boston

Koutsoudas, A and Koutsoudas, O 1962 A contrastive analysis of the segmental phonemes of Greek and English. *Language Learning* **12**: 211–30

Krashen, S 1973 Lateralization, language learning and the critical period: some new evidence. *Language Learning* **23**: 63–74

Krashen, S 1975 Language learning and language acquisition. Unpublished manuscript, Queens College, New York

Krashen, S 1976 Formal and informal linguistic environments in language acquisition and language learning. *TESOL Quarterly* **10**: 157–68

Krashen, S 1977 Some issues relating to the Monitor Model. In Brown, H, Yorio, C, and Crymes, R (eds.) *On TESOL '77*, pp. 144–58. TESOL, Washington, D.C.

Krashen, S 1978 Individual variation in the use of the monitor. In Ritchie, W (ed.) *Second language acquisition research*, pp. 175–83. Academic Press, New York

Krashen, S 1979 A response to McLaughlin, 'The Monitor model: some methodological considerations'. *Language Learning* **29**: 151–67

Krashen, S 1980 The input hypothesis. In Alatis, J (ed.) *Current issues in bilingual education*, pp. 168–80. Georgetown University Press, Washington, D.C.

Krashen, S 1981a *Second language acquisition and second language learning.* Pergamon

Krashen, S 1981b The 'fundamental pedagogical principle' in second language teaching. *Studia Linguistica* **35** (1–2): 50–70

Krashen, S 1982a *Principles and practice in second language acquisition.* Pergamon

Krashen, S 1982b Accounting for child–adult differences in second language rate and attainment. In Krashen, S, Scarcella, R and Long, M (eds.) *Child–adult differences in second language acquisition*, pp. 202–26. Newbury House, Rowley, Mass.

Krashen, S 1983 Newmark's ignorance hypothesis and current second language acquisition theory. In Gass, S and Selinker, L (eds.) *Language transfer in language learning*, pp. 135–53. Newbury House, Rowley, Mass.

Krashen, S 1984 Response to Ioup. . . *TESOL Quarterly* **18** (2): 350–2

Krashen, S 1985 *The Input Hypothesis: issues and implications.* Longman, New York

Krashen, S, Butler, J, Birnbaum, R and Robertson, J 1978 Two studies in language acquisition and language learning. *ITL: Review of Applied Linguistics* **39-40**: 73–92

Krashen, S and Galloway, L 1978 The neurological correlates of language acquisition. *SPEAQ Journal* **2**: 21–35

Krashen, S, Jones, C, Zelinski, S and Usprich, C 1978 How important is instruction? *English Language Teaching Journal* **32** (4): 257–61

Krashen, S, Houck, N, Giunchi, P, Birnbaum, R, Butler, J and Strei, G 1977 Difficulty order for grammatical morphemes for adult second language performers using free speech. *TESOL Quarterly* **11**: 338–41

Krashen, S, Long, M and Scarcella, R 1979 Age, rate, and eventual attainment in second language acquisition. *TESOL Quarterly* **13**: 573–82

Krashen, S and Pon, P 1975 An error analysis of an advanced ESL learner. *Working Papers on Bilingualism* **7**: 125–9

Krashen, S and Scarcella, R 1978 On routines and patterns in language acquisition and performance. *Language Learning* **28**: 283–300

Krashen, S, Scarcella, R and Long, M (eds.) 1982 *Child–adult differences in second language acquisition*. Newbury House, Rowley, Mass.

Krashen, S and Seliger, H 1975 The essential contributions of formal instruction in adult second language learning. *TESOL Quarterly* 9: 173–83

Krashen, S and Seliger, H 1976 The role of formal and informal linguistic environments in adult second language learning. *International Journal of Psycholinguistics* 3: 15–21

Krashen, S, Seliger, H and Hartnett, D 1974 Two studies in second language learning. *Kritikon Litterarum* 3: 220–8

Krashen S, Sferlazza, V, Feldman, L and Fathman, A 1976 Adult performance on the SLOPE test: more evidence for a natural sequence in adult second language acquisition. *Language Learning* 26 (1): 145–51

Krashen, S and Terrell, T 1983 *The natural approach*. Pergamon, New York

Kubota, R 1987 Analysis of the learning problems experienced by Japanese LEP students and suggestions for global bilingual assessment. MAT Thesis, School for International Training

Kufner, H 1962 *The grammatical structures of English and German*. University of Chicago Press

Kumpf, L 1983 A case study of temporal reference in interlanguage. In Campbell, C, Flashner, V, Hudson, T and Lubin, J (eds.) *Proceedings of the Los Angeles Second Language Research Forum*, Vol. II, pp. 179–92. Department of English, University of California at Los Angeles

Kumpf, L 1984 Temporal systems and universality in interlanguage: a case study. In Eckman, F, Bell, L and Nelson, D (eds.) *Universals of second language acquisition*, pp. 132–43. Newbury House, Rowley, Mass.

Labov, W 1969 Contraction, deletion and inherent variability of the English copula. *Language* 45: 715–62

Labov, W 1970 The study of language in its social context. *Studium Generale* 23: 30–87

Lachter, J and Bever, T 1988 The relationship between linguistic structure and associative theories of language learning: a constructive criticism of some connectionist learning models. *Cognition* 28 (1–2): 195–247

Lado, R 1957 *Linguistics across cultures*. University of Michigan Press, Ann Arbor

Lakoff, R 1973 Language and woman's place. *Language in Society* 2: 45–79

Lambert, R and Freed, B (eds.) 1982 *The loss of language skills*. Newbury House, Rowley, Mass.

Lambert, W 1967 The social psychology of bilingualism. *Journal of Social Issues* 23: 91–109

Lambert, W, Hodgson, R, Gardner R and Fillenbaum, S 1960 Evaluation reactions to spoken languages. *Journal of Abnormal and Social Psychology* 60: 44–5

Lambert, W and Tucker, G 1972 *Bilingual education of children: the St. Lambert experiment*. Newbury House, Rowley, Mass.

Lamendella, J 1977 General principles of neurofunctional organization and their manifestations in primary and non-primary language acquisition. *Language Learning* 27: 155–96

Lamotte, J, Pearson-Joseph, D and Zupko, K 1982 A cross-linguistic study of the relationship between negation stages and the acquisition of noun phrase morphology. Unpublished manuscript, University of Pennsylvania

Landes, J 1975 Speech addressed to children: issues and characteristics of parental input. *Language Learning* 25 (2): 355–79

Lantolf, J and Frawley, W 1983 Second language performance and Vygotskyan psycholinguistics: implications for L2 instruction. LACUS

Lantolf, J and Frawley, W 1984 On communication strategies: a functional perspective. Paper presented at the AILA Conference, Brussels

Lantolf, J and Frawley, W 1988 Proficiency: understanding the construct. *Studies in Second Language Acquisition* 10 (2): 181–95

Larsen-Freeman, D 1975a The acquisition of grammatical morphemes by adult learners of English as a second language. Unpublished Ph.D. dissertation, University of Michigan

Larsen-Freeman, D 1975b The acquisition of grammatical morphemes by adult ESL students. *TESOL Quarterly* 9: 409–30

Larsen-Freeman, D 1976a Evidence of the need for a second language acquisition index of development. In Ritchie, W (ed.) *Second language acquisition research: issues and implications*. Academic Press, New York

Larsen-Freeman, D 1976b Teacher speech as input to the ESL learner. *UCLA Workpapers in TESL* 10: 45–9

Larsen-Freeman, D 1976c An explanation for the morpheme acquisition order of second language learners. *Language Learning* 26 (1): 125–34

Larsen-Freeman, D 1978 An ESL index of development. *TESOL Quarterly* 12: 439–48

Larsen-Freeman, D (ed.) 1980a Editorial. *Language Learning* 30: i

Larsen-Freeman, D (ed.) 1980b *Discourse analysis in second language research*. Newbury House, Rowley, Mass.

Larsen-Freeman, D 1982 The 'what' of second language acquisition. In Hines, M and Rutherford, W (eds.) *On TESOL '81*, pp. 107–28. TESOL, Washington, D.C.

Larsen-Freeman, D 1983a Assessing global second language proficiency. In Seliger, H and Long, M (eds.) *Classroom-oriented research in second language acquisition*. Newbury House, Rowley, Mass.

Larsen-Freeman, D 1983b The importance of input in second language acquisition. In Andersen, R (ed.) *Pidginization and creolization as language acquisition*, pp. 87–93. Newbury House, Rowley, Mass.

Larsen-Freeman, D 1983c Second language acquisition: getting the whole picture. In Bailey, K M, Long, M and Peck, S (eds.) *Second language acquisition studies*, pp. 3–22. Newbury House, Rowley, Mass.

Larsen-Freeman, D (ed.) 1985a Editorial. *Language Learning* 35: i-ii

Larsen-Freeman, D 1985b Considerations in research design in second language acquisition. In Celce-Murcia, M (ed.) *Beyond basics: issues and research in TESOL*. Newbury House, Rowley, Mass.

Larsen-Freeman, D 1986 *Techniques and principles in language teaching*. Oxford University Press

Larsen-Freeman, D 1988 Research on language teaching methodologies: a review of the past and an agenda for the future. Paper presented at the European–American Conference on Empirical Research on Second Language Learning in Instructional Settings, Bellagio, Italy

Larsen-Freeman, D (in press) Teaching grammar. In Celce-Murcia, M (ed.)

Teaching English as a second or foreign language, 2nd edition. Newbury House/Harper and Row, New York

Larsen-Freeman, D and Long, M (To appear) *Foreign language education: towards a national research agenda.* National Foreign Language Center, Washington, D.C.

Larsen-Freeman, D and Strom, V 1977 The construction of a second language acquisition index of development. *Language Learning* 27: 123–34

Larson, P, Judd, E and Messerschmitt, D (eds.) 1984 *On TESOL '84.* TESOL, Washington, D.C.

Lehtonen, J and Sajavaara, K 1985 The silent Finn. In Tannen, D and Saville-Troike, M (eds.) *Perspectives on silence*, pp 193–201. Ablex, Norwood, N. J.

Leiter, K L 1980 *Primer on ethnomethodology.* Oxford University Press, New York

Le Mahieu, J 1984 The differential effect of attitudes and motivation on competence and control in second language acquisition. *Interlanguage Studies Bulletin* 8: 24–57

Lenneberg, E 1967 *Biological foundations of language.* John Wiley, New York

Leontiev, A 1981 *Psychology and the language learning process.* Pergamon

Lepke, H 1977 Discovering student learning styles through cognitive style mapping. In Schulz, R (ed.) *Personalizing foreign language instruction: learning styles and teacher options.* National Textbook Co., Skokie, Ill.

Levin, J, Divine-Hawkins, P, Kerst, S and Guttman, J 1974 Individual differences in learning from pictures and words: the development and application of an instrument. *Journal of Educational Psychology* 66

Levitt, E 1953 Studies in intolerance of ambiguity, I: the Decision Location Test with grade school children. *Child Development* 26: 263–8

Lewis, N and Rosenblum, L 1977 *Interaction, conversation, and the development of language.* Wiley, New York

Liceras, J 1985 The role of intake in the determination of learners' competence. In Gass, S and Madden, C (eds.) *Input in second language acquisition*, pp. 354–73. Newbury House, Rowley, Mass.

Liceras, J 1986 *Linguistic theory and second language acquisition.* Gunter Narr, Tubingen

Liceras, J (in press) L2 learnability: delimiting the domain of core grammar as distinct from the marked periphery. In Flynn, S and O'Neil, W (eds.) *Linguistic theory in second language acquisition.* Reidel, Dordrecht

Lightbown, P 1980 The acquisition and use of questions by French L2 learners. In Felix, S (ed.) *Second language development*, pp. 151–75. Gunter Narr, Tubingen

Lightbown, P 1983 Exploring relationships between developmental and instructional sequences in L2 acquisition. In Seliger, H and Long, M (eds.) *Classroom-oriented research in second language acquisition*, pp. 217–43. Newbury House, Rowley, Mass.

Lightbown, P 1985 Great expectations: second language acquisition research and classroom teaching. *Applied Linguistics* 6: 173–89

Lightbown, P and Barkman, B 1978 Interactions among ESL learners, teachers, texts, and methods. Report to the Department of the Secretary of State of Canada, ED 166 981

Lightbown, P and Spada, N 1978 Performance on an oral communication task by francophone ESL learners. *SPEAQ Journal* 2 (4): 34–54

Lightbown, P, Spada, N and Wallace, R 1980 Some effects of instruction on child and adolescent ESL learners. In Scarcella, R and Krashen, S (eds.) *Research in second language acquisition*, pp. 162–72. Newbury House, Rowley, Mass.

Lightbown, P and White, L 1987 The influence of linguistic theories on language acquisition research. *Language Learning* 37: 483–510

Lococo, V 1976 A comparison of three methods for the collection of L2 data: free composition, translation and picture description. *Working Papers on Bilingualism* 8: 59–86

Long, M 1977 Teacher feedback on learner error: mapping cognitions. In Brown, H, Yorio, C and Crymes, R (eds.) *On TESOL '77*, pp. 278–93. TESOL, Washington, D.C.

Long, M 1980a *Input, interaction and second language acquisition*. Unpublished Ph.D. dissertation, University of California at Los Angeles

Long, M 1980b Inside the 'black box': methodological issues in classroom research on language learning. *Language Learning* 30 (1): 1–42

Long, M 1981a Input, interaction and second language acquisition. In Winitz, H (ed.) *Native language and foreign language acquisition*, pp. 259–78. *Annals of the New York Academy of Sciences* 379

Long, M 1981b Questions in foreigner talk discourse. *Language Learning* 31 (1): 135–57

Long, M 1983a Native speaker/non-native speaker conversation and the negotiation of comprehensible input. *Applied Linguistics* 4 (2): 126–41

Long, M 1983b Native speaker/non-native speaker conversation in the second language classroom. In Clarke, M and Handscombe, J (eds.) *On TESOL '82*, pp. 207–25. TESOL, Washington, D.C.

Long, M 1983c Linguistic and conversational adjustments to non-native speakers. *Studies in Second Language Acquisition* 5 (2): 177–93

Long, M 1983d Does second language instruction make a difference? A review of research. *TESOL Quarterly* 17 (3): 359–82

Long, M 1983e Training the second language teacher as classroom researcher. In Alatis, J, Stern, H, and Strevens, P (eds.) *Applied linguistics and the preparation of second language teachers: toward a rationale. GURT '83*, pp. 281–97. Georgetown University Press, Washington, D.C.

Long, M 1984 Process and product in ESL program evaluation. *TESOL Quarterly* 18: 409–25

Long, M 1985a A role for instruction in second language acquisition: task-based language teaching. In Hyltenstam, K and Pienemann, M (eds.) *Modelling and assessing second language development*, pp. 77–99. Multilingual Matters

Long, M 1985b Input and second language acquisition theory. In Gass, S and Madden, C (eds.) *Input in second language acquisition*, pp. 377–93. Newbury House, Rowley, Mass.

Long, M 1988a Maturational constraints on language development. *UHWPESL* 7 (1): 1–53

Long, M 1988b Instructed interlanguage development. In Beebe, L (ed.) *Issues in second language acquisition: multiple perspectives*, pp. 115–41. Newbury House, Cambridge, Mass.

Long, M and Crookes, G 1986 Intervention points in second language classroom processes. Paper presented at the 1986 RELC Seminar, Singapore

Long, M, Ghambiar, S, Ghambiar, V, and Nishimura, M 1982 Regularization in foreigner talk and interlanguage. Paper presented at the 17th annual TESOL convention, Toronto, Canada, March 15–20

Long, M and Porter, P 1985 Group work, interlanguage talk, and second language acquisition. *TESOL Quarterly* 19: 207–28

Long, M and Sato, C 1983 Classroom foreigner talk discourse: forms and functions of teachers' questions. In Seliger, H and Long, M (eds.) *Classroom-oriented research in second language acquisition*, pp. 268–85. Newbury House, Rowley, Mass.

Long, M and Sato, C 1984 Methodological issues in interlanguage studies: an interactionist perspective. In Davies, A, Criper, C and Howatt, A (eds.) *Interlanguage*, pp. 253–79. Edinburgh University Press

Lukmani, Y 1972 Motivation to learn and language proficiency. *Language Learning* 22: 261–73

Lynch, B 1983 A discourse-functional analysis of interlanguage. In Campbell, C, Flashner, V, Hudson, T and Lubin, J (eds.) *Proceedings of the Los Angeles Second Language Research Forum*, Vol. II, pp. 216–25. Department of English, University of California at Los Angeles

Mace-Matluck, B 1977 The order of acquisition of certain oral English structures by native-speaking children of Spanish, Cantonese, Tagalog and Ilokano learning English as a second language between the ages of five and ten. Unpublished Ph.D. dissertation, University of Texas at Austin

McClelland, J, Rumelhart, D and the PDP Research Group 1986 *Parallel distributed processing: explorations in the microstructures of cognition*, Vol. 2: *Psychological and biological models*. MIT Press, Cambridge, Mass.

MacCorquodale, K 1970 On Chomsky's review of Skinner's *Verbal behavior*. *Journal of the Experimental Analysis of Behavior* 13: 83–99

McGroarty, M 1984 Some meanings of communicative competence for second language students. *TESOL Quarterly* 18: 257–72

McLaughlin, B 1978 The Monitor model: some methodological considerations. *Language Learning* 28: 309–32

McLaughlin, B 1980 On the use of miniature artificial languages in second-language research. *Applied Psycholinguistics* 1: 353–65

McLaughlin, B 1984 *Second-language acquisition in childhood*, 2nd edition, Vol. 1: *Preschool children*. Lawrence Erlbaum Associates, Hillsdale, N.J.

McLaughlin, B 1987 *Theories of second language learning*. Edward Arnold

McLaughlin, B 1990 Restructuring. *Applied Linguistics* 11 (2): 113–28

McLaughlin, B, Rossman, T and McLeod, B 1983 Second language learning: an information-processing perspective. *Language Learning* 33: 135–58

McLeod, B and McLaughlin, B 1986 Restructuring or automaticity? *Language Learning* 36: 109–23

Macnamara, J 1973 Nurseries, streets and classrooms: some comparisons and deductions. *Modern Language Journal* 57: 250–5

Macnamara, M 1973 Attitudes and learning a second language. In Shuy, R and Fasold, R (eds.) *Language attitudes: current trends and prospects*, pp. 36–40. Georgetown University Press, Washington, D.C.

Madsen, H 1982 Determining the debilitative impact of test anxiety. *Language Learning* 32: 133–43

Mahoney, G 1975 Ethnological approach to delayed language acquisition. *American Journal of Mental Deficiency* 80: 139–48

Major, R 1987 Phonological similarity, markedness, and rate of L2 acquisition. *Studies in Second Language Acquisition* 9: 63–82

Makino, T 1979 English morpheme acquisition order of Japanese secondary school students. *TESOL Quarterly* 13: 428

Makino, T 1980 Acquisition order of English morphemes by Japanese secondary school students. *Journal of Hokkaido University of Education* 30: 101–48

Mallinson, G and Blake, B 1982 *Language typology*. North Holland, Amsterdam

Mannon, T 1986 Teacher talk: a comparison of a teacher's speech to native and non-native speakers. Unpublished MA TESL thesis, University of California at Los Angeles

Maple, R 1982 Social distance and the acquisition of English as a second language: a study of Spanish-speaking adult learners. Unpublished doctoral dissertation, University of Texas at Austin

Mason, C 1971 The relevance of intensive training in English as a foreign language for university students. *Language Learning* 21: 197–204

Master, P 1987 Acquiring the English article system: a cross-linguistic interlanguage analysis. Paper presented at the 8th Second Language Research Forum, University of Southern California

Matsunobu, J 1981 A sore thumb?: identifying the ESL writer. Term paper, Ed 676, University of Pennsylvania, Philadelphia

Mazurkewich, I 1984 The acquisition of the dative alternation by second language learners and linguistic theory. *Language Learning* 34: 91–109

Mazurkewich, I 1985 Syntactic markedness and language acquisition. *Studies in Second Language Acquisition* 7 (1): 15–35

Mazurkewich, I and White, L 1984 The acquisition of the dative alternations: unlearning overgeneralizations. *Cognition* 16: 261–83

Mehan, H 1978 Structuring school structure. *Harvard Educational Review* 48: 32–64

Mehan, H and Wood, H 1975 *The reality of ethnomethodology*. Wiley, New York

Mehrabian, A 1970 The development and validation of measures of affiliative tendency and sensitivity to rejection. *Educational and Psychological Measurement* 30: 417–28

Meisel, J 1975 *The language of foreign workers in Germany*. Unpublished manuscipt, Wuppertal

Meisel, J 1977a The language of foreign workers in Germany. In Molony, C, Zobl, H and Stolting, W (eds.) *Deutsch im Kontakt mit anderen Sprachen (German in contact with other languages)*, pp. 184–212. Scriptor, Kronborg, Ts.

Meisel, J 1977b Linguistic simplification: a study of immigrant workers' speech and foreigner talk. In Corder, S and Roulet, E (eds.) *The notions of simplification, interlanguages and pidgins, and their relation to second language pedagogy*, pp. 88–113. Droz, Genève

Meisel, J 1983a Transfer as a second language strategy. *Language and Communication* 3: 11–46

Meisel, J 1983b Language development and linguistic theory: review of Derek Bickerton, *Roots of language*. *Lingua* 61: 231–57

Meisel, J 1983c Strategies of second language acquisition: more than one kind of simplification. In Andersen, R (ed.) *Pidginization and creolization as language acquisition*, pp. 120–57. Newbury House, Rowley, Mass.

Meisel, J 1987 Reference to past events and actions in the development of natural second language acquisition. In Pfaff, C (ed.) *First and second language processes*, pp. 206–24. Newbury House, Cambridge, Mass.

Meisel, J, Clahsen, H and Pienemann, M 1981 On determining developmental stages in natural second language acquisition. *Studies in Second Language Acquisition* 3 (1): 109–35

Messer, S 1976 Reflection-impulsivity: a review. *Psychological Bulletin* 83: 1026–52

Miller, G 1969 A psychological method to investigate verbal concepts. *Journal of Mathematical Psychology* 6: 169–91

Milon, J 1974 The development of negation in English by a second language learner. *TESOL Quarterly* 8: 137–43

Missler, R 1986 Analytic and synthetic cognitive functioning: a critical review of evidence bearing on field dependence. *Journal of Research in Personality* 20: 1–33

Mitroff, I and Kilman, R 1978 *Methodological approaches to social science*. Jossey-Bass, San Francisco

Moerk, E 1974 Changes in verbal child-mother interactions with increasing language skills of the child. *Journal of Psycholinguistic Research* 3: 101–16

Moerk, E 1980 Relationships between parental input frequencies and children's language acquisition: a reanalysis of Brown's data. *Journal of Child Language* 7: 105–18

Montgomery, C and Eisenstein, M 1985 Real reality revisited: an experimental course in ESL. *TESOL Quarterly* 19 (2): 317–34

Morrison, D and Low, G 1983 Monitoring and the second language learner. In Richards, J and Schmidt, R (eds.) *Language and communication*, pp. 228–49. Longman

Morsley, D and Vasseur, M 1976 L'emploi des verbes français par des travailleurs immigrés arabophones et portugais. *Langue française* 29: 80–92

Moulton, W 1962 *The sounds of English and German*. University of Chicago Press

Mowrer, D 1950 *Learning theory and personality dynamics*. Ronald Press, New York

Mueller, T and Miller, R 1970 A study of student attitudes and motivation in a collegiate French course using programmed language instruction. *International Review of Applied Linguistics in Language Teaching* 8: 297–320

Muhlhausler, P 1981 The development of the category of number in Tok Pisin. In Muysken, P (ed.) *Generative studies in creole languages*. Foris, Dordrecht

Myhill, J 1982 The acquisition of complex sentences: a cross-linguistic study. *Studies in Second Language Acquisition* 4: 193-200

Naiman, N 1974 The use of elicited imitation in second language acquisition research. *Working Papers on Bilingualism* 2: 1–37

Naiman, N, Fröhlich, M, Stern, H and Todesco, A 1978 *The good language learner*. Research in Education Series No. 7, The Ontario Institute for Studies in Education, Toronto

Natalicio, D and Natalicio, L 1971 A comparative study of English pluralization by native and non-native English speakers. *Child Development* 42: 1302–6

Nation, R and McLaughlin, B 1986 Experts and novices: an information-processing approach to the 'good language learner' problem. *Applied Psycholinguistics* 7: 41–56

Nemser, W 1971 Approximative systems of foreign language learners. *International Review of Applied Linguistics* 9: 115–24

Neufeld, G 1977 Language learning ability in adults: a study on the acquisition of prosodic and articulatory features. *Working Papers on Bilingualism* 12: 45–60

Neufeld, G 1978 On the acquisition of prosodic and articulatory features in adult language learning. *Canadian Modern Language Review* 34 (2): 163–74

Neufeld, G 1979 Towards a theory of language learning ability. *Language Learning* 29 (2): 227–41

Newport, E 1984 Constraints on learning: studies in the acquisition of American Sign Language. *Papers and Reports on Child Language Development* 23: 1–22

Newport, E, Gleitman, H, and Gleitman, L 1977 'Mother, I'd rather do it myself': some effects and non-effects of maternal speech styles. In Snow, C and Ferguson, C (eds.) *Talking to children: language input and acquisition*, pp. 109–49. Cambridge University Press

Nicholas, H 1984 Individual differences in interlanguage use. Paper presented at the 9th annual Conference of the Applied Linguistics Association of Australia, Alice Springs

Nicholas, H 1985 Individual differences in interlanguage use. *Australian Review of Applied Linguistics* 8 (1): 70–86

Nicholas, H 1987 Contextually defined queries: evidence for variation in orientations to second language acquisition processes? In Pfaff, C (ed.) *First and second language acquisition processes*, pp. 81–102. Newbury House, Cambridge, Mass.

Nicholas, H and Meisel, J 1983 Second language acquisition: the state of the art. In Felix, S and Wode, H (eds.) *Language development at the crossroads*, pp. 63–89. Gunter Narr, Tubingen

Nixon, J 1981 *A teacher's guide to action research*. Grant McIntyre

Norton, R 1975 Measurement of ambiguity tolerance. *Journal of Personality Assessment* 39: 607–18

Nunan, D (ed.) 1987 *Applying second language acquisition research*. National Curriculum Resource Centre, Adult Migrant Education Program, Adelaide

Nunan, D 1988 *Learner-centered curriculum design*. Cambridge University Press

Obler, L 1981 Right hemisphere participation in second language acquisition. In Diller, K (ed.) *Individual differences and universals in language learning aptitudes*, pp. 53–64. Newbury House, Rowley, Mass.

Ochs, E 1979 Planned and unplanned discourse. In Givon, T (ed.) *Syntax and semantics*, Vol. 12: Discourse and semantics, pp. 51–80. Academic Press, New York

Ochs, E 1982 Talking to children in Western Samoa. *Language in Society* 11: 77–104

Ochs, E and Schieffelin, B (eds.) 1979 *Developmental pragmatics*. Academic

Press, New York

Ochsner, R 1979 A poetics of second-language acquisition. *Language Learning* 29 (1): 53–80

Odlin, T 1989 *Language transfer: cross-linguistic influence in language learning.* Cambridge University Press

O'Grady, W 1987 *Principles of grammar and learning.* University of Chicago Press

O'Grady, W (to appear) The optional subject stage. In *The joy of grammar: a Festschrift for James D. McCawley.*

Oller, J 1976 Evidence for a general language proficiency factor: an expectancy grammar. *Die Neuren Sprachen* 2: 165–71

Oller, J 1979 *Language tests at school: a pragmatic approach.* Longman, New York

Oller, J 1981a Language as intelligence? *Language Learning* 31: 465–92

Oller, J 1981b Research on the measurement of affective variables: some remaining questions. In Andersen, R (ed.) *New dimensions in second language acquisition research*, pp. 14–27. Newbury House, Rowley, Mass.

Oller, J 1982 Gardner on affect: a reply to Gardner. *Language Learning* 32: 183–9

Oller, J 1984 Communication theory and testing: what and how. Paper presented at the 2nd TOEFL Invitational Conference, October 19–20

Oller, J, Baca, L and Vigil, F 1977 Attitudes and attained proficiency in ESL: a sociolinguistic study of Mexican-Americans in the Southwest. *TESOL Quarterly* 11: 173–83

Oller, J, Hudson, A and Liu, P 1977 Attitudes and attained proficiency in ESL: a sociolinguistic study of native speakers of Chinese in the United States. *Language Learning* 27: 1–27

Oller, J and Perkins, K 1978a Intelligence and language proficiency as sources of variance in self-reported affective variables. *Language Learning* 28: 85–97

Oller, J and Perkins, K 1978b Language in education: testing the tests. Newbury House, Rowley, Mass.

Olshtain, E 1985 Language policy and the classroom teacher. In Celce-Murcia, M (ed.) *Beyond basics: issues and research in TESOL.* Newbury House, Rowley, Mass.

Olson, L and Samuels, S 1973 The relationship between age and accuracy of foreign language pronunciation. *Journal of Psycholinguistic Research* 66: 263–7

O'Malley, J 1987 The effects of training in the use of learning strategies. In Wenden, A and Rubin, J (eds.) *Learning strategies in language learning*, pp. 133–44. Prentice-Hall, Englewood Cliffs, N.J.

O'Malley, J and Chamot, A 1990 *Learning strategies in second language acquisition.* Cambridge University Press

O'Malley, J, Chamot, A, Stewner-Manzanares, G, Küpper, L and Russo, R 1985a Learning strategies used by beginning and intermediate ESL students. *Language Learning* 35: 21–46

O'Malley, J, Chamot, A, Stewner-Manzanares, G, Russo, R and Küpper, L 1985b Learning strategy applications with students of English as a second language. *TESOL Quarterly* 19: 557–84

Onaha, H 1987 Foreigner talk in Japanese: a comparison of ellipsis of particles and noun phrases between foreigner talk and speech to native speakers. *JACET Journal* 18: 89–107

Oppenheim, A 1966 *Questionnaire design and attitude measurement.* Basic Books, New York

Orlovic, M 1984 Das Gasterbeiterdeutsch: Versuch einer Analyse. Unpublished manuscript, University of Mainz

Osgood, C 1953 *Method and theory in experimental psychology.* Oxford University Press, New York

Oskarsson, M 1972 Comparative method studies in foreign language teaching. *Moderna Sprak* 66: 350–66

Oxford-Carpenter, R 1988 *A new taxonomy of second language learning strategies.* ERIC Clearinghouse on Languages and Linguistics, Washington, D.C.

Oyama, S 1973 A sensitive period for the acquisition of a second language. Unpublished Ph.D. dissertation, Harvard University

Oyama, S 1976 A sensitive period in the acquisition of a non-native phonological system. *Journal of Psycholinguistic Research* 5: 261–85

Oyama, S 1978 The sensitive period and comprehension of speech. *Working Papers on Bilingualism* 16: 1–17

Oyama, S 1985 *The ontogeny of information: developmental systems and evolution.* Cambridge University Press

Palmberg, R 1976 A select bibliography of error analysis and related topics. *Interlanguage Studies Bulletin* 1: 340–89

Palmberg, R 1977 Bibliography additions. *Interlanguage Studies Bulletin* 2: 91–9

Pankhurst, J, Sharwood-Smith, M and van Buren, P (eds.) 1988 *Learnability and second languages.* Foris, Dordrecht

Parker K, 1989 Learnability theory and the acquisition of syntax. *University of Hawaii Working Papers in ESL* 8: 49–78

Parker, K and Chaudron, C 1987 The effects of linguistic simplifications and elaborative modifications on L2 comprehension. *UHWPESL* 6 (2): 107–33

Parrish, B and Tarone, E 1986 Article use in interlanguage: a study in task-related variability. Paper presented at the TESOL Convention, Anaheim, Calif.

Patkowski, M 1980 The sensitive period for the acquisition of syntax in a second language. *Language Learning* 30: 449–72. Reprinted in Krashen, S, Scarcella, R and Long, M (eds.) 1982 *Child–adult differences in second language acquisition,* pp. 52–63. Newbury House, Rowley, Mass.

Paulston, C 1980 *Bilingual education: theories and issues.* Newbury House, Rowley, Mass.

Pavesi, M 1984 The acquisition of relative clauses in a formal and in an informal setting: further evidence in support of the markedness hypothesis. In Singleton, D and Little, D (eds.) *Language learning in formal and informal contexts,* pp. 151–63. IRAAL, Dublin

Pavesi, M 1986 Markedness, discoursal modes, and relative clause formation in a formal and an informal context. *Studies in Second Language Acquisition* 8 (1): 38–55

Payne, A 1980 Factors controlling the acquisition of the Philadelphia dialect by out-of-state children. In Labov, W (ed.) *Locating language in time and space*, pp. 143–78. Academic Press, New York

Peck, S 1978 Child–child discourse in second language acquisition. In Hatch, E (ed.) *Second language acquisition: a book of readings*, pp. 383–400. Newbury House, Rowley, Mass.

Peck, S 1980 Language play in child second language acquisition. In Larsen-Freeman, D (ed.) *Discourse analysis in second language research*, pp. 154–64. Newbury House, Rowley, Mass.

Pelto, G and Pelto, P 1978 *Anthropological research: the structure of inquiry.* Cambridge University Press

Penfield, W and Roberts, L 1959 *Speech and brain mechanisms.* Atheneum Press, New York

Perdue, C (ed.) 1982 *Second language acquisition by adult immigrants: a field manual.* European Science Foundation, Strasbourg, France

Perkins, K and Larsen-Freeman, D 1975 The effect of formal language instruction on the order of morpheme acquisition. *Language Learning* 25 (2): 237–43

Peters, A 1977 Language learning strategies: does the whole equal the sum of the parts? *Language* 53: 560–73

Pettigrew, T 1958 The measurement and correlates of category width as a cognitive variable. *Journal of Personality* 26: 532–44

Pfaff, C (ed.) 1987 *First and second language acquisition processes.* Newbury House, Cambridge, Mass.

Philips, S 1972 Participation structures and communicative competence: Warm Springs children in community and classroom. In Cazden, C, John, V and Hymes, D (eds.) *Functions of language in the classroom*, pp. 370–94. Teachers College Press, New York

Piaget, J 1929 *The child's conception of the world.* Routledge & Kegan Paul

Pica, T 1982 Second language acquisition in different language contexts. Unpublished Ph.D. dissertation, University of Pennsylvania

Pica, T 1983a Adult acquisition of English as a second language under different conditions of exposure. *Language Learning* 33 (4): 465–97

Pica, T 1983b The article in American English: what the textbooks don't tell us. In Wolfson, N and Judd, E (eds.) *Sociolinguistics and second language acquisition*, pp. 222–33. Newbury House, Rowley, Mass.

Pica, T 1983c The role of language context in second language acquisition. Review article, *Interlanguage Studies Bulletin* 7: 101–23

Pica, T 1984 Methods of morpheme quantification: their effect on the interpretation of second language data. *Studies in Second Language Acquisition* 6 (1): 69–78

Pica, T 1985 The selective impact of classroom instruction on second language acquisition. *Applied Linguistics* 6 (3): 214–22

Pica, T and Doughty, C 1985 Input and interaction in the communicative language classroom: a comparison of teacher-fronted and group activities. In Gass, S and Madden, C (eds.) *Input in second language acquisition*, pp. 115–32. Newbury House, Rowley, Mass.

Pica, T, Doughty, C, and Young, R 1986 Making input comprehensible: do interactional modifications help? *I.T.L. Review of Applied Linguistics* 72: 1–25

Pienemann, M 1980 The second language acquisition of immigrant children.

In Felix, S (ed.) *Second language development*, pp. 41–56. Gunter Narr, Tubingen

Pienemann, M 1981 *Der Zweitsprachenerwerb auslandischer Arbeiterkinder.* Bouvier, Bonn

Pienemann, M 1984 Psychological constraints on the teachability of languages. *Studies in Second Language Acquisition* 6 (2): 186–214

Pienemann, M 1985a Psycholinguistic principles of second language teaching. Unpublished manuscript, Department of German, University of Sydney

Pienemann, M 1985b Learnability and syllabus construction. In Hyltenstam, K and Pienemann, M (eds.) *Modelling and assessing second language development.* Multilingual Matters

Pienemann, M 1986 L'effeto dell'insegnamiento sugli orientamenti degli apprendenti nell'acquisizione di L2. (The effect of instruction on learners' orientations in L2 acquisition.) In Ramat, A (ed.) *L'apprendimiento spontaneo di una seconda lingua*, pp. 307–26. Mulino, Bologna

Pienemann, M 1987 Determining the influence of instruction on L2 speech processing. *Australian Review of Applied Linguistics* 10 (2): 83–113

Pienemann, M 1988 Psychological constraints on the teachability of languages. In Rutherford, W and Sharwood-Smith, M (eds.) *Grammar and second language teaching: a book of readings*, pp. 85–106. Newbury House/Harper and Row, New York

Pienemann, M 1989 Is language teachable? *Applied Linguistics* 10 (1): 52–79

Pienemann, M and Johnston, M 1985 Towards an explanatory model of language acquisition. Paper presented at the Second Language Research Forum, University of California at Los Angeles, February 22–24

Pienemann, M and Johnston, M 1986 An acquisition-based procedure for second language assessment. *Australian Review of Applied Linguistics* 9: 92–122

Pienemann, M and Johnston, M 1987 Factors influencing the development of language proficiency. In Nunan, D (ed.) *Applying second language acquisition research*, pp. 45–141. National Curriculum Resource Centre, Adult Migrant Education Program, Adelaide

Pienemann, M and Johnston, M (in progress) A predictive framework for language acquisition/processing contraints and learnability. Unpublished manuscript, University of Sydney

Pienemann, M, Johnston, M and Brindley, G 1988 Constructing an acquisition-based procedure for second language assessment. *Studies in Second Language Acquisition* 10 (2): 217–43

Pierson, H, Fu, G and Lee, S 1980 An analysis of the relationship between language attitudes and English attainment of secondary students in Hong Kong. *Language Learning* 30: 289–316

Pimsleur, P 1966a *The Pimsleur language aptitude battery.* Harcourt Brace Jovanovich, New York

Pimsleur, P 1966b Testing foreign language learning. In Valdman, A (ed.) *Trends in language teaching*, pp. 175–214. McGraw-Hill, New York

Pinker, S 1984 *Language learnability and language development.* Harvard University Press, Cambridge, Mass.

Pinker, S and Prince, A 1987 On language and connectionism: analysis of a parallel distributed processing model of language acquisition. Occasional paper #33, Center for Cognitive Science, MIT

Pinker, S and Prince, A 1988 On language and connectionism: analysis of a parallel distributed processing model of language acquisition. *Cognition* 28 (1–2): 73–193

Plann, S 1977 Acquiring a second language in an immersion situation. In Brown, H, Yorio, C and Crymes, R (eds.) *On TESOL '77*, pp. 213–23. TESOL, Washington, D.C.

Politzer, R 1977 Foreign language teaching and bilingual education: implications of some recent research findings. Paper presented at the ACTFL annual conference, San Francisco, November

Politzer, R and McGroarty, M 1985 An exploratory study of learning behaviors and their relationship to gains in linguistic and communicative competence. *TESOL Quarterly* 19: 103–23

Politzer, R and Weiss, L 1969 An experiment in foreign language learning through learning of selected skills associated with language aptitude. ERIC Document Reproduction Service, ED 046261. Stanford University

Porter, J 1977 A cross-sectional study of morpheme acquisition in first language learners. *Language Learning* 27 (1): 47–62

Porter, P 1983 Variations in the conversations of adult learners of English as a function of the proficiency level of the participants. Unpublished Ph.D. dissertation, Stanford University

Povey, J (ed.) 1980 *Language planning and language teaching: essays in honor of Clifford H. Prator.* English Language Services, Culver City, Calif.

Purcell, E and Suter, R 1980 Predictors of pronunciation accuracy: a reexamination. *Language Learning* 30 (2): 271–87

Purves, A (ed.) 1987 *Writing across languages and cultures: issues in contrastive rhetoric.* Sage Publications, Beverly Hills

Raimes, A 1983 Tradition and revolution in ESL teaching. *TESOL Quarterly* 17: 535–52

Ramamurti, R 1977 How do Americans talk to me? Term paper, Folklore Department, University of Pennsylvania

Ramirez, M, Herold, P and Castaneda, A 1974 Cognitive styles of children of three ethnic groups in the United States. *Journal of Cross-Cultural Psychology* 5: 212–19

Ravem, R 1968 Language acquisition in a second language environment. *International Review of Applied Linguistics* 6: 165–85

Ravem, R 1970 The development of Wh-questions in first and second language learners. *Occasional Papers*, Language Centre, University of Essex. Also in Richards, J (ed.) 1974 *Error analysis*, pp. 134–55. Longman

Reber, A, Kassin, S, Lewis, S and Cantor, G 1980 On the relationship between implicit and explicit modes in the learning of a complex rule structure. *Journal of Experimental Psychology: Human Learning and Memory* 6: 492–502

Reichardt, C and Cook, T 1979 Beyond qualitative versus quantitative methods. In Cook, T and Reichardt, C (eds.) *Qualitative and quantitative methods in education research.* Sage Publications, Beverly Hills

Reid, J 1987 The learning style preferences of ESL students. *TESOL Quarterly* 21: 87–111

Reinecke, J 1935/1969 *Language and dialect in Hawaii.* University of Hawaii Press, Honolulu (reprinted 1988)

Reinert, H 1976 One picture is worth a thousand words? Not necessarily!

Modern Language Journal **60**: 407–42

Reinert, H 1977 ELSIE is no bull! or: on utilizing information concerning student learning styles. In Schulz, R (ed.) *Personalizing foreign language instruction: learning styles and teaching options.* National Textbook Company, Skokie, Ill.

Remick, H 1971 The maternal environment of linguistic development. Unpublished Ph.D. dissertation, University of California at Davis

Reves, T 1982 What makes a good language learner? Unpublished Ph.D. dissertation, Hebrew University, Jerusalem

Reynolds, P 1971 *A primer in theory construction.* Bobbs-Merrill, Indianapolis

Richards, D 1980 Problems in eliciting unmonitored speech in a second language. *Interlanguage Studies Bulletin* **5**: 63–98

Richards, J 1971 Error analysis and second language strategies. *Language Sciences* **17**: 12–22

Richards, J (ed.) 1974 *Error analysis.* Longman

Richards, J (ed.) 1978 *Understanding second and foreign language learning.* Newbury House, Rowley, Mass.

Richards, J and Schmidt, R (eds.) 1979 Speech acts and second language learning. *Applied Linguistics* **1**: 129–57

Ringbom, H 1978 The influence of the mother tongue on the translation of lexical items. *Interlanguage Studies Bulletin* **3**: 80–101

Ringbom, H (ed.) 1983 *Psycholinguistics and foreign language learning.* Abo Akademi, Abo

Ringbom, H 1987 *The role of the first language in foreign language learners.* Multilingual matters

Rist, R 1977 On the relations among educational research paradigms: from disdain to detente. *Anthropology and Education Quarterly* **8**: 42–9

Ritchie, W 1978a The right roof constraint in an adult-acquired language. In Ritchie, W (ed.) *Second language acquisition research*, pp. 33–63. Academic Press, New York

Ritchie, W (ed.) 1978b *Second language acquisition research: issues and implications.* Academic Press, New York

Ritchie, W 1983 Universal grammar and second language acquisition. In Rogers, D and Slovoda, J (eds.) *The acquisition of symbolic skills.* Plenum Press, New York

Rivers, W 1964 *The psychologist and the foreign language teacher.* University of Chicago Press

Rivers, W 1979 Learning a sixth language: an adult learner's diary. *Canadian Modern Language Review* **36**: 67–82

Rivers, W 1980 *Teaching foreign language skills.* University of Chicago Press

Rizzi, L 1982 *Issues in Italian syntax.* Foris, Dordrecht

Roach, D 1985 Effects of cognitive style, intelligence, and sex on reading achievement. *Perceptual and Motor Skills* **61**: 1139–42

Robinett, B and Schachter, J (eds.) 1983 *Second language learning: contrastive analysis, error analysis and related aspects.* University of Michigan Press, Ann Arbor

Roeper, T 1973 Connecting children's language and linguistic theory. In Moore, T (ed.) *Cognitive development and the acquisition of language*, pp. 187–96. Academic Press, New York

Romaine, S 1988 *Pidgin and creole languages.* Longman

Rondal, J 1978 Patterns of correlations for various language measures in mother–child interactions for normal and Down's syndrome children. *Language and Speech* 21 (3): 242–52

Rondal, J 1979 On the nature of linguistic input to language-learning children. *International Journal of Psycholinguistics* 8-1 [21]: 75–107

Rosansky, E 1975 The critical period for the acquisition of language: some cognitive developmental considerations. *Working Papers on Bilingualism* 6: 10–23

Rosansky, E 1976 Methods and morphemes in second language acquisition research. *Language Learning* 26 (2): 409–25

Rosenberg, S 1982 The language of the mentally retarded: development processes and intervention. In Rosenberg, S (ed.) *Handbook of applied psycholinguistics: major thrusts of research and theory.* Lawrence Erlbaum Associates, Hillsdale, N.J.

Rosenblum, D and Dorman, M 1978 Hemispheric specialization for speech perception in language deficient kindergarten children. *Brain and Language* 6: 378–89

Rossier, R 1976 Extroversion–introversion as a significant variable in the learning of oral English as a second language. Unpublished Ph.D. dissertation, University of Southern California

Rubin, J 1975 What the 'good language learner' can teach us. *TESOL Quarterly* 9: 41–51

Rubin, J 1981 Study of cognitive processes in second language learning. *Applied Linguistics* 11: 117–31

Rumelhart, D and McClelland, J 1986 On learning the past tenses of English verbs. In McClelland, J, Rumelhart, D and the PDP Research Group, *Parallel distributed processing: explorations in the microstructures of cognition*, Vol. 2: *Psychological and biological models*, pp. 216–71. MIT Press, Cambridge, Mass.

Rutherford, W 1982 Markedness in second language acquisition. *Language Learning* 32 (1): 85–108

Rutherford, W 1983 Language typology and language transfer. In Gass, S and Selinker, L (eds.) *Language transfer in language learning*, pp. 358–70. Newbury House, Rowley, Mass.

Rutherford, W (ed.) 1984 *Language universals and second language acquisition.* John Benjamins, Amsterdam

Rutherford, W 1986 Grammatical theory and L2 acquisition: a brief overview. *Second Language Research* 2 (1): 1–15

Rutherford, W 1987 *Second language grammar: learning and teaching.* Longman, New York

Rutherford, W and Sharwood-Smith, M (eds.) 1988 *Grammar and second language teaching: a book of readings.* Newbury House/Harper and Row, New York

Sachs, J, Bard, B and Johnson, M 1981 Language learning with restricted input: case studies of two hearing children of deaf parents. *Applied Psycholinguistics* 2 (1): 33–54

St. Martin, G 1980 English language acquisition: the effects of living with an American family. *TESOL Quarterly* 14: 388–90

Sajavaara, K 1978 The monitor model and monitoring in second language speech communication. In Gingras, R (ed.) *Second language acquisition and foreign language teaching*, pp. 51–67. Center for Applied Linguistics, Arlington, Va.

Sajavaara, K 1981 The nature of first language transfer: English as L2 in a foreign language setting. Paper presented at the first European–North American Workshop on Cross-Linguistic Second Language Acquisition Research, Lake Arrowhead, Calif.

Sajavaara, K 1986 Transfer and second language speech processing. In Kellerman, E and Sharwood-Smith, M (eds.) *Cross-linguistic influence in second language acquisition*, pp. 66–79. Pergamon Press

Samarin, W 1971 Salient and substantive pidginization. In Hymes, D (ed.) *Pidginization and creolization of languages*, pp. 117–40. Cambridge University Press

Sampson, G 1987 Parallel distributed processing. Review article, *Language* **63**: 871–86

Saracho, O 1981 Teachers' cognitive styles: educational implications. *The Educational Forum*, January: 152–9

Sato, C 1982a Form and function in the English interlanguages of two Vietnamese children. Paper presented at the Georgetown University Round Table, pre-conference session on the Analysis of Spoken Discourse, March

Sato, C 1982b Ethnic styles in classroom discourse. In Hines, M and Rutherford, W (eds.) *On TESOL '81*, pp. 11–24. TESOL, Washington, D.C.

Sato, C 1984 Phonological processes in second language acquisition: another look at interlanguage syllable structure. *Language Learning* **34** (4): 43-57. Also in Ioup, G and Weinberger, S (eds.) 1987 *Interlanguage phonology*, pp. 248–60. Newbury House, Cambridge, Mass.

Sato, C 1985a Task variation in interlanguage phonology. In Gass, S and Madden, C (eds.) *Input in second language acquisition*, pp. 181–96. Newbury House, Rowley, Mass.

Sato, C 1985b The syntax of conversation in interlanguage development. Unpublished Ph.D. dissertation, University of California at Los Angeles

Sato, C 1986 Conversation and interlanguage development: rethinking the connection. In Day, R (ed.) *'Talking to learn': conversation in second language acquisition*, pp. 23–45. Newbury House, Rowley, Mass.

Sato, C 1988 Origins of complex syntax in interlanguage development. *Studies in Second Language Acquisition* **10** (3): 371–95

Sato, C (to appear) *The syntax of conversation in interlanguage development*. Gunter Narr, Tubingen

Savignon, S 1972 *Communicative competence: an experiment in foreign language teaching*. Center for Curriculum Development, Philadelphia

Scarcella, R 1983 Discourse accent in second language performance. In Gass, S and Selinker, L (eds.) *Language transfer in language learning*, pp. 306–26. Newbury House, Rowley, Mass.

Scarcella, R 1984 Cohesion in the writing development of native and non-native English speakers. Unpublished Ph.D. dissertation, University of Southern California

Scarcella, R and Higa, C 1981 Input, negotiation and age differences in second language acquisition. *Language Learning* **31**: 409–38

Scarcella, R and Higa, C 1982 Input and age differences in second language acquisition. In Krashen, S, Scarcella, R and Long, M (eds.) *Child–adult differences in second language acquisition*, pp. 175–201. Newbury House, Rowley, Mass.

Scarcella, R and Krashen, S (eds.) 1980 *Research in second language acquisition.* Newbury House, Rowley, Mass.

Schachter, J 1974 An error in error analysis. *Language Learning* **24**: 205–14

Schachter, J 1983 A new account of language transfer. In Gass, S and Selinker, L (eds.) *Language transfer in language learning*, pp. 98–111. Newbury House, Rowley, Mass.

Schachter, J 1986a In search of systematicity in interlanguage production. *Studies in Second Language Acquisition* **8**: 119–34

Schachter, J 1986b Three approaches to the study of input. *Language Learning* **36**: 211–25

Schachter, J 1988 Second language acquisition and its relationship to Universal Grammar. *Applied Linguistics* **9**: 219–35

Schachter, J 1989 Testing a proposed universal. In Gass, S and Schachter, J (eds.) *Linguistic perspectives on second language acquisition*, pp. 73–88. Cambridge University Press

Schachter, J and Celce-Murcia, M 1977 Some reservations concerning error analysis. *TESOL Quarterly* **11**: 441–51

Schachter, J and Rutherford, W 1979 Discourse function and language transfer. *Working Papers on Bilingualism* **19**: 3–12

Schachter, J, Tyson, A and Diffley, F 1976 Learner intuitions of grammaticality. *Language Learning* **26**: 67–76

Schaffer, J (ed.) 1977 *Studies in mother–infant interaction.* Academic Press, London

Scherer, G and Wertheimer, F 1964 *A psycholinguistic experiment in foreign-language teaching.* McGraw-Hill, New York

Schinke-Llano, L 1983 Foreigner talk in content classrooms. In Seliger, H and Long, M (eds.) *Classroom-oriented research in second language acquisition*, pp. 146–64. Newbury House, Rowley, Mass.

Schlue, K 1976 An inside view of interlanguage: consulting the adult learner about the second language acquisition process. Unpublished MA in TESL thesis, University of California at Los Angeles

Schmeck, R 1981 Improving learning by improving thinking. *Educational Leadership* **38**: 384–5

Schmidt, M 1980 Coordinate structures and language universals in interlanguage. *Language Learning* **30**: 397–416

Schmidt, R 1977 Sociolinguistic variation and language transfer in phonology. *Working Papers on Bilingualism* **12**: 79–95

Schmidt, R 1981 Interaction, acculturation and the acquisition of communicative competence. *University of Hawaii Working Papers in Linguistics* **13** (3): 29–77

Schmidt, R 1983 Interaction, acculturation, and acquisition of communicative competence. In Wolfson, N and Judd, E (eds.) *Sociolinguistics and second language acquisition*, pp. 137–74. Newbury House, Rowley, Mass.

Schmidt, R 1988a The potential of PDP for SLA theory and research. *UHWPESL* **7** (1): 55–66

Schmidt, R 1990 The role of consciousness in second language learning. *Applied Linguistics* **11** (2): 129–58

Schmidt, R and Frota, S 1986 Developing basic conversational ability in a second language: a case study of an adult learner of Portuguese. In Day, R (ed.) *'Talking to learn': conversation in second language acquisition*, pp. 237–326. Newbury House, Rowley, Mass.

Schmidt, R and McCreary, C 1977 Standard and super-standard English. *TESOL Quarterly* 11: 415–30

Schneider, W and Shiffrin, R 1977 Controlled and automatic processing. 1: Detection, search and attention. *Psychological Review* 84: 1–64

Schneiderman, E and Wesche, M 1983 The role of the right hemisphere in second language acquisition. In Bailey, K M, Long, M and Peck, S (eds.) *Second language acquisition studies*, pp. 162–74. Newbury House, Rowley, Mass.

Schumann, F 1980 Diary of a language learner: a further analysis. In Scarcella, R and Krashen, S (eds.) *Research in second language acquisition*, pp. 51–7. Newbury House, Rowley, Mass.

Schumann, F and Schumann, J 1977 Diary of a language learner: an introspective study of second language learning. In Brown, H, Yorio, C and Crymes, R (eds.) *On TESOL '77*, pp. 241–9. TESOL, Washington, D.C.

Schumann, J 1975 Affective factors and the problem of age in second language acquisition. *Language Learning* 25: 209–35

Schumann, J 1978a *The pidginization process: a model for second language acquisition.* Newbury House, Rowley, Mass.

Schumann, J 1978b The relationship of pidginization, creolization and decreolization to second language acquisition. *Language Learning* 28: 367–79

Schumann, J 1978c The acculturation model for second language acquisition. In Gingras, R (ed.) *Second language acquisition and foreign language teaching*, pp. 27–50. Center for Applied Linguistics, Arlington, Va.

Schumann, J 1978d Social and psychological factors in second language acquisition. In Richards, J (ed.) *Understanding second and foreign language learning*, pp. 163–78, Newbury House, Rowley, Mass.

Schumann, J 1979 The acquisition of English negation by speakers of Spanish: a review of the literature. In Andersen, R (ed.) *The acquisition and use of Spanish and English as first and second languages*, pp. 3–32. TESOL, Washington, D.C.

Schumann, J 1982 Simplification, transfer, and relexification as aspects of pidginization and early second language acquisition. *Language Learning* 32: 337–65

Schumann, J 1983 Art and science in second language acquisition research. In Clarke, M and Handscombe, J (eds.) *On TESOL '82*. TESOL, Washington, D.C. Also in *Language Learning* 33, Special Issue No. 1: 49–76

Schumann, J 1986 Research on the acculturation model for second language acquisition. *Journal of Multilingual and Multicultural Development* 7: 379–92

Schumann, J 1987a The expression of temporality in basilang speech. *Studies in Second Language Acquisition* 9 (1:) 21–41

Schumann, J 1987b Utterance structure in basilang speech. In Gilbert, G (ed.) *Pidgin and creole languages: essays in memory of John E. Reinecke*. University of Hawaii Press, Honolulu

Schumann, J, Hinofotis, F, McGroarty, M, Erickson, M, Hudson, T, Kimbell, L and Scott, M 1982 Grammatical correlates of FOPT (FSI) ratings. Paper presented at Second Language Research Forum, University of California at Los Angeles, April 28–29

Schumann, J, Holroyd, J, Campbell, R and Ward, F 1978 Improvement of foreign language pronunciation under hypnosis: a preliminary study. *Language Learning* 28: 143–8

Schwartz, B 1986 The epistemological status of second language acquisition. *Second Language Research* 2 (2): 120–59

Schwartz, J 1980 The negotiation for meaning: repair in conversations between second language learners of English. In Larsen-Freeman, D (ed.) *Discourse analysis in second language research*, pp. 138–53. Newbury House, Rowley, Mass.

Scollon, R 1973 A real early stage: an unzippered condensation of a dissertation on child language. *University of Hawaii Working Papers in Linguistics*

Scollon, R 1974 One child's language from one to two: the origins of construction. Unpublished Ph.D. dissertation, University of Hawaii at Manoa, Honolulu

Scollan, R 1976 *Conversations with a one-year old*. The University of Hawaii Press, Honolulu

Scott, M and Tucker, G 1974 Error analysis and English language strategies of Arab students. *Language Learning* 24 (1): 69–97

Scovel, T 1969 Foreign accents, language acquisition, and cerebral dominance. *Language Learning* 19: 245–54

Scovel, T 1978 The effect of affect on foreign language learning: a review of the anxiety research. *Language Learning* 28: 129–42

Scovel, T 1981 The recognition of foreign accents in English and its implications for psycholinguistic theories of language acquisition. In Savard, J-G and Laforge, L (eds.) *Proceedings of the 5th Congress of AILA*, pp. 389–401. University of Laval Press, Laval

Scovel, T 1988 *A time to speak: a psycholinguistic inquiry into the critical period for human speech*. Newbury House/Harper and Row, New York

Segal, J, Chipman, S and Glaser, R (eds.) 1985 *Thinking and learning skills*. Lawrence Erlbaum Associates, Hillsdale, N.J.

Segalowitz, N and Gatbonton, E 1977 Studies of the nonfluent bilingual. In Hornby, P (ed.) *Bilingualism: psychological, social, and educational implications*. Academic Press, New York

Seliger, H 1975 Inductive method and deductive method in language teaching: a re-examination. *International Review of Applied Linguistics* 13 (1): 1–18

Seliger, H 1977 Does practice make perfect?: a study of interaction patterns and L2 competence. *Language Learning* 27 (2): 263–78

Seliger, H 1978 Implications of a multiple critical periods hypothesis for second language learning. In Ritchie, W (ed.) *Second language acquisition research*, pp. 11–19. Academic Press, New York

Seliger, H 1979 On the nature and function of language rules in language teaching. *TESOL Quarterly* 13: 359–70

Seliger, H 1982 On the possible role of the right hemisphere in second language acquisition. *TESOL Quarterly* 16: 307–14

Seliger, H 1983 The language learner as linguist: of metaphors and realities. *Applied Linguistics* 4: 179–91

Seliger, H 1984 Processing universals in second language acquisition. In

Eckman, F, Bell, L and Nelson, D (eds.) *Universals of second language acquisition*, pp. 36–47. Newbury House, Rowley, Mass.

Seliger, H and Long, M (eds.) 1983 *Classroom-oriented research in second language acquisition*. Newbury House, Rowley, Mass.

Selinker, L 1969 Language transfer. *General Linguistics* 9: 67–92

Selinker, L 1972 Interlanguage. *International Review of Applied Linguistics* 10: 209–31

Selinker, L and Douglas, D 1985 Wrestling with 'context' in interlanguage theory. *Applied Linguistics* 6: 190–204

Selinker, L and Gass, S 1984 *Workbook in second language acquisition*. Newbury House, Rowley, Mass.

Selinker, L and Selinker, P 1972 *An annotated bibliography of U.S. Ph.D dissertations in contrastive linguistics*. Center for Applied Linguistics, Washington, D.C.

Selkirk, E 1983 *The syntax of words*. MIT Press, Cambridge, Mass.

Seright, L 1985 Age and aural comprehension achievement in francophone adults learning English. *TESOL Quarterly* 19 (3): 455–73

Sharwood Smith, M 1981 Consciousness-raising and the second language learner. *Applied Linguistics* 11: 159–68

Sharwood Smith, M 1983 Cross-linguistic aspects of second language acquisition. *Applied Linguistics* 4: 192–9

Sharwood Smith, M 1986 The competence/control model, crosslinguistic influence and the creation of new grammars. In Kellerman, E and Sharwood Smith, M (eds.) *Cross-linguistic influence in second language acquisition*, pp. 10–20. Pergamon Press

Shavelson, R 1979 *Introduction to statistical reasoning*. Allyn and Bacon, Boston

Shavelson, R, Hubner, J and Stanton, G 1976 Self-concept: validation of construct interpretations. *Review of Educational Research* 46: 407–41

Shiffrin, R and Schneider, W 1977 Controlled and automatic human information processing. 2: Perceptual learning, automaticity, attending, and a general theory. *Psychological Review* 84: 127–90

Shuy, R, Wolfram, W and Riley, W 1967 *Linguistic correlates of social stratification in Detroit speech*. Michigan State University, East Lansing

Sinclair, J and Coulthard, M 1975 *Towards an analysis of discourse: the English used by teachers and pupils*. Oxford University Press

Singh, R, d'Anglejan, A and Carroll, S 1982 Elicitation of inter-English. *Language Learning* 32 (2): 271–88

Singleton, D and Little, D (eds.) 1984 *Language learning in formal and informal contexts*. IRAAL, Dublin

Sjoholm, K 1983 Problems in 'measuring' L2 learning strategies. In Ringbom, H (ed.) *Psycholinguistics and foreign language learning*. Abo Akademi, Abo

Skehan, P 1982 Memory and motivation in language aptitude testing. Unpublished Ph.D. dissertation, University of London

Skehan, P 1985 Where does language aptitude come from? Paper presented at the BAAL 1985 Seminar, University of Edinburgh

Skehan, P 1989 *Individual differences in second-language learning*. Edward Arnold

Skinner, B 1957 *Verbal behavior*. Appleton-Century-Crofts, New York

Slobin, D 1973 Cognitive prerequisites for the development of grammar. In Ferguson, C and Slobin, D (eds.) *Studies of child language development*.

Appleton-Century-Crofts, New York

Slobin, D (ed.) 1982a *The cross-linguistic study of language acquisition*. Lawrence Erlbaum Associates, Hillsdale, N.J.

Slobin, D 1982b Universal and particular in the acquisition of language. In Wanner, E and Gleitman, L (eds.) *Language acquisition: state of the art*. Cambridge University Press

Slobin, D (ed.) 1985 *The cross-linguistic study of language acquisition*. Lawrence Erlbaum, Hillsdale, N.J.

Slobin, D and Bever, T 1982 Children use canonical sentence schemes: a cross-linguistic study of word order and inflections. *Cognition* 12 (3): 229–65

Smith, D 1972 Some implications for the social status of pidgin languages. In Smith, D and Shuy, R (eds.) *Sociolinguistics in cross-cultural analysis*. Georgetown University Press, Washington, D.C.

Smith, K and Braine, M 1972 Miniature languages and the problem of language acquisition. In Bever, T and Weksel, W (eds.) *The structure and psychology of language*, Vol. 2. Holt, Rinehart and Winston, New York

Snow, C 1977 The development of conversations between mothers and babies. *Journal of Child Language* 4 (1): 1–22

Snow, C 1983 Age differences in second language acquisition: research findings and folk psychology. In Bailey, K M, Long, M and Peck, S (eds.) *Second language acquisition studies*, pp. 141–50. Newbury House, Rowley, Mass.

Snow, C 1987 Relevance of the notion of a critical period to language acquisition. In Bernstein, M (ed.) *Sensitive periods in development: an interdisciplinary perspective*, pp. 183–209. Lawrence Erlbaum Associates, Hillsdale, N.J.

Snow, C, Arlman-Rupp, A, Hassing, Y, Jobse, J, Joosten, J, and Vorster, J 1976 Mothers' speech in three social classes. *Journal of Psycholinguistic Research* 5: 1–20

Snow, C and Ferguson, C (eds.) 1977 *Talking to children: language input and acquisition*. Cambridge University Press

Snow, C and Hoefnagel-Hohle, M 1977 Age differences and the pronunciation of foreign sounds. *Language and Speech* 20: 357–65

Snow, C and Hoefnagel-Hohle, M 1978 The critical age for language acquisition: evidence from second language learning. *Child Development* 49: 1114–28

Snow, C, van Eeden, R, and Muysken, P 1981 The interactional origins of foreigner talk. *International Journal of the Sociology of Language* 28: 81–92

Snow, M with Shapira, R 1985 The role of social-psychological factors in second language learning. In Celce-Murcia, M (ed.) *Beyond basics: issues and research in TESOL*, pp. 3–15. Newbury House, Rowley, Mass.

Sorensen, A 1967 Multilingualism in the Northwest Amazon. *American Anthropologist* 67: 670–684

Spada, N 1986 The interaction between types of content and type of instruction: some effects on the L2 proficiency of adult learners. *Studies in Second Language Acquisition* 8: 181–99

Spada, N 1987 Relationships between instructional differences and learning outcomes: a process-product study of communicative language teaching. *Applied Linguistics* 8: 137–61

Speidel, G, Tharp, R, and Kobayashi, L 1985 Is there a comprehension problem for children who speak nonstandard English? A study of children with Hawaiian-English backgrounds. *Applied Psycholinguistics* 6 (1): 83–96

Spielberger, C, Gorusch, A and Lushene, B 1970 *State-trait anxiety inventory.* Consulting Psychologist Press, Palo Alto, Calif.

Spolsky, B 1969 Attitudinal aspects of second language learning. *Language Learning* 19: 271–85

Spolsky, B 1979 The comparative study of first and second language acquisition. In Eckman, F and Hastings, A (eds.) *Studies in first and second language acquisition.* Newbury House, Rowley, Mass.

Spolsky, B 1989 *Conditions for second language learning.* Oxford University Press

Springer, S and Deutsch, G 1981 *Left brain, right brain.* W.H. Freeman Co., San Francisco

Sridhar, J 1980 Contrastive analysis, error analysis, and interlanguage. In Croft, K (ed.) *Readings on ESL for teachers and teacher trainees.* Winthrop Publishers, Inc., Cambridge, Mass.

Stansfield, C and Hansen, J 1983 Field dependence–independence as a variable in second language cloze test performance. *TESOL Quarterly* 17: 29–38

Stauble, A 1977 *An exploratory analogy between decreolization and second language learning.* MA TESL thesis, University of California at Los Angeles

Stauble, A 1978 Decreolization: a model for second language development. *Language Learning* 28: 29–54

Stauble, A 1980 Acculturation and second language acquisition. In Scarcella, R and Krashen, S (eds.) *Research in second language acquisition*, pp. 43–50. Newbury House, Rowley, Mass.

Stauble, A 1981 A comparative study of a Spanish–English and Japanese–English second language continuum: verb phrase morphology. Unpublished Ph.D. dissertation, University of California at Los Angeles

Stauble, A 1984 A comparison of the Spanish–English and Japanese–English interlanguage continuum. In Andersen, R (ed.) *Second language: a crosslinguistic perspective*, pp. 323–53. Newbury House, Rowley, Mass.

Stauble, A and Larsen-Freeman, D 1978 The use of variable rules in describing the interlanguage of second language learners. *Workpapers in TESL*, University of California at Los Angeles

Stauble, A and Schumann, J 1983 Towards a description of the Spanish–English basilang. In Bailey, K M, Long, M and Peck, S (eds.) *Second language acquisition studies*, pp. 68–82. Newbury House, Rowley, Mass.

Stenson, N 1974 Induced errors. In Schumann, J and Stenson, N (eds.) *New frontiers in second language learning.* Newbury House, Rowley, Mass.

Stern, H 1967 *Foreign languages in primary education.* Oxford University Press

Stern, H 1983 *Fundamental concepts of language teaching.* Oxford University Press

Stevick, E 1976 *Memory, meaning and method.* Newbury House, Rowley, Mass.

Stevick, E 1980 The Levertov Machine. In Scarcella, R and Krashen, S (eds.) *Research in second language acquisition*, pp. 28–35. Newbury House, Rowley, Mass.

Stevick, E 1986 *Images and options in the language classroom*. Cambridge University Press

Stockwell, R and Bowen, J 1965 *The sounds of English and Spanish*. University of Chicago Press

Stockwell, R, Bowen, J, and Martin, J 1965a *The grammatical structures of English and Spanish*. University of Chicago Press

Stockwell, R, Bowen, J, and Martin, J 1965b *The grammatical structures of English and Italian*. University of Chicago Press

Strevens, P 1978 *New orientations in the teaching of English*. Oxford University Press

Strevens, P 1980 *Teaching English as an international language*. Pergamon

Strickland, D 1988 The teacher as researcher: toward the extended professional. *Language Arts* 65 (8): 754–64

Strong, M 1983 Social styles and the second language acquisition of Spanish-speaking kindergartners. *TESOL Quarterly* 17: 241–58

Strong, M 1984 Integrative motivation: cause or result of successful second language acquisition? *Language Learning* 34 (3): 1–14

Strong, M (ed.) 1988 *Language learning and deafness*. Cambridge University Press

Suter, R 1973 Predictors of pronunciation accuracy in second language learning. Unpublished Ph.D. dissertation, University of Southern California

Suter, R 1976 Predictors of pronunciation accuracy in second-language learning. *Language Learning* 26: 233–53

Swain, M 1981 Immersion education: applicability for nonvernacular teaching to vernacular speakers. *Studies in Second Language Acquisition* 4 (1): 1–17

Swain, M 1985 Communicative competence: some roles of comprehensible input and comprehensible output in its development. In Gass, S and Madden, C (eds.) *Input in second language acquisition*, pp. 235–53. Newbury House, Rowley, Mass.

Swain, M and Burnaby, B 1976 Personality characteristics and second language learning in young children. *Working Papers on Bilingualism* 11: 115–28

Swain, M and Lapkin, S 1982 *Evaluating bilingual education: a Canadian case study*. Multilingual Matters

Swain, M, Naiman, N and Dumas, G 1974 Alternatives to spontaneous speech: elicited translation and imitation as indicators of second language competence. *Working Papers on Bilingualism* 3: 68–79

Tahta, S, Wood, M and Lowenthal, K 1981a Foreign accents: factors relating to transfer of accent from the first language to a second language. *Language and Speech*, 24: 265–72

Tahta, S, Wood, M and Lowenthal, K 1981b Age changes in the ability to replicate foreign pronunciation and intonation. *Language and Speech*, 24 (4): 363–72

Tanaka, S and Kawada, S 1982 Politeness strategies and second language acquisition. *Studies in Second Language Acquisition* 5: 18–33

Tarallo, F and Myhill, J 1983 Interference and natural language processing in second language acquisition. *Language Learning* 33 (1): 55–76

Tarone, E 1977 Conscious communication strategies in interlanguage: a progress report. In Brown, H, Yorio, C and Crymes, R (eds.) *On TESOL '77*, pp. 194–203. TESOL, Washington, D.C.

Tarone, E 1979 Interlanguage as chameleon. *Language Learning* 29: 181–91

Tarone, E 1980a Some influence on the syllable structure of interlanguage phonology. *International Review of Applied Linguistics* 18: 139–52

Tarone, E 1980b Communication strategies, foreigner talk and repair in interlanguage. *Language Learning* 30: 417–31

Tarone E 1982 Systematicity and attention in interlanguage. *Language Learning* 32: 69–82

Tarone, E 1983 On the variability of interlanguage systems. *Applied Linguistics* 4: 142–63

Tarone, E 1984 On the variability of interlanguage systems. In Eckman, F et al. (eds.) *Universals of second language acquisition*, pp. 3–23. Newbury House, Rowley, Mass.

Tarone, E 1985 Variability in interlanguage use: a study of style-shifting in morphology and syntax. *Language Learning* 35: 373–404

Tarone, E 1988 *Variation in interlanguage*. Edward Arnold

Tarone, E, Frauenfelder, V and Selinker, L 1976 Systematicity/variability and stability/instability in interlanguage systems. *Language Learning*, Special Issue No. 4: 93–134

Tarone, E, Swain, M and Fathman, A 1976 Some limitations to the classroom applications of current second language acquisition research. *TESOL Quarterly* 10: 19–32

Taylor, B 1974 Toward a theory of language acquisition. *Language Learning* 24: 23–36

Taylor, B 1975 The use of overgeneralization and transfer learning strategies by elementary and intermediate students in ESL. *Language Learning* 25 (1): 73–107

Taylor, L, Guiora, A, Catford, J and Lane, H 1969 The role of personality variables in second language behavior. *Comprehensive Psychiatry* 10: 463–74

Thiem, R 1969 Bibliography of contrastive linguistics. *PAKS-Arbeitsbericht* 2,3,4: 79–86 and 93–120

Thomas, J 1983 Cross-cultural pragmatic failure. *Applied Linguistics* 4: 91–112

Titchener, E 1912 The scheme of introspection. *American Journal of Psychology* 23: 485–508

Tomlin, R 1984 The treatment of foreground–background information in the on-line descriptive discourse of second language learners. *Studies in Second Language Acquisition* 6: 115–42

Torrey, J 1971 Second language learning. In Reed, C (ed.) *The learning of language*. Appleton-Century-Crofts, New York

Toutaiolepo, V 1984 Stalking the wild ESL writer. Term paper, ESL 672, University of Hawaii at Manoa, Honolulu

Tsang, W-K 1987 Text modifications in ESL reading comprehension. Scholarly paper, Department of ESL, University of Hawaii at Manoa, Honolulu

Tucker, G, Hamayan, E and Genesee, F 1976 Affective, cognitive and social factors in second language acquisition. *Canadian Modern Language Review* 32: 214–26

Tucker, G and Lambert, W 1973 Sociocultural aspects of language study. In Oller, J and Richards, J (eds.) *Focus on the learner.* Newbury House, Rowley, Mass.

Tucker, G, Lambert, W and Rigault, A 1977 *The French speaker's skill with grammatical gender: an example of rule-governed behavior.* Mouton, The Hague

Tucker, G and Sarofim, M 1979 Investigating linguistic acceptability with Egyptian ESL students. *TESOL Quarterly* 13: 29–39

Tuckman, B 1978 *Conducting educational research,* 2nd edition. Harcourt Brace Jovanovich, New York

Tumposky, N 1984 Behavioral objectives, the cult of efficiency, and foreign language learning: are they compatible? *TESOL Quarterly* 18: 295–310

Turner, R 1978 *The structure of sociological theory.* The Dorsey Press, Homewood, Ill. Underwood, B 1966 *Experimental psychology.* Appleton-Century-Crofts, New York

Underwood, B 1966 *Experimental psychology.* Appleton-Century-Crofts, New York

Upshur, J 1968 Four experiments on the relation between foreign language teaching and learning. *Language Learning* 18: 111–24

Upshur, J, Acton, W, Arthur, B and Guiora, A 1978 Causation or correlation: a reply to Oller and Perkins. *Language Learning* 28: 99–104

Valdman, A (ed.) 1966 *Trends in language teaching.* McGraw-Hill, New York

Valdman, A and Phillips, J 1975 Pidginization, creolization and the elaboration of learner systems. *Studies in Second Language Acquisition* 1: 21–40

Valette, R 1964 Some reflections on second language learning in young children. *Language Learning* 14: 91–98

Van Buren, P and Sharwood-Smith, M 1985 The acquisition of preposition-stranding by second language learners and parametric variation. *Second Language Research* 1 (1): 18–46

Vander Brook, S, Schlue, K and Campbell, C 1980 Discourse and second language acquisition of yes/no questions. In Larsen-Freeman, D (ed.) *Discourse analysis in second language research,* pp. 56–74. Newbury House, Rowley, Mass.

van Els, T, Bongaerts, T, Extra, G, van Os, A, and Janssen-van Dieten, A 1984 *Applied linguistics and the learning and teaching of foreign languages.* Edward Arnold

van Lier, L 1988 *The classroom and the language learner.* Longman

van Naerssen, M 1980 How similar are Spanish as a first and foreign language? In Scarcella, R and Krashen, S (eds.) *Research in second language acquisition,* pp. 146–54. Newbury House, Rowley, Mass.

van Naerssen, M 1986 Hipotesis sobre la adquisición de una segunda lengua, consideraciones interlenguaje: comprobación en el español. In Meisel, J (ed.) *Adquisición de Lenguaje.* Vervuert, Frankfurt

Van Patten, B 1988 How juries get hung: problems with the evidence for a focus on form in teaching. *Language Learning* 38: 243–60